OPERA 101

A COMPLETE GUIDE TO LEARNING

AND LOVING OPERA

FRED PLOTKIN

HYPERION

NEW YORK

F O R   A N D R E I   M A R K ,

W H O   I S   A   P A R T   O F   T H I S   B O O K

I N   S O   M A N Y   W A Y S

Verse from Leoncavallo's *Pagliacci* on page xvii © EMI Recording, Electrical
Musical Industries (U.S.) Ltd. 1954. Courtesy of EMI Classics.

Library of Congress Cataloging-in-Publication Data
Plotkin, Fred.
Opera 101 : a complete guide to learning and loving opera / by Fred Plotkin.
p. cm.
Includes bibliographical references, discography and videography, and index.
ISBN 0-7868-8025-2
1. Operas—Analysis, appreciation. I. Title.
MT95.P675 1994
782.1—dc20   94-9477
                                              CIP
                                              MN

Designed by Ann Gold

FIRST EDITION
10 9 8 7 6 5 4 3 2 1

CONTENTS

FOREWORD

One cannot help falling in love with opera all over again reading this book. I also venture to say that if someone is a stranger to opera, he or she will have become a convert by the final page.

Fred Plotkin asks his readers to open their hearts without inhibitions to let music flow through them. That, indeed, is the real secret to becoming a music enthusiast, because reacting emotionally to music is more important than analyzing it mentally. But in order to break down all the barriers, the writer—in brilliant fashion—first guides the reader through a discussion of many different aspects of opera until a better understanding of it is achieved. Just a look at the table of contents shows the reader that by the end of the book many topics will have been discussed—the origin and history of opera (from Baroque court opera to present-day composers such as John Corigliano, Philip Glass, and even Stephen Sondheim), the excitement of going to the opera, the drama *and* the comedy in opera, Italian opera in contrast to French opera, the path from chamber opera to grand and even epic opera, a history of important opera houses, a guide of important recordings and videos, and suggestions for books or periodicals to read about this art form and its artists.

I've spent practically my entire life with music and in the theater (having been born to parents who were zarzuela performers), and I can say honestly that nothing in this book was redundant for me but proved a fascinating journey through the world that means so much to me.

PLÁCIDO DOMINGO

ACKNOWLEDGMENTS

Just as an opera is the product of the participation and goodwill of many individuals, a book such as this one has been made better by the assistance the author received from many kind people.

Brian Kellow was a faithful source of advice and humor as the book was being written. At a crucial point during the book's development, the manuscript was read by Nancy Bachrach, Jennifer Josephy, Valerie Saalbach, Marylis Sevilla-Gonzaga, and Len Horovitz. All provided valuable insights when they were most needed.

Alison Ames of Deutsche Grammophon, Nancy Zannini of Philips, Tony Caronia of EMI/Angel, and Sean O'Sullivan of CBS/Sony offered early help as the musical selections for this book were being made. Thanks also to the press representatives of BMG, Deutsche Grammophon, EMI/Angel, London/Decca, Philips, and Teldec.

The press and education departments of many major opera companies were also quite helpful, especially the following: the Metropolitan Opera, the New York City Opera, the Lyric Opera of Chicago, the Santa Fe Opera, the San Francisco Opera, the Los Angeles Music Center Opera, the Dallas Opera, the Houston Grand Opera, the Icelandic Opera, il Teatro alla Scala, il Teatro Comunale di Bologna, il Teatro La Fenice di Venezia, the Rossini Festival of Pesaro, the Royal Opera House at Covent Garden, and the Royal Danish Opera.

I was able to construct the detailed listing of the world's opera houses with help from the national tourist offices and consulates of the nations I included.

Special thanks to Edward Sorel, the artist who created this book's cover, and Plácido Domingo, who wrote the foreword. Each man synthesized and expressed the many ideas in *Opera 101* with concision and great feeling. They made me see yet again why I love opera so. Edgar Vincent, Paul Garner, James Cope, and Henry Cuevas also deserve my thanks.

David Black, my tenacious yet tender agent, and his able staff, Lev Fruchter and Susan Raihofer, are constant sources of support and advice. They bring much happiness to my life as an author.

Richard Kot, this book's editor, shares my love of opera, of words, and of a good laugh. He arrived in this book's life like a great operatic knight, turning a potential ugly duckling into a *lieber Schwan*. He has my great admiration. Patrick Dillon was the knowledgeable and sensitive copy editor of *Opera 101*. He sets a standard of excellence that others should aspire to. Particular thanks also to David Cashion, and to all the other people at Hyperion who worked on this book.

Finally, my mother, Bernice, my father, Edward, and my grandmother Rose surrounded me with love and music in my very young years. Because of them, opera has given me a lifetime of pleasure and fulfillment that I am happy to share with others.

INTRODUCTION

Si può? May I?

This is what Tonio, one of the itinerant players in Leoncavallo's *Pagliacci,* asks the public before the opera begins. While the curtain is still down, he says, permit me to step forward to speak to you, the audience, and tell you about the special world you are about to enter. And now I, as your guide to the passionate, exotic world of opera, invoke Tonio in asking your indulgence for a few words before we begin our journey.

The fact that you chose to read this book means that you have become interested in opera and would like to start learning more about it. The best way to do this is to have a knowledgeable friend teach you about it. The important thing to know is not only which opera to see first but how to see it. To launch a person on a lifetime of operagoing takes a lot of time and effort, and not every friend has the resources to do that. So I hope you will consider me that friend and let me guide you. I have introduced many people to opera and have developed a method which is the basis of this book. When my friend Susan wept twice during her first opera, *Rigoletto,* I saw again how a person who is well prepared for her first performance, yet allows herself to be open to whatever happens once the curtain rises, can have a memorable experience that will be the first of many treasured nights at the opera.

To paraphrase Anna Russell, whose priceless comic routines on disk and video you should hear once you become an opera regular, the beauty of opera is that you can do anything you want as long as you sing it. To the person with only a casual knowledge of opera, this art form is riddled with clichés such as overweight sopranos, bellowing tenors, preposterous plots, and long hours spent crammed into uncomfortable seats. While these clichés do represent a small segment of opera, they do not in any way suggest what is beautiful and glorious about it.

To me, opera is about consideration of the human experience. Opera audiences become so involved with performances because they face emotional truths most of us don't confront in daily life. The late twentieth century, with its rapid-fire information flow, does not make room for the reflection that opera affords. During a three-hour operatic performance one can focus on the issues that opera explores and find personal meaning in them. Every human emotion and activity—love, lust, incest, hatred, fidelity, bravery, fear, humor—is enacted in opera, but on a grand scale. It's like going to an amusement park and looking at yourself in one of those elongated fun-house mirrors. What we see in opera is ourselves, as long as we are honest enough to admit it.

Operagoing at its best is about the rekindling of the soul, about having an open window into what makes us human. The transfixing melodies, the tragedies and dilemmas that confront our operatic heroes, the throbbing orchestras and booming choruses—all of these take us into the realm of our feelings. While music is a pure, sublime abstraction that speaks to us in places that other messages cannot reach, and drama is the use of recognizable symbols— words—that speak to us directly, opera is something altogether different. Opera puts drama on musical wings and speaks to us simultaneously in literal and intangible ways. Once you are capable of receiving its messages, you discover the capacity to live on an emotional level that many nonoperagoers will never experience. That is what this book is about: learning how to listen to opera, whether on the radio, on a recording, in full production in an opera house, or even in concert form, and to experience a rekindling of the soul.

Many of the performances we operagoers cherish are those that first made us love the art form. This period of infatuation, as in love, is one of all feelings writ large. Every older operagoer you meet will say, "There are good singers and conductors today, but they can't compare with [fill in names], who were singing when I began to go to the opera. Now *that* was the Golden Age." You should smile and ask the older operagoer about his memories, but don't feel short-changed. This is *your* Golden Age, and the memories you build will be recounted with pleasure to the next generation. Now that we have nearly a century of recorded performances, you have the unique opportunity to go back and hear how Caruso, Gigli, di Stefano, Bergonzi, Domingo, and *your* golden tenor all sing a partic-ular aria. Unfortunately, we don't necessarily give equal affection to more recent great performances.

Once the infatuation period is passed, however, this does not mean you will become blasé about opera. What makes it so special is that for audiences and artists alike, there is always room to grow and there are new things to discover. I have seen operas such as *Don Carlo* and *La Traviata* at least fifty times each, and they still fasci-nate me. My memories of past performances enable me to make comparisons of the choices made by the performers, directors, de-signers, and conductors considering these masterpieces. Similarly, as I get older, my experiences in life become more varied, and the pathos of a particular moment I never noticed before may suddenly touch me deeply.

There are many other factors that will make a particular per-formance memorable. For example, who was on your arm the night of that *Tristan und Isolde* with Birgit Nilsson and Jon Vickers? What did you do afterward? Certain music will always have partic-ular associations that come to mind whenever that music is heard. I first made love with someone I cherish as the strains of the Act I love duet from *Otello* played on my stereo. So when I hear Mirella Freni sing that music, as she did on that video recording with Plácido Domingo, is my heart warmed in a special way? Of course. This is an example of how deeply opera can permeate one's thought and feeling and how on re-encountering particular music, one's feelings can again be aroused.

By their very nature, opera lovers are a subjective, opinionated lot. What touches me most deeply may have little meaning to you. For example, I am mightily moved by operas such as *Fidelio, Tannhäuser,* and *Andrea Chénier* in which the hero ardently defends his or her ideals despite inevitable condemnation and punishment. A more cynical operagoer may find such utopianism unrealistic and will not have the transcendent experience I do. Conversely, that person may identify with the fatalism of Carmen and feel vindicated in his attitude toward life when the gypsy is stabbed to death outside the bull ring in Seville. A person going through a rough patch in a romance will find special resonance in Mimì's and Rodolfo's bittersweet reconciliation during Act III of *La Bohème,* while someone in a more placid relationship may not be affected. As I suggested, one of the glories of a lifetime of operagoing is that while at one stage in your life a particular emotional chord will not be struck, twenty years later you will suddenly experience a revelation at the same moment in an opera that failed to move you before.

Operagoers are not only opinionated about what moves them but also about who does the moving. Let us take, for example, the Marschallin in *Der Rosenkavalier.* This is a multifaceted character, by turns joyous and introspective, bound by custom and position to maintain a cool and regal public bearing, but privately passionate and fearful over passing into middle age. The role requires great skills in physical *and* vocal acting to make these quicksilver changes in mood felt by an audience. The Marschallin is a character to love and care about, but not one to pity. Many great opera singers have made the role their own by bringing their particular strengths and frailties to it. Among the great Marschallins of recent times, I have been especially moved by Régine Crespin, Evelyn Lear, Elisabeth Söderström, and Kiri Te Kanawa. Each woman created a different Marschallin, but so great is the role that there was room for all of them. Another opinionated opera lover may feel that these portrayals all pale in comparison to those of Christa Ludwig or Anna Tomowa-Sintow. While these two are also great artists, they did not, on the evenings when I heard them, strike the same chords in me that the others did. It could be that they were having an off-night—or that I was. The variables of attending a live performance are such that a great performance "on paper" may be disappointing

in fact, while a less promising performance may turn out to be unforgettable. So each operagoer has his own cherished performers,
performances, and recordings, and there is very little right and
wrong about this subjectivity.

When I told friends which operas and recordings I chose to present in this book, I encountered both admiring praise and scathing
criticism. How could I pick the James Levine–conducted *Die Walküre* over the magnificent Georg Solti recording of thirty years ago?
Do I really think *Don Giovanni* is better than *Le Nozze di Figaro*
for discussing Mozart? How could I leave *Madama Butterfly* off the
list of operas to teach you? How come I selected the *Tosca* of Maria
Callas rather than that of Renata Tebaldi, Zinka Milanov, Leontyne Price, Eva Marton, or someone else?

Let me explain my method. I am as subjective and opinionated as
the next opera lover, but I like to think that I am open to every
interpretation and opinion about an opera or a performer. With
each hearing of *Rigoletto,* for example, thanks to the interpretation
of a conductor, singer, stage director, set designer, or costumer, I
find something new that serves to make me better understand the
genius of Verdi, the composer, and Piave, the librettist. In fact, I
have selected *Rigoletto* as the work with which we will begin our
study of opera. This does not mean that *Rigoletto* is the best opera
(there is no such thing), but simply that it has many of the components of opera that I wish to reveal to you first. The fact that I picked
the recording of *Rigoletto* conducted by Richard Bonynge and sung
by Joan Sutherland, Luciano Pavarotti, and Sherrill Milnes does not
mean that this is the best recording or the only one you should listen
to. My choice of each recording in this book was based on two
factors: that the recording is easily found wherever you might live
and that it contains good examples of things I want to teach you. So
while the Solti *Die Walküre* is a landmark recording that I cherish
and encourage you to listen to, I selected Levine's version because
the more modern recording techniques reveal orchestral nuances
that cannot be heard on the Solti and because I want you, the listener, to pay special attention to Hildegard Behrens's use of the German language. While the legendary Birgit Nilsson is a fabulous
Brünnhilde on the Solti recording, in linguistic terms I give Behrens

the edge, and language is one of the things I will talk about in that chapter. Similarly, many friends thought I should have selected the Callas *Lucia di Lammermoor* over Sutherland's. I chose the latter because I want to explore particular characteristics of Sutherland's Lucia that cannot be found in Callas's. But I love both interpretations and hope that after learning the one you will seek out the other for comparison.

The goal of this book is that with each opera we explore, you will learn more about the operatic art than you knew before. The first five operas we will learn in this book are all frequently performed "chestnuts," so it is likely that you will be able to attend a performance wherever you might live or travel. After studying the first three operas in this book, you should be able to attend most any opera and get something meaningful out of it. After studying the eleven operas we will look at, you should be able to attend any opera and fully enjoy and appreciate the experience. This book is not only for people who live in major metropolitan areas; anyone with access to a radio or to recordings (in the store, in the library, or by mail) will be able to use it. If you like to travel, you might plan vacations to places where operas are being performed. Devoted operagoers visit famous theaters with the awe that the deeply religious experience when they go to an important church, synagogue, mosque, temple, or shrine. I will never forget the first performances I saw in Milan's La Scala, at the Vienna State Opera, the opera houses in Munich, Paris, London, and, of course, my home theater, the Metropolitan Opera. Appendix C will give you the names, addresses, and phone numbers for major opera houses around the world.

Before we actually start studying *Rigoletto* and the operas that follow it, I want you to learn about the elements that go into making an opera, how to listen to and look at an opera, and how to attend a performance. Once you know about buying tickets (not always easy), what to wear, when to applaud, and what to look at, you will feel very much at home in the opera house.

My prologue is nearly finished and the curtain is about to rise. Let me close as I opened, with Tonio's words to his audience:

Please? May I?
Ladies! Gentlemen! Excuse me
If I appear here thus alone.
I am the Prologue.
Since our author is reviving on our stage
The masks of ancient comedy,
He wishes to restore for you, in part,
The old stage customs, and once more
He sends me to you.
But not, as in the past, to reassure you,
Saying, "The tears we shed are false,
So do not be alarmed by our agonies
Or violence." No! No!
Our author has endeavored, rather,
To paint a slice of life,
His only maxim being that the artist
Is a man, and he must write
For men. Truth is his inspiration.
Deep-embedded memories stirred one day
Within his heart, and with real tears
He wrote, and marked the time with sighs!
Now, then, you will see men love
As in real life they love, and you will see
True hatred and its bitter fruit. And you will hear
Shouts of both rage and grief, and cynical laughter.
Mark well, therefore, our souls,
Rather than the poor players' garb
We wear, for we are men
Of flesh and bone, like you, breathing
The same air of this orphan world.
This, then, is our design. Now give heed
To its unfolding.
(Shouting toward the stage):
On with the show! Begin!

OPERA 101

1.

400 YEARS OF OPERA

Opera is a still-evolving art form that is almost four hundred years old. It is generally said that the first opera, *Dafne,* was written in Florence in 1597. But *Dafne* did not appear from a void. It was just another step, albeit a major step, in the history of the theater. Opera, in Italian, is called *opera lirica,* or lyric work. "Lyric" is defined as "appropriate for song," so *opera lirica* is a work of theater that is set to song. And whatever the era of its composition, an opera reflects the political currents and attitudes of its time.

In ancient times, Greek theater was a forum for examining moral issues as exemplified by the characters in the tragedies of Aeschylus, Sophocles, Euripides, and other playwrights. Most Greek theatergoers knew the stories of Orpheus and Eurydice, of Electra, Medea, Alceste, Iphigenia, Oedipus, and all the other personages of mythology. Greek theater was not merely an enactment of these characters' stories but served to instruct and remind audiences of the consequences of the characters' actions.

We know that Greek theater had a strong musical component. Typically, the verses written for the chorus—which served as the moral teacher that commented upon the action—were set to music. Many speeches by individual characters were actually sung. Incidental music played on instruments of the time often accompanied certain passages of the play, bringing to it the abstract, though emotional, element that is unique to music.

To an audience member, whether in ancient Greece or in the modern world, music has a direct line to the soul in a way that more literal art forms cannot achieve. So while the spoken word may *describe* an emotion, the music played while those words are spoken may more effectively enable an audience member to identify with that emotion and sympathize with the character who is experiencing it onstage.

Roman theater, especially the comedies, drew upon the Greek model in many ways, one being the inclusion of music. Some of the comedies were about contemporary themes in Roman society, such as family relations, lust, greed, and other vices. Usually, one of the characters got his comeuppance at the end of the play, so that moral issues were examined in a humorous context.

Following the fall of Rome, there was not any significant theatrical activity until the Middle Ages. As in other areas of medieval culture, there seems to have been little contact with the ancients but, rather, a point of view based on Christian religious doctrine.

One of the most important, and forgotten, figures in musical history was a medieval Benedictine monk named Guido d'Arezzo (992?–1050). In his *Prologus in Antiphonarium,* Guido set forth the principles of musical notation that are still used today, allowing music to be preserved and passed down to succeeding generations. In his *Micrologus,* he wrote of musical theory and aesthetics, which are now the points of departure for all musical instruction.

In the eleventh century, liturgical drama developed as a theatrical form designed to convey the teachings of the Church. Officiating priests would enact the stories of prophets, saints, and apostles; of the Nativity; and of the trial of Christ, the Crucifixion, the Resurrection, and all the other episodes of the Passion Week. These "Passion plays" were first performed in Latin, but, by the fifteenth century they often were performed in the vernacular, especially German. The most famous surviving Passion play is the one performed in Oberammergau, Germany.

Most liturgical dramas had musical components. The acoustics of Gothic cathedrals were kinder to song than they were to the spoken word, so music became the more effective means of communication. Gregorian chant is probably the most famous musical form to come out of the Middle Ages, although there were other types as well, some of which had instrumental accompaniment. More than two hundred liturgical dramas survive from medieval times.

Other theatrical forms developed in the late Middle Ages and the early Renaissance. One of these was called the mystery (according to some, from the Latin *ministerium,* or "service"; others say the source is *mestier*—metier, trade). While liturgical dramas were performed in churches, mysteries were done in other public places. It was necessary to have the permission of the local bishop to stage a mystery, but they were performed by professional actors (rather than church officials) for the community at large. It was customary to perform a mystery in the local language instead of Latin. Mysteries were visually oriented, presenting literal depictions of the events being recounted. So angels flew, natural disasters such as flood and fires were enacted, and tortures and beheadings were actually staged. The mysteries represented a step forward in stagecraft as imagination and rudimentary technology were required to make many of the onstage effects plausible.

Music was largely incidental to mysteries, and little of it survives. These plays were significant departures from the pious liturgical dramas in which word and music served to represent the stories being told. As the Renaissance dawned and the ideals of the ancients were being stressed, the often gruesome spectacle of the mysteries was condemned by the Church and shunned by aesthetes.

The other chief theatrical form of the Middle Ages was the secular music drama. *Le Jeu de Robin et de Marion,* by Adam de la Halle, is the earliest-known of these to use a lot of music. First performed at the court of Naples in 1282, this work is sort of a pastoral comedy that naively extols simple virtues in song, speech, and dance.

As the Middle Ages gave way to the Renaissance, the secular use of music evolved. The masquerade (the *mascherata* in Italian, the *mascarade* in French, and the *masque* in England) was originally a festive spectacle staged at Carnival time (when people wore masks) in which the exploits of figures from mythology and pagan tales and of popular medieval personages would be enacted.

Dance was a key component of the masquerade, which served as the forerunner to ballet. This French word comes from the Italian *balletto,* or "little dance." What is significant about ballet, and made it different from everything that preceded it, was that it was a sustained form of storytelling through music and dance—a new art form based on, but not confined to, the movements developed over centuries in rustic and courtly dances for pleasure. Ballet was especially popular in France, so it should not surprise you to discover that, through the centuries, dance would play a greater role in French opera than in operas produced in Italy, Germany, and other lands.

While music supported the spectacle of the dance in the masquerade, it was used to comment upon and accompany dramatic action in a theatrical form known as the *intermedio.* The *intermedii* were plays with music that were often written for special occasions held in the courts of Italian city-states, including those of Rome, Florence, Ferrara, Mantua, and Venice. They were performed in either Latin or Italian, and included solo songs and choral works that would be interspersed with spoken dialogue. The music was accompanied by orchestras containing instruments such as lutes, harps, lyres, viols, trombones, horns, and organs.

What had not yet appeared, in all of these uses of word and music from antiquity until the early Renaissance, was an art form that married words and music in a way in which each exalted the other, creating a whole that was more than the sum of the two parts.

In Italy, toward the end of the fifteenth century, the *pastorela* (pastorale), was a form of entertainment that drew inspiration from idyllic and bucolic scenes of nature. Many of the musical sounds in pastorales came from instruments used by shepherds, some of which can still be heard today in pastures in central and southern Italy. The *Favola d'Orfeo,* staged in the court of Mantua in 1480, is an early example of the Italian pastorale in which shepherd's pipes were used. This interest in nature (look at the paintings of that time) was not a new concept in the Renaissance but was also found in the writings of Virgil and other poets of antiquity who were being rediscovered. Pastorales were combinations of words, dance, and song that prefigured the earliest operas.

The representation of nature in music is a continuous thread that goes from the pastorales through Vivaldi (think of *The Four Seasons*), Handel, Bach, Mozart, Beethoven, Rossini, Verdi, Wagner, and up to Benjamin Britten and other twentieth-century composers.

THE CAMERATA FIORENTINA

In the 1560s, in Florence, a group known as the Camerata Fiorentina, or Florentine Academy, was created. This group of literati and musicians met in the home of Count Giovanni Bardi del Vernio (1534–1612), a leading patron of the arts in Renaissance Florence. Their goal was to cast aside the musical and dramatic art forms of the time and go back to the spirit of the ancient Greeks. One member of the Camerata, Vincenzo Galilei (1532–91), was the father of the astronomer Galileo and was also one of Florence's leading musical theoreticians. Along with a Roman scholar, Girolamo Mei (1519–94), he created the *Dialogue About Ancient and Modern Music* (1581), a utopian vision of a new music. Since no Greek music was available to them, they had to imagine what it was like as they attempted to create a new music based on a Greek model. They believed that their new music would be a combination of words and music in which each served the other.

It was deemed essential that the words be understood. To this end, the solo voice was brought forward and the instrumental accompaniment was subordinated. The voice, in effect, was the leading instrument in a group of instruments. The Camerata theorists felt that the music should reflect the cadences of the spoken word rather than those of dance, so their new music did not have the steady beat that one hears in dance music. Of utmost importance, the Camerata stressed that the music should not simply underscore the words in the text but explore the feelings and emotions inherent in them. Here, then, is the germ for the new art form, opera.

While these ideas were crucial to the creation of opera, what was still missing was the creative genius who could put them to use. Various members of the Camerata Fiorentina set about to create works based on their theories. Most scholars consider the first true opera to be *Dafne,* based on Greek myth, with lyrics by Ottavio Rinuccini (1562–1621) and music by Jacopo Peri (1561–1633) and

Jacopo Corsi (1561–1602). Documents from that time report that the new work received an enthusiastic reception; unfortunately, only fragments of the music survive.

Peri and Rinuccini later wrote *Euridice,* about the story of Orpheus and Eurydice. Unlike certain later operas based on these ill-fated lovers, in which Orpheus fails to lead Eurydice out of Hades because he cannot resist looking back upon her, this version has a happy ending. Perhaps this was because *Euridice* was staged for the wedding of Marie de' Medici and King Henri IV of France (on October 6, 1600). Most of this opera has been preserved.

What was lacking in the early operas produced in Florence was characterization. The operas were rather staid and passionless. While the members of the Camerata were able to articulate the theories that would ultimately create opera, they did not have the skills to create an enduring masterpiece that would still have meaning for audiences of today. This task fell to Claudio Monteverdi (1567–1643), the first great operatic composer.

Monteverdi was different from those who preceded him because, whether by instinct or by training, he understood that opera was more about the search for musical and dramatic meaning than about fitting a paradigm devised by a bunch of theoreticians. In other words, an opera had to be a living, breathing thing that captured the feelings and imaginations of audiences.

His first opera, *Orfeo,* again based on the ever-popular myth of Orpheus and Eurydice, was produced in the court of Mantua in 1607. In this case Eurydice dies; but, to suit the tastes of the time, the ending of the opera has Orpheus taken to Parnassus, from where he can see Eurydice in the sun and the stars—they are reunited musically.

In this book I will use a term, "musical painting," to describe the ways each great composer depicts the actions and feelings of operatic characters. From Monteverdi onward, operatic composers selected particular instruments and wrote specific music for the sounds those instruments can produce in order to describe the actions and emotions occurring onstage.

Monteverdi had a full understanding of the range of musical instruments available to him for use in an opera orchestra. These included early versions of violins, violas, cellos, basses, wood organs, reed organs, the clavicembalo (a forerunner of the harpsichord), trombones, flutes, and trumpets. Each instrument was brilliantly used by Monteverdi to create orchestral color and describe character. When you listen to a recording of *Orfeo,* pay special attention to the sounds of different instruments selected for accompaniment of a solo voice and ask yourself, as you read the libretto, what effect these instrumental sounds have upon what you feel. For example, Orpheus is typically accompanied by a harp, shepherds by flutes, lutes, and harpsichord, and the gods of the underworld by the bellowing of trombones. Imagine if Orpheus were accompanied by a trombone and the underworld gods by a harp. How would the effect differ? Notice in particular how carefully Monteverdi paints Orpheus' joys and suffering. You should be aware that the instrumentation used in many recordings of early music varies according to the taste and judgment of the conductor. This is because not every surviving musical score includes the composer's original instrumentation.

The Florentine composers and Monteverdi used particular singing forms that remain a part of opera today, although they have evolved through the centuries. The best-known is the *aria* (air), a song sung by one singer. The *recitativo* (recitative, in English) was a semisung passage that came between set pieces of music. The recitative was one of Monteverdi's great technical innovations. The purpose of the recitative was to advance the action by having one or more characters more or less talk as they would in a play. So-called *recitativo secco* (dry recitative) was done to the accompaniment of harpsichord or selected string instruments. *Recitativo accompagnato* (accompanied recitative), which was not very common in early opera, was sung to full orchestra. After a recitative, a full musical section would be performed (whether by one voice or chorus), and the action of the story would usually come to a halt. The musical selection often explored the feelings or intentions of the character at that point in the opera. It was not until the time of Mozart (1756–91) that music sung by one, two, or more singers would significantly advance the action.

The *arioso* is a form of singing that was especially popular in early opera. It is sort of a cross between an aria and a recitative. The arioso is usually accompanied by full orchestra, it advances the action, and it is more melodic than a *recitativo accompagnato,* which can often seem rather singsong and uninventive musically. In fact, poorly trained singers who sing less-than-scintillating recitatives often give them a let's-get-this-over-with-and-get-to-my-aria rendition. So the arioso was a more interesting way to advance the plot. Among the composers of later times, Richard Wagner made the arioso an important component of his nineteenth-century music dramas.

Soon after Monteverdi's success with *Orfeo,* he set to work on another opera, *Arianna.* This was to be performed at the wedding feast of Francesco di Gonzaga (of the ruling family of Mantua) to Marguerite of Savoy. As he began writing *Arianna,* Monteverdi's wife became ill and soon died. It is said that the grief he experienced was poured into the music of *Arianna,* an opera that was referred to as *una tragedia in musica.* Unfortunately, only one fragment of the opera remains, the famous "Lamento di Arianna," which is still performed today by singers in concert. This aria is powerfully dramatic and is sung in a declamatory style that makes it different from the fluid, beauty-for-beauty's-sake type of music that came before it. In the "Lamento," Monteverdi skillfully employed dissonance to create poignancy in the sound. The technical definition of dissonance is quite involved, but in simple terms dissonance occurs when notes are sounded together in such a way that they sound discordant and not what the ear and the mind would immediately expect. Dissonance is not necessarily unpleasant but, rather, serves to communicate a different emotion than the straightforward beauty of music without it. Great composers, in opera and otherwise, have employed dissonance with great effect ever since Monteverdi, and it is a regular feature of modern music. A famous example of its use is in the opening notes of Wagner's *Tristan und Isolde* (1865), which often are said to contain the seeds of modern music. But the seeds of the dramatic use of dissonance actually are found in Monteverdi.

In 1613, following the death of the Duke of Mantua, Monteverdi moved to Venice to become the *maestro di cappella*—sort of the master musician—of the Church of San Marco and, by extension, of the Venetian Republic. San Marco was second only to Rome Peter's in Catholic Europe in terms of its financial resources and its capacity to commission artists of all types. The history of music is full of composers who were able to live and work thanks to the support of civic governments, the Church, or wealthy private patrons. The absence of this kind of support today makes it increasingly difficult for most composers to create music unless they are independently wealthy. But a composer who became a *maestro di cappella,* or *Kapellmeister* in German-speaking lands, was able to flourish and produce. Such composers included Monteverdi, Vivaldi, Bach, Haydn, and Salieri, who, as Kapellmeister of Vienna, made life very difficult for the struggling Mozart.

When Monteverdi moved to Venice, he devoted himself to the composition of exquisite religious music for San Marco. In fact, Monteverdi became a priest in 1632. Yet he also composed works to be performed outside a religious setting. In Venice he wrote for a broader, more sophisticated audience than the one he knew at the court of Mantua. Before Venice, Monteverdi focused on setting text to music. But as his art developed and his audiences changed, he became ever more focused on the emotional power that music could give to a text. Aside from the oratorios, vespers, and other religious music he created for his "day job," Monteverdi continued to write operas. Unfortunately, only two of these survive: *Il Ritorno di Ulisse in Patria* (1641) and *L'Incoronazione di Poppea* (1642, less than a year before Monteverdi's death). *Poppea,* which is considered Monteverdi's masterpiece, is also notable because it is based on a historical, rather than mythological or literary, source. The use of known *human* characters from history created an immediacy that mythic personages could not rival. Monteverdi's Venetian successors went on to create more operas with real people as subjects, further secularizing the art form and making it open to new themes and styles, including comedy. With Monteverdi and his successors, Venice became the first great city of opera.

Venice was the New York City of its day, a vibrant, worldly port that grew thanks to the entrepreneurial spirit of its citizens. It was governed by an ever-changing Council of Ten that selected the Doge, or leader, who acted in the best interests of the mercantile class. While opera had previously been an entertainment for the rulers of various cities, with the opening of the Teatro San Cassiano in Venice in 1637, the art form became popular with merchants and professionals in Venetian society. To satisfy the great demand for opera by Venetian audiences, seventeen theaters for the ticket-buying public were opened, and 388 operas had been produced by the year 1700. These audiences were less interested in the arioso and more eager for fuller scores, so you will notice this major difference in listening to *Orfeo* and the two surviving operas from the end of Monteverdi's career.

Other major Venetian composers included Francesco Cavalli (1602–76), who wrote more than forty operas. From 1660 to 1662 he worked in Paris. While the opera he composed there is now lost, it is important to note that he was among the first Italians active in bringing their art form to France.

Antonio Cesti (1623–69) was a Tuscan who had worked in Florence and Rome before coming to Venice. By the end of his life, public opera houses had been opened in most major Italian cities, and his experience in various centers permitted him to amalgamate various styles (from the formality of Florence to the spontaneity of Venice) and move opera a little bit forward. Cesti's other main contribution was that he brought Italian opera to various cities in the German-speaking world during his many periods of employment abroad. Most notable was his stay in Vienna (1667), which would soon become one of the greatest musical centers in Europe.

Cesti's operas expanded the use of choruses for dramatic emphasis. He also loved spectacle and large productions. Importantly, Cesti emphasized vocal ornamentation in the arias he wrote. By "ornamentation" I mean the often rapid movement up and down the scale surrounding a note to give it, and the person singing it, more character and drama. Imagine that instead of singing the note C in a straight line or tone, a singer will start with C and "ornament" it to create a sense of the personality or emotional state of the character. This ornamentation is hardly unique to opera. The scat singing of Ella Fitzgerald is a brilliant example of ornamentation that achieves incredible response from audiences.

What is notable about ornamentation, whether in Cesti's time or today, is the degree of skill with which singers can achieve it. Composers from Cesti onward are known to have written music with particular singers in mind, matching the singer's voice and skill to the score. Some of the best practitioners of ornamentation in the seventeenth and eighteenth centuries were the castrati, who made up for what they were lacking in some areas by having the skill to sing across a three-octave (twenty-four-tone) range with fluidity and power. Castrati usually began as musically talented boys from poor families, who would be castrated to create this special type of voice, which never deepened during puberty. These men were also known as the *voci bianchi* (white voices) and were objects of great adoration wherever they appeared. The practice of castration, abhorrent though it might have been, continued until the early nineteenth century. Mozart and Rossini were among the last composers to write for castrati. Both composers were attracted to the more "natural" sound of lower female voices, so the demand for castrati gradually diminished. When early operas are performed today, women with soprano and mezzo-soprano voices or the high-voiced though unadulterated men called countertenors assume the castrato roles.

The next great composer of Italian opera was, in fact, a German who ultimately would have his greatest success in England. George Frideric Handel (1685–1759) moved to Italy in 1706 and became a wildly popular composer of operas and oratorios (religious works with singers, orchestra, and chorus that differed from operas in that they usually were sung in churches in concert form rather than staged in theaters). Handel's operas often drew upon mythological subjects or great heroic characters from ancient Greece and Rome, while his oratorios were based on characters in the Bible. His greatest Italian success was *Agrippina,* which premiered in Venice in 1707. Handel moved to England in 1711 and stayed there for most of the remainder of his life, obtaining English citizenship in 1726. His musical output included forty operas in Italian and twenty-two oratorios (twenty in English, two in Italian). The most famous Handel oratorio is, of course, *Messiah.*

Handel made great strides forward in musical coloration by using dazzling vocal ornamentation accompanied by brilliant orchestral comment to create remarkable effects. A good example is in his first English hit, *Rinaldo* (1711). Rinaldo is a brave warrior who in Act III goes into battle with the aria "Fammi combattere," a call-and-response in which trumpeter and singer imitate one another with blazing skill. Handel's genius here was in creating an effect that gives a sense of battle.

The notable English composer of a slightly earlier era was Henry Purcell (1659–95). While Handel was English by adoption, Purcell was a Londoner by birth and outlook. His main job was as the church organist at Westminster Abbey, where he is buried. London was a great theater town then, as it has remained ever since. Purcell was steeped in the great English choral tradition, and this is reflected in his operas, which have a sensuality both in music and in text. His most famous work in England is probably *The Fairy Queen* (1692), which is a loose adaptation of Shakespeare's *Midsummer Night's Dream*. In addition, he composed music for John Dryden's *King Arthur, or the British Worthy* (1691). These works were not opera in the Italian or French sense but, rather, spectacles that combined dialogue, dance, elaborate scenic design, orchestral music, and song.

Purcell's only work that resembles European opera is *Dido and Aeneas* (1689), which is thought to have been composed for a performance at Josias Priest's School for Young Gentlewomen in Chelsea. All the roles, male and female, were sung by girls, making it distinct from continental operatic tradition, where the noble male role might have been written for a castrato. Recent scholarship suggests that the opera was written for an earlier court performance sung by men and women. The greatness of *Dido and Aeneas* was not fully appreciated and the opera was not staged again until 1895, the bicentennial of Purcell's death.

At the start of the eighteenth century, while Handel was blazing the operatic path in England, the art form continued to develop in Europe. In Venice, the great successor to Cavalli and Cesti was Antonio Vivaldi (1678–1741). While he is most famous for his more than four hundred and fifty concertos and his religious music, Vivaldi also wrote forty-six known operas, and scholars suggest that he may have produced nearly twice that amount. Vivaldi is important because he kept the Venetian opera tradition alive and flourishing and also because he traveled widely throughout Europe, especially to Prague, Amsterdam, and Vienna, where he died. His travels helped spread Italian opera and sparked the imaginations of young composers who heard his works in northern Europe.

After Venice, the second great Italian city of opera was Naples. It had excellent schools to train composers, musicians, and singers. Among the leading composers of early Neapolitan opera were Arcangelo Corelli (1653–1713; in Naples from 1702 to 1708), Egidio Duni (1708–75), Francesco Durante (1684–1755), Niccolò Jommelli (1714–74), Leonardo Leo (1694–1744), Davide Perez (1710–78), Giovanni Battista Pergolesi (1710–36), and Leonardo Vinci (1690–1730), who entered the service of the court of Naples toward the end of his life. What was notable about opera in Naples is that it embraced the various styles of opera that had been created from 1600 on. Neapolitan composers experimented with melody, orchestral color, stagecraft, and the blending of tragic and comic elements. The other great contribution of Naples is that its composers traveled throughout Europe, taking their art with them. Neapolitan opera reached Spain and Portugal to the west, Saint Petersburg to the north, and France, where a notable operatic culture had already developed by the mid-1650s.

The most important Neapolitan opera was Pergolesi's *La Serva Padrona* (1733), which most scholars consider the first great comic opera. In its title character, the serving girl Serpina, there is the prototype for the wise, capricious young woman who is always two steps ahead of a lecherous, bumbling old man, who in this case employs her.

The role of Serpina was the first *soubrette,* a lighthearted but always in-control young woman who in opera usually has a piping soprano voice. In most operas with soubrette parts that followed *La Serva Padrona,* the role is written for this type of soprano voice. "Soubrette" means a lady's maid, and many, though not all, soubrettes fit that description. Famous soubrette roles include Mozart's Susanna *(Le Nozze di Figaro),* Zerlina *(Don Giovanni),* and Despina *(Così fan tutte),* Beethoven's Marzelline in *Fidelio,* a few Rossini characters, Adina in Donizetti's *L'Elisir d'Amore,* and Nannetta in Verdi's *Falstaff*. The typical soubrette is a practical person who is in charge of her own life and does not allow herself to be taken advantage of and is often fickle in love. (Typically, too, these characters' names often end in the diminutive *-ina* or *-etta*.) Famous soubrettes in recent times include Roberta Peters and Kathleen Battle.

Uberto in *La Serva Padrona* is the prototype of the *basso buffo,* or comic bass, a stock character in most every opera that has a soubrette. Rossini used many a basso buffo, in operas such as *L'Italiana in Algeri* (Taddeo and Mustafà), *Il Barbiere di Siviglia* (Dr. Bartolo and Don Basilio), as did Mozart: Osmin in *Die Entführung aus dem Serail* and Bartolo in *Le Nozze di Figaro*. Although they were created much later, the title characters in Verdi's *Falstaff* (1893) and Puccini's *Gianni Schicchi* (1918), although written for baritones, show the influence of the basso buffo.

As this style of opera emerged, terms had to be created to distinguish between the forms of opera that were based on humor and those that were not. While older operas may have had moments of comic relief or, at least, mild diversion, their main thrust was usually tragic or deeply emotional. *Opera seria* suggested serious opera—that is, stories that did not attempt to provoke laughter in the audience. *Opera buffa,* in contrast, was opera that was comic in intent.

Opera buffa often drew its themes from contemporary life and used texts by the great writers of the day. The foremost comic playwright was the Venetian Carlo Goldoni (1707–93), whose texts were set by most of the great composers of the eighteenth century. Baldassare Galuppi (1706–85), Goldoni's favorite, was a Venetian opera composer who was the other leading exponent of comic operas. However, Goldoni also supplied libretti—texts—to many other composers, including Antonio Salieri (1750–1825), and even the young Mozart, who wrote *La Finta Semplice* in 1769. What is amazing about Goldoni is that in his long life he worked with composers who were active in the seventeenth, eighteenth, and nineteenth centuries.

Galuppi's heirs to the tradition of comic opera composition were Niccolò Piccini (1728–1800) and Giovanni Paisiello (1740–1816).

Piccini completed his studies in Naples and quickly had a raging success with his first opera, *Le Donne Dispettose* (1754). He moved to Rome, where he wrote *La Buona Figliuola* (1760) to a libretto by Goldoni, and remained there until 1774, composing operas that brought him great acclaim. Following a brief return to Naples, he moved to Paris, where his particular style was greatly appreciated. Italian comedies were thought to have a slight emotional tug under the brilliant humor, and Piccini's style was known as the *comédie larmoyante,* which translates loosely as "tearful comedy." He remained in Paris until 1791, when the unsettled atmosphere compelled him to return to Naples. There, he was suspected of being in sympathy with the Jacobins of the French Revolution and was imprisoned for four years. In 1798 he returned to Paris, where he died. In all, Piccini wrote 120 operas, both comic and tragic. While he is little remembered today, he was very influential in his time.

Paisiello is notable because he traveled widely, absorbing different styles and tastes that he incorporated in his own musical idiom. Following study and early success in Naples, he worked in Bologna and, in 1775, was summoned to the court of Catherine the Great in St. Petersburg to run the Italian opera house as maestro di cappella. Paisiello later worked in Vienna and Paris, in the process absorbing and adapting to the ideas of these two important cities. In St. Petersburg he composed his version of *La Serva Padrona* (1781), based on the same libretto used by Pergolesi fifty years earlier, and *Il Barbiere di Siviglia* (1782), a charming comedy that probably would have an audience today if it had not been eclipsed by Rossini's marvelous version (1816). In fact, when Rossini's *Barbiere* had its premiere at the Teatro Argentina in Rome, admirers of Paisiello turned out to boo the singers and throw objects at the stage. The first performance was a fiasco because of the disturbances, but the second performance was a brilliant success, and Rossini's *Barbiere* was destined to become the most popular comic opera of all time.

EARLY OPERA IN FRANCE

By the time Pergolesi's *La Serva Padrona* came to Paris in 1752, there had already been a flourishing operatic scene there for nearly a century. Francesco Cavalli had worked there in 1660, and a Florentine named Giovanni Battista Lulli (1632–87) had established a brilliant career as the court composer for King Louis XIV, the Sun King. Lulli renamed himself Jean-Baptiste Lully. This was the period of great writers, and the tragedians Corneille (1606–84) and Quinault (1635–88) and the more humorous Molière (1622–73) all supplied texts set to music by Lully.

While France drew musical inspiration from Italy, it was the first country to develop an autonomous style that would continue to grow in its own different directions. Lully, by now thoroughly French in outlook, was the first composer to establish certain traditions that would become hallmarks of French opera through the years. The French term for his works was *tragédie-lyrique,* which suggests that these works were really plays set to music. The most important tradition created by Lully is the greater emphasis given in French opera to enunciation of the words. This meant that the arioso style, which allowed words to be sung along a melodic line that made them comprehensible, had greater influence in France than it did in the more rapidly evolving Italian opera scene.

In service to the tastes of his royal employer, Lully composed operas based on stories that included great spectacle. This required the inclusion of long dance sequences, which have always been more prized in France than in other countries. The productions of Lully operas were full of dramatic stage effects, elegant costumes, and beautiful scenery. Lully operas, such as *Alceste* (1674), *Atys* (1676), and *Armide* (1686), all are notable for the intense participation the orchestra has in the dramatic action, commenting upon and underlining the feelings of the characters and providing the audience with gripping dramatic impulse.

In fact, Lully was a rather imposing and dramatic type himself, an autocrat who ran the musical life at court with a very tight rein. He personally oversaw the rehearsals of orchestras and choruses at court—and met his end in the process: while pounding out the beat with a large pole during a rehearsal, he drove the pole through his foot. The resultant gangrene proved fatal.

The next great French composer was Jean-Philippe Rameau (1683–1764), a student of Lully. He was a great theoretician who published several treatises about musical theory and performance practice. He attempted to break with the formal traditions of Lully, just as the Venetians and Neapolitans had broken with the earlier tradition of the Florentines. Voltaire asked Rameau to compose a score to his *Samson* in 1731. The opera was banned by censors, but Rameau went on to write *Hippolyte et Aricie* (1733), *Les Indes Galantes* (1735), and *Castor et Pollux* (1737). Just as Lully was a man of the Baroque era, Rameau was an exponent of the Enlightenment philosophy of eighteenth-century Europe. In response to Lullian excesses, Rameau sought balance among opera's various components: words, vocal music, dance, orchestration, scenery, costumes, and special effects. Above all, he gave greater emphasis than Lully to melody as an expressive form and worked to further the use of the orchestra as an active participant in the storytelling of opera.

Pergolesi's *La Serva Padrona* triggered a great debate among the French about comic opera. French comic opera based on Molière found humor primarily in the words of the text, while Italian comedies found humor in the situations that would be expressed primarily in the music.

During the latter part of the eighteenth century, the French came up with the term *opéra comique*. This does not mean comic opera but, rather, opera (usually based on rustic, pastoral, or contemporary themes) that combines sung music with spoken text as opposed to recitative, which has at least the underpinning of a harpsichord. This is not unlike our modern Broadway musical in which characters talk before breaking into song and then return to speaking when the song is over. The prototype for the opéra comique was *Richard Coeur de Lion* (1784) by André Ernest Modeste Grétry (1741–1813); although largely forgotten today, it remained a standard repertory work for nearly a century. Subsequent opéras comiques were written by Italians such as Rossini (*Le Comte Ory,* 1828) and Gaetano Donizetti (*La Fille du Régiment,* 1840) and by many Frenchmen, most notably François Adrien Boieldieu (1775–1834), Daniel François Esprit Auber (1782–1871), and Adolphe Charles Adam (1803–56).

This digression into the future should not distract us from looking at where opera had arrived by the 1770s. The intentions of the

Camerata Fiorentina were all but forgotten. In many places opera was a business as well as an art form, and public taste became as important as pure artistic sensibility. In other words, many composers sought to give the people what they wanted.

Opera composers in this era and for many years to come did not write with the idea that their works would be revived. They composed to make money and for artistic expression, but they thought in terms of producing a new work for the latest court event or empty slot in a theater's schedule. If they compared themselves with their predecessors and rivals, it was primarily to blaze a new path and give expression to their particular artistic point of view. Only as musical history became longer did composers begin to look backward for inspiration.

Paris and other cities had by now witnessed the opening of public opera houses. In addition, the Enlightenment and social unrest were creating the groundswell that would lead to the French Revolution in 1789. This radical change in European history meant that opera librettists and composers became interested in exploring contemporary social and moral issues in addition to drawing their subjects from ancient and classical sources. In Italy particularly the interest in the ancients declined, although opera seria still was important in Paris and Vienna. As political configurations changed across the Continent, and certain cities, such as Paris and Vienna, became the seats of empires, composers were no longer assured of court patronage in the provinces. Paris and Vienna became two of the leading opera centers, rivaling Venice, Naples, and other Italian cities, including Milan.

The Venetian empire waned during much of the eighteenth century and the city finally fell, weakly, to Napoleon in 1797. Many of its opera houses were converted to sites for plays or were closed altogether. Most of the glorious city-states of the Italian peninsula were by now under the domination of other powers, such as Spain, France, and Austria-Hungary. Rome and other Italian cities became sources of artistic inspiration for visitors from northern Europe, and though Italy continued to produce many of the greatest operatic composers, opera was now a European art form with composers, librettists, and singers working in Italian, French, German, and, to a lesser extent, Spanish, English, Russian, and other languages.

In 1778 the Teatro alla Scala opened in Milan with the first performance of *L'Europa Riconosciuta* by Antonio Salieri. While opera had been performed in Milan for many years, La Scala would come to occupy a special place in opera history as the national stage of Italy, rivaling Covent Garden in London, the Staatsoper in Vienna, and the Palais Garnier in Paris, which is also known as the Paris Opéra. Later, the Metropolitan Opera, which opened in 1883, would assume a comparable status as the national operatic stage of America.

EARLY OPERA IN GERMANY

Only Germany among the major operatic countries does not have one preeminent theater. This is due largely to the fact that the golden age of German opera would come in the nineteenth century, as well as the fact that the geographic and political entity we call Germany only came into being around 1870.

In the first 175 years of opera history, opera in Germany was for the most part Italian opera. Italian subject matter and musical styles came to the courts of the more than seventeen hundred small German states in the persons of composers and singers who were brought north to provide entertainment.

The first great German opera composer, Handel, wrote his operas in Italian. Before Handel, the musical-theatrical form that predominated was the *Singspiel,* which more or less means a "sung play." Early singspiel was either completely sung or had passages that were spoken, like the later French opéra comique. By 1750, though, all singspiels were a combination of spoken dialogue and music. The word *Oper* (opera) was not consistently used in Germany until about 1720, by which time Handel was busy in England, and Italy and France had thriving operatic traditions.

The first known singspiel or opera in German is probably *Dafne* (1627), which was translated and adapted by the foremost German poet, Martin Opitz (1597–1639), from the text by Peri's librettist, Rinuccini. Its music, composed by Heinrich Schütz (1585–1672), has disappeared. Other German composers followed with operas of their own, but there was not yet really a German style to speak of.

A major change came with the opening of the first public opera house outside of Italy, in Hamburg in 1678. Hamburg, like Venice, was a major mercantile center, and its ships plied the North Sea as Venice's boats sailed the Adriatic. The opera house in Hamburg presented the work of German composers, starting with Johann Theile (1646–1724), a pupil of Schütz's, whose *Der Erschaffene, Gefallene, und Wieder Aufgerichte Mensch* (loosely, The Creation, Fall, and Redemption of Man) told the story of Adam and Eve. This religious theme was in deference to the Lutheran Church, which was suspicious of the pagan and sometimes immoral themes explored in some Italian and French operas. But Italian and French works soon came to Hamburg, often translated into German for local audiences.

The next important Hamburg composer was Reinhard Keiser (1674–1739), who is thought to have written about eighty operas, twenty-five of which have survived. His works are an eclectic mix of Italian and French influences along with a strong emphasis on exploiting the expressive means of the orchestra. A generalization that can be made about German opera through the centuries is the particularly rich texture that German composers attempted to create in their orchestras, which would provide a more telling account of the action onstage. Keiser sought to create this orchestral color while eliminating the excessive heaviness he heard in French orchestras. His sparkling lightness prefigured the operatic orchestra of Mozart, which always combined the meaningful with the ethereal.

Keiser did draw from Lully by including choruses and ballets in his operas, but he departed from tradition by giving different styles to the basic aria. Traditionally, an aria was a declamatory song performed by a singer who would communicate in words and music the particular situation his character was in. Keiser was one of the first composers to make the aria more flexible, permitting it to be shorter or longer than was customary in order to suit the needs of the drama.

It is important to remember that Theile, Keiser, and other German composers dealt with a new operatic variable that the French and Italians did not face: the German language. Because German words often end in consonants rather than vowels and have a harsher sound than the Latin languages, the music that would couch these words had to sound different. This is certainly not meant to imply that German music was less pretty; but just as the Italian language requires a loose jaw and an open mouth and French needs a smaller mouth and a tighter jaw, the mandibular movements required to speak German resulted in a different sound in sung German. In fact, spoken and sung German often requires the looser mouth of Italian and the tighter muscles of the French mouth. Whenever you approach an opera, you must keep in mind that the language in which it is sung will have a major influence on the sound of the music. This is why opera in translation is a questionable practice. Composers heard the words as they created the music, and those same sounds can seldom be reproduced in another language.

The first German to have an undeniably important impact on opera as an art form was Christoph Willibald Gluck (1714–87). Gluck was washed with all of the musical waters of Europe, and through him opera took a major step forward. At the age of seventeen he enrolled at the University of Prague to study logic. A few years later he went to Vienna to work as a musician in the service of an Austrian prince. At the age of twenty-four he went to Milan for more musical study and began writing operas there four years later. He spent 1745–46 in London, where he had contact with Handel. After further travels, he moved to Vienna in 1750, where he married a wealthy woman and remained until 1774. In 1750 he came into contact with several French operas when he was asked to conduct their first Vienna performances. In 1774 he left for a five-year sojourn in Paris, returning to Vienna in 1779 for his last years.

Having experienced all of the major operatic styles, Gluck was in a unique position to evaluate the state of the art form. In his first twenty years of composing (1741–61), Gluck created thirty operas in the styles that were then in favor in Italy and France. He wrote his first ten operas in Milan in just four years (between 1741 and 1745) before leaving for London. By 1760 Gluck had come to believe that the Italian, French, and Handelian styles of opera were full of excesses that betrayed the reasons for which the art form was invented. When he met the Italian poet Ranieri de Calzabigi (1714–

95), he found a like-minded thinker who could give words to the kind of music Gluck sought to create.

The changes Gluck envisioned for opera came to be known as the Gluckian reforms. First of all, Gluck was in agreement with the Camerata Fiorentina in his interest in returning to Greek theater as the major source of subject matter. Opera, he felt, should offer the emotional transport and purification that was inherent in the great theater works of antiquity. He sought to restore balance between vocal music, words, orchestral accompaniment, and a more restrained style of stagecraft that enhanced the drama rather than overwhelmed it. Following the example of the Greeks, Gluck made extensive use of the chorus as an additional character in his post-1760 reformist operas. Before Gluck, the overture that preceded operas was a piece of music composed to entertain but did not necessarily relate to the opera's story. Gluck believed that the overture should introduce audiences to the atmosphere of the music and story that would follow. He was displeased with excessive ornamentation, which he believed was more of a showcase for a singer's talents than a service to an opera's creators. He emphasized the orchestra's independent expressive function, commenting upon rather than simply accompanying the singing and the action. He also sought scenic designers who created sets that permitted continuous flow of action rather than frequent stopping and starting for scene changes. Gluck's ideals are summed up well in the following excerpt from his preface to the score of *Alceste* (1767): "I have striven to restrict music to its true office of serving poetry by means of expression and by following the situations of the story, without interrupting the action or stifling it with useless superfluity of ornaments; and I believe that it should do this in the same way as telling colors affect a correct and well-ordered drawing; by a well-assorted contrast of light and shade, which serves to animate the figures without altering their contours."

It should not surprise you that, in seeking to re-establish contact with opera's beginnings, Gluck and Calzabigi chose the story of Orpheus and Eurydice as the plot for their first reformist opera. To hear their *Orfeo ed Euridice* (1762) after listening to Lully or Handel is to find a work stripped of everything except the essentials of opera. It is like looking at a perfect nude from which clothing or jewels would only detract, or perhaps a Christmas tree with no lights or ornaments; the tree itself is a miraculous thing of beauty. This rediscovery of the essence of music and poetry can be very bracing. All of the Gluckian reforms would influence the operatic composers who followed him. Whether or not these composers incorporated the reforms into their own art, they had to be given consideration.

Orfeo ed Euridice was widely heard and studied, although many composers and patrons resisted the reforms and sought to continue the excesses that brought them fame and fortune. Gluck and Calzabigi followed this success with two more landmark operas, *Alceste* and *Ifigenia in Aulide,* which put the Gluckian reforms to further use. All three works were revised for performances in French during Gluck's Paris period. The composer also added ballets to suit French tastes, yet these dance sections were made integral to the story rather than serving as interludes that separated the music that preceded and followed them. This integration of dance into action, though it had precedents in theater and opera, was startling to the eyes of audiences who had become used to spectacle for spectacle's sake. In Paris Gluck also wrote *Iphigénie en Tauride* (1779), with a powerfully dramatic libretto by Nicolas-François Guillard.

Among the composers who drew inspiration from Gluck—whether they acknowledged it or not—were Luigi Cherubini (1760–1842), Mozart, Beethoven, Wagner, Berlioz, and Richard Strauss.

MOZART

Wolfgang Amadeus Mozart (1756–91) was the greatest composer of his time, a singular genius whose work towered above that of everyone around him. While most earlier and subsequent composers distinguished themselves primarily in one form of composition, Mozart excelled at anything he touched: opera, symphonies, concertos, sonatas, chamber music.

Mozart's greatest feat as an opera composer is his mastery of so many different styles, almost always producing works superior to those of other composers. *Die Entführung aus dem Serail* (The Abduction from the Seraglio) and *Die Zauberflöte* (The Magic Flute) are among the finest singspiels ever written. *Mitridate, Rè di Ponto* and *Lucio Silla* were his teenage attempts at opera seria, a form he returned to with assurance and brilliance in *Idomeneo* and his last opera, *La Clemenza di Tito.* He dabbled early with pastoral opera *(Il Rè Pastore)* and opera buffa *(La Finta Giardiniera).* And the three works he wrote to librettos by Lorenzo da Ponte—*Le Nozze di Figaro, Don Giovanni,* and *Così fan tutte*—are among the greatest of all marriages of words and music. While Gluck was very much the theorist who fashioned his operas to his idea that the drama was foremost, Mozart worked with intuitive understanding of human motivations to create deeper psychological depictions of his characters than Gluck, with all of his rationality, ever achieved. To hear Mozart's music with da Ponte's brilliant and witty words is to understand how musical "paint" can create a stunning canvas when the "painter" is one of the finest composers of all time. Just as it took a Monteverdi to make the goals of the Camerata Fiorentina real, Mozart, in his best work, unintentionally realized the goals of Gluck. The elements of music, drama, characterization, dance, spectacle, and orchestral color converge with near-perfection in the mature works of Mozart.

Mozart and da Ponte were men of their age. In adapting Beaumarchais's 1778 play, *Le Mariage de Figaro,* they took one of the most controversial plays ever written and turned it into a truly revolutionary opera in 1786, just three years before the French Revolution. While the play and the opera are comic tales about the love between a servant (Figaro) and a maid (Susanna) in the home of the Count and Countess Almaviva, it was also the story of the servile classes outwitting and rebelling against the ruling classes. Audiences who see *Le Nozze di Figaro* nowadays without an awareness of the background of the story might think they are witnessing a charming entertainment about fidelity set to gorgeous music. Mozart viewed all of the characters in this opera as real people with real feelings rather than simply comic figures. When the Countess, one of Mozart's most beautiful creations, laments her husband's infidelities and wonders whether she is still desirable, the beauty and pathos of her music affects the listener far more than the literal message of the words alone would. Herein we are reminded that in the great debate over the pre-eminence of words or music, the finest operatic moments are those in which music is inextricably wedded to the words, a sublime combination that reaches the listener on both rational and purely emotional levels.

In *Figaro* we see Mozart at his most overtly political. *Don Giovanni* and *Così fan tutte* are brilliant studies of human behavior, especially human sexuality. Politics in these operas is more about the flouting of convention and how the social restraints of the time affected the search for sexual gratification and emotional fulfillment. These were hot topics in that era and no less so in our own times. In the character insights that we hear in Mozart's music we discover the constants as well as the quicksilver changes in human desire.

In the composer's penultimate opera, *Die Zauberflöte,* Mozart, who was desperately poor and nearing the end of his short life (he died of typhus), went beyond the discussion of sexual love to explore the lofty human values of bravery and, especially, the search for truth and, to use a modern phrase, to find out what it all means. Again, the uninformed might see this opera as a playful fairy tale with lots of pretty music, but it is also about the human quest for spiritual peace. How this story must have found resonance in Mozart!

I consider Mozart's last opera, *La Clemenza di Tito,* to be his most underrated. With its formal conventions of arias, duets, and choruses, this is a perfect example of opera seria rather than the through-composed character of *Nozze* or *Così fan tutte.* Yet the characters in *Tito* burn with a kind of passion that one seldom finds so overtly in opera seria. This opera is about the power of forgiveness even in the face of extreme wrongdoing and injustice. Whenever I hear it, I think of the dying Mozart trying to reconcile his feelings. Why were composers of marginal quality whose music and ideas were safer than Mozart's allowed to lead comfortable lives with abundant patronage, while this genius was always in debt and ultimately so sick? Mozart's last two operas, I believe, were about his efforts to understand his fate, while his beautiful Requiem mass, his last work, was his acknowledgment that death would quickly claim him. His widow could not afford the funeral costs, and Mozart was buried in a potter's field among the destitute of Vienna. No one seems to know where his remains wound up, but his operas are still with us, representing both a pinnacle of musical accomplishment and the crossroads between early opera and the nineteenth century, the golden age of opera.

It is remarkable that most of the operas referred to as the "standard repertory"—works that are the bread and butter of most theaters—come from the nineteenth century. It is safe to say that the overwhelming majority of works presented on the world's stages appeared in just 140 years, between 1786 *(Le Nozze di Figaro)* and 1926 *(Turandot,* Puccini's last opera).

The styles that had evolved in opera up to the time of Mozart were viewed as old-fashioned in post-1789 Europe. The philosophers and poets who led revolutions in America and France helped wipe out all of the old assumptions about the human condition. Mozart was the first composer to recognize this; and his works, combined with the Gluckian reforms, meant that opera in the nineteenth century was destined to take a different course. It is probable that the standard repertory of today speaks to audiences in deeper ways because it was created in an environment that produced many of the political and social institutions under which we still live.

In the early twentieth century, some of these institutions and assumptions began to break down. Empires and monarchies gave way to the spread of constitutional democracy or totalitarianism. The United States and the Soviet Union became poles that split Europe ideologically. Freud, Jung, and the rise of psychoanalysis gave new language to the description and understanding of human motivations. The invention of film, radio, the phonograph, and television changed the way people got their entertainment. All of these developments had a profound impact on opera's growth.

BEETHOVEN'S INFLUENCE

Any mention of the composers who were directly affected by, and sought to influence, the political and social movements of their times, immediately brings Ludwig van Beethoven to mind. He was born in the German city of Bonn in 1770 to a family of modest means. He attracted the attention of the Breuning family, which engaged him to teach piano. In this cultured family, Beethoven was exposed to discussions of the leading contemporary writers and thinkers, including Goethe, Schiller, Herder, and Kant. These men, all of whom were eloquent in their loathing of tyranny and their exalting of the nobility of man, were members of an artistic movement known as *Sturm und Drang* (Storm and Stress), which advocated youthful revolt against existing standards.

In 1787, full of talent and revolutionary ideals, young Beethoven went to Vienna for further musical training, but he soon had to return to Bonn because of the death of his mother. He returned to Vienna in 1792 to study with Antonio Salieri and the famous Franz Joseph Haydn (1732–1809), who was the composer of numerous operas, now seldom produced, but is best remembered for his 104 symphonies.

In this post-1789 era, Beethoven felt that a musician did not exist simply to please a royal patron, but was endowed with gifts that should be spread to the public at large. In 1795, he gave his first public concerts, a practice that continued until 1815, when his advancing deafness (first detected in 1798) became so severe that he was compelled to stop.

In listening to Beethoven's music, one hears a passion and nobility that few other composers have ever approached. One of the reasons he achieved this was his use of larger orchestras than his predecessors. By adding more instruments, he was able to achieve a greater variety of orchestral color and, quite simply, more sound. Beethoven's wider palette and greater sonic range, from the softest *pianissimo* to the loudest *fortissimo,* gave him expressive possibilities that were new to audiences. This was impressive in the concert hall, but it had different implications in the opera house.

The thrilling possibilities of a bigger orchestra made for greater dramatic potential, but it also meant that singing styles would begin to change. In opera's first two hundred years, the human voice served as the leading instrument in an ensemble of sound. Singing was fluid and a natural extension of speaking. Beauty of sound, excellent diction, and skill of ornamentation were the major expres-

sive tools required for singers. When projection over a greater number of instruments becomes part of a singer's task, singers need to be
trained to meet this additional requirement. In addition, theaters
have gradually become larger, which means that singers need to
project further. The Vienna State Opera has approximately sixteen
hundred seats, as did La Scala until a recent renovation removed
some to make wider, safer aisles. By contrast, modern American
opera houses have up to four thousand seats.

Opera singing is a taxing physical feat, requiring a strong diaphragm, great lung power and breath control, and healthy vocal
cords. The goal of an opera singer is to combine beauty of tone,
expressiveness, and accurate reflection of the written musical score
with projection that can reach every ear in the theater.

So when you listen to nineteenth-century opera and compare it
with works from Monteverdi through early Mozart, you will notice
that it sounds fundamentally different. Early orchestras may have
had up to forty instruments, but opera orchestras in the past two
hundred years can have twice that number and in some exceptional
cases (Richard Strauss's *Elektra,* for example) even exceed one hundred musicians. Combine a large orchestra with a fifty-member
chorus in operas such as Verdi's *Aïda,* and you can imagine the
vocal power the title character must achieve to be heard above everyone else. But, despite the stereotypes, opera singing is not only
about volume. The greater sonic range of the orchestra means that
an opera singer's character might sing softly over quieter orchestral
passages in moments of sadness or tenderness and then be asked to
sing louder in moments of great passion or stress. All of these requirements are placed in the score by the composer, and it is the job
of the conductor to keep the correct balance of volume and tempo
for all the musical elements: orchestra, chorus, and solo singers.

Beethoven wrote only one opera, *Fidelio,* but it is a work of such
beauty and significance that it deserves mention in any discussion of
the great operas. *Fidelio* is not a perfect opera. Beethoven wrestled
with it for years: it was first presented in 1805 (when it was deemed
a failure), but he continued to revise it until 1814, writing four versions of the opera's overture. Beethoven used various existing operatic conventions, some of which do not fit together comfortably.

Fidelio is essentially a "rescue opera," similar in theme to the many tellings of the Orpheus and Eurydice story and many other tales of bravery that appeared during opera's first two hundred years. It tells the story of a woman, Leonore, whose husband, Florestan, has been imprisoned because of his revolutionary activities. In an attempt to save him, Leonore disguises herself as a young man, Fidelio (derived from the same linguistic root as "fidelity"), and hires on as the jailer's assistant. The jailer's daughter, Marzelline (a soubrette), is attracted to the "young man," who resists the girl's flirtations. This initial part of the opera, in the style of the comic mistaken identity, does not effectively lead to the story that will follow. The opera has a lot of spoken dialogue, in the style of the singspiel, and this makes it somewhat less accessible to audiences who don't speak German.

Following the opera's comic first scene, there is a relatively clumsy presentation of some of the other characters as the action moves disjointedly along. Toward the end of the act, Leonore sings a long and very difficult aria that bespeaks her pain and anguish. This aria is unlike anything heard before in opera history because of what may sound like rawness in its musical palette. The first act ends with a gorgeous choral scene in which the prisoners (mostly jailed for political reasons) pine for freedom. In a tradition going back through Gluck to the Camerata Fiorentina, the chorus has an actual role rather than being there simply to offer commentary. Nowhere in the first act do we see Florestan, the object of Leonore's concern and affection. Despite the unwieldy dramaturgy, audiences become deeply engrossed in the story because of Beethoven's powerful music.

The start of Act II is rather unorthodox. The curtain rises to reveal almost total darkness. Only gradually, during an excruciatingly emotional orchestral passage of almost four minutes, does the audience discover Florestan chained to the floor of his subterranean cell. The character's first pained note is a cry, "Gott!" (God!), which rivets the audience when sung by a great artist. Florestan's music depicts the hallucinations of the desperate prisoner who suddenly "sees" an angel, Leonore. We in the audience know that she is soon to arrive on the scene to rescue him, but this does not detract from the pain and suffering we are witnessing.

In fact, this opera, with a very simple story and very little action, achieves astonishing emotional heights and, in good performances, can grip audiences as few other theatrical or musical works can. Through his effective use of the orchestral and vocal elements at his disposal, Beethoven makes audiences feel uplifted and ennobled by the bravery of Leonore and Florestan.

Beethoven's only opera was a great inspiration to many composers, especially Gioacchino Rossini (1792–1868) and Wagner. When we think of Rossini, we think of sparkling comedies set to fluid, lilting, almost Mozartian melodies. But what Rossini learned from Beethoven was the great expressive power of the orchestra to act as one voice or many voices in the total musical picture.

Rossini was the first great Italian composer of the nineteenth century. The sparkling sound of his music, and the alleged facility with which he wrote it, are prime reasons for its being discounted by "serious" music lovers. Add to this the fact that his best-known works are comedies, which are wrongly considered by many to be poor cousins of serious opera, and Rossini is frequently undervalued. But L'Italiana in Algeri (1813) and Il Barbiere di Siviglia (1816) are supreme examples of opera buffa, while La Cenerentola (1817), Rossini's version of the Cinderella story, combines buffa elements with tender sentimentality.

Yet Rossini also created some of the greatest opera seria works, including Tancredi (1813), Mosè in Egitto (1818), and Semiramide (1823). Because castrati were a rare commodity by Rossini's time, the composer chose to cast a mezzo-soprano in the role of the heroic male. These roles are called "travesti" or "trouser" parts.

Except for the comedies, most Rossini operas disappeared from the world's stages following his death. With the advent, since 1950, of singers such as Maria Callas, Joan Sutherland, Marilyn Horne, Montserrat Caballé, and Samuel Ramey, we have seen an amazing resurgence in Rossini's stature. Marilyn Horne is probably the century's greatest Rossini singer, and she has recorded many of his great mezzo-soprano roles. Additionally, scholars such as Philip Gossett and conductors such as Claudio Abbado and Alberto Zedda have championed the rediscovery of Rossini, and many of his works have been dusted off, re-evaluated, produced onstage, and recorded. Each August, Rossini's hometown of Pesaro holds a festival in which at least one rarity is staged.

Rossini moved from Italy to Paris in 1823 and immersed himself in the French musical world. Paris was the operatic capital of Europe for most of the nineteenth century, attracting great composers and singers from throughout Europe. Rossini was swept up in Romanticism, the century's dominant artistic current. A reaction to the rationalism of the eighteenth century, Romanticism not only was about love but was a glorification of nature and of the simpler life. You probably have noticed that throughout artistic and philosophical history there has been a continuous pendular shift between overriding interest in the mind (ancient Greece, the Renaissance, the Enlightenment, the rise of Freudianism) and an interest in the soul (the Middle Ages, the seventeenth-century Baroque, Romanticism). Gluck, Mozart, Beethoven, and Rossini were all in the middle of one of these great shifts, although Rossini lived long enough to see it completed.

In 1829, at the age of thirty-seven, Rossini wrote the last of his approximately forty operas ("approximately" because of rewrites and what he called "pastiches"). *Guillaume Tell* (William Tell) is remembered today primarily for its wonderful overture, but in its time it was one of the most popular operas. By 1868, the year of Rossini's death, it had already been given five hundred performances at the Paris Opéra. It remained active in the repertory in Paris until 1932, by which time it had received 911 performances. Although composed to a French libretto, it often has been staged outside of France in Italian translation. *Guillaume Tell* is a large-scale romantic drama that foreshadows many of the works of Verdi, Berlioz, and Wagner in its use of nature almost as a character and in its majestic sweep coupled with precise character delineation. This opera is notable as an example of grand opera, which we will talk about later on.

Rossini, along with Vincenzo Bellini (1801–35) and Gaetano Donizetti (1797–1848), was a leading exponent of the musical style known as *bel canto*. This term means simply "beautiful singing," but it implies much more than that. In some ways it recalls the ornamentation found in Handel and Mozart, but it was a distinct artistic movement. While Gluck and Beethoven pointed opera in one direction, these Italian composers sought a different way of employing the human voice. Actually, bel canto was a reassertion of the emphasis on the voice as the most important expressive element in opera, more important than words or the orchestra. The words of some bel canto operas are rather mundane, but their open vowels allow talented singers to float beautiful melody that effectively expresses the feelings of the character.

A particular specialty in bel canto is the mad scene, a solo set piece in which a soprano enacts insanity or despair in musical terms by using effects such as rolling up and down the musical scale on a single breath or repeating a previously heard melody in a distorted way. While the sound of these mad scenes is invariably beautiful, they amazingly communicate dementia. The most famous mad scene is from Donizetti's *Lucia di Lammermoor* (1835), which I will discuss further in chapter 6.

The bel canto composers generally eschewed recitativo secco in favor of recitativo accompagnato. The vocal line in bel canto scores calls for soft, rounded notes and great agility in ornamentation and phrasing. Big bel canto arias often have two parts, the *cavatina* and the *cabaletta*. The former is often slow, melodic, expressive and sometimes allows for ornamentation. The latter is a different melody in a contrasting (usually faster) tempo and allows the singer even more room for bravura display. The cabaletta usually ends with a great soaring note which if well sung will drive audiences into a frenzy. In many of these arias, the chorus interrupts the singer after the cavatina to agree with or perhaps comment on what has just been said by the singer. The chorus plays a large role in bel canto, often seconding or underscoring melodies as orchestras might do in other operas. The effect is to suggest that this crowd of people onstage understands or endorses what the solo character is singing. Rather than merely commenting, as other choruses generally do, the bel canto chorus often interacts musically and dramatically with the soloist. While Donizetti's and Bellini's orchestras lack the complexity of Rossini's, they nonetheless create a pronounced mood. Bellini in particular was a sublime melodist, and his *Norma* (1831) is considered by many to be the greatest bel canto opera, although *Lucia di Lammermoor* is more popular.

Donizetti also wrote bel canto comedies, including *L'Elisir d'Amore* (The Elixir of Love, 1832), which includes one of opera's greatest tenor arias, "Una furtiva lagrima"; *La Fille du Régiment* (The Daughter of the Regiment), written for Paris in 1840; and the great opera buffa *Don Pasquale* (1843). Bellini's last opera, the wonderful *I Puritani* (1835), was also written for Paris. It contains gorgeous music, including "Suoni la tromba," a thrilling duet for baritone and bass, and the heroine's mad scene, from which she later recovers to join the tenor for a happy finale.

Bel canto is a touchstone for anyone who loves opera because it shows the great glory of a beautiful human voice and because the listener learns to find drama primarily in music rather than words.

VERDI

The inheritor of the Italian opera mantle was Giuseppe Verdi (1813–1901), who is often referred to as the greatest Italian artist since the Renaissance. Verdi and his German counterpart, Richard Wagner (1813–83), were the twin colossi of nineteenth-century opera. More has been written about these two than any other opera composers, and their great works are the anchors of the standard repertory.

Verdi began to write opera in an Italy that was largely under foreign domination, broken into many little pieces occupied by Austria, France, and Spain. The house of Savoy in Piedmont was the seat of a monarchical family that sought to unify Italy under its rule. Patriots such as Cavour and Garibaldi led the struggle for unification through oratorical and military means, but Verdi's contribution was at least as important.

It has often been said that Verdi led the fight for unification from the stage of La Scala. Many of his early operas, such as *Nabucco, I Lombardi alla Prima Crociata, Ernani, I Due Foscari, Attila, La Battaglia di Legnano,* and *Rigoletto,* had themes about oppressed people rising up and claiming freedom or (in the case of *Rigoletto*) presented a ruler in an unflattering light. The popular chorus from *Nabucco,* "Va, pensiero, sull'ali dorate" (Go, thought, on golden wings), is a moving evocation of yearning for freedom. It was sung throughout the Italian peninsula and even today is the unofficial national anthem of Italy. Italian audiences often sing along when that chorus is performed. In the opera houses of Italy in the 1840s, 1850s, and 1860s it was common for Italians seeking freedom from the yoke of foreign dominance to cry "Viva Verdi!"—not only as a tribute to the composer but as a veiled declaration of allegiance to Victor Emmanuel, the Savoy king—Vittorio Emanuele, Re d'Italia, or Victor Emmanuel, King of Italy. Unification finally came in 1870.

Yet it would be unfair to ascribe Verdi's popularity to his politics alone. One senses while listening to Verdi his unerring sense of drama. He knew how to have a single anguished voice float over a roaring orchestra or how to communicate every emotion, from love to fear to resignation. In his music and in his own life, he grappled with great issues in very profound ways: church vs. state, parental love, responsibility vs. desire, accountability for one's actions, and so on. His letters vividly show that his ability to feel for characters in traumatic situations was directly linked to his own profound responses to personal misfortune.

Unlike many other famous composers, Verdi was not a child prodigy who was put on a course that led him to early success. He was born into a family of modest circumstances in Roncole, a tiny hamlet in the province of Parma. His first contact with music were lessons on a spinet piano from the organist at the local church. He began writing music at the age of fifteen, but he could not convince any local patrons to aid him financially, and his attempt to find a job as a church organist failed. His application to the Milan Conservatory of Music was rejected.

Finally, he convinced Vincenzo Lavigna, a harpsichordist at La Scala, to give him private lessons. This brought him into the great Milanese theater, and Verdi quickly absorbed the music he heard (Rossini, Bellini, and especially Donizetti) and the ways of the opera house. He married in 1836 and soon was the father of two children. He wrote two operas, the successful *Oberto* (1839) and *Un Giorno di Regno* (1840), which was deemed a failure. During the writing of the latter, his wife and children all died and Verdi was left, at the age of twenty-seven, alone and in profound grief.

To confront his misfortune, Verdi decided to throw himself into his work. In what he later called his *anni di galera* (galley years),

Verdi pushed himself artistically and emotionally to create his unique brand of fiery musical theater. Modern-day psychologists may describe this effort as survivor's guilt, but whatever his motivation, the years of rejection and loss obviously touched him. I believe that they created in Verdi a Beethovenian empathy for the rigors of the human condition, though Beethoven's point of departure was in philosophy while Verdi's was forged in personal experience.

The first product of the galley years was *Nabucco* (1842), in some ways Verdi's *Fidelio*. The story of Nebuchadnezzar, king of Babylonia, and the vanquished Israelites who yearned to be free struck deep chords in the Italian public. But the opera also showed great musical promise and sophistication, and Verdi was finally given significant recognition at the age of twenty-nine. Remember that Mozart, Rossini, Bellini, and Donizetti all had written many glorious works by that age.

Verdi continued writing: *I Lombardi alla Prima Crociata* (1843), *Ernani* (1844), *I Due Foscari* (1844), *Giovanna d'Arco* (1845), *Alzira* (1845), *Attila* (1846), *Macbeth* (1847), *I Masnadieri* (1847), *Jérusalem*, a reworking of *I Lombardi* for the Paris Opéra (1847), *Il Corsaro* (1848), *La Battaglia di Legnano* (1849), *Luisa Miller* (1849), and *Stiffelio* (1850). He worked with various librettists during this period and developed a sure sense of what made for good drama. Verdi was an active force in the creation of his librettos, prodding his writers for improvements and tickling their imaginations for ideas for future projects.

Through the years his fame increased and, with Rossini in retirement in Paris and Donizetti mentally and physically incapacitated (he died in 1848), Verdi was unchallenged as Italy's leading composer well before he had written the works that would bring him worldwide fame.

Shakespeare always held a special allure for Verdi, who read and reread all of the Bard's plays throughout his life. While he managed to produce brilliant operas based on the stories of Macbeth, Othello, and Falstaff, he never realized his long-held dream of writing an opera about King Lear. In *Macbeth*, Verdi and Francesco Maria Piave, his librettist, decided that Lady Macbeth was a character at least as interesting as her husband, so she is given a larger role in the opera than in the play. Their mad scene for the sleepwalking Lady as she relives the preceding horrors is still a chilling moment in the theater. What is fascinating about Verdi and Shakespeare is how the composer managed to isolate the most riveting moments in the plays and, through his music, make them even more memorable in the opera house.

Luisa Miller was an impressive step forward in character development. Instead of the great sweeping battles of Verdi's earlier works, we find a story of jealousy and doomed love. The opera includes an aria, "Quando le sere al placido," that many consider the finest moment for tenor that Verdi ever produced. This opera also has a loving but complicated relationship between father and daughter—a theme that would recur in many of his works, including *Rigoletto, Simon Boccanegra, Aïda,* and, in a somewhat different form, *La Traviata.*

After *Stiffelio* came three masterpieces that are among the most popular of all operas: *Rigoletto* (1851), *Il Trovatore* (1853), and *La Traviata* (1853). *Rigoletto,* to my mind, is the perfect first opera for a neophyte to attend. It has all the elements of opera: gorgeous and passionate music, a compelling story, great roles for soprano, mezzo-soprano, tenor, baritone, bass, and chorus, all fitting compactly into three hours, including intermissions. There is a cliché about a great work of music that says it has "not one extra note in it" and this is certainly true of *Rigoletto.* This opera and *La Traviata* brought Verdi into great conflict with censors, a group he fought throughout his career. In the former we have a libertine duke who seduces and rapes and a court jester who plots to kill the duke (a dangerous prospect in the turbulent political climate of that era). *La Traviata* is the famous retelling of *La Dame aux Camélias* by Alexandre Dumas the younger, which years later became the famous Greta Garbo film *Camille.* This true story of a prostitute who died young and destitute after a brief period in the upper echelons of Parisian life was deemed scandalous in its overt acknowledgment of sex, prostitution, and lifestyles that were less than pure.

In Verdi's private life, he was living out of wedlock with the singer Giuseppina Strepponi (1815–97). They met when she was in the cast of *Nabucco* and lived "in sin" from 1848 on, only marrying in 1859. Recent scholarly research has revealed that they had a daughter during the early years of their relationship. The girl was given up for adoption as an infant, though she lived near Verdi. It is not known if she ever learned the identity of her natural father. This story may explain Verdi's particular obsession with father-daughter relationships in his operas.

After the success of these three operas, Verdi slowed down his production, choosing to look back at some of his works to make revisions. He selected subject matter more carefully and labored to make each new opera a masterpiece. He wrote *Les Vêpres Siciliennes* for Paris in 1855 (it later was produced in Italy as *I Vespri Siciliani*); then came *Simon Boccanegra* (1857; substantially revised 1880–81). These fine operas often are overshadowed by the three wildly popular works that preceded them and by the masterpieces that followed: *Un Ballo in Maschera* (1859), *La Forza del Destino* (1862), *Don Carlos* (1867), and *Aïda* (1871). In 1874 Verdi wrote his famous Requiem in memory of Alessandro Manzoni (1785–1873), considered by many to be Italy's greatest novelist. Verdi's mass stunned listeners in the way it raged against death rather than embracing it as a road to the afterlife.

Verdi then retired, only to be lured away from the life of the gentleman farmer by Arrigo Boito (1842–1918), a brilliant librettist who also composed *Mefistofele* (1868), an excellent interpretation of the Faust legend as viewed from the devil's side. Boito challenged Verdi to create an opera based upon *Othello*. The result was *Otello* (1887). Although he was an old man, Verdi did not rely on old tricks. In his earlier works, the operas were divided into scenes that contained arias, duets, trios, choruses, and so on, one following the next and most with a stirring climax that would be greeted with applause. In *Otello,* Verdi and Boito created a form similar to that used by Wagner: sustained drama through an entire act, with no stopping or significant scenic changes. The result was that the drama would hurtle toward its inevitable tragic conclusion, all the more powerful for not being interrupted. Verdi insisted that they were not copying Wagner but simply creating an opera appropriate to the dramatic dictates of Shakespeare's play.

In 1890 Boito again used Shakespeare to lure Verdi back to composing. This time it was the comic and sympathetic character of Falstaff that captured Verdi's fancy, leading him to create, in his very old age, one of opera's most brilliant comedies. He crafted it for three years before its sensationally received opening at La Scala in February 1893. *Falstaff* is a true ensemble piece, basically devoid of solo arias as we usually think of them. It is more a musical continuum that beautifully blends music, words, and action. The character Falstaff's "Va, vecchio John," in which he finds justification in his behavior to keep on living life with spirit, must have appealed mightily to old Verdi.

Following the death of Strepponi, Verdi spent most of his last years in Milan as a beloved national hero. He endowed a rest home for retired musicians, La Casa di Riposo Giuseppe Verdi, which still functions today. (If your video store has a copy of a film called *Tosca's Kiss,* you should rent it to enjoy this affectionate, bittersweet visit to old musicians who have stopped performing but for whom the music never ends.)

VERISMO

In Verdi's later years a new artistic movement rose in Italian opera: *verismo.* The word comes from *vero,* true, or *verità,* truth. We might call it realism. The first great verismo opera was probably *Cavalleria Rusticana* (1890) by Pietro Mascagni (1863–1945). This seventy-minute, one-act opera takes place in a small Sicilian town on Easter Sunday. The passions of the characters are those of real people. Unlike most operas, whose characters are larger than life, this one is peopled with men and women whom audience members might have known personally. They made wine, went to church, combed their hair, and worked for a living. Audiences no longer could create a psychological distance between themselves and the gods, kings, queens, dukes, and great literary characters portrayed onstage. What they saw in verismo was a re-enactment of real life.

Another great verismo opera is *Pagliacci* (1892) by Ruggero Leoncavallo (1857–1919), a tragic tale of love, jealousy, and murder among a band of touring clowns that was drawn from an actual incident reported in the newspapers of the day. It too is only seventy minutes long and ends with a play within a play: the clowns Nedda and Canio are performing before an onstage audience. He, in real life, is convinced that she is having an affair with another performer and stabs her to death before the horrified onlookers, to whom he then cries, "La commedia è finita!" (The show is over!)—perhaps the most famous closing line in all of opera. *Cavalleria Rusticana* and *Pagliacci* often presented as a double bill, offering a powerfully dramatic evening in the theater.

Other Italian composers at the end of the nineteenth century worked in the verismo style, though usually they dealt with stories from other eras rather than their own. These composers included Francesco Cilea (1866–1950), most famous for his *Adriana Lecouvreur* (1902), and Umberto Giordano (1867–1948), whose *Andrea Chénier* (1896) concerned a famous poet during the French Revolution whose independence made him untrustworthy to both the revolutionary and the royalist forces. Giordano embraced realism by setting the real André Chénier's poems to music and by re-enacting the trial in which he was sentenced to death. The one major distortion in the opera was the decision to have the poet's beloved Maddalena choose to die with him. This did not really happen, but it makes for a moving finale, including one of the greatest love duets in all of opera. Chénier is one of the best tenor roles in the repertory, which is the chief reason for this opera's enduring popularity.

In less than seventy years, Italian opera had gone from the comedies of Rossini and the dreaminess of bel canto to the grandeur of emotion and spectacle of Verdi to the razor-sharp psychological realism of verismo.

PUCCINI

The last great Italian composer in the unbroken line that began with Monteverdi was Giacomo Puccini (1858–1924). The mere mention of three of his works, *La Bohème* (1896), *Tosca* (1900), and *Madama Butterfly* (1904), confers upon him the stature of one of the most popular composers in opera history. Puccini had a great gift for perfumed melody and a special sympathy for his women characters. He had particular insights into many of these women's psyches and was able to explore them with effective musical and dramatic strokes.

Puccini had a sharp instinct for effective theatricality. *Tosca,* probably the most veristic of all of his works, contains in its second act one of the most compelling scenes in all of opera. Although a few other characters come in and out, the act is primarily a confrontation between Tosca, a high-strung, passionate opera singer, and Baron Scarpia, the sadistic chief of police in Rome in Napoleonic times, as she bargains for the life of her imprisoned lover, a painter and political dissident. While this scene is inherently dramatic, Puccini's music gives it great artistic stature. Almost every stage action is signaled musically, so that here, more than just about anywhere else in opera, you can shut your eyes and know exactly what is happening onstage.

Another characteristic of Puccini is his interest in the exotic. While most of Verdi's stories were anchored in Europe and dealt with subject matter that was familiar to European audiences, Puccini's imagination wandered to far corners of the globe. This is due in part to the wave of orientalism—a fascination with the art and cultures of China, Japan, India, and parts of the Arab world—that swept intellectual circles in Europe at the start of the twentieth century. Three of the greatest Puccini characters, Cio-Cio-San *(Madama Butterfly)* and Liù and Turandot (from *Turandot*), are Asian women. We might look at them with our politically correct eyes and deem them caricatures, but the Western view of the East was different one hundred years ago. So we listen to these operas to see how delicately Puccini delineates their moments of elation and despair. Whenever I have attended performances of *Madama Butterfly* in Italy, I have always been impressed by the fact that audiences begin to cry in the second act, even though the truly sad moments don't come until Act III. Puccini foreshadows the tragedy musically so well that they cry in anticipation. By Act III, the sniffling is sometimes so loud that it becomes hard to hear the singer. But for an audience member, this is an irreplaceable experience. The collective sharing of an emotional catharsis is one of the unique aspects of operagoing.

One other bit of exoticism was Puccini's *La Fanciulla del West,* about Minnie, a tough-talking but sexually naive woman who lives in the High Sierras of California during the years of westward expansion when cowboys and criminals ruled the range. Modern Americans often find Puccini's Italian-singing miners, Indians, and Wells Fargo agents unintentionally hilarious, but to Puccini these people were just as exotic as the Chinese. And as is always the case with Puccini, the heroine does have complexity and depth of feeling.

La Fanciulla del West was commissioned by and given its world premiere at the Metropolitan Opera. It was conducted by Arturo Toscanini, who played a crucial role in popularizing Italian opera in America. Although works of Italian composers had been performed in America, especially New York, since the days of the American Revolution, Toscanini was a singular figure in our nation's musical development. In his long life (1867–1957), he knew Verdi and conducted many of his works; he led premieres of many verismo operas, including *Pagliacci,* and had a very close working relationship with Puccini that began with the premiere of *La Bohème.* When Toscanini was engaged to conduct at the Metropolitan Opera in 1908, he brought his prowess in the Puccini repertory with him. The house tenor at the Met in those years was the legendary Enrico Caruso, who sang most of the great roles of Verdi, Puccini, and the verismo composers. This was also the dawn of the age of the phonograph, so that recordings of Caruso singing music of Puccini, among others, became enormously popular, further spreading the composer's fame.

It was Toscanini who conducted the first performance of *Turandot,* at La Scala in 1926. While Puccini managed to compose most of the work, he died before finishing the third act, composing only up through the death of Liù, one of his favorite characters. Another composer, Franco Alfano (1875–1954), was chosen to complete the opera based on Puccini's sketches. At the premiere, following the death of Liù, Toscanini stopped the performance, turned to the audience, and said, "Here the Maestro laid down his pen." Only in later performances were the Alfano additions used.

After the rise of fascism in Italy, Toscanini spent most of his life in New York, conducting the Philharmonic and the NBC Symphony. His radio and television broadcasts carried music to millions, popularizing an art form that until that time was available to only a comparatively few persons in major metropolitan centers. He became the first superstar conductor in the modern sense of the term.

For neophyte operagoers, a Puccini opera—especially *La Bohème*—is often their first opera. Unfortunately, in my opinion, these operas' main strengths for the newcomer are pretty music and short running time. A first opera should be something to grab the listener's imagination, and among Puccini's operas, I think, only *Tosca* is an excellent pick, with *Turandot* a decent second choice. So think twice if a well-meaning friend proposes any other Puccini work for your maiden operatic voyage.

GERMAN OPERA

While opera was evolving in its own way in Italy, other significant developments were happening elsewhere in Europe. One of the great political movements of the nineteenth century was nationalism, as each nation and ethnic group sought to define itself. Part of this self-definition came with the creation of national operas in the local language with subjects drawn from national literature and folklore. In Eastern Europe, many composers included folk melodies in their scores. The most formidable national opera styles developed in Germany, France, Russia, and Czechoslovakia, although many other countries have produced native operas. In England, opera was an essentially Continental, especially Italian, art form, although operettas by Gilbert and Sullivan developed a very popular following among British audiences.

German opera was the great polar opposite of Italian opera. Beethoven composed only one opera, but he was a great source of inspiration for several generations of German composers that followed him. What they learned from Beethoven is that the work of a musician was self-expression: to communicate private passions and ideals in a theatrical form. While Verdi and other Italians applied this philosophy to a certain extent, the Germans embraced it completely. In operas created before Beethoven, one had a sense of beautiful craftsmanship, but only Mozart ever gave glimpses of deeply personal feeling. Handel, Monteverdi, and others managed to communicate action, drama, and emotions; but one senses the composers of the seventeenth and eighteenth centuries as being separate from their characters. In the nineteenth and twentieth centuries, composers often had deep attachments to their characters: Beethoven loved Leonore and Florestan, Verdi loved Falstaff, Puccini loved Butterfly and Liù, and Wagner saw himself in Tannhäuser, Siegfried, and Parsifal.

Carl Maria von Weber (1786–1826) was born in Lübeck, in northern Germany, and grew up in a theatrical family. His earliest musical efforts were not well received, but he continued to work and study. When he was offered the chance to conduct an opera house orchestra in Breslau (1804–06), he used the opportunity to gain further insights into orchestration. He then composed various symphonic works and operas such as *Silvana* (1810) and *Abu Hassan* (1811). During this period he had more success as a conductor, and in his travels around Europe he met many cultural luminaries, including Goethe, the composer Giacomo Meyerbeer, the poet and composer E. T. A. Hoffmann, the composer-conductor Carl Friedrich Zelter, and the clarinettist Heinrich Bärmann, for whom he wrote several brilliant works. His exposure to these individuals expanded his aesthetic scope and he became caught up in the burgeoning artistic movement of Romanticism.

In music, one could generally say that Romanticism emphasized content over form, but certain Romantic composers, especially the Germans, strived to create a fully realized entirety in an opera that employed music, words, dance, scenic effects, costumes, and staging to create a complete work of art. Nonoperatic Romantic composers, such as Brahms and Chopin, also strove for the emotional power of their music.

An essential component of Romanticism was the strong emphasis placed on nature. Romantics spoke of the *Urklang,* or original sound, in describing music. They believed that music was the original sound of nature, the sound that gave life to the world. For many artists this love of nature was particularized as a love for the nature of their own country. The blend of Romanticism and the rise of nationalism resulted in a curious mixture in which national characteristics were often described as originating in the natural endowments of particular countries. Nowhere was this Romantic-nationalistic marriage more potent than in Germany. Implicit in the work of some German artists of the last two centuries is the idea of German superiority. Adolf Hitler found great inspiration in the music and literature of certain nineteenth-century German artists, especially Wagner. Yet it should never be said that all German Romantic art promoted negative ideals in the heads of madmen. Beethoven and Schiller were Romantic artists who produced some of the most humane and noble works of art that exist.

The heady philosophical milieu in which Carl Maria von Weber found himself in the second decade of the nineteenth century had a profound influence upon him. From 1813 to 1820, as a conductor at the opera houses of Prague and Dresden, he devoted himself to developing greater public interest in the new German music while further honing his considerable theatrical skills. From 1817 to 1820 he spent much of his time writing *Der Freischütz,* which would become the first great German Romantic opera. Its plot is too intricate to describe here, but what is notable in this opera is its profoundly German sensibility. The characters dwell in wild forests rather than the manicured, well-tended nature of the Classical era. There are forest spirits and a healthy dose of the supernatural—all part of the German folk tradition. There is a virtuous heroine, a brave if somewhat suspect hero, a father figure represented by a prince who supplies guidance, meaning, and justice. Good battles evil; religion comes into conflict with the supernatural spirits.

Musically, Weber created a score that was powerfully evocative of the elements that exist in the libretto. The overture includes many themes used in the opera and introduces the listener to the special quiet of the forest. In setting the mood and using such themes, Weber created a model that would be followed by Wagner and other composers. In effect, the overture lays out many of the musical and dramatic themes of the opera, so that when they are heard again during the performance, they are already familiar as ideas and symbols. When two of these themes are sounded together (such as themes we associate with the characters of Agathe and Caspar), they suggest something different than either would alone. This use of themes, or *leitmotivs,* to suggest a character or an idea—was the core of Wagner's construction of his music dramas. While the term *leitmotiv* was coined well after Wagner began to use them, it is applied to his work and to Weber's before him.

Throughout *Der Freischütz,* there are many folk melodies that Weber orchestrates in such a way that they retain their fresh simplicity while still fitting into the grander operatic context. This use of folk melody to convey national character was a hallmark of Romantic composers and, especially, those who created national operatic styles: Tchaikovsky in Russia; Smetana, Dvořák, and Janáček in Czechoslovakia and later on, Martinů and Enescu in Romania; Bartók in Hungary; Delius and Britten in England; and George Gershwin in America.

In the famous "Wolf's Glen" scene in the second act of *Der Freischütz,* Weber masterfully employs musical instruments and voices to paint the action and emotions of the scene. He creates chilling supernatural effects by using choruses of spirits singing in monotone while an air of mystery is created with the quivering sounds of string instruments. Horns, clarinets, and oboes suggest various sounds of nature.

Weber went on to write *Euryanthe* (1823), his only opera not to have spoken dialogue. He had been criticized by some for having too much talk, in the style of a singspiel, in *Der Freischütz,* so *Euryanthe* was "through-composed"—that is, every note was set to music. This meant the reintroduction of the arioso, which had been popular at the beginnings of opera. The arioso, a sung form of speech, would become a major component in nineteenth-century Romantic opera, especially in Wagner. *Euryanthe* is an early example of the Romantic ideal called the *Gesamtkunstwerk*—the all-encompassing art work that seamlessly blends music, drama, scenery, lighting, special effects, and philosophical underpinnings. This *Gesamtkunstwerk* concept, like much else in Weber, would have a profound influence on Wagner.

Weber's final opera, *Oberon* (1826), was written in English for a premiere at London's Covent Garden. The opera is a melange of spoken dialogue, dance, and magical music that evokes fates, fairies, and water sprites. It is seldom performed today and is best remembered for its overture and its stirring soprano aria "Ocean, thou mighty monster." The composer died shortly after completing *Oberon,* ending the trailblazing path he had forged and leaving the way open for Richard Wagner, the colossus of German opera and probably the most controversial composer of all time.

WAGNER

Everything Richard Wagner (1813–83) thought, did, and created was characterized by a hugeness of scope and ambition. He grappled with the most universal themes of human existence yet seldom settled for easy answers or soothing moral pieties. Not content to use someone else's librettos, Wagner wrote his own texts, so that he was responsible for the sound and meaning found in the words as well as the music. Most of his operas are four to five hours in length, including intermissions, and require enormous commitment and active participation on the part of the audience as well as of every performer and artist involved in creating the production. By the time he was thirty-seven, Wagner had deemed it necessary to build his own theater—a sort of shrine to his artistic vision. While this dream would not be realized until he was fifty-nine, the theater whose construction he oversaw in Bayreuth, Germany, is still a mecca for thousands of opera lovers and aesthetes, who come to drink at the Wagnerian source and debate the significance of every detail they see and hear.

Wagner was very much a man of his time, in both the good and bad senses of that concept. He was a political revolutionary who fled from the police in Dresden. He was perpetually in debt and had to appeal to royalty and to wealthy patrons to keep him afloat. He was ambivalent about the virtues of capitalism versus a more communal form of economics. He sought in German myth and contemporary philosophers a justification for his beliefs that the German people were superior to all others. He was rabidly anti-Semitic, yet it was a Jew, Herman Levi, whom he chose to conduct *Parsifal,* the most Christian of his works. Women in his operas often embody virtues and wisdom that his shortsighted men lack, yet there is little indication that he regarded most of the real women in his life with the same reverence he bestowed upon his characters. He had a complicated relationship with his second wife, Cosima, the daughter of the famous pianist and composer Franz Liszt. She was a spiritual model and a protector, but many observers think Wagner used her shamelessly to advance his own goals. In fact, Wagner used many people, men and women, expediently getting from them what he needed and then moving on.

Wagner also has a unique legacy among artists. Because he so carefully documented his beliefs on matters artistic, political, and philosophical, he made it very easy and tempting to analyze his work based on his writings and statements. Since he wrestled with great existential issues in his operas, his work was viewed as greater, or at least more important, than the operas of Verdi and other contemporary composers. In fact, Verdi dealt with many of the same issues Wagner did, but with a lighter hand and without leaving such a long paper trail. But most major critics, including George Bernard Shaw in his amusing yet insightful book *The Perfect Wagnerite,* did much to enshrine Wagner further by considering him more serious and more worthy of discussion than other artists. Wagner did a very good job of creating the cultism that still encircles him today.

There are Wagner societies around the world, many filled with profoundly philosophical individuals who find great spiritual meaning in Wagner's operas. They return to his works often to reconsider what the composer intended in his words and his music. There is also, unfortunately, a lunatic fringe among Wagner cultists, who treat him as a spiritual leader and who justify rather dastardly beliefs and behaviors in his name. Hitler was surely an example of this: he found in Wagner a confirmation of his own beliefs in German superiority and justification for the murder and torture of Jews, Gypsies, homosexuals, and millions of other people. Wagner died fifty years before Hitler came to power, but the association of Wagner and Nazism still exists. In fact, his music has effectively been banned from public performance in Israel since 1938. While members of the Israel Philharmonic voted to lift the ban in 1992, the outcry was so strong among many Holocaust survivors that the management and musicians of the orchestra decided to respect their wishes on this sensitive issue.

Many performers and composers who were alive during the Nazi era and, in some cases, sympathetic to the Nazi cause have been treated less harshly than Wagner. Richard Strauss remained in Germany throughout the war, yet his works are not greeted with the same degree of anger abroad that Wagner's receive. It is a question as old as art and creativity whether to judge a work of art on strictly aesthetic terms or whether the personality and values of the artist should also be included in the evaluation. It is probable that Wagner was not a person whose values and opinions would be respected by decent, fair-minded people. But it is also true that he wrote some of the most sublimely beautiful music ever written, and that his ideas about man's relationship to God, nature, and other human beings are provocative and require ongoing consideration and discussion.

While Wagner's first operatic efforts, *Die Feen* (1834) and *Das Liebesverbot* (1835), were written in styles imitating the German Romantic idiom and Italian comedy, respectively, he was already preparing for bigger things. *Rienzi* (1840) was a French-style grand opera (to be discussed later on in this chapter). Its overture and Rienzi's prayer are popular concert hall and recording pieces today, but, like most of the operas on which it was modeled, it is seldom seen today because its demands are beyond the reach of the average opera company.

On a trip to London in 1839, Wagner encountered terrible storms in the North Sea, which came to influence him as he drafted his libretto for *Der Fliegende Holländer* (The Flying Dutchman), completed in Paris in 1841. Just as Weber had dazzlingly depicted the sounds of the forest in *Der Freischütz,* Wagner in *Der Fliegende Holländer* wrote some of the most pictorially descriptive music ever created to describe the sea. The opera is about salvation through love: specifically, how a doomed man is saved by a woman's love and sacrifice. The theme of love and salvation recurs in nearly all of Wagner's works.

Der Fliegende Holländer gave Wagner some fame and prestige and resulted in an appointment as the kapellmeister to the court of

Dresden (1843–49). During this fertile creative period, Wagner wrote *Tannhäuser* (1845) and *Lohengrin* (1850), two of the most gorgeously lyrical operas ever written. The beauty of these works further spread his fame. Both dealt with themes from German literature and myth, and their German-ness became part of their appeal. His key artistic development during this period was that he began to diminish the importance of the aria, replacing it with arioso and extended musical passages in the orchestra. Wagner used the orchestra to create potent images, colors, and tension. The chorus, particularly in *Lohengrin,* serves to comment but also plays roles in the opera, as soldiers, crowds, wedding guests, and so on. *Lohengrin* is probably the last opera written in the great German Romantic tradition; afterward Wagner departed toward a more personal style.

The year 1848 was one of great political upheaval in Europe. The last revolutionary fervor was vented, after which nations began to form and capitalism began to rise. Wagner was involved in political activity in Dresden and had to flee before being arrested. He moved to the safety and serenity of Zurich, where he found a patroness and gradually began to distance himself from his first wife, Minna. He began to write the poem that would become the text for his four-opera cycle, *Der Ring des Nibelungen.* He completed the poem in 1852. The *Ring* cycle, as it is often called, is quite simply the most ambitious accomplishment in the history of opera, and for many people the greatest. Drawing from Nordic and Germanic myths, Wagner created a society of gods and mortals who vie for the power and control conferred by possession of the cursed gold ring. The cycle depicts great acts of love, greed, and violence, and it has been interpreted by scholars and stage directors through various lenses: as a treatise for or against capitalism, as a Romanticist's appeal for the restoration of harmony to nature, as a revolutionary's call for the overthrow of society, even as a diatribe against the Jews. Over the next twenty years—with breaks to write other operas—he wrote the music for the four operas—*Das Rheingold, Die Walküre, Siegfried,* and *Götterdämmerung*—and the first complete cycle was staged at Bayreuth in 1876. A notable feature of the *Ring* cycle is Wagner's expanded use of what he called the *Hauptmotiv* and what subsequently came to be known as leitmotivs, which had appeared in embryonic form in Weber's operas. Depending upon whose judgment you accept, the *Ring* cycle contains anywhere between seventy and two hundred leitmotivs, representing everything from the ring itself and the curse placed on it to the love that eventually redeems the world. As Wagner blends and weaves these leitmotivs together in various ways throughout the fifteen hours of the cycle, the orchestra creates a texture and fabric that go a long way toward unifying this magnum opus. You will notice, in attending Wagner performances, that the audience gives the orchestra a much more rousing ovation than you will hear at performances of Mozart or Puccini operas. This is because, rightly or wrongly, there is the perception that the orchestra has more to do or has played a greater role. In fact, opera orchestras always play a huge role, but their work, unfortunately, is usually more noted when they don't do well. Every composer from Monteverdi to Philip Glass creates demands for an orchestra that must be met if an opera performance is to succeed.

The four operas of the *Ring* cycle are customarily performed over six days, and the whole experience is much greater than the sum of its parts. The work's implications and meanings carry much more weight when they can be considered over a short period of time. *Ring* cycles are performed almost every summer in Bayreuth and Seattle, and have begun to appear with increasing regularity in New York, Chicago, San Francisco, Munich, and Vienna.

During composition of *The Ring*, Wagner wrote *Tristan und Isolde*. In its famous dissonant opening notes many musicologists claim to hear the beginning of modern music. Though Monteverdi and many other composers knew how to use dissonance effectively, Wagner made great strides forward, and in this opera he created an erotic, sexually charged world for his characters. As in the *Ring* cycle, we see Wagner attempting with all of his force to understand the meaning of existence. While the Romantics in the early part of the nineteenth century often idealized the human condition, by the second half of the century artists had seen revolutionary ideals fail, wars rage, and human misery accelerate, so Wagner's view became dark and tragic.

Wagner's two other late works, *Die Meistersinger von Nürnberg* (1867) and *Parsifal* (1882), curiously reflect a certain return to optimism on the part of the composer. *Die Meistersinger* is a five-and-a-half-hour comedy (including intermissions) that attempts to create an ideal world of harmonious spirit in which the artist has a significant place in society, where work is appreciated and accomplishment rewarded. This is perforce a simplistic description of a very complex work, but this opera is singular in Wagner's oeuvre, like Verdi's *Falstaff,* in being a comedy written by an older man looking back on what life has taught him and trying to find humor in it. On the other hand, *Parsifal* is a profoundly serious exploration of pure simplicity in a person as a virtue and a gift. World-weary Wagner was detaching himself from all of the grinding political and social issues, attempting to find truth in Christian myth, the eternal peace that comes with redemption and the stripping away of all earthly concerns. The fundamentally tragic viewpoint of the *Ring* cycle is replaced in *Parsifal* by the desire to be cleansed by faith. Wagner referred to his last opera as a "consecration festival for the stage" and insisted in its performances at Bayreuth that there be no applause following its two-hour first act. With intermissions, the opera is almost six hours long, and at a good performance an audience member feels as if he or she has been on a long journey to an unfamiliar place. The musical pacing is very slow, with few of the rousing sections found in other operas. But if concentration can be sustained, this journey permits reflection and introspection and can be very meaningful.

When Wagner died in 1883, the year after *Parsifal*'s first performance, he left an enormous void in German opera. While Verdi was still holding forth in Italy and other artistic movements moved apace in Europe, Wagner's giant shadow over German musical life required time before perspective could be regained.

Not all Teutonic opera was heavy. Germany had two popular composers of lighter operas that were comic or sentimental in spirit: Gustav Lortzing (1801–51) and Friedrich von Flotow (1812–83), whose *Martha* (1847) is still very much loved today.

The most direct heir to Wagner was Engelbert Humperdinck (1854–1921). (If this name conjures up someone you might have heard sing in Las Vegas, the truth is that the British crooner who sports it borrowed it from the German composer.) Humperdinck studied in Cologne and Munich and met Wagner in southern Italy, where he was working on the second act of *Parsifal*. Wagner invited Humperdinck to Bayreuth to assist on the first production of the opera. Humperdinck was infused with Wagnerian orchestral scoring, which he used to great effect in *Hänsel und Gretel* (1893), his operatic rendering of the popular fairy tale. Under all of that gingerbread is an extraordinarily elaborate score, with beautiful solos, choruses, and orchestral passages. Because of its subject matter, many adults bypass this opera, which is a shame. Although Humperdinck never equaled his achievement with *Hänsel und Gretel,* it stands as a great work that reflects the influence of Richard Wagner yet is very much an original, not an imitative, work. The opera's premiere was conducted by Richard Strauss.

RICHARD STRAUSS

Just as Puccini was to twentieth-century Italian opera what Verdi was to the nineteenth century, Richard Strauss (1864–1949) became Wagner's great twentieth-century operatic heir. His musical output can be classified largely in three very distinct areas: the symphonic poem, opera, and song. In all three camps Strauss showed an acute sensitivity to literature and the word. Strauss's symphonic poems are essays for orchestra in which he drew from literary or philosophical sources—Shakespeare, Cervantes, Nietzsche—and communicated them in musical terms. His art songs, of which there are hundreds, are masterpieces of intimacy and delicate communication, and most recitalists count them as part of their basic repertory.

Like most great artists who created works of universal appeal, Strauss was a product of and a reflection of his time even though he made timeless art. As Romanticism ebbed and other movements in art and literature—impressionism, expressionism, orientalism—rose, Strauss incorporated some of these influences into his work while rejecting others.

Perhaps the biggest influence on his work was scientific. As Sigmund Freud developed a vocabulary to explain the passions of the mind, artists embraced or rejected his theories, but in the process had to reexamine any assumptions they had made about human motivation. While Mozart and Lorenzo da Ponte could write *Così fan tutte* with a knowing nod and wink toward feminine behavior, their twentieth-century counterparts would have a whole series of questions about women's intentions and motivations that would never have been posed in Mozart's time.

Like Mozart, Strauss too enjoyed collaboration with a librettist who was one of the greatest writers of his time. Just as da Ponte furnished Mozart with three libretti that became powerful stimuli for the composer's imagination, Hugo von Hofmannsthal (1874–1929) provided the libretti for Strauss's *Elektra* (1909), *Der Rosenkavalier* (1911), *Ariadne auf Naxos* (1912), *Die Frau ohne Schatten* (1919), *Die Aegyptische Helena* (1928), and *Arabella* (1933). Hofmannsthal wrote in a very beautiful German, incorporating the burgeoning Freudian psychology into his characters while seldom burdening them with it.

Strauss's operatic output can be divided into two basic categories: the mythic and the nostalgic. He often wrote about mythical figures, whether from the ancients, from the Bible, or from other sources. In this vein he evoked Wagner by giving his characters symbolic meaning that went beyond the actual events of the story. In his mythic operas he dealt with issues of love, lust, fertility, death, renewal, fidelity, family, and the transient nature of physical beauty juxtaposed against enduring spiritual beauty. Some of these operas are composed in a slashing, powerfully modern musical idiom that startled and outraged many listeners when the works had their premieres.

Strauss's first two operas, *Guntram* (1894) and *Feuersnot* (1901), are seldom performed today. Major fame came with his third opera, *Salome* (1905), a setting of Oscar Wilde's play, which involved erotic obsession, incest, and necrophilia. The opera was not for the faint of heart at its premiere in Dresden, and it still quickens the pulse today. It is interesting that Strauss was not being intentionally revolutionary in the manner of Wagner or Verdi; rather, he recognized the dramatic potential of the story and he composed music appropriate to it. The score of *Salome* continues Wagner's emphasis on the orchestra as the primary expressive voice of the opera (as opposed to the Italian style of Verdi and Puccini), and the vocal line alternates between the declamatory style common in Wagner and a passionate outpouring of sound that many nineteenth-century composers employed. There is also a certain gripping verismo in the bloody realism of this opera.

Just as *Fidelio* opened the door to varying operatic styles in the nineteenth century, *Salome* and Strauss's next opera, *Elektra*, would contain certain keys to the twentieth century. The emotional directness of these two works cast aside any pretense of politeness or formality that had attended opera until that point. They also demanded, as Wagner's operas did, a more active intellectual participation on the part of the audience. This new approach to hearing opera meant that older works would be reconsidered from a more analytical perspective.

Somewhere toward the end of Wagner's time and the beginning of Strauss's career, opera starting moving from being an art of the people to being something more exclusive. Part of this was Wagner's doing; he wrote many essays about art, culture, and philosophy, and critics and scholars who wrote about opera found it necessary to use his theories as a point of departure. Shaw and others wrote brilliant commentaries in newspapers and books, and opera became subject matter for study at universities. There were, by now, three hundred years of opera history, and it was possible to look backward and explore opera's progression. Composers from earlier times, such as Purcell, were rediscovered and their works were staged, giving composers, critics, and audiences the chance to reconsider these ancient works. And with the last vestiges of old Europe being eradicated in the First World War, composers felt they had to reflect the issues and perspectives of their times.

But Strauss's times were not only forward-looking. With the profound changes happening politically in Europe, many people were jolted from everything that was familiar and comfortable. Strauss's other style was the cozy nostalgia of *Der Rosenkavalier* (1911), *Arabella* (1933), and *Capriccio* (1942), in which he evoked longings among some audience members for the vanished eras of great empires and cultural dominance. In the years immediately before, during, and after World War I, as the Austrian empire crumbled and Germany saw its aspirations quashed, many German-speaking people found comfort in the funny, bittersweet *Rosenkavalier,* the story of a relationship between a seventeen-year-old man and a thirty-two-year-old woman. Hofmannsthal and Strauss beautifully delineated the yearnings of the Marschallin, the older woman, who felt her youth and allure slipping away and of young Octavian, her eager lover. The opera opens with the two characters in bed (Octavian, by the way, is sung by a mezzo-soprano), and the music, though sweet, is powerfully erotic. Full of waltzes and naughty comedy, *Der Rosenkavalier* entranced audiences, and in the Marschallin Strauss created one of the most affecting characters in all of opera.

In this idiom, as well as in his songs, Strauss was a master at tinging music of great beauty with sadness. The vehicle for these bittersweet feelings, as well as for the emotions in his mythic operas, was the soprano voice, of which Strauss was particularly enamored. He greatly admired Mozart, and sopranos who specialize in Mozart often find many Strauss roles particularly congenial. In fact, the Marschallin and Octavian are direct descendants of the wistful Countess and the amorous Cherubino in *Le Nozze di Figaro.*

It is interesting that the German-language opera that followed World War I was a direct response to what was perceived as Strauss's prim conservatism. Although *Salome, Die Frau ohne Schatten,* and *Elektra* remained highly charged and provocative for composers and audiences alike, the hugely successful and melodic *Der Rosenkavalier* seemed too old-fashioned in the period of inflation, privation and decadence that characterized postwar Europe.

Musical composition since World War I has been characterized by experimentation, the search for new forms, and reinterpretation of the classical tradition. In Germany and Austria, the two leading names were Arnold Schoenberg (1874–1951) and his pupil Alban Berg (1885–1935), both of whom were influenced by expressionism, the artistic movement in figurative arts, literature, and film that emphasized the expression of raw emotions and spiritual sensations without the prettification that might have happened in Romanticism. Schoenberg experimented with atonality that moved beyond the dissonance Strauss effectively used in *Salome* and *Elektra*. Schoenberg's operas *Erwartung* (Expectation, 1909), a vocal monologue for soprano and orchestra, and *Moses und Aron* (1932) are brilliant musical and intellectual exercises, but they require a great deal of familiarity and patience on the part of an audience. They are performed infrequently and really require a thorough background in opera and music before they can be approached.

Conversely, Berg's two operas, *Wozzeck* (1925) and *Lulu* (1935), are among the most highly charged music dramas ever composed, and they have continued to develop an audience since their premieres. Berg died of an infected abscess, presumably from an insect sting, around the time Hitler came to power. The Nazis banned Berg's operas, which were considered anathema to the mythology they were attempting to create about the superiority of the German character.

Wozzeck is based on the play *Woyzeck,* written in 1836 by the revolutionary playwright Georg Büchner (1813–37), which was one of the first plays to explore the tragedy of the common man. Wozzeck, a downtrodden soldier, feels abused by society and by his mistress, Marie. Near the end of the opera Wozzeck explodes, murders Marie, and drowns himself. The chilling finale shows Marie and Wozzeck's child riding a hobby horse as children run in with the news of Marie's death. "Your mother is dead!" one of them tells him, but he continues to play, mindlessly singing "hop, hop—hop, hop," not old enough to understand. This opera touched a very deep nerve in 1920s Germany and Austria as those countries picked up the pieces of their shattered societies.

Lulu in some ways picks up where *Salome* left off. The opera is based on two plays, *Die Buchse der Pandora* and *Erdgeist,* by the German expressionist playwright Frank Wedekind (1874–1918). The character of Lulu is one of the most fascinating and complex in all of opera. She has sex with both men and women. She seems oblivious to the consequences—or is she? Men kill each other to have her. Her intentions are hotly debated and subject to many interpretations. There are those who think she is a man-hating lesbian. There are others who think she sadistically abuses anyone who comes near her, while others claim she is a masochist who searches for her own demise. What is significant about Lulu is not that she is so ambiguous but that what we see in her is a reflection of what we see in ourselves, whether our hopes or our fears.

In their peculiar ways, Wozzeck and Lulu are the Everyman and Everywoman, timeless artistic creations who touch our fears and make us question our assumptions. You can imagine why Berg's operas were so threatening to the Nazi sensibility.

A contemporary of Schoenberg and Berg was Kurt Weill (1900–50), a believer in the *Zeitoper,* or opera of the times. In 1920s Berlin, where Weill first worked, he met the playwright Bertolt Brecht (1898–1956). Brecht believed that music and theater had a didactic use. He felt that one form should not support the other, but that they should work side by side to bring across a moral or political message. The two most important products of the Weill-Brecht collaboration were *Die Dreigroschenoper* (The Threepenny Opera, 1928) and *Aufsteig und Fall der Stadt Mahagonny* (Rise and Fall of the City of Mahagonny, 1930). These pessimistic works describe a society that is rotting and crumbling because of decadence, greed, and violence. One of the most haunting lines in *Mahagonny,* oft-repeated, is "Nothing you can do can help a dead man."

Both Weill and Brecht had to flee the rise of Nazism, and Weill traveled to France, England, and finally the United States. In America, Weill wrote some masterful works for stage and film: *Knickerbocker Holiday* (1938), *Lady in the Dark* (1941), *One Touch of Venus* (1943), the more operatic *Street Scene* (1947), and *Lost in the Stars* (1949). After Weill's death his widow, the great singer-actress Lotte Lenya, carried his artistic torch, appearing in a landmark production of *Threepenny Opera* in the 1950s, doing concert performances of his music, and preserving it in a pioneering series of recordings.

The most famous German opera composer of the postwar era is Hans Werner Henze (b. 1926), whose operas include *Boulevard Solitude* (1952), *König Hirsch* (1956), *Der Prinz von Homburg* (1960), and *Die Bassaridin* (1966). His works are well crafted musically and theatrically.

We have looked at the beginnings of opera in Italy in the Renaissance and Baroque eras and then the spread of opera in the Classical era. We have seen how the Classical era gave way to Romanticism, verismo, expressionism, and other movements in Italy and Germany in the nineteenth and twentieth centuries. We have yet to explore the third main pillar in the operatic temple, French opera, as well as the rise of national styles in other countries, including Russia, Czechoslovakia, England, and the United States.

FRANCE: GRAND OPERA AND BEYOND

France was the second home of opera. Just as Catherine de' Medici brought her cooks from Italy and helped launch French cuisine, the Italian Lully brought opera to France. An ongoing trend in French history and culture is that France has been the great assimilator, gathering culture and ideas from abroad and blending them with other currents that already had been introduced there.

So when Lully came to France, he imparted his taste and ideas to Rameau, who would encounter the continuing stream of Italians (especially Neapolitans) who arrived throughout the Baroque and Classical eras. Most major German and Austrian composers, from Gluck and Mozart through Weber and Wagner (with *Rienzi* and *Tannhäuser*), spent time in Paris, imparting their talents and drawing inspiration and ideas from other artists and their works. Two Germans in particular, Giacomo Meyerbeer (1791–1864) and Jacques Offenbach (1819–80), were so successfully assimilated into Parisian musical life that they are generally thought of as French composers.

Most of the great Italian composers of the late eighteenth through mid-nineteenth centuries experienced their first international recognition in Paris. Rossini spent the last forty-five of his seventy-six years in France, where he was a leading musical luminary and social lion. Donizetti *(La Favorite, La Fille du Régiment)* and Verdi *(Les Vêpres Siciliennes, Don Carlos)* were commissioned to create new operas for Paris. Two Italians, Luigi Cherubini (1760–1842) and Gaspare Spontini (1774–1851), had their major successes in France.

From the time of Lully, Parisians loved grand spectacle, elaborate stage machinery, and the incorporation of dance in their operas. In the nineteenth century, after the fall of Napoleon, this particularly French style became known as *grand opera*. In the strictest sense, grand operas were the works commissioned between 1828 and 1870 by the Académie Royale de la Musique (the Paris Opéra) based on guidelines by the French writer Eugène Scribe (1791–1861), who produced the first grand-opera libretto, *La Muette de Portici* (1828) for composer Daniel François Esprit Auber (1782–1871). Grand opera usually featured a broad scenic tableau, great heroic feats, large passions, great suffering, all attached to a religious or romantic story. As often as not, the stories came from medieval and modern history rather than from ancient times.

Essential to grand opera were huge crowd scenes for weddings, processions, wars, coronations, and miraculous events. These scenes were distasteful to Verdi and Wagner, who believed in crowds onstage only when the drama demanded it. It is notable that these two great composers had little success in Paris, while lesser composers were acclaimed. Each had developed his own style and theories, and these did not easily merge with Parisian preference for gratuitous grandeur.

Grand opera was an expression of the taste of the large bourgeoisie that was the heart of the Parisian audience. Because most of the Opéra's administrators and the funds for these expensive productions came from the government, there was a great deal of state influence on which composers and operas were selected for performance and what the subject matter would be. Operas were chosen far in advance of their presentation so that public opinion could be molded, with great help from the press, to accept the ideas in these works. The operas chosen tended to reinforce bourgeois values and were not critical of the French regime.

In spite of Verdi and Wagner, Paris was the operatic capital of Europe in the nineteenth century. In addition to the foreign composers who proved themselves there, the Paris Opéra also presented the works of many Frenchmen. Auber's *La Muette de Portici* got the grand opera movement off to a roaring start in 1828. This five-act opera, based on an uprising in Naples in 1647, is full of hot-blooded passion and concludes with a real coup de théâtre, an onstage eruption of Mount Vesuvius. The opera actually helped set off a revolution: following a performance in Brussels on August 25, 1830, the people of that city started a protest that resulted in the establishment of the country of Belgium.

Guillaume Tell (1829) by Rossini and *La Juive* (1835) by Jacques Halévy (1799–1862) were two of the most popular successors to Auber's hit. But the most famous composer of grand opera was surely Giacomo Meyerbeer. Born in Berlin as Jakob Liebmann Meyer Beer in 1791, Meyerbeer showed early prowess as a pianist and composer. By 1815, his works had been staged in Berlin, Munich, Stuttgart, and Vienna and he had visited Paris and London. But he yearned to go to Italy to absorb the style of Rossini, whom he met in Venice in 1815. In Italy he wrote several operas, culminating with *Il Crociato in Egitto* (1824), which is in the Rossinian opera seria style. When Rossini moved to Paris, he saw to it that *Il Crociato* was produced there in 1827. Meyerbeer's first great success was *Robert le Diable* (1831) to a libretto by Eugène Scribe. Other important Meyerbeer operas are *Les Huguenots* (1836), considered his masterpiece, *Le Prophète* (1849), *Dinorah* (1859), and *L'Africaine* (1864).

The operas of Meyerbeer were extraordinarily popular but are seldom seen today. This is the fate of most French grand operas: They often are very long and with their scenic demands and pageantry are expensive to produce. Also, the French singing style, precise yet passionate, with great attention paid to language, is not taught as widely as those of the Italian and German repertory, whose operas are the bread and butter of most singers. Finally, Wagner's open contempt of Meyerbeer, a Jew—even though Meyerbeer had championed Wagner and his ideas—infected the critical community, and was reflected in the commentary of those who advocated Wagner's art.

Hector Berlioz (1803–1869) was probably the greatest French composer of the nineteenth century, yet he failed to garner the acclaim in France that other grand opera composers achieved. The fact that for much of his early career he worked as a critic did not endear him to his colleagues. He also had a rather difficult temperament which cast him into long periods of elation and depression.

Berlioz did have influential admirers abroad, including Liszt and

Wagner. He was considered by many to be the musical heir to Bee-thoven thanks to his extraordinary understanding of the many in-strumental voices in the symphony orchestra; his *Symphonie Fan-tastique* (1830) is one of the most popular symphonies ever written. Beginning in 1842, with Liszt's encouragement, Berlioz made fre-quent concert tours around Europe, and his fame as a masterful composer spread far and wide.

Berlioz wrote only three operas: *Benvenuto Cellini* (1838), *Les Troyens* (1856–58) and *Béatrice et Bénédict* (1862). All three are rich in melody and drama, but Berlioz the opera composer will al-ways be associated with the stupendous achievement of *Les Troy-ens,* probably the greatest grand opera ever composed. It is an opera of epic proportions and is to Berlioz what the *Ring* cycle is to Wag-ner. By "epic" I wish to suggest heroic, not long and boring.

Berlioz wrote his own libretto for *Les Troyens,* based on parts of Vergil's *Aeneid.* As created by Berlioz, the work is actually made up of two operas: the two-act *La Prise de Troie* (The Capture of Troy) and the three-act *Les Troyens à Carthage* (The Trojans at Car-thage). The second part received twenty-one performances in Paris in 1863; the first part was not staged until 1890, in Karlsruhe, Ger-many. Since that time, *Les Troyens* has been staged infrequently, although it has received a number of performances in which both operas are given on the same night, an event that (uncut and with intermissions) takes nearly six hours.

Les Troyens is different from most grand operas in that the crowds, the grandeur, the ballets, the love scenes, the painful death of Dido, the battle scenes, and the famous "Royal Hunt and Storm" are all integral to the action. Nothing was done just to suit the taste of the time; as in the *Ring* cycle all of the action has dramatic mean-ing. Its music is remarkably sophisticated and expressive. Indeed, this is a music drama of the highest order. Because it is expensive to produce *Les Troyens* and hard to find singers who are up to the challenge of its length and difficulty, any production of it should command your attention. Even a new operagoer will find things to appreciate and will feel fortunate to have had the rare treat of seeing one of the greatest achievements in musical history.

French opera since Berlioz has been an almost uninterrupted

stream of singular achievements by composers who were as eclectic and unique as any group could be. While all of them are distinctly French in their pursuit of the new, the vivid, the palpable and the expressive, each one represents a step in a direction different from any path charted before.

Jacques Offenbach (1819–80) was the master of a kind of opéra comique known as *opéra bouffe,* a blend of music, dance, and spoken dialogue that combines elements of Italian-style opera buffa with Gallic joie de vivre and witty parody of Parisian life in the second half of the nineteenth century. *Orphée aux Enfers* (Orpheus in the Underworld, 1858) is a rollicking send-up of Gluck's serious-minded account of Orpheus and Eurydice. Offenbach is also well remembered for *La Belle Hélène* (1864), *La Vie Parisienne* (1866, from which the famous "can-can" music is derived), *La Grande-Duchesse de Gérolstein* (1867), and *La Périchole* (1868). These works are performed frequently in France, but they require a fluent knowledge of French to be fully appreciated.

Offenbach's most famous work is his least typical: *Les Contes d'Hoffmann* (1880) is a genuine opera, an ambitious work that we will discuss in chapter 9.

Charles Gounod (1818–1893) and Léo Délibes (1836–1891) created many operas that were very popular in their time, but most of them are seldom seen today. Gounod's *Faust* (1859) is probably the most famous rendition of Goethe's tale of the man who sells his soul to the Devil to regain his youth. The opera has stirring choruses, soaring arias and a thrilling trio near the end. It was the opera chosen to inaugurate the Metropolitan Opera in 1883. While it is still a work of great musical interest, the opera's story may seem dusty and archaic to audiences on the threshold of the twenty-first century.

Délibes is better known for his ballet music for *Coppélia* (1870) and *Sylvia* (1876) than for his operas, but *Lakmé* (1883) must be noted in passing. Set in India, this work is a prime example of the orientalism that captivated French artists of all types at the close of the 1800s. The first-act soprano–mezzo-soprano duet, "Dôme épais" is instantly recognizable to most people from a popular British Airways commercial.

Georges Bizet (1838–75) also dabbled in orientalism in *Les*

Pêcheurs de Perles (The Pearl Fishers, 1863), set in Ceylon. The story is foolish, but the music has a steamy sensuality which particularly characterizes the famous tenor-baritone duet. But Bizet staked his claim to eternal fame as the composer of *Carmen* (1875). Probably no opera can boast more music that is familiar to nonoperagoers than this one. *Carmen,* with its extensive spoken dialogue, was in the classic tradition of opéra comique. In its own way it too drank from the cup of exoticism that so enthralled the French. Here the exotic locale (from the book by Prosper Mérimée) was Spain, a different country from the somber, at times brutal kingdom that appears in Verdi's *Don Carlos* and Beethoven's *Fidelio.*

But the great feature of *Carmen* is the story's gripping realism. Women in the chorus smoke cigarettes and brawl, and the title character drinks, swears, and leads a very active sex life. It is a brilliant role, and a gifted singer can impart her own special flavor to it: some accentuate the sexuality, others the inherent tragedy; some even portray Carmen as vulnerable and pitiable. Bizet's vivid and dramatic music so effectively evokes the story and the Spanish locale that few audiences are untouched by a performance. At the end, when Carmen is stabbed by Don José, her frustrated lover, the moment is as powerful as any to be felt in a theater. The realism of *Carmen* pointed the way to Italian verismo, and its finale would be echoed by that of *Pagliacci.*

Bizet died three months after the premiere of *Carmen,* which was greeted with a mixed reception. Many critics found the orchestration too overpowering for the story. Some audiences found the long passages of spoken dialogue to be tedious. When *Carmen* received its Vienna premiere four months after Bizet's death, it contained sung recitatives composed by Bizet's friend Ernest Guiraud (1837–92). The opera gained worldwide acceptance in this form, although some recent productions have returned to the original spoken dialogue.

Jules Massenet (1842–1912) nourished a taste for sensual lyricism, his scores are full of color and pictorial details, and he enjoyed setting his operas in exotic locales. Drawing a page from Meyerbeer's book, Massenet wrote most of his operas with an eye to box-office appeal rather than following his own particular artistic imperatives à la Berlioz. *Le Roi de Lahore* (1877) was Oriental; *Le Cid* (1885) had a heavily Spanish flavor (drawing from *Carmen*); and *Cendrillon* (1899) was a Gallic take on the story of Cinderella. Yet in many of his works Massenet showed a deep sensitivity to his women characters that marks him as the French counterpart of Puccini and Richard Strauss. His *Manon* (1884) is in many ways superior to Puccini's later *Manon Lescaut* (1893). Massenet also created a Salome, in *Hérodiade* (1881), although Strauss's version made most people forget Massenet's very different slant on the character. Probably the most affecting and endearing woman in Massenet's canon is Charlotte in *Werther* (1892), drawn from Goethe. Both she and the title character are yearning, passionate and poetic, and audiences love them.

Several French composers are famous for a single opera. Camille Saint-Saëns (1835–1921) was a remarkably versatile and prolific musician whose *Samson et Dalila* still provides a lushly melodic, somewhat kitschily entertaining evening in the theater. Gustave Charpentier's (1860–1956) *Louise* (1900), which features the famous soprano aria "Depuis le jour," is a rather realistic evocation of the pleasures and adversities of working-class and bohemian life in turn-of-the-century Paris, somewhat reminiscent of Puccini's *La Bohème*. And although Claude Debussy (1862–1918) succeeded in many areas of musical composition, he completed only one opera, *Pelléas et Mélisande,* written between 1892 and 1902. Yet it is a landmark work in its musical style and language.

What makes Debussy distinct is that while he carefully listened to and assimilated all the music he heard, he forged his own distinct, nonderivative musical language. He was a man of his time in his interest in the Orient, particularly in his case the music of Java. But ultimately Debussy's music could not be confused with anyone else's.

Debussy is the principal exponent of impressionism in music. Most of us think of impressionism primarily in the context of the paintings of Claude Monet and other artists, who sought pure color, rather than literal depiction of objects, as a communicative means. But impressionism appeared in other art forms. For poets such as Verlaine, Rimbaud, and Mallarmé, impressionism (or symbolism) was an encounter between the meaning of the words and their sounds, which jointly would create the desired sensation.

Debussy's version of impressionism was to find pure color in the sound of voices and instruments and in the subject matter, and then to wed the color to the meaning and sound of the words. In creating his sound, Debussy did not feel constrained to follow the traditional models he learned in school and in his study of the world's music. He would, for example, use the meandering melodic line of certain Asian music to produce a musical and emotional effect that he felt could not be achieved through traditional Western composition.

Pelléas et Mélisande is a musical setting of a play by the Belgian Maurice Maeterlinck (1862–1949), who was an exponent of the artistic movement known as symbolism, which believed in conveying ideas through suggestion rather than direct discussion. A symbol was like a Wagnerian leitmotiv, which would allude to an idea or a feeling as a way of bringing it to the mind of the listener.

Unlike other composers, who *adapted* works of theater and literature to create an opera, Debussy took the play as it was, made minimal changes in the text, and created a musical landscape to support and surround the words. The music of this opera is not one of instant images; the gradual progression of sound and color ultimately creates a total impression. Think of it as looking at an impressionist painting: the more you look, the more you discover. Gradually, certain images come forth which will have particular meaning to you based on your own aesthetic. For example, rather than bringing the action to a halt between scenes, Debussy makes subtle and gradual transitions to orchestral interludes which transport the listener from the mood and the colors of one scene to those of the next. There are almost no arias in the traditional sense, and only one brief choral section. The action moves forward like the dialogue in a play, except that it is sung and the orchestra delicately paints around the vocal line.

Pelléas et Mélisande is one of the most difficult works for a new operagoer, so you should reserve it for when you have become deeply involved in opera. It was a turning point in music for the way it shattered rules and gave twentieth-century composers the courage to experiment rather than seek a continuum with the past.

Eric Satie (1866–1925) and Maurice Ravel (1875–1937), the next two great names in French music, are both much better known for their orchestral and piano compositions than for their operatic works. The music of Satie has the particular characteristic of attracting the listener but at the same time keeping him at a certain respectful distance. Satie played around with musical chords and dissonances in ways that would affect many twentieth-century composers. It would stretch a metaphor a bit, but not too far, to liken his music to cubism in art, in which familiar elements are reconfigured just enough to allow us to recognize them but in such a way as to tell us something new. In 1899, Satie wrote an opera, *Geneviève de Brabant,* to be performed with marionettes, with the singers offstage. This three-act work lasts less than fifteen minutes and was in fact intended as a parody of all the traditions of French opera that preceded it. Satie went on to work with many of the great artistic figures who frequented Paris in the first decades of the twentieth-century: the writer Jean Cocteau, Léonide Massine, the impresario Serge Diaghilev, the painter Pablo Picasso, and others. This phenomenon is notable because it brought together giants from several fields to produce a complete work of art. The previous model of creating for the stage began with the composer and perhaps the librettist; a designer and a choreographer would come into the picture only after an opera was completely written. The Diaghilev-Satie-Cocteau-Picasso-Massine work *Parade* (1917), which was called a "ballet réaliste," was written to provoke outrage at the war that was ravaging Europe; though pleasing and pretty on the surface, it actually had a dark view of the future. *Relâche* (1924), a two-act "ballet instantaneiste," as he and the painter-designer Francis Picabia called it, included a film by René Clair that was shown between the acts. In these ballets one can discern a shift from familiar opera and dance to something new. They are the early forerunners of what we at the end of the twentieth century call performance art. Included in these forms are song, dance, design, stage effects, and dialogue—the same elements one saw in ancient Greece and Rome, in the Middle Ages, in the Camerata Fiorentina and Monteverdi, in Lully, Mozart, Meyerbeer, Wagner, and just about every other operatic innovator.

Maurice Ravel was also immersed in the cultural and political ambience that influenced Debussy and Satie. Ravel distinguished himself with rich orchestrations and vibrant rhythms that stirred audiences. Ravel and Richard Strauss were probably the foremost orchestrators (creators of great and varied orchestral color) of the early twentieth century. These qualities are especially palpable in Ravel's *L'Heure Espagnole* (The Spanish Hour, 1911), a one-act comic opera set in a clockmaker's shop in which the orchestra humorously evokes the many sounds of that room. The opera combines great charm and humor—especially for French speakers—and is a priceless piece of musical invention that continually delights the ear.

Ravel's other opera, which he called a "lyrical fantasy," is *L'Enfant et les Sortilèges* (The Child and the Sorceries, 1925). The opera, set to a libretto by Colette, is yet another example of a work of art dismissed as a piece for children that has great resonance for adults as well. It is a masterful exploration of interior life, in this case the fantasy of a child. Certainly the Freudian winds blowing from Vienna had an influence on Colette and Ravel, but this opera is composed with great delicacy and a variety of orchestration that suits the quicksilver changes of mood and action and reflects the short attention span of a small boy.

L'Enfant et les Sortilèges, with its child protagonist and singing teacups, chairs, and animals, is radically different in flavor and subject from anything else we have examined—far from the heroes and heroines of mythology and ancient times and the characters of Verdi, Wagner, Berlioz, and most other composers. And even operas that have very "human" stories—*Le Nozze di Figaro, Il Barbiere di Siviglia, Carmen, Cavalleria Rusticana*—deal with interaction among characters rather than the inner workings of one mind, especially that of a child.

Francis Poulenc (1899–1963) is the heir to the French composers of the first three decades of the twentieth century. His *Les Mamelles de Tirésias* (The Breasts of Tiresias, 1947) is an ironic and surrealist one-act work written as France and Europe rose from the ashes of World War II. The story includes role reversal between the sexes and touches upon the desire to have lots of babies to repopulate the world after the war. But who will raise these babies, and with what values will they be raised? The Metropolitan Opera has in its repertory a triple bill of *Parade, Les Mamelles de Tirésias,* and *L'Enfant et les Sortilèges.* While these works may not seem to have much in common, they all make one think of childhood in its innocence and its terror—and also about the childish and dastardly deeds of adults who should know better.

La Voix Humaine (The Human Voice, 1959), based on a play by Jean Cocteau, is a forty-five-minute tour de force for a soprano. It is the story of a woman who has just seen her relationship with her lover end: as she breaks down while talking on the telephone, alternately imploring, rejecting, and vainly hoping to reconcile with her lover, she goes through a broad range of emotions that are vividly explored in the music and text. The opera is basically one long, psychologically calibrated mad scene that is riveting when entrusted to a great singing actress.

Poulenc's masterpiece, however, is *Les Dialogues des Carmélites* (The Dialogues of the Carmelites)—probably the most recently composed opera to hold a solid place in the standard repertory; most of the world's top companies have presented it often since its premiere at La Scala in 1957. Set during the Reign of Terror following the French Revolution, it is the story of a group of Carmelite nuns who are persecuted and ultimately put to death at the guillotine. Written in a period when the horrors of World War II were still strongly felt, it is an exploration of fear in life that somehow results in courage and grace in death. It is musically and dramatically powerful, and the final scene is one of the most gripping in all of opera. To the relentless cadence of the offstage guillotine, the condemned nuns bravely sing in a chorus as they go to their deaths, and eventually their voices are reduced to three, then two, then one.

Darius Milhaud (1892–1974) wrote twenty operas, drawing subject matter from Greek tragedy and more contemporary influences. His operas are seldom staged outside of France but are interesting for true devotees of twentieth-century French music.

Olivier Messiaen (1908–92) was another singular voice in French music, one who was inspired by mysticism and by a lifelong fascination with stories and events in the history of the Catholic Church.

He wrote many liturgies, piano works, and pieces for large orchestra. His only opera, *Saint François d'Assise* (Saint Francis of Assisi, 1983), is a summation of many of the themes that fascinated Messiaen; for example, he loved describing the sounds of birds in his music, and this opera gave him the chance to study the life of the saint who communicated with birds. This opera has just begun to gain acceptance following two major productions in 1992. At more than five hours and with music that is not easily accessible to many listeners, it is a daunting, though towering, work that will eventually find an audience.

France's role as the great assimilator of culture is sure to point opera in new and challenging directions in the future. This is due in part to the great emphasis the French put on the creation and promotion of the arts. Note in appendix C how many opera theaters exist in the city of Paris alone.

RUSSIAN OPERA

Now that we have explored the three main pillars of the temple of lyric art—Italian, German, and French—it bears repeating that opera has many homelands. The national operatic styles of Russia and Czechoslovakia are probably the most significant outside the big three, but many other lands have seen native opera take its place alongside the standard repertory of works from Italy, Austria, Germany, and France. Finland, for example, has one of the most vibrant contemporary opera scenes. In the twentieth century England has seen many of its finest composers take an active interest in opera. And the United States has proved a special and fertile ground for opera that seldom receives the credit it deserves.

Before there ever was a United States, opera had already reached Russia. The first public theater in Russia was in St. Petersburg in 1703. This imperial city, which has always viewed itself as Russia's window to the West, welcomed Italian composers who brought the lyric art with them. Later, the imperial court sent Russians to Italy and other countries in Western Europe to study with the leading composers there.

Most of the early operas staged in St. Petersburg were in Italian.

By the end of the eighteenth century, however, native composers began creating music for Russian-language librettos. The most famous Russian composer of the eighteenth century was Evstigney Ipatovich Fomin (1761–1800), whose best work was *Orfey i Evridika* (1792), based on the story of our old friends Orpheus and Eurydice. Many of the early Russian operas were comical and drew upon local characters and folk melodies. As often as not, the eighteenth-century Russian operas combined vocal music and spoken dialogue, much like the Singspiels in Germany.

The Romanticism and nationalist sentiment that swept Europe in the early nineteenth century was also felt in Russia. Just as German composers sought to extol German values, Russian composers were encouraged by these trends to explore Russian character, history, and folklore. Most of these works are now only known from the history books, although *Askoldova Mogila* (Askold's Grave, 1835) by Alexey Verstovsky (1799–1862) was performed consistently well into the twentieth century.

Russian opera as we think of it today is generally said to have begun with Mikhail Ivanovich Glinka (1804–57). Glinka received private musical education from German and Italian teachers. During his travels in Germany, Switzerland, and Italy from 1830 to 1834, he came to know Mendelssohn, Bellini, and Donizetti and saw performances of many operas. *Fidelio* and *Der Freischütz* in particular had a profound influence upon him. He returned to Russia imbued with Italian lyricism and German Romanticism. In Russia he came to know Pushkin and Gogol, whose writings renewed his interest in Russian subjects.

The confluence of all of these artistic influences made Glinka the ideal transitional figure from the "Euro-Russian" opera to a more distinctly Russian national style. In 1835 he wrote *A Life for the Tsar*, the first great Russian opera. Actually, this is a work that shows both Russian and Western influences: the vocal line is reminiscent of Italian bel canto, the orchestral texture is markedly Germanic, and the large scale of the choral scenes brings to mind French grand opera, a style that was just coming to the fore. Yet Glinka also shared with his eighteenth-century Russian predecessors a delight in Russian folklore. The folk song that opens the opera is repeated throughout to represent Russian heroism. In contrast, mazurkas and polonaises, which are traditional Polish musical styles, are used to represent the outside Polish forces. The counterpoint between Russian and Polish themes is an effective form of musical story-telling.

The story is an involved tale about a peasant, Ivan Susanin, who sacrifices his life to save the tsar's. The relationship between the tsar and the masses is a theme that may be found in many Russian operas. *A Life for the Tsar* was a great success at its first performance, in St. Petersburg in 1836.

Later, Glinka wrote a second opera, *Ruslan and Lyudmila* (1842). This opera did not enjoy much success at its premiere, perhaps because audiences hoped for another large historical epic. With *Ruslan,* Glinka dug deeper into the Russian folkloric patrimony, with its pronounced veins of fantasy and moralism based on peasant values, which will be familiar to any reader of Russian folk stories. There is also a large element of exoticism in the opera, at least to Western European eyes and ears. This is the sort of subject matter and music that French composers of a later time sought to emulate as part of their interest in orientalism. But Russian exoticism came in the use of music and subjects native to the lands of Eastern Europe and Central Asia that were under Russian sway and therefore part of Russian culture. Listening to the music of *Ruslan and Lyudmila,* one hears the vivid melodies of these Russian lands.

Although this opera failed at its premiere, its influence on the future of Russian opera was profound. Later composers reveled in its liberal use of native elements; it made them realize that they did not have to imitate Western European styles to produce an opera of musical value. The features of *A Life for the Tsar* and *Ruslan and Lyudmila* combined to create the distinctive Russian style that would be built upon by the next generations of Russian composers.

Modest Mussorgsky (1839–81) is the foremost example of a purely Russian composer. His *Boris Godunov* premiered in St. Petersburg in 1874 after earlier versions of the opera were rejected. Based on a story by Pushkin, the opera is a searing psychological study of the half-mad Tsar Boris, who reigned from 1598 to 1605—a character that must have had great meaning for Mussorgsky, who suffered deep bouts of depression. (He was a hopeless alcoholic as well, which made his outlook even gloomier.)

The chorus plays a crucial role in *Boris Godunov,* representing the abused and oppressed Russian people, who were always the worst victims of the struggles of powerful forces going on above them. Both *Boris Godunov* and Mussorgsky's later *Khovanshchina* are notable for their exploration of the yearnings of common people. The operas were written at the dawning of a new era in Russian society, as serfdom was abolished by the edict of Tsar Alexander II in 1861. The Russian people were just beginning to explore freedom after centuries of oppression, and Mussorgsky was very much attuned to their feelings. The choral music in *Boris Godunov* is as detailed and emotional as anything Mussorgsky created for Boris or the other characters.

The great achievement of *Boris* is how emotionally specific the music is. The effect is not one of repetitive music or leitmotivs (which are little used) but rather of music written with a very close eye to the text. The opera underwent various revisions, both by Mussorgsky himself and by several well-meaning champions who sought to "improve" his score. For many decades Nikolai Rimsky-Korsakov's rearranged, reorchestrated *Boris* was the standard version of the opera. Recently, though, Mussorgsky's original scoring, long thought to be crude and ineffective, has gained new respect for its originality and stark power.

Rimsky also had a hand in the completion of *Khovanshchina,* which was not yet finished at the time of the composer's death. While *Boris* took hold in the repertory almost from its first performance in the West, *Khovanshchina,* first seen in St. Petersburg in 1886, has had to struggle for recognition. A story of the Old Believers in the Russian church who resisted the westernizing reforms of Peter the Great in 1689, *Khovanshchina* is rich in Russian musical flavor, with abundant choral music and several vividly drawn characters. In recent years *Khovanshchina* has been produced with greater frequency.

While Mussorgsky was creating his great epics, Alexander Borodin (1833–87) was pursuing a career in science; he was never a full-time composer. He lacked the great melodic genius of Tchaikovsky and the emotional force and involvement of Mussorgsky. His one opera of note, *Prince Igor* (first performed in 1890), took him seventeen years to write, and in fact it too was completed by Rimsky-Korsakov. The opera is a blend of Asian, Russian, and European sounds and is awash in beautiful music (much of which was adapted for use in the Broadway musical *Kismet*), but it has not had wide appeal outside Russia.

By the time Peter Ilyich Tchaikovsky (1840–93) began working, the Russian folkloric style had become the dominant influence. But some Russian composers still drew some inspiration from Western Europe, and Tchaikovsky certainly was among them.

Tchaikovsky is the Russian composer whose music is best known outside Russia. His ballets (including *Swan Lake* and *The Nutcracker*), piano works, symphonies, and orchestral show-stoppers (such as the *1812 Overture*) make him one of the most frequently heard of all creators of music. The fact that Tchaikovsky was not primarily an opera composer means that his works for the lyric theater are often undervalued. His first three operas, *Voyevoda* (1869), *The Oprichnik* (1874), and *Vakula the Smith* (1876), are nationalist in flavor but are seldom heard today. Tchaikovsky hit his stride with *Eugene Onegin* (1879).

Eugene Onegin is based on a popular poem by Pushkin; though Russian in subject matter, it is really a universal meditation on the many aspects of love. We should note here that Tchaikovsky had traveled widely in Europe and admired the music of Mozart, Beethoven, Mendelssohn, and Schumann—especially Mozart, whose music represented brilliance and invention as well as psychological insight into character. Tchaikovsky was drawn particularly to characters who were victims of destiny and of societal conventions to which they were unhappily bound.

The Queen of Spades (often called by its French title, *Pique Dame,* 1890) is his other most popular opera. It has many of the same elements found in *Eugene Onegin* and has much to offer the listener. *The Maid of Orleans* (1881) is a little sluggish in its plotting, but it contains thrilling choruses and a well-drawn title role in Joan of Arc.

Glinka, Tchaikovsky, and most Russian operatic composers

were masters of the use of the chorus and the inclusion of dance. In many Russian operas, the chorus represents the Russian people, the great masses who have been oppressed and ennobled and profoundly shaped by the sweeping events of Russian (and, later, Soviet) history. When you see a Russian opera, the singers in the chorus often seem to be playing roles to a much greater extent than in Western European operas, in which they merely comment upon or underscore the actions and ideas of the principal characters. This is not to say that chorus members in Western European operas never have roles, but simply that in Russian opera the role of the chorus is often as important as that of the principal characters.

Dance has always been an important part of the Russian popular and classical tradition. Russian composers have produced many of the greatest ballet scores, and Russian folk dancing is among the world's best. In some Russian operas dance is not merely spectacle that brings the action to a halt, as is often the case in French opera, but is rather an element that advances the action. There are three scenes containing dance in *Eugene Onegin,* two in the countryside and one in St. Petersburg. Each is distinct in musical and dramatic tone and reveals much about the feelings of the principal characters.

For a man who was so crucial to the preservation and promotion of operas by other Russian composers, Nikolai Rimsky-Korsakov (1844–1908) is interesting in that outside Russia his own operas are seldom seen today. Perhaps this is because he was drawn to the mystical and fantastic aspects of Russian life and literature, and the stories he selected seem to have less of a hold on modern audiences than the emotional dramas of Tchaikovsky and the political-historical epics of Mussorgsky.

Rimsky-Korsakov had great feeling for the capacity of individual instruments to provide particular voices or color, a trait he shared with Rossini (to whom I have never seen him compared), Debussy, and Ravel. Most of his operatic output was based on Russian folk material. *The Snow Maiden* (1882) is a fairy legend; *Mlada* (1892) is drawn from village tales. His greatest works, *Sadko* (1898) and *The Golden Cockerel* (often called *Le Coq d'Or,* 1909) also came from folk sources but manage to be more appealing to modern audiences. In terms of the history of opera, Rimsky-Korsakov's place is in his championing of the works of other Russians and in his influence as teacher and orchestrator on future composers in Russia and abroad.

When one brilliant pupil of Rimsky's, Igor Stravinsky, met another, the impresario Serge Diaghilev, the course of musical history would never be the same. At the time, early in 1909, Stravinsky was at work on his opera *Le Rossignol,* based on a fable by Hans Christian Andersen. Diaghilev commissioned Stravinsky to orchestrate a Chopin waltz for the finale of the ballet *Les Sylphides,* which was presented by the Ballets Russes in Paris in the spring of 1909. This was immediately followed by a commission for *The Firebird,* which was a huge success the next year in Paris, where audiences were dazzled by the orchestral color that Stravinsky had been so effectively taught by Rimsky-Korsakov.

By now Stravinsky was firmly established in France, where he met Debussy, Satie, Ravel, and the other great French composers of the time. Two more ballets drawn from Russian themes, *Petrouchka* (1911) and *Le Sacre du Printemps* (The Rite of Spring, 1913), were extraordinary successes. Although the latter caused riots at its premiere in Paris—some people found the music jarring and violent—it established Stravinsky definitively among the great composers of this century.

Stravinsky would go through many artistic phases in his career, parallelling the artist Pablo Picasso (1881–1973). Stravinsky's early impressionistic phases were similar to the rose and blue phases of Picasso. Stravinsky's take on fauvism (the artistic movement exploring the wild and savage in color and emotion) occurred with *Le Sacre du Printemps.* Elements of Picassian cubism and neoclassicism could also be identified in Stravinsky's work. What these two great artists shared was an endless desire to experiment and create new forms. They also had in common the fact that no matter how different in style all of their works might be, Picasso's art and Stravinsky's music could never be confused with anyone else's work.

In 1914 Stravinsky permanently left St. Petersburg to live on the banks of Lake Geneva in Switzerland, the neutral nation that served as a refuge for so many during World War I. He returned to composing *Le Rossignol,* which was successfully presented in Paris as a short three-act opera in 1920. After the war Stravinsky moved to Paris, and later he became a French citizen. At the outset of World War II he moved to the United States, where he was granted citizenship in 1945. In both countries he continued to write all kinds of music, but his operatic output was limited to *Mavra,* a one-act comic work written in 1922, *Oedipus Rex* (1927), and *The Rake's Progress* (1951). The static *Oedipus Rex* is more like an oratorio than a real opera, but it is performed in opera houses as well. In keeping with his experimental nature, Stravinsky chose to use a libretto in Latin, a language he thought would better communicate the weight of history and antiquity in this tragic story of man's impotence in the face of a larger, divine plan. *The Rake's Progress* was given its world premiere at the Teatro La Fenice in Venice in 1951. It has a libretto by W. H. Auden and Chester Kallman and was inspired by the famous prints by William Hogarth (1697–1764). In this opera Stravinsky uses what could be called a neo-Mozartean style. There is recitative accompanied by a harpsichord, arias, duets, trios, quartets, and ensembles. Audiences at the premiere could look at the opera's eighteenth-century mores and values through war-weary twentieth-century eyes; some critics declared it derivative and irrelevant while others thought it to be meaningful and of great beauty. After a slow start, *The Rake's Progress* has gained steadily in popularity.

While Stravinsky left his homeland early in his career, Sergei Prokofiev (1891–1953) and Dmitri Shostakovich (1906–75) can accurately be described as Soviet composers. Most audiences know Prokofiev for his ballet music *(Romeo and Juliet, Cinderella)* and orchestral pieces, but he also created significant operas that are not produced as often as they should be. Immediately before and for some time after the Russian Revolution, Prokofiev lived in Paris, where he wrote *The Gambler* (1917) and the comic, fantastical *Love for Three Oranges,* which had its world premiere in Chicago in 1921 and whose colorful orchestration recalls Rimsky-Korsakov. For most of the 1920s, Prokofiev labored on *The Fiery Angel* (1927). This opera takes a very dark view of life, and that—along with its final scene, an orgy of crazed nuns—rendered it unsuitable for presentation at the time, at least in the Soviet Union, where the state wanted art to project only positive ideals to the proletariat. The opera had to wait until 1955 for its first performance, in Venice.

Prokofiev decided to return to the Soviet Union, but in the process he had to mold his talents and his voice to the requirements of the Soviet system. He wrote his famous ballets and the beloved children's work *Peter and the Wolf* but fared less well operatically. Neither *Semyon Kotko* (1940), about a hero of the Russian Revolution, nor *The Story of a Real Man* (1948), about a heroic World War II fighter pilot, met with much official favor, despite their pro-Soviet themes.

The composer's masterpiece would be *War and Peace* (1943; revised version, 1952), after Tolstoy. This massive historical opera in thirteen scenes follows the dramatic tradition of Mussorgsky with its vivid characters and extensive use of the chorus. Written during Russia's heroic struggle in the Second World War, it tapped into the nation's deep patriotism but also stands powerfully as a universal work of art. Like Berlioz's *Les Troyens, War and Peace* is large, ambitious, and expensive to produce, so a staging of it is a welcome event.

Another composer who struggled under the Soviet system was Dmitri Shostakovich. He is best known as a symphonic composer, probably because symphonic music is more abstract than opera, whose words and story leave it more open to criticism and censorship. The official Soviet view of art was that it belonged to all the people, not merely a "cultural elite."

Shostakovich's surreally comic *The Nose,* based on the story by Gogol, was well received when it premiered in 1930. When his second opera, *Lady Macbeth of Mtsensk,* was staged in 1934, it too was a success and soon had productions in several Western countries. But when Stalin saw it in 1936, he deemed it degenerate, and the opera was not performed in the Soviet Union for nearly thirty years, when it was staged in Moscow in a revised version prepared by Shostakovich. The opera is based upon a novella written in 1865 by Nikolai Leskov about a woman named Katerina Izmailova, whose restlessness with provincial life leads her to adultery, murder, and suicide. While the composer toned down some of the text, the full meaning of the story can be heard in the music, which creates a feeling of real sexual tension. Only lately has the opera begun to have a presence on the international opera scene.

CZECH OPERA:
SMETANA, DVOŘÁK, JANÁČEK

Czechoslovakia was, until its division on January 1, 1993, into the Czech Republic and Slovakia, a small country whose composers rivaled those in neighboring Germany, Austria, and Russia. Prague had always been a great musical capital, notable especially for commissioning Mozart to write *Don Giovanni* and welcoming performances of many of his other compositions.

What we now call the Czech Republic is composed of two distinct regions, Bohemia and Moravia. The two most important Czech composers of opera in the nineteenth century were both Bohemians: Bedřich Smetana (1824–84) and Antonín Dvořák (1841–1904). Smetana was to Czech opera what Weber was to German opera, Auber to French grand opera, and Glinka to Russian opera: the groundbreaker who created the conditions in which the great composers who followed him could produce their masterworks.

Smetana, the son of a brewer, showed early prowess in music and was encouraged to develop his skills. He studied intensively from 1834 to 1843 in different Czech towns, in the process coming into close contact with local music and folkways. In 1840, in Prague, he met Liszt, who was impressed with Smetana's talents and was generous in his encouragement. Smetana came to believe that it was important to create an academy in Prague for musical instruction, and in 1848 Liszt sent him money to start the school. The succeeding years were ones of political turmoil in Europe and hard work for Smetana, who had to take various teaching positions and other jobs in order to fund his school. He spent part of his time in Sweden heading the orchestra in Göteborg. A visit to Weimar in 1857 at Liszt's invitation reignited Smetana's desire to compose. Most of Smetana's compositions in the preceding years had been didactic, used for teaching in his school; they were standard structural pieces that did not reveal much of his soul and feelings. After Weimar, however, he showed an interest in self-expression in his music and an eagerness to champion Czech aspirations. At the time, the Czech regions were about to receive certain concessions of self-rule from Austria, among them permission to use the Czech language in schools and in official documents. (Only in 1918, in the wake of the First World War, would Bohemia, Moravia, Slovakia, and a small part of Silesia join to become the independent Czechoslovakia.)

Smetana established permanent residence in Prague and gained a platform to articulate his ideas of Czech musical nationalism. His first opera, in Czech, was *The Brandenburgers in Bohemia* (1863). It inspired great admiration at the time for its use of native language and folk themes, but it is dramatically unwieldy and seldom is presented today.

Smetana's next opera, his masterpiece, was *The Bartered Bride,* (1866). This folk opera takes place in a Bohemian village and is the comic telling of a young woman's betrothal. More importantly, it was an assertion of pride in Czech language, music, and values at a time when the nation was young and struggling. The opera was not an immediate success, in part because it did not have enough dance in it to suit Czech audiences, who were following dictates of taste that came from faraway Paris. Smetana later added dance sequences, a soprano aria, and a chorus and, later still, recitatives to replace the original spoken dialogue, but even before it reached its final form the opera had achieved a permanent place in the hearts of the Czech people. It quickly entered the international repertory—where, ironically, it was usually performed in German translation. Only in recent years have international audiences begun to hear the opera in its original language.

Smetana wrote several operas after *The Bartered Bride,* but few of them are now seen outside of the Czech-speaking lands. *Libuše* (1872) was a more serious work that was an ode to the developing Czech nation. But his most famous expression of Czech nationalism is *Má Vlast* (My Homeland), a six-part symphonic essay that evokes the rivers, fields, mountains, and people of Bohemia.

In his later years Smetana grew deaf and suffered from ill health and depression, yet he continued to compose. His place in Czech history was assured, and he received many honors in his last years.

While Smetana remained a largely nationalistic composer, Antonín Dvořák was an internationalist who incorporated his Czech roots. Dvořák was one of the great melodists, and much of his music is part of the standard repertory in the world's concert halls: symphonies, tone poems, chamber music, a famous cello concerto. He is known to a much lesser extent for his ten operas. He traveled widely in his lifetime, visiting most of Europe and spending the years 1892–95 in the United States, where he discovered music and rhythms that he wove into his most famous piece, the "New World" Symphony, whose premiere he conducted at New York's Carnegie Hall in 1893.

In his international travels, Dvořák saw many of the works of Wagner and Meyerbeer, and his early operas reflect the influence of these two composers. These are seldom seen today. But his nationalist style, under the influence of Smetana, resulted in *The Cunning Peasant,* (1878), which was very much in the style of *The Bartered Bride,* and his finest opera, *Rusalka,* first produced in 1901. Dvořák's operas were difficult to find outside of Czechoslovakia in his day but were well known to Czechs.

Many other composers were creating operas in the Czech language in the second half of the nineteenth century and the early part of the twentieth. These composers, whom we can think of as Smetana's children, helped make Prague one of the foremost musical centers of Europe; Paris and Vienna were probably its only rivals in this regard. The composer who gathered the best of all of this musical ferment and brought Czech opera fully into the twentieth century was Leoš Janáček (1854–1928). Born to a poor Moravian family, Janáček was largely self-taught, although he did spend some time in his twenties in Prague, Leipzig, and Vienna. For the first half of Janáček's life he was deeply involved in Moravian folk music and tradition, dedicating himself to learning as much of it as he could. He also absorbed the music of Smetana, Dvořák, and other Czech composers. He made his money teaching music and leading orchestras and choruses in the city of Brno. From 1885 to 1901 he wrote ballets, piano pieces, orchestral works, and attempted an opera, *Sarka,* all in a Moravian vein.

Janáček is different from many composers in that his first great opera did not appear until he was fifty years old. *Jenůfa* (1904) opened with great success and represented the beginning of a period of intense creativity that Janáček maintained until his death. *Jenůfa* gradually developed an international audience, following a famous production in Prague in 1916, and in recent years it has been acclaimed as one of the great operas in the world repertory.

Janáček combined the native melodies of Moravia with subject matter that was much more adult and psychologically rooted than anything Czech opera had seen before. Premarital sex, teenage pregnancy, infanticide, and many forms of human cruelty were explored often, in the same rural setting that lent rustic charm to earlier Czech operas. In all of Janáček's operas the composer grappled with moral questions frankly and directly, making him different from Verdi, Wagner, and other composers who explored morality on large musical and dramatic canvases. In Janáček's search for truth in the ideas and structure of his operas, he follows in the great tradition of Monteverdi, Gluck, and Mussorgsky, among others.

Of great concern to Janáček was moral integrity. Jenůfa, a girl who lives in a traditional provincial town, is impregnated by a handsome wastrel who then wants little to do with her. His half brother, Laca, loves Jenůfa, but she spurns his affections. She is hidden by her stepmother, Kostelnička, and secretly delivers the baby. Kostelnička feels that they have been shamed and fears for their standing in the eyes of the community. She drugs Jenůfa and cries, "I shall take this child and give him back to God!" She wraps the baby in a shawl and runs out of the house. Months later, the infant's body is found in an icy bank of the river. The community accuses Jenůfa, but Kostelnička finally confesses that she killed the child. Jenůfa makes the unusual gesture of asking the community to let Kostelnička make her own peace with God. She then tells Laca to leave her, saying that he could not marry a woman who has been so disgraced. He insists that his love is greater than any disgrace that may befall them.

This may sound like a strange and unfulfilling ending to an opera that is full of the violation of "moral values," as they are traditionally described, but Janáček was intrigued by the Wagnerian notion of redemption through love. Where he went beyond Wagner is that

Wagner's characters were mythic and larger than life, while the characters in *Jenůfa* were people that anyone in the opening night audience in Brno might have known in rural Czechoslovakia.

He wrote six subsequent operas, including four more towering achievements: *Káťa Kabanová* (1921), *The Cunning Little Vixen* (1924), *The Makropulos Affair* (1926), and *From the House of the Dead* (1928). *Káťa Kabanová* is an attack on bourgeois society and its values that is full of incisive psychological portraits. *The Cunning Little Vixen* is a comic parable set in a Moravian forest in which animals can talk and humans discover the special wonder of renewal in nature. Like *Jenůfa*, this opera grew out of Janáček's keen interest in the consequences of love, death, redemption, and renewal. *The Makropulos Affair* and *From the House of the Dead* are deeper, more pessimistic explorations of these same themes.

Janáček's operas are difficult for newcomers to the art form, but his works are among the greatest, and it is he, rather than the more famous Smetana and Dvořák, who is often regarded as the greatest Czech operatic composer.

OPERETTA

One area of opera that we have not yet explored is operetta. The word means "little opera," and in fact lovers of "serious" opera often turn up their noses at operetta. We have looked at opéra comique (not necessarily funny) and opera buffa (definitely funny). Operetta is a slightly different entity. It evokes distinctly *national* feelings and humor rather than exploring universal themes. The two leading styles of operetta were French and Austro-Hungarian, or "Viennese," operetta.

French operetta usually falls into the larger category of opéra comique, but without the serious overtones that many composers brought to that form. The leading composer of French operetta was Offenbach. His operettas are spirited and humorous, full of frothy music, but really meaningful only to audiences who speak French and know about the ambience of the Paris of his time. They are often staged abroad but lose much in translation.

Viennese operetta is generally better known. It is characterized by lilting melodies, naughty humor, and heavy dollops of nostalgia. Richard Strauss evoked much of this in *Der Rosenkavalier.* The leading composers of Viennese operetta were Franz von Suppé (1819–95) and Johann Strauss, Jr. (1825–99—no relation to Richard). Strauss was nicknamed "the Waltz King" for the swirling dance melodies that made him among the most popular of Viennese composers. He wrote the most famous operetta of all, *Die Fledermaus* (The Bat, 1874), a work that is performed in most of the world's opera houses in repertory with all of the "serious" works from Monteverdi to the present day. In Vienna, there is a special company, the Volksoper, that performs most of the beloved Viennese operettas, while the nearby Staatsoper does "serious" opera, though *Die Fledermaus* is a fixture there, too.

The Hungarian Franz Lehár (1870–1948) had great international success with *Die Lustige Witwe* (The Merry Widow, 1905) and *Das Land des Lächelns* (The Land of Smiles, 1929).

The Spanish version of operetta is called *zarzuela.* Although they were not always comic, the zarzuelas often have spoken dialogue and very local roots and ideas. There were zarzuelas in the seventeenth century, and the style rose and fell in popularity many times during the centuries. Foreign opera, especially Italian, made inroads in Spanish musical life, and generations of Spanish singers have distinguished themselves in mainstream European operatic styles. Another Spanish theatrical form, the *tonadilla,* was typically a short comic piece using local music, language, and humor that would be performed in between the acts of an opera in many Spanish theaters.

In 1857, the Teatro de la Zarzuela opened in Madrid. In artistic circles at that time, there was a desire to reintroduce Spanish flavor to opera, and two new forms of zarzuela were born: *zarzuela grande,* a Spanish equivalent of French grand opera, and *genero chico,* which is the Spanish take on operetta. Both are still performed regularly throughout Spain, particularly in Madrid. The foremost Spanish opera composer of the twentieth century was Manuel de Falla (1876–1946), whose best-known works were *La Vida Breve* (1905), famous for its dance music, and *El Retablo de Maese Pedro* (1923), an opera for three voices and marionettes.

The most famous manifestation of operetta came in England and, later, in the United States. W. S. Gilbert (1836–1911) wrote thirteen wonderfully witty texts that were set to music by Arthur Sullivan (1842–1900). These included *H.M.S. Pinafore* (1878), *The Pirates of Penzance* (1880), *Iolanthe* (1882), and *The Mikado* (1885). These works were immensely popular in England and gained a huge following in the United States as well. They exercised a profound influence on the development of the American musical theater, more popularly known as the Broadway musical.

BRITISH OPERA

Sullivan was only the most popular of a whole generation of English composers in the nineteenth century, most of whose operas and operettas are seldom heard nowadays. Two later Englishmen whose works have endured provided an important transition to the twentieth century: Gustav Holst (1874–1934) and Ralph Vaughan Williams (1872–1958). Both were composers of "serious" music (even if it was used in comedies) in styles reminiscent of those found on the Continent. Holst is best known for his symphonic suite *The Planets* (1916), a concert-hall staple, but he also wrote seven operas, the most famous of which is a one-act comedy, *The Perfect Fool* (1923). Some of his operas attempted to create an English idiom that drew on native literary sources, such as Shakespeare for *At the Boar's Head* (1923), adapted from the Falstaff scenes of *Henry IV*. Vaughan Williams wrote six operas, including *The Shepherds of the Delectable Mountains* (1922) and *Hugh the Drover* (1924), which use folk melody to evoke rural, pastoral England, and *Sir John in Love, his* Falstaff opera.

Another important English composer was Frederick Delius (1862–1934). He lived most of his life abroad, first in Florida, then in Germany, and finally in France. He greatly admired the nationalist style of the Norwegian Edvard Grieg (1843–1907), who did not write any operas, and was also influenced by the musical impressionism of Debussy. The most famous of Delius's six operas is *A Village Romeo and Juliet* (1907), which uses Celtic musical themes. Although Delius did not spend much time in England, he is considered an important transitional figure leading up to the most important operatic composer England has produced: Benjamin Britten (1913–76).

Britten's operas include many of the finest music dramas of the twentieth century: *Peter Grimes* (1945), *The Rape of Lucretia* (1946), *Albert Herring* (1947), *The Little Sweep* (1949), *Billy Budd* (1951), *Gloriana* (1953), *The Turn of the Screw* (1954), *A Midsummer Night's Dream* (1960), and *Death in Venice* (1973). For more than thirty years, Britten shared his life with Peter Pears, a tenor who was one of England's most sensitive and thoughtful singers. Whereas Mozart, Rossini, Verdi, and other composers created music for certain women in their lives, Britten is unusual in having created so many roles for a particular man. While Mozart and others composed music with particular voices—male or female—in mind, Britten often chose subjects that would suit Pears's talents. Three of the most interesting and psychologically tormented characters in opera were created specifically for Pears: Peter Grimes, Captain Vere in *Billy Budd,* and Aschenbach in *Death in Venice.* (Because these were written during the era of the phonograph, we have the unique opportunity to hear Pears in these roles, all conducted by Britten.)

These are characters who carry large moral burdens, whether for actions taken or those that were avoided—reflective characters who speak in searching monologues about personal responsibility. To play these roles, a singer must have a fluid command of the subtleties of the English language as well as a reservoir of emotions to tap. It is possible to find a link to certain Janáček characters, except that the Czech composer often used his protagonists as models for the exploration of ideas, while Britten's characters verbalize the issues rather than simply illustrate them.

Another feature of these three Britten operas and several of his others is the presence of the sea. *Peter Grimes* is set in Aldeburgh in East Anglia, and part of its appeal for Britten was his affection for that seaside town. He and Pears lived there for most of their lives and started a music festival there that continues today.

Peter Grimes is notable for its six orchestral interludes that connect certain scenes. Four of these interludes evoke the rhythms of the sea and the changing moods of the town. The other two, much more wrenching, interludes describe the psychological torment of the fisherman Peter Grimes. Britten wrote an extraordinary scene depicting Grimes's mental collapse that both Pears and Jon Vickers (in different ways) made memorable.

Peter Grimes was an instant success and quickly appeared in many of the world's great opera houses, becoming the first English-language work to win international acclaim and recognition. Other significant English opera composers were Sir William Walton (1902–83), who used a Shakespeare play for *Troilus and Cressida* (1954) and Michael Tippett (b. 1905), whose works include *The Midsummer Marriage* (1955), *King Priam* (1962), *The Knot Garden* (1970), and *The Ice Break* (1977).

AMERICAN OPERA

In the years since 1945, opera in English has slowly entered the standard repertory. Many of these works were by Britten, yet a good deal more were by composers in the United States. While English will probably never challenge the Italian-German-French linguistic hegemony, it has gained a secure place in the second tier of operatic languages alongside Russian and Czech.

A significant factor in the evolution of American opera, as in every aspect of American life, was immigration. As a nation that has received shiploads of new citizens from throughout the world for centuries, the United States is distinctive in that its national operatic style is a blend of the many foreign elements that arrived on American shores and the uniquely American values that are a product of the nation's landscape, political philosophy, and particular energy.

The earliest opera performance on the American continent is thought to have been *Flora* by the English composer John Hippesley, first seen in Charleston, South Carolina, in 1735. English and French operas (the latter usually in translation) were seen in the colonies on a regular basis. Not surprisingly, New Orleans was the hub of French-language opera in the New World. New York was America's leading city of theater and music then as it is now, and many opera performances were given there during the eighteenth and nineteenth centuries.

Operas by native composers appeared as early as 1767. *Darby's Return* by William Dunlap (1766–1839) had its premiere in New York on November 24, 1789, in the presence of the newly elected President, George Washington. Many early American operas were based on patriotic themes, while others recounted the stories of Native Americans, especially Pocahontas.

Throughout the nineteenth century, immigrants from Italy, France, and Germany brought their national art form with them to the New World. These European styles dominated American stages, inhibiting development of an American operatic idiom. Italian opera was the first great style to sweep America in the nineteenth century. In 1805 Lorenzo da Ponte, the librettist of *Le Nozze di Figaro, Don Giovanni,* and *Così fan tutte,* moved to New York, where he became the first professor of Italian at Columbia University and helped introduce the city to Italian culture, including opera. Italian-language operas by Mozart, Rossini, and others were first given in New York in 1825, and their success led to the establishment of a series of opera companies that vied for audiences by bringing the newest operas and the greatest singers from Europe. Operas by American composers appeared throughout the nineteenth century, although most of them were influenced by the German style. With political unrest in Germany bubbling over, the 1850s and 1860s saw massive waves of German arrivals.

Many opera companies existed in New York before the Metropolitan Opera was created in 1883. The Academy of Music, on Fourteenth Street at Irving Place, was built in 1854 specifically for the presentation of opera. It had only eighteen boxes in its loge, the section where the bluebloods of New York society chose to sit. The Metropolitan was created by members of New York's upper crust who had trouble gaining admittance to the choice boxes in rival theaters. An architect was engaged to build the Metropolitan Opera House, on Broadway at Thirty-ninth Street, with the express mandate of designing an auditorium with many more boxes (there were 122 of them) to accommodate New York's burgeoning population of nouveau millionaires. Because social prominence was more important at the time than what was presented onstage, the design of the stage itself was shortchanged: there was not enough room in the wings, so scenery had to be placed on Thirty-ninth Street, no matter the weather.

Very quickly, the Metropolitan, the Academy of Music, and other theaters had to compete for audiences, and the way to accomplish this was to outdo one another in the grandeur of the productions and the quality of the singers engaged. New York audiences became more discerning, fueled by the competition and by the ever-increasing waves of immigrants, who often compared what they saw in New York with what they knew in Europe. It became clear that the Metropolitan needed a new theater to stage worthy productions, although, because of years of wars and economic depressions, the new Met did not open until 1966. But the board members of the Metropolitan Opera Association had deep pockets, so the world's finest singers were engaged, and the Met came to be known as a "singers' house." This meant that, because of scenic limitations, the focus of Met productions was more on talented vocalists who would stand and sing. This may not sound like a bad state of affairs, but the consequence was that American audiences essentially came to believe that opera was voice and only voice, instead of being a combination of forces that together produce a work of art. Don't misunderstand: you can't do an opera if you don't have talented, intelligent singers with beautiful voices, but opera is musical *theater,* and for the event to be complete, the orchestral, choral, and scenic elements must count too.

New York musical audiences had other venues for hearing operatic music as well. The New York Philharmonic was born in 1842, a few months after the founding of the Vienna Philharmonic. New York's orchestra regularly programmed orchestral and vocal segments from the newest European operas, which meant that this music was introduced to New York audiences soon after being heard in Europe. This happened in part because newly arrived immigrant musicians brought sheet music with them of the newest works. In addition, composers such as Tchaikovsky and Dvořák came to the United States to compose and perform. The opening of Carnegie Hall in 1891 featured the New York Philharmonic under the baton of Tchaikovsky.

Other American cities received large groups of German and Italian immigrants and saw the development of orchestras and opera companies that performed the classics and newer works. Cincinnati, with its large German population, was an early leader in classical music, and it has a fine orchestral, choral, and operatic tradition as well as an excellent conservatory of music. Philadelphia, Boston, Baltimore, Cleveland, Chicago, and Milwaukee were other American capitals of classical music and opera. Singers such as Enrico Caruso arrived just as phonograph recordings and later radio helped spread their sound and their fame.

Arturo Toscanini conducted at the Metropolitan from 1908 to 1915. In 1928 he became music director of the New York Philharmonic. He spent most of his career, until his death in 1957, leading American orchestras and was a pioneer in broadcasting classical music on television.

While "serious" opera in America was based on the European model, Gilbert and Sullivan–style "light" opera and operetta soon developed a distinctly American flavor. From the end of the Civil War until the end of World War I, music-hall entertainments, tent shows, minstrel shows, Negro spirituals, the humor of vaudeville and the Yiddish theater of Jewish immigrants, and the uniquely American musical elements of ragtime and jazz all contributed to an emerging style known as the American musical theater. Because so many of these shows were first seen in the theaters of New York's Times Square, which is bisected by that great thoroughfare Broadway, the form came to be called the Broadway musical.

Early composers of the Broadway musical included George M. Cohan, Jerome Kern, Irving Berlin, and George Gershwin. Kern and Gershwin were especially taken with American stories and native musical styles, and they produced musicals that could really be called folk operas, as American in flavor as *The Bartered Bride* was Czech. In Europe, Kern's *Show Boat* (1927) and Gershwin's *Porgy and Bess* (1935) are usually performed in opera houses and are accorded the respect that works by the great European composers receive. (I once spent a weekend in Budapest hearing *Così fan tutte* on Saturday and *Porgy and Bess* on Sunday—both in Hungarian!) In recent years, American opera companies, especially the New York City Opera and the Houston Grand Opera, have begun to give classic American musicals the credit and the productions they deserve, and leading record companies have begun to record musicals by Kern, Berlin, Gershwin, Cole Porter, Richard Rodgers, Leonard Bernstein, and others, using opera singers in the roles formerly sung by Broadway stars such as Mary Martin, Gertrude Lawrence, and Barbara Cook.

(It is unfortunate that young audiences today think of the Broadway musical as an art form in which singers are amplified. This recent development is the product of poor vocal training for young performers and the tastes of audiences who have become used to loud rock and roll. In fact, until the early 1970s, Broadway musical comedy stars sang without microphones, and the orchestras that accompanied them were not amplified, either. The new operagoer at the end of the twentieth century is often startled to discover that opera does not use microphones. This sound, strangely enough, is jarring to some listeners because it is *not* artificially loud and distorted.)

Although Toscanini, Mahler, and others had been in New York earlier, a new phase in American operatic life began toward the end of World War I. The war and subsequent privation in Europe meant that many composers and performers could have more work and income in the United States. Their influence and contact with the old tradition elevated the quality of performances in American theaters.

As Nazism rose in the 1930s, many more artists and composers came to America, including Igor Stravinsky, Kurt Weill, Arnold Schoenberg, Erich Wolfgang Korngold (1897–1957), Béla Bartók (1881–1945), and Benjamin Britten, who drafted *Peter Grimes* in the United States before returning to England in 1942. Korngold was a talented Austrian whose best-known opera, *Die Tote Stadt,* was written when he was only twenty-three years old. In America he became one of the finest composers of film scores and guided a whole generation of Hollywood composers. Bartók was a Hungarian whose opera *Bluebeard's Castle* (1911) has been a popular vehicle recently for Samuel Ramey, Eva Marton, and Jessye Norman. He was the greatest Hungarian composer, with a marvelous feeling for the potential in an orchestra to express mood, color and emotion. He also brought Hungarian folk melody into his music and played a key role in developing musical education in his country. His life ended sadly and without much recognition in New York, where he lived close to Carnegie Hall. Bartók spent his last years anonymously, teaching music at Columbia University.

This inundation of great talent meant that American music schools and performing arts institutions benefited from the knowledge that the artists from the Old World could impart. In addition to composers, conductors, singers, dancers, and instrumentalists, many of Europe's top stage directors and scenic designers arrived and gradually began to shape twentieth-century American operatic production. This mass artistic immigration was different from previous waves of immigration, in which people arrived who wanted to preserve art as they had known it in Europe. By contrast, the 1930s and '40s saw the arrival of artists who intended to create art for audiences in the United States. These artists helped launch a distinctly American style of classical music and opera that has continued unabated ever since.

One of the most successful émigré composers was Gian Carlo Menotti (b. 1911). Born in Varese, Italy, he began his studies in Milan and continued them at the Curtis Institute in Philadelphia. Although an Italian by birth, he deeply felt American style and idiom. His early operas were highly successful. They included *Amelia Goes to the Ball* (1937), *The Old Maid and the Thief* (1939), *The Medium* (1946), and *The Telephone* (1947). Later works, including *The Consul* (1950), *Amahl and the Night Visitors* (1951, a beloved children's opera, written for television), and *The Saint of Bleecker Street* (1954), all added to his reputation. Menotti is a complete man of the theater who directs and conducts performances of his and other composers' works. Among his greatest achievements was the creation of one of the world's foremost arts events, the Festival of the Two Worlds, held in Spoleto, Italy, since 1958. In recent years an American edition of the festival has taken place each May in Charleston, South Carolina, site of the first known opera production in the New World more than 250 years ago.

Since the 1930s, many American composers have written brilliant works, often with American settings and themes and tailored to the talents of specific American singers. These composers and their operas include: Leonard Bernstein (1918–90), *Trouble in* *Tahiti* and *A Quiet Place;* Douglas Moore, *The Ballad of Baby Doe* (1956) and *Carrie Nation* (1966); Jack Beeson, *Lizzie Borden* (1965); Aaron Copland (1900–90), *The Tender Land;* Carlisle Floyd, *Susannah* (1955) and *Of Mice and Men* (1970); Marc Blitzstein (1905–64), *Regina* (1949); Virgil Thomson, *Four Saints in* *Three Acts* (1934) and *The Mother of Us All* (1947), to librettos by Gertrude Stein; Stephen Paulus, *The Postman Always Rings Twice* (1982); William Bolcom, *McTeague* (1992); John Adams, *Nixon in* *China* (1987) and *The Death of Klinghoffer* (1991); and Samuel Barber (1910–81), whose *Vanessa* (1958) is one of the most popular and enduring American operas. Barber's *Antony and Cleopatra* (1966), commissioned for the opening of the new Metropolitan Opera House at Lincoln Center, has only recently begun to be given the credit it is due.

Stephen Sondheim, who wrote the lyrics for Bernstein's *West* *Side Story* (1957), is now one of the greatest composers for the American musical theater. While some of his works are superb examples of the Broadway musical, two Sondheim works from the 1970s, *A Little Night Music* and *Sweeney Todd,* are more like operettas or even operas and have received numerous performances in opera houses.

Other American composers whose work has covered a wide range of musical styles include: Roger Sessions (1896–1985), Hugo Weisgall (1912–), John Corigliano, and Philip Glass. Corigliano's *The Ghosts of Versailles,* which had its world premiere at the Metropolitan Opera in 1991, was one of the most wildly successful new operas in many years. Corigliano and his librettist, William Hoffman, used characters from Beaumarchais's *Le Barbier de Seville* and *Le Mariage de Figaro* to create something new. *The Ghosts of Ver-* *sailles* draws both from the plays and from the operas they inspired in Rossini and Mozart, but we look back at them with modern, weary eyes. The opera is brilliant and sentimental in music and atmosphere, and it proved yet again that engaging and meaningful new operas can still be created and still attract audiences.

The contemporary American opera composer who is probably

best known around the world is Philip Glass (1937–). His musical style, which is characterized by repetition and by the rhythms and cadences of the music of India, has divided audiences and critics. Just as Satie and Stravinsky worked with talented collaborators from all of the arts to produce their music dramas, Glass has sought the leading contemporary writers, directors, and designers. His works may be difficult to comprehend for the opera newcomer, but they should be approached with an open mind and revisited as one's knowledge of opera grows. His leading works include *Einstein on the Beach, Satyagraha, Akhnaten,* and *The Voyage,* which was commissioned for its world premiere in 1992 at the Metropolitan Opera to observe the five hundredth anniversary of Christopher Columbus's voyage to America. The opera is a sophisticated meditation on the way travel changes our sense of ourselves, of others and our world. Columbus is but one protagonist in this challenging opera that uses music to encourage audiences in self-discovery.

Although my intention in this chapter was to give an overview of the growth of opera, many fine composers were given little or no coverage and many operas were not mentioned. The important thing is to understand how opera has evolved due to the political, psychological, social, and artistic forces that have shaped four hundred years of Western history. Opera existed long before Mozart and did not die with Puccini. Importantly, the art form is still vibrant and growing and if opera composition in the United States and Britain continues to evolve, English may well be the future great language of opera.

Today opera lovers have the unique opportunity to learn more works than ever before. There are a few reasons for this. The first is the increase in musical scholarship in the past forty years. Composers whose lives were only sketchily documented have been rediscovered by researchers. Knowledge of these composers has meant that seldom-seen scores have been tracked down by scholarly detectives and have been newly published.

Opera singers and companies have attempted to revive these lost operas in concerts and full productions. For example, many of the long-ignored bel canto classics were revived in the 1950s and 1960s when singers capable of performing them came into prominence. In recent years there has been a keen interest, especially in England and France, in works from the first century of opera, which means that Monteverdi and Lully can now be heard more frequently.

We now are building permanent documentation of four hundred years of opera as recording companies preserve audio and video performances of an ever-expanding repertory of newly composed works and rediscovered masterpieces. This means that you, the opera lover, can see and hear new works all the time. When you realize that even as recently as the 1970s most audiences could get to know unusual works only if they were staged in a local opera house, the audio and video boom represents a revolution that should both increase the art form's audience and change the way we look at opera.

Ultimately, the way you look at an opera will have a lot to do with what that opera can tell you about yourself. Whether the message comes purely in the music or in a particularly affecting dramatic moment that combines words and music, you will find yourself being touched and moved and, in the process, will discover your deepest self. As you continue to explore works from Monteverdi to Glass, familiar operas will give you unexpected insights and new operas will make you face ideas and feelings that you may not yet have considered.

Let us now look at the various components of an opera and see how they combine to make what Wagner called a *Gesamtkunstwerk,* a complete work of art. Or, to pose the eternal question central to opera's addictive appeal, how does the combination of music and words become something greater than the sum of the two parts?

2.

BECOMING AN OPERA COGNOSCENTE

1. MUSIC, WORDS, AND MORE: WHAT IS AN OPERA MADE OF?

Sind es die Worte, die mein Herz bewegen, oder sind es die Töne, die stärker sprechen? . . .

Vergebliches Müh'n, die beiden zu trennen.
In eins verschmolzen sind Worte und Töne—
zu einem Neuen verbunden.
Geheimnis der Stunde—
Eine Kunst durch die andere erlöst!

Whether the words touch my heart more, or whether it is the music that speaks more strongly? . . .

In vain do I try to separate them, yet words and music are combined to form a single creation. A mysterious experience—one art being restored by the other!

—*from the Countess's closing monologue in* Capriccio, *called "A Conversation Piece for Music," words by Clemens Krauss, music by Richard Strauss* (1942)

In these few words, set to touching music, the most essential operatic conundrum is expressed. If you come to opera as a classical music fan, then what you witness is a sung concert to which words, scenery, and costumes have been added. If you see your first opera with the eyes and ears of a theater devotee, then opera is a play set to music.

But opera is neither a concert nor a play. It is, as we learn in *Capriccio,* a mysterious combination of words and music that produces a singular creation in which each component enhances the other. The way to understand this better is to acknowledge that music and words are each a *language,* one abstract and emotional, the other literal and rational. Central to both languages is that they are based in *sound.* When we hear the Italian word for love, *amore,* there is not only the meaning of the word but the three syllables— *ah-moh-ray*—that create the sound that we associate with love. Compare that sound to those in other languages:

> French: amour *(ah-moor)*
> German: Liebe *(lee-beh)*
> Russian: lyubov *(liu-bov)*
> English: love *(luv)*

You notice that in English it takes one syllable to bring love to mind, while in French, German, and Russian it takes two, and in Italian it takes three. Each syllable in each language has a distinct sound. For example, in French, Russian, and English the word ends with a consonant, while the Italian and German end in a vowel; in four of the five languages the final syllable has a different sound.

So if you need to describe that very operatic emotion called love, the language you choose is the first way you will differentiate among sounds. Then, if you set that word to music, you are combining two sounds, the spoken language and the musical language. Depending upon which notes a composer selects, how many notes are assigned to each syllable, and how long the notes are held, a different feeling can be created that tells us a lot about the love being described. In *Carmen,* the title character sings about love in a languorous, sensual fashion, making the first syllable, *ah,* soar upward through several notes before purring the second syllable, *moor,* on a lower note. By contrast, the title character of *Tosca,* upon greeting her lover Mario, sings the three Italian syllables, *ah-moh-ray,* with equal emphasis on each syllable. This creates a wistful sound that could not be more different from Carmen's frankly erotic *amour*. The lesson here is that while the meaning of these words is always *love,* the nature of the love being described can be made specific by the musical sound to which the word is set.

Here we run into the much-debated issue about the virtues of opera in translation. In almost every case, I am against translating the words of a libretto into another language. The sound of the language a composer worked with when he created the music cannot be replaced by using translated words.

To understand how different languages can sound when describing the same thing, take, for example, the title of an opera by Giuseppe Verdi, *La Forza del Destino*. In German, this translates as *Der Macht des Schicksals*. Even if you don't speak German, you need only look at the words to realize how different they sound. To appreciate an opera effectively as its creators made it, the audience cannot hear it in any way other than in its original form; otherwise, they are just not receiving the message the composer and librettist hoped to be sending.

There is only one circumstance in which I condone opera in translation: performances for children. Since children are still forming their own linguistic skills, it is important that they be exposed to sounds and ideas that are familiar so that they can draw from their knowledge in attempting to understand the rather unusual thing called opera. Children pay more attention when they hear familiar words. But most teenagers and adults have the skills and maturity to confront opera on its own terms.

Once you understand how composers and librettists select the words and sounds to communicate the feelings that will be expressed by one singer in an aria, you know what is the most fundamental component of an opera. The solo aria is the use of one voice to communicate the feelings of one operatic character. The human voice is the world's oldest musical instrument. Because every voice is unique, the sound of the same note and syllable will be different according to who is singing it.

By extrapolating from this information, you can see how an opera—a drama expressed in musical and verbal terms—is created. For example, if you have a scene in which a man and a woman are having an argument, how can this scene be constructed? The first decision the composer makes concerns what voice types the singers in this scene have. Let us assume, say, that the woman is the daughter of the man. She loves a young man, but her father disapproves of him. Young, romantic characters often have higher voices, and older, parental characters frequently have lower voices. So our daughter in this example is a soprano and our father is a baritone.

How will this argument be created in musical and verbal terms? There could be two solos ("Father, I love him" followed by "Daughter, he will do you harm"). This may work, but how often do you have an argument in which one person speaks for five uninterrupted minutes, followed by an uninterrupted five-minute response? This is not particularly realistic, but opera is not necessarily about realism. Our scene might start with an aria by each character describing his or her feelings. These arias might be followed by a *duet*—that is, music sung by the two of them.

Duets can be constructed in several ways. In one, the two characters will sing the same words to the same music, thus reinforcing one another's ideas ("I love you—I know you care about me"). Or the pair might sing different words but to the same music. The contrasting words would indicate conflict, as in "I love him—I want to be with him" versus "You love him, but duty prevents you from being with him," but the use of the same music would indicate a common interest or shared feeling. A third type of duet might feature the same words ("I love you—I know you care about me") but different music for each singer. This might suggest either irony or a lack of mutual comprehension—that is, they echo one another's words, but the contrasting music suggests different internal feelings that are not being openly expressed. A fourth type of duet might include different words and different music ("Father, I am old enough to decide for myself" versus "You bring shame on the family and your dead mother"). This is the most assertive form of argument, as both the musical and verbal elements express conflict.

In the course of a scene, it is possible to shift from one form of duet to another as the debate changes. Obviously, duets can be used for all forms of interaction between two characters: love, hatred, departures, arrivals, and so forth.

Let us now assume that the lover arrives on the scene. Since young romantic roles are often assigned to higher voices, this character will likely be a tenor. Another reason for this is that the composer has a large palette of vocal color to use in "painting" the scene. With a high female voice and a high male voice joined in expressing love and devotion, the contrasting lower voice of the dissenting father will come through clearly to the audience. This use of three voices is called a *trio*. The types of duets described above (same words and music; same words, different music, etc.) can be used to form a trio. But there is an additional variable: the third voice can sing along with one of the others, expressing agreement with one person and disagreement with the other. It can also represent a third point of view. Of course, a trio can be about agreement among three characters or about the contrasting feelings that they have.

To take the example further, let us assume that the tenor is in fact a two-timer and has another woman, who is overtly sexy and of loose morals, contrasting with the innocent goodness of our soprano. For dramatic and musical purposes the composer might decide that this woman is a mezzo-soprano, whose sultry lower voice clearly contrasts with the virtuousness the soprano voice might suggest. So our scene is now a *quartet,* with four voices. Each character has his or her own goals and intentions, and as the four of them sing, their words and music will contrast to make these intentions clear.

To go even further, the mezzo-soprano has an older brother who wants, for his own reasons, to kill the tenor. He hopes that his sister will attract the tenor to facilitate the murder. This older brother—a bass—might be hiding on the other side of a wall, expressing his separate intentions while the other characters sing together. Thus, the booming bass may fit in with the other four voices or it may contrast with the combined sound produced by the four voices. In either case, this ensemble would be called a *quintet.*

Lest you think I have invented an improbable scene, what you have just read is the basic story of the five central characters in *Rigoletto.*

(Let me digress briefly to remind you that high voices are not necessarily the good guys and low voices the bad guys. Our tenor, as we know, is unfaithful. The girl's father, a baritone, only wants the best for his daughter. The mezzo-soprano may want her man, but she doesn't know that he is romancing the soprano. She is sexually free, but she is not a bad person, merely different than the more virginal character played by the soprano.)

If our scene added a sixth character, it would be a *sextet*. A seventh voice would make a *septet*, an eighth an *octet*, etc. But in every case, each voice expresses the ideas and feelings of a different character.

The other vocalists onstage in an opera are the members of the chorus. The chorus may represent a crowd that is a protagonist who interacts with solo characters (as in many Russian operas) or that simply echoes and reinforces the words and music (that is, the thought) of a single character. The chorus can also be offstage, creating a sound effect (such as the storm in *Rigoletto*). Each chorus member can play a distinct character (a farmer, a sailor, a grandmother, a priest). It is also possible for chorus members to play more than one role during the course of an opera. For example, in Verdi's *Il Trovatore*, women choristers who play Gypsies in one scene might play nuns in the next.

The chorus contains all vocal types: sopranos, mezzo-sopranos, contraltos (the lowest female voice), tenors, baritones, basses, and, often, children's voices. These many voices can blend to sing the same words with the same message. Or there can be contrasting dialogue in the chorus—between, for example, men going off to war and the women and children they leave behind: all have different ideas and feelings to be expressed. The chorus is trained by the chorus master.

The music composed for the orchestra provides a contrasting tonal or pictorial sensation to what is happening onstage. If characters such as Hansel and Gretel are in the woods, the orchestral music may suggest a sylvan atmosphere while the two children's solo lines will concern the events in the story. If a character is singing about a person or a place that is not onstage at the moment, certain instruments in the orchestra may play music that evokes that absent element. Orchestral passages without singing, such as overtures or the sea interludes in Britten's *Peter Grimes,* can set a mood or advance the action.

Just as there are different singing voices, there are many instrumental voices, colors, and textures in the orchestra. The string instruments—violins, violas, cellos, basses, and harps—often provide the basic melody and in many ways resemble the vocal line being sung onstage. The strings can suggest delicacy, power, and a whole range of sonic effects, such as thumping and pounding, which can be dramatically suggestive. The winds—piccolos, flutes, oboes, clarinets, English horns, bassoons—and brass instruments—trumpets, French horns, trombones, tubas—provide volume, dramatic force, and a great deal of individual color. Each of these instruments has a particular voice, which often is associated with particular characters and emotions. The flute, for example, can be used to suggest delicacy and humor, but it is famous also for suggesting insanity in *Lucia di Lammermoor.* Trumpets are used to herald battles, wars, and the arrival of kings and to lend a particular excitement to the orchestra. Then there are the percussion instruments—drums, triangles, gongs, xylophones, etc.—which provide special effects such as thunderclaps, the shaking of skeletons, and anything else an inventive composer might create. Drums may imitate the heartbeat of a particular character.

The combination of all of these musical forces is called orchestration. This implies a knowledge of the capabilities of the different instruments and a sense of what they can achieve. When a composer orchestrates his music, he must decide how many of each instrument should be used. In general there is a preponderance of strings, since they often carry the basic melody and some of the contrasting melodies. But the use of other instruments may vary greatly. Handel and Wagner both enjoyed using the trumpet, so their orchestras often have more trumpeters than one might find in those of other composers. Doubling the number of kettle drums can create a powerful pounding that may provoke certain sonic effects. When I speak in this book of the composers who are great orchestrators, including Rossini, Berlioz, Wagner, Rimsky-Korsakov, Ravel, and Richard Strauss, I refer to composers who achieve maximum dramatic and psychological effect in their orchestral colors.

There is one special instrument that appears in most operatic orchestras from the Camerata Fiorentina through early Rossini: the harpsichord (or, in some cases, the fortepiano). This instrument, which in former times was usually played by the conductor, provided the *continuo* (continuity), or underlying music, that accompanied the recitatives. As recitatives came to be fully scored for orchestra in the nineteenth century, the use of the harpsichord declined.

There are also nonmusical performers onstage in an opera. Dance has been an important component of opera almost since the beginning of the art form. Dance can be used as part of a celebration scene in the story of an opera or can be used to advance the action. As I have mentioned, huge ballet scenes are especially prized in French grand opera. There was always a segment in the audience in nineteenth century Paris that arrived just in time to see the ballet and left soon thereafter. These audience members were often men-about-town who had ballerinas as mistresses.

Dance tends to be more interesting in operas in which it serves dramatic purposes rather than simply being empty though eye-filling spectacle. In *Eugene Onegin,* Tchaikovsky used three dance scenes—two in the country, one in the city—to create different environments in which the characters must interact. Composers often write a particular kind of dance to create a specific mood or evoke a specific region: for example, the polkas found in certain Eastern European works and the waltzes in the Vienna of *Der Rosenkavalier.* (Waltzes did not exist in mid-eighteenth-century Vienna, but they appealed to Richard Strauss's audiences in the early twentieth century.) Modern opera may contain more abstract choreography, subject to the tastes of the composer, the choreographer, or the stage director.

In operas with large crowd scenes, there are many people onstage who do not sing but merely occupy space or perform small functions. These might be dancers or people hired specially as extras. In opera, extras are known as *supernumeraries,* usually shortened to "supers." In addition to swelling the population of big scenes, these nonsinging characters can serve as spear carriers or ladies-in-waiting for the lead characters. Many supers get their starts as the lowly types armed with a broom and dustpan, ready to clean up every time an onstage horse or elephant leaves his calling card.

The one performer we have not yet discussed is probably the most crucial of all. When you attend your first opera, you may be surprised to see that the performer who takes the final, and most important, bow is not the leading singer but the conductor. It is the conductor's responsibility, during rehearsals, to shape all of the musical and musico-dramatic elements of the production. During the performance, he or she controls everything done by the performers, onstage and in the orchestra pit.

In the early days of orchestras, the conductor was primarily responsible for beating time. This was done by stamping one's foot on the floor or pounding a stick or cane. As you may recall, this tradition faded after Lully stabbed himself in the foot and died from the subsequent infection. Gluck and Mozart conducted with their hands, often while seated at the harpsichord. Nowadays, when an opera with continuo is performed, there often is a conductor leading the orchestra and an instrumentalist playing the keyboard.

Before 1800, it often was the case that the composer of a piece of music would conduct the first performance. In the early Romantic era, conductors who were not necessarily the composer of a work began to have more importance. Conducting became a talent distinct from composition. Since Romantic opera has more variation in beat and tempo than Classical opera, the interpretive abilities of a conductor became more vital. In Romantic opera, especially French grand opera, the large forces of orchestra, chorus, ballet, and many soloists all had to be kept under control. Berlioz was probably the first composer to demand separate rehearsals for chorus, for orchestra, and for individual singers, which required one individual to supervise the overall musical development. This enabled a conductor to mold every component and shape a total vision of an opera. Wagner, who concentrated more of the drama in the orchestra pit than any previous composer, insisted on a more prominent role for the conductor.

In addition to having total knowledge of the score, the successful operatic conductor must have a strong point of view. In order to shape the sound of orchestra, chorus, and soloists, he or she must study the score and the libretto for clues to the meaning of particular passages or characters. How does this shaping happen? By holding a note a little longer; by playing passages louder or softer; by bringing forward certain instruments and toning down others; by playing certain passages a little more slowly or quickly than marked in the score. Importantly, there are many conductors who keep the orchestra too loud, forcing singers to scream in an effort not to be drowned out. This sounds ugly and leaves the impression that the singer is bad. Some singers, when conductors blast the orchestral sound, refuse to scream for fear of wrecking their voices, which can give the mistaken impression that they are not capable of singing audibly. When you realize that a conductor can alter and shape *all* the solo, choral, and orchestral voices, you realize how much he can affect the flavor and temperament of a performance.

During the preparatory and rehearsal period of a new production, a common artistic vision is forged by the conductor in concert with the stage director, the singers, the choreographer, the chorus master, and the designers of the scenery, costumes, and lighting. It is important that a conductor have a realistic sense of the quality of the talent he is working with. If young singers are cast in major roles, they may not have the experience or insights of more mature artists. It is often up to the conductor to impart wisdom to the young performers. Similarly, older singers may no longer have complete command of their voices, and may even have to sing some of their music in a lower key. The conductor will have to instruct the orchestra about key changes and make sure that everything jells. I once attended a performance of *Il Barbiere di Siviglia* in which a mezzo-soprano sang Rosina in Act I and, when she took ill, was replaced by a soprano in Act II; the conductor had to ensure that the orchestra and the other singers were aware of the key changes that would occur. A conductor without a point of view, a mere time beater, cannot give special character to an opera, and the resulting performances can be deadly. I'm afraid that many people attempting to discover opera have been turned off by performances that were poorly conducted rather than poorly sung.

There are some famous cases in opera history of singers and con-

ductors working together consistently, such as Maria Callas and
Tullio Serafin, and Joan Sutherland and her husband, Richard Bonynge. These collaborations were successful because both partners
were talented and serious in purpose. Callas had a strong artistic
point of view, that often rankled conductors, but with Serafin she
found someone who understood what she had to offer and shaped
performances to bring out her best—along with the best of the orchestra and the other singers. In Sutherland, Bonynge found a singer
of awesome talent and great discipline. He taught her the bel canto
repertory, and through the course of their long careers they deepened these portrayals musically and dramatically.

On the other hand, there have always been cases in which a star
singer will insist that an opera house use his or her pet conductor
simply because the conductor will defer to that singer's wishes,
often at the expense of the overall performance. Sometimes the result is not even what is most flattering, simply what the singer thinks
is so. I have been to many of these vanity performances, and while
the star may sound great, the total production is usually unbalanced
and unsatisfactory because the orchestra, the chorus, and the other
singers have been given only perfunctory attention. The key to a
successful performance is that the opera be served before the egos of
the performers, including that of the conductor.

Up to now, this chapter has been devoted mostly to the musical
aspects of opera. The music is the most complex component in telling the story, yet the words are also vital for their sound and their
meaning. The sum of these words is the libretto. This may be a
poem, as in many early operas or in Wagner, or it may be a play, as
in *Pelléas et Mélisande*. In many cases the libretto is a combination
of free verse and poetry, in which the poems are the arias and the
verses are the spoken dialogue or sung recitatives. But always the
libretto is a work of theater that requires all the elements of a theatrical production.

Everyone who works on an opera production—conductors, singers, directors, designers—needs to explore the meaning of the
drama. The ideas need to be explored in both the music (what the
composer says to you) and the words. In studying a score, the singer
will see where musical emphasis is placed on specific words, and

then further explore the libretto to decide where other coloring and inflection might be placed. It is important for all involved in an opera production to read about the attitudes and philosophy of the composer and librettist and to do research into the period in which the opera is set. In some operas, certain characters are symbols as much as full-fledged characters, so the meaning of these symbols must be understood in order for the performance to be effective. In addition, a singer must consider the physical aspects of acting a role: how a character moves and thinks is an important step toward plumbing the role's psychological depths. Costumes also help developing a character. If a bass is given ceremonial robes and imposing headgear to play Boris Godunov, these clothes promote a sense of who the character is.

Singers often work with coaches and conductors to develop the musical and dramatic components of a role. In every production of a particular opera, the serious singer will endeavor to deepen her understanding of her character rather than simply repeating what has already been done. This is crucial because each production has new singers, conductors, stage directors and audiences, all of which require spontaneity from a singer, even if she has sung a role a hundred times.

The other principal shaper of an opera production is the stage director. (In opera this person is often called the producer.) In the past, very few stage directors had the power and influence to demand control of an operatic staging. But things have changed in the last fifty years. Nowadays, it is not uncommon to hear talk of the Ponnelle *Nozze di Figaro,* the Sellars *Così fan tutte,* the Chereau *Ring,* or the Corsaro *Carmen.* Stage directors have increased their power, to the pleasure of some audience members and the dismay of others. There are a few reasons for this. The first is television. Since television purports to present realism, or at least its version of realism, its audiences have become more literal-minded and less reliant on their own fantasy and imagination. When the television generation goes to a performance of live theater, dance, or opera, it often expects realism in acting and scenery. In some cases, this may serve an opera well, but in many instances it can flatten out the rich texture that is part of many operatic works. To me, one of the great tragedies in the contemporary performing arts is the erosion of fantasy on the part of audiences.

Many directors, too, have sought to make opera "relevant" to contemporary audiences. A standard way of doing this is to update it in terms of time and place. So a recent production of Wagner's *Tannhäuser* made the title character a Jimmy Swaggart–type American preacher rather than a German poet-singer from centuries ago who struggled with his own moral and ethical issues. A confession of sin in late-twentieth-century America is not the same as one in Germany six hundred years ago. To set the opera's last act in a modern airport waiting room rather than in a German valley completely denies the impact of nature on this opera and its characters. Audiences who saw this production and had no prior knowledge of *Tannhäuser* would find it nearly impossible to understand its meaning.

While few stage directors who "translate" an opera to make it "relevant" ever manage to capture the real essence of that work, I do not wish to imply that all updatings are bad, or that I adhere only to conservative methods of stagecraft. What I insist is most important is that a stage director attempt to bring to audiences the meaning of a work of art *as created by the composer and librettist*. If a director understands the meaning of an opera as intended by the creators, he or she may present that opera in a variety of styles or contexts. So when a recent production of *La Traviata* updated the story to 1990 and the unnamed illness that afflicts Violetta became AIDS rather than tuberculosis, the production still honored the intentions of the opera's creators: the issues of promiscuity, the abandonment of the sick and dying, and the power of love to reconcile differences in the face of death are as relevant today as they were in the 1850s.

Another reason for the rise of stage directors is the belief (mistaken or not) by many opera company executives that there are less good singers now than at any time in history. I think that there are many wonderful singers now, but they have not achieved the level of fame that translates into ticket sales every time they appear in a production. Only very few of today's stars instantly sell out a four-thousand-seat house. So there is the currently popular notion of designing and staging productions that are "singer-proof." In other words, if a good singer is not available, at least the show looks good. This is another example of how television and film have changed audience perceptions and how many creative people in opera underestimate audiences. In the long run, this will be a negative phenomenon, because audiences will pay less and less attention to what they hear and more to what they see.

A good stage director *can* make the difference between a ho-hum, routine performance and a great one. If a singer has made a career of singing the title role in *Madama Butterfly,* her interpretation may become stale unless her ideas are challenged every so often. A conductor with a good ear and a stage director with a good eye can help deepen her performance of Cio-Cio-San. The best operatic stage directors are successful because they understand the meaning of a libretto; they feel what the characters feel, hear meaning in the music, and know how to merge their ideas with those of their colleagues.

When a conductor and a stage director plan a production, they have specific ideas and goals that need to be realized musically, dramatically, and visually. The production designers, especially the scenic designers, take part in this planning. (A few notable stage directors are also talented designers—the most famous example is Franco Zeffirelli—so that they create scenery to support their view of a particular opera.) If realism is preferred, the designers will be charged with making stage pictures that represent places and objects that are familiar. In these productions, mountains look like mountains, churches look like churches, and chairs look like chairs. But there are many other interesting and viable approaches in selecting the style and tone of a production.

One that is often used is implication or suggestion. This is a viable choice financially as well as dramatically, since opera productions can be very expensive. For example, instead of a real-looking house onstage, there may be a set with two walls. We see objects that suggest a particular room, but the room does not have to be fully furnished for us to deduce what else is there. This is where our imagination comes into play.

The production team may opt for a completely abstract setting in which everything familiar is absent. If the conducting and the stage direction are excellent, an abstract production that minimizes the visual can help focus the audience's attention on the music and the ideas of an opera. This is tricky; such a performance can be very dull if it is not done with great skill. Yet the results can be revelatory. I once saw a production of *Elektra* that consisted simply of three descending tiers of gray platforms. Each platform had thin blood-red stripes at its edges, whose practical purpose was to keep the singers from accidentally falling off but which also made perfect dramatic sense in this story of family ties and murder. As the characters, all clad in black or gray, moved from upper to lower platforms, our eyes were completely riveted on them and our ears were focused on the sounds they made. This was a great production for the simple reason that it honored the intentions of the librettist and the composer.

A costume designer, who usually works in tandem with the scenic designer, must also be intimately acquainted with the opera. If, in reading the libretto, the designer sees a mention of a particular garment or color, then that must be included in the costume design. If the designer "hears" colors in the music (not a farfetched idea), those colors, too, might be included. A designer should understand the historical context of an opera and know the fashions of that time; the best costume designers are also historians.

It is not a given that costumes must be realistic or of a certain era. In the abstract *Elektra* I described above, Aegisth, the husband of Klytämnestra, wore a tuxedo, a garment that certainly never existed in ancient Greece; yet it gave him the frivolous, decadent, slightly disengaged air that is part of the character. Another choice that many designers make is to use costumes of the time when the opera was written rather than of the era in which the opera is set, usually in an effort to evoke older productions. This is particularly common in productions of seventeenth- and eighteenth-century works based on classical themes: a Roman emperor or Greek god may appear in powdered wig and breeches.

Operatic costumes must be designed for durability and flexibility. It is common for several singers to play a role during the life of a production, and so opera costumes often have an intricate system of hooks and zippers that allow them to become larger or smaller, shorter or longer. These costumes are built to last: they can weigh twenty to thirty pounds and can be highly decorated. Wardrobe staffs in opera houses are responsible for cleaning and repairing these costumes for the life of the production—often as long as twenty-five or thirty years.

Without the contribution of a lighting designer, you would not be able to see the scenery, costumes, and staging created by the production team. But theatrical lighting is not simply about illumination. Lighting can evoke the mood of music, the words, and the action. In a love scene, the two characters might be bathed in pinkish light; in a storm scene, darker colors might be used to suggest the gathering clouds.

To create certain settings without building sets, scenic designers may work with the lighting designer to produce slides that will suggest that setting. If, in the third act of *Tosca,* you want to put the Roman skyline of the year 1800 in the background, you can build that skyline of scenery or design a slide that will evoke the scene. By changing the amount of light projected through the slide, the designer can suggest different times of the day: dawn, morning, high noon, dusk, and night.

Many other people than the ones we have looked at animate the life of an opera house, and without them the opera could not get onstage. Stage managers run onstage traffic, ensuring that soloists, chorus, dancers, and supers are all in the right places at the right times. In many opera houses, centered at the front of the stage right above the orchestra pit is a small shell or box. Inside is the prompter, who follows the performance with the score, calling out cues or assisting a singer with a temporary mental lapse. (Singers are human, and such things do occur.)

In the wings (sides) of the stage are stagehands, who set up and take down scenery. Stage carpenters and electricians keep everything in shape and running. Property masters are responsible for laying out props and removing them at the end of a scene. Any non-costume item smaller than fourteen feet (4.3 meters) is considered a prop—a chair, a book, a bottle, a knife. Scene painters and carpenters produce and maintain the sets. Makeup artists and wigmakers complete the costume and the look of all the onstage performers.

Dressers help performers in and out of costumes. All of the staff on and near the stage comes under the purview of a technical director.

The artistic director of an opera company (working with a staff) selects repertory, singers, designers, and conductors, administers the orchestra, chorus, and corps de ballet, and handles all the performers' contracts. A librarian is responsible for the scores, placing them on the music stands in the orchestra pit before every performance.

Most opera companies in North America have a board of directors and one or more chief executives to run all operations. An opera company also has box office staff, a marketing department, fund-raisers, a press and public relations department, and a house manager, whose staff includes ushers, ticket takers, matrons, security guards, a house doctor, checkroom attendants, and a cleaning crew. There are often restaurants and bars to serve the public as well as eating facilities backstage for company members.

And then there is the audience, without whom all of this effort and expense would be pointless. The audience is one of the special protagonists who make each performance unique. For example, in a run of seven performances of *Il Barbiere di Siviglia,* each will be distinctive because of the audience's mood and responsiveness to the humor and the music. But this does not apply only to comedy. In Wagner's somber *Parsifal,* the conductor, the orchestra, and the singers onstage can sense the involvement of the audience and are affected by it.

How do audiences differ? First, certain audiences are more attracted to particular operas. Popular works by Verdi and Puccini will pull in a broad cross section, from the most devoted opera lovers to those who listen only to standard Italian repertory to those who are just testing the operatic waters. By contrast, people attending a work by Wagner or something in Russian probably planned to be there and are more ready for what they will see. And depending upon the day of the week and the hour of the performance, the audience will have a different character. On Mondays and Tuesdays at the Metropolitan, one tends to find dedicated, lifelong operagoers. Wednesdays and Thursdays have a cross section of devoted operagoers and those who attend occasionally. In the first four nights of the week, audiences listen carefully and may be somewhat reserved in their applause. Some of these audience members leave before the opera ends because they have to get up early.

On Fridays and Saturdays (and Sundays in some theaters), one sees subscription audiences who go to the opera as much because of the night of the week as because of what is onstage. These audiences, who are out for a good time, are often noisier and more demonstrative than their midweek counterparts. They may even applaud the scenery—something you really shouldn't do, since it usually disrupts the flow and the mood of the music.

Matinee audiences tend to be much older than others. They often have long memories and are delightful to talk to at intermission about performances from their own golden age.

It is possible, at a great performance or one featuring a major star, to sense the electricity that courses through the audience. Singers and musicians sense this, too, and tend to give more. On the other hand, if a listless performance is making its audience restless or sleepy, this too can be felt onstage. Part of the thrill of operagoing, for better or worse, is that no two performances are ever alike. You never know when you might be present at a moment of greatness.

Before we leave our discussion of what makes up an opera, there is the delicate issue of the opera critic. Since the earliest human artistic expression, there has always been someone else around who had an opinion about it. Don't forget that "opinion" does not necessarily imply negative feelings, and that a critic's judgment does not necessarily have to be negative. You also should realize that ultimately, any critic's evaluation is just one person's opinion. Reviews are too often taken as gospel. Try to read critics whose love and support for opera are apparent even when they're giving something a bad review. Draw from their wisdom but never be afraid to question their opinions.

You will notice that every opera fan, in his or her own way, is a critic. For you to take part in this ritual, you must come prepared. So let's find out what to do.

2. LEARNING THE STORY

The first step you must take in discovering an opera is to learn the story. There is a short way and a long way to do this. The short way is to read the synopsis, a summary of usually a page or two, which will give you the framework of the story. After reading a synopsis of an opera, you can see a performance and have a general idea of what is going on.

To understand an opera more deeply, however, you must take time to read the libretto. The libretto, as you know, is the play, poem, or text that is set to music to create an opera. When you read a libretto, you will notice that the first pages usually contain a synopsis and a list of characters, including the voice categories the composer has assigned to them. There may also be some historical and critical essays about the opera, especially in the libretto that comes with a recording.

Before reading the text, take time to read the synopsis and learn the names and voice types of the principal characters. You know that the same words and music can have different impact depending on what kind of voice is singing. Then, as you read the libretto, try to envision what is going on, and what the settings look like.

Libretti come in many styles. In this regard they are like spoken theater. Shakespeare or Molière wrote in rhymed verse with a particular meter. Some opera libretti are written in rhymed verse, with the difference that the spoken meter often goes by the wayside and is replaced by a meter or rhythm imposed by the music. A whole opera in the same meter would be terribly boring. Other libretti use free verse or even the most conversational dialogue.

Whatever the format, a libretto on the page is only part of the librettist's conception. Reading a libretto, like reading a play, can take the operagoer only so far. When you read Shakespeare, you admire the writing and storytelling, but you must use your imagination to sense how it will play on stage.

In writing *Lucia di Lammermoor*, the librettist, Salvatore Cammarano, and the composer, Gaetano Donizetti, put stage directions into the libretto and score to guide singers, conductors, directors, and designers. For Lucia's entrance for her mad scene, they wrote:

> Lucia enters disheveled and her deathly pale face makes her look more like a ghost than a living being. Her glassy stare and convulsive movements demonstrate clearly that she is out of her senses, and that her life is drawing to its close.

These evocative words enable you to see exactly what Lucia's state is; they offer guidance to everyone involved in staging this scene. Compare them to those by Arrigo Boito and Verdi for the opening of the last act of *Otello:*

> Desdemona's bedchamber. A bed, a prie-dieu, a table, a mirror, some chairs. A lamp hangs burning before a picture of the Madonna which is above the prie-dieu. There is a door on the right, a lighted candle on the table. It is night.

The virtual absence of adjectives means that a lot has to be left to the imagination. The creators have given us only the most salient pieces of information for the scene. We know that it is night, but we do not know if the room has a window. If it does not, then how does the audience know it is night? And so a designer might include a window in the set even though it is not specifically called for.

To take another example: does it matter how many chairs there are? Perhaps not, but it mattered to the creators that there be chairs. This might be because of the custom of the time that there be chairs in a bedchamber, or it might be that they have decided that someone will sit in a chair later on. If it never is addressed in the libretto, then it is up to the director to decide when and where a singer might sit down. In fact, one chair might be for Emilia, Desdemona's confidante, who otherwise would have to stand through Desdemona's Willow Song.

In imagining the scene, we will find that the prie-dieu (a bench suitable for kneeling for prayer) is a central piece of furniture. Therefore, the director and the scenic designer must position it as a point of focus for the audience, and the lighting design must be geared to this spot. Boito and Verdi did not tell us any of this, but with careful reading and creative thinking we can see what the set looks like before Desdemona and Emilia enter.

Perhaps my favorite scenic indication in a libretto comes from Wagner, who opens *Das Rheingold,* the first opera of the four-opera *Ring* cycle, with these words: "At the bottom of the Rhine." Period. While we all have a sense of what the bottom of a river looks like, this scant indication is both very specific and impossibly general. Very few scenic designers would think to journey to the Rhine, put on diving gear, and find out what the bottom of the river looks like. Here, a director and a designer would listen to the music to get a sense of what Wagner envisioned. And that is what you should do, too.

Wagner was even less helpful for the other scenes of *Das Rheingold.* Scene 2 occurs in "an open space on the mountaintops," scene 3 in "a subterranean cavern," and scene 4 in the same setting as scene 2.

As you might imagine, elsewhere Wagner was actually quite thorough in describing what the Rhine should look like, and wrote separate, specific indications for the scenic aspect of the river. An excerpt:

> A greenish twilight, brighter toward the top, darker toward the bottom. The upper part is filled with swirling waters that flow restlessly from right to left. Lower down, the waves dissolve into an increasingly fine, damp mist. . . . In all directions, steep rocky cliffs rear up from the depths. . . . The whole riverbed is broken up into wild, craggy confusion. There is a reef in the middle of the stage which points a slender finger up into the denser water where the light is brighter. . . .

These directions are very specific, but if you don't have access to all of Wagner's writings or the time to read them, you are left with "at the bottom of the Rhine" from the libretto.

If you read a libretto without listening to a recording, you will reach your understanding of the visual and dramatic content of an opera strictly through the librettist's words and your own imagination. An even better way to learn an opera is to listen to a recording or broadcast while reading a libretto. This need not cost a lot of money. Major libraries in most cities have libretti and some have recordings as well. In addition, residents in most of North America have a Saturday afternoon opera broadcast for much of the year on their classical or public radio station. Canadians have the same on the CBC. Readers of this book who live elsewhere (especially Europe) have many opera broadcasts on the radio from their own great companies and occasionally from the Metropolitan Opera in New York. With a libretto from the library and the opera on the radio, you have not spent anything. In this book, for teaching purposes, we will be using specific recordings which you might have to purchase if your local library doesn't have them. A suggestion if your funds are limited and your library does not have the recording is to study opera with one or more friends. This will enable you to split the costs of the recordings and will probably result in companions to attend performances with once that time comes.

When you read a libretto to learn the story, you will read it in your native language unless you know the original. Let us assume, for example, that you are reading the libretto of *Carmen,* but since you do not know French you need to read it in English. While listening to a recording of the opera, however, you should try to read both the French and the English columns. This is not as difficult as it seems once you get the hang of it. In reading the English, you will know what is happening when, and which music relates to those events. By reading the French while listening to the singer, you will learn what the words sound like and better understand the art of the composer.

3. LISTENING TO THE MUSIC

When you listen to an opera, more important than being able to recognize an instrument is hearing the sound and feeling whatever it is that you feel. The sound of the music had specific meaning for the composer and it has specific meaning for every listener. Each of us makes a personal connection to the music, and the sensations we derive from it are uniquely ours.

Try to disconnect yourself from literal, rational thought; where music is concerned, allowing yourself to feel it without the encumbrance of analysis is crucial. When you feel music, you will find meaning in it that has nothing to do with words or events.

As we have discussed before, we can describe sound in terms of color—not necessarily in blues, browns, or yellows as we know them (although these are there as well) but in musical colors. A great flowing stream of violins is a different color than the rapid bowing or plucking of the same instruments. A great flowing stream of cellos and basses is a different color than our stream of violins. While the violins may suggest wind and a blue sky, the cellos might be the undercurrent in the darker blue of the Rhine.

We have discussed earlier how orchestration works and the way orchestra, soloists, and chorus can combine for an endless variety of musical and dramatic effects. We know that a conductor can control the total sound of these effects by emphasizing or playing down certain elements in the orchestral or singing voices. But we have not yet explored how a singer can affect the sound of the drama.

4. THE SINGERS

The ability to sing is an extraordinary thing, but it is exceedingly difficult to explain or quantify. Even a person with a gloriously beautiful voice may not know how to sing. The most important requirement for an opera singer is the actual act of producing sound in such a way that its beauty and volume fairly represent the composer's intentions without causing physical harm to the singer. In a four-hour opera, a singer might be onstage for more than half the time, singing the music over an eighty-piece orchestra to a four-thousand-seat auditorium. The ability to do this is called a *technique*.

A singer may have a good or a bad technique, but everybody has one. The first thing opera singers learn is technique, and they must spend much of their time assiduously maintaining it. Singers do exercises each day to keep the technique in shape. These may involve singing scales or loosening and tightening muscles in the facial mask, mouth, jaw, throat, chest, diaphragm, and buttocks. What all of this leads to is breath control, or the ability to allow as much or as little breath as is necessary to pass through the throat and out of the mouth as required to bring forth the sound being made by the vocal cords. This enables them to sustain the vocal line longer or to increase or decrease volume for dramatic effect. Short spurts of breath will produce the rapid-fire effect that is part of coloratura singing. Listen to a recording of Marilyn Horne singing Rossini arias and you will understand what great breath control is.

The best singers not only have beautiful voices and an innate sense of drama in music but have outstanding breath control as well. The absence of breath control results in a dryness of sound or a lack of flexibility. Some singers wind up sounding underpowered, while others become uncontrollably loud. Breath control must come from the diaphragm, which is one of the reasons why singers exercise this part of their bodies.

Breath control is central to the singer's education, yet many observers feel that this fundamental of good technique is dying out.

I believe that the modern problem is not so much that we have forgotten how to teach technique but that with more opera houses producing more works than ever before and the demand for singers increasing, singers are subject to all sorts of temptations. Managers want them to start singing even though their teachers tell them to wait; too many singers take on roles they are not prepared for because of the excitement of being offered important parts and the lure of money. Many leading singers in their late thirties and early forties experience vocal problems that were rare years ago in artists of that age. The problem is especially acute among singers of Verdi and Wagner who push themselves to sing roles that are too demanding.

Young voices are being consumed too quickly, which means that few new singers will have careers such as those of Leonie Rysanek, Alfredo Kraus, and Leontyne Price, all of them in their sixties and still doing great singing as of this writing. In singing, as in much of life, young people need to learn how to say no until the time is right.

Even if a singer shows intelligence and restraint in the selection of roles in terms of technique, there is also the issue of style. In the 1920s there were still people around who knew Rossini and Wagner. They passed their wisdom about how to sing those composers' music down to people who today are very old. Toscanini, who was a direct link to Verdi and Puccini, influenced generations of singers, conductors, and instrumentalists until his death in 1957. Now these people are passing from the scene, having taught what they learned. There are still some people around who had direct contact with Richard Strauss, Mascagni, Gershwin, Poulenc, Stravinsky, and Britten, but their number is dwindling. The wave of immigrants to the United States between the two world wars filled American music schools and opera companies, but the people who constituted it are also disappearing. We have nearly a century of recordings to let us know how the likes of Enrico Caruso, Rosa Ponselle, Lauritz Melchior, and Maria Callas sounded, but we may not know how they did what they did. You have learned that there are several operatic languages, especially Italian, German, French, and Russian. These come from national traditions in Italy, Austria, Germany, France, and Russia that developed over centuries. Yet war, political realignments, and immigration have diluted many national characteristics, producing what we might call the international style of singing. This means that a Spaniard such as Plácido Domingo or an American such as Jessye Norman can be considered among the foremost interpreters of some French and German roles. These singers bring good voices, intelligence, and versatility to whatever roles they play, yet purists would argue that only a French artist could bring truth and authenticity to a French role.

What is probably more important is whether an "international" singer has endeavored to learn the intricacies and historical legacy of a particular national style. With immigrant teachers spreading their craft in the United States, the chief beneficiaries of this instruction have been young American singers, who draw from all styles rather than from one national tradition. Their versatility and good work habits have put them in great demand around the world. But there is a difference between knowing foreign languages just well enough to understand and correctly pronounce the words and being able to give them meaning. This is another thing that separates good singers from great ones, and surprisingly few singers do it well. Despite all the excitement about the voice and persona of Luciano Pavarotti, it is seldom noted how exquisitely he uses the Italian language in his singing. Words are shaped and caressed so they achieve extra beauty and emotional effect. This is part of his greatness.

Hildegard Behrens extracts great meaning from the German language in every character she essays. You can hear, even on record, how distinct each one of her characters is. In French, José van Dam is exemplary.

As if this were not enough to deal with, singers must also understand at least the fundamentals of acting. Years ago I was an acting coach for opera singers in Italy and was constantly reminded of the inhibition many of them felt onstage. So much of their training had been geared to sound production and musical and linguistic phrasing that the notion of acting seemed daunting. In olden days, it is generally (and perhaps mistakenly) assumed, all an opera singer had to do was "stand and sing." But a great singing performance takes on even greater dimensions when the artist is also a riveting actor.

While every operatic era has had its excellent actors, ours seems to be blessed with more than in the past. This is because young singers, especially Americans, are given more acting training. The rise of the stage director has also contributed to a heightened theatrical aesthetic. Then, too, the postwar operatic generation was weaned on the incendiary acting talent of Maria Callas. Although hers was not the most beautiful voice, when her technique was at its peak in the 1950s and was combined with her extraordinary musicianship, use of language, fiery temperament, and insightful acting abilities, the result was consummate artistry. She was also fortunate to work with great conductors, fellow singers such as the baritone Tito Gobbi who could match her in dramatic terms, and stage directors such as Luchino Visconti. Callas seldom overacted; through study and genius she understood the meaning of her characters and brought dramatic and emotional truth to them.

Among the numerous singers in recent years who have also shone as actors, we should first note Leonie Rysanek and Teresa Stratas. Rysanek has the power to move audiences to tears, chills, or elation with her extraordinary skills. Stratas is her match. This special artist, who learned the repertory of Kurt Weill from his widow, Lotte Lenya, has created a gallery of unforgettable portrayals. In Franco Zeffirelli's film of *La Traviata,* despite the presence of Plácido Domingo and scene after scene of gorgeous costumes and sets, all one really remembers is Stratas's achingly pathetic and beautiful Violetta. Stratas has been an incomparable Lulu, Mimì, Liù, Suor Angelica, and Nedda in *Pagliacci,* among many others.

Other great singing actresses have included Renata Scotto (who now directs operatic productions), Régine Crespin (in *Carmen* and *Der Rosenkavalier*), and Hildegard Behrens in *Fidelio, Elektra,* and Wagner's *Ring* cycle. Also worth noting are Maria Ewing, Evelyn Lear, Shirley Verrett, Fiorenza Cossotto, Regina Resnik, and the late Tatiana Troyanos. Among the great male singing actors, the recently retired Jon Vickers was unbeatable in great heroic, psychological, and emotional roles such as Otello, Canio in *Pagliacci,* Peter Grimes, Aeneas in *Les Troyens,* Florestan in *Fidelio,* Tristan in *Tristan und Isolde,* and Samson in Handel's *Samson* and Saint-Saëns' *Samson et Dalila.* Other great actors include Ruggero Raimondi (a superb Don Giovanni, Figaro, and Boris Godunov), José van Dam, and the late Tito Gobbi and Martti Talvela.

The polar opposite to Maria Callas was Renata Tebaldi. Although they sang many of the same roles, Tebaldi was not the actress Callas was. Instead she offered a beautiful voice and gloriously creamy singing that bewitched lovers of pure sound. Her expressiveness in her native Italian was also proficient, and she could arouse the requisite passion when needed. There was great animosity in the 1950s and 1960s between fans of Callas and those of Tebaldi, and, as in an ancient blood feud worthy of an operatic plot, tempers still flare today when discussions of "Maria" and "Renata" come up.

In the Tebaldi category of singers who are prized strictly for their vocal beauty and rapturous singing, pride of place belongs to Montserrat Caballé. Her vast repertory, which you can hear in her many recordings, ranges from Handel to Puccini, with most of the great Mozart, bel canto, Verdi, and Wagner roles included. Caballé's hallmarks are her gorgeous voice and unmatched pianissimi, those endlessly floating soft high notes that she spins out with masterful breath control. Caballé's diction is seldom deserving of praise, but she creates more drama through sound than just about anyone else. Other singers in the postwar years who have been admired, rightly or wrongly, mainly for vocal radiance rather than additional attributes include Zinka Milanov, Bidù Sayão, Joan Sutherland, Kiri Te Kanawa (who effectively brings great physical beauty to her well-chosen stage portrayals in *Le Nozze di Figaro, Così fan tutte, Don Giovanni, Der Rosenkavalier,* and *Arabella*), Leontyne Price, Margaret Price, Victoria de los Angeles, Edita Gruberová, June Anderson, Leona Mitchell, Deborah Voigt, Luciano Pavarotti, Alfredo Kraus, Carlo Bergonzi, Jussi Bjoerling, Lauritz Melchior, and Ettore Bastianini.

In between the two poles we find the majority of top singers, those who possess special voices, solid technique, distinctive personality, and capable acting ability. The best of these, including Birgit Nilsson, Marilyn Horne, Mirella Freni, Beverly Sills, Elisabeth Söderström, Martina Arroyo, Eva Marton, Christa Ludwig, Elisabeth Schwarzkopf, Frederica von Stade, Richard Tucker, Nicolai Gedda, Plácido Domingo, José Carreras, Franco Corelli, Ezio Pinza, Sherrill Milnes, Samuel Ramey, and James Morris, have been stars of the first order who are every bit as good as the singers mentioned in the Callas and Tebaldi camps. Others in this group include Kathleen Battle, Dawn Upshaw, Roberta Peters, Lucia Popp, Gabriela Benačková, Cheryl Studer, Carol Vaness, Jessye Norman, Anna Tomowa-Sintow, Aprile Millo, Katia Ricciarelli, Lucia Valentini-Terrani, Grace Bumbry, Agnes Baltsa, Cecilia Bartoli, Siegfried Jerusalem, René Kollo, Bernd Weikl, Thomas Allen, Thomas Hampson, Piero Cappuccilli, Matti Salminen, Aage Haugland, and Nicolai Ghiaurov.

A final group of singers to consider are those that specialize in playing small character roles which are nonetheless essential to an opera's success. These are people who seldom get the acclaim they deserve, but they are an important part of the operatic landscape. They play mothers and fathers, trusted servants and advisers, or the comic foils who provide the material for the stars to win laughter. These secondary roles, all of which fall under the general term *comprimario,* have been capably assumed by many special artists. While many singers devote their entire careers to playing such roles, often they are taken by either young singers on their way up or seasoned professionals who use their experience to memorably delineate older characters—and lengthen their careers in the process.

We have been talking about vocal categories in general terms, but we should devote a little time to defining what we mean when we use certain terminology. I should caution you that within these categories there are many subcategories and some degree of overlap.

When we talk about a singer's *Fach,* we are referring to that group of roles most congenial to a singer's voice and temperament. We can group singers by *Fach* and say, for example, that Birgit Nilsson, Hildegard Behrens, and Eva Marton all share the "heavy" German *Fach* that includes Leonore in *Fidelio,* the major dramatic roles in Wagner, and Strauss's Elektra and Salome. But within this *Fach,* each of these sopranos brings her own characteristics that make her better or less suited to particular roles. It is probably fair to say that Behrens is the best Leonore, Nilsson the strongest Salome, and Marton the most suitable Elsa in Wagner's *Lohengrin.* But beyond these, one could make provocative arguments, depending upon your personal preferences, for any one of these singers in the other roles in their *Fach.* This is why opera fans can debate endlessly about who is the greatest singer in any role.

And this is why, when people ask who my favorite singer is, I can fairly answer that there are so many vocalists with different *Fachs* that it is impossible to name just one singer. For example, in naming sopranos I like, I could quickly reel off the names Sutherland, Te Kanawa, Freni, Caballé, Rysanek, Stratas, Nilsson, Behrens, Lear, Söderström, and de los Angeles and still feel that I have left out many more. Yet isn't it better that so many different singers can give me aural pleasure? The names above cover several *Fachs* and vocal types, yet they are all sopranos.

The soprano is the highest female voice and the one for which the most roles exist in opera. Within the category of soprano, however, we have at least five subgroups.

The *soprano leggiero* or *soubrette* is the lightest voice. These roles are often maids and servants, pert, bright young women who are always one step ahead of the men who pursue them. There are relatively few tragic soubrette parts, even in operas that are ultimately tragic. Mozart has at least one soubrette in most of his operas, including Blonde in *Die Entführung aus dem Serail,* Susanna in *Le Nozze di Figaro,* Zerlina in *Don Giovanni,* and Despina in *Così fan tutte.* Other notable soubrette parts include Adina in Donizetti's *L'Elisir d'Amore* and Norina in *Don Pasquale,* Marzelline in *Fi-*

delio, Adele in *Die Fledermaus,* Oscar the page in *Un Ballo in Maschera,* Nannetta in *Falstaff,* and Sophie in *Der Rosenkavalier.* Leading soubrette singers include Roberta Peters and Kathleen Battle.

The *coloratura soprano* may be the most misunderstood. To the uninformed, this is the operatic canary, who chirps mindlessly, producing lots of high-flying, meaningless sounds. It is often thought that term means "colored" in Italian, thus implying giving color to singing. Actually, the origin seems to be the German *Koloratur.* In medieval German, this referred to ornamentation of an idea using the main line of thought as a point of departure. In applying this metaphor to song, a coloratura singer will start with the melody and then ornament by singing above, below, and around the melody to create various musical and dramatic effects. Coloratura (the Italianization of *Koloratur*) singing is hardly birdsong. The great coloratura soprano—Joan Sutherland being the prototype—can ornament in such a way as to suggest happiness, sadness, despair, infatuation, and many other emotions. In the first opera we study, *Rigoletto,* you will hear a fine example of coloratura singing as Gilda (the soprano) sings dreamily of the man she has just met. Maria Callas and Montserrat Caballé also did coloratura singing. You need only listen to their Gildas, Lucias, or Normas (the last two being the greatest coloratura soprano roles) in comparison with Sutherland's and you will understand how great a variety can exist in fine coloratura singing. Each singer brings her own style of ornamentation to the same roles. In general, Callas was the most impassioned, Caballé the most honeyed, and Sutherland the most virtuosic. All three approaches are valid. Younger exponents of this repertory include June Anderson, Ruth Ann Swenson, Edita Gruberová, and Mariella Devia. Most of the coloratura soprano roles are in the bel canto works of Donizetti, Bellini, and Rossini, although a few can be found elsewhere: in many Handel operas, Mozart's Konstanze *(Die Entführung aus dem Serail)* and Queen of the Night *(Die Zauberflöte),* Verdi's Gilda, Strauss's Zerbinetta *(Ariadne auf Naxos),* and Offenbach's Olympia in *Les Contes d'Hoffmann.*

Some coloratura sopranos also venture into the soubrette repertory and vice versa. You should know, too, that coloratura singing is not the exclusive province of the soprano; there is similar ornamentation in music for mezzo-sopranos, tenors, baritones, and basses.

In his wonderful book *Voices: Singers & Critics* (Amadeus Press, 1992), J. B. Steane describes the *lyric soprano* as "the world's girlfriend." Such roles include Mimì in *La Bohème* and Tatyana in *Eugene Onegin,* Micaëla (the "good girl" in *Carmen*), Marguerite in *Faust,* and Liù in *Turandot.* Another strain of the lyric soprano repertory is in Mozart (Donna Elvira in *Don Giovanni,* Fiordiligi in *Così fan tutte,* and the Countess in *Le Nozze di Figaro*) and Richard Strauss (the Marschallin and Arabella). The prototype in the girlfriend category is Mirella Freni, while Kiri Te Kanawa is best suited for the Mozart-Strauss roles; but these two fine artists could share some of these parts (Te Kanawa has done many of the girlfriend roles). And there are other roles that can be explored as well. For example, Verdi created classic lyric parts such as Violetta in *La Traviata,* which combines lyric and coloratura requirements, Amelia in *Simon Boccanegra,* and Desdemona in *Otello.* Antonia in *Les Contes d'Hoffmann* and Jenůfa are other prime lyric parts.

The lyric soprano is seldom required to consistently hit the high notes of the soubrette and the coloratura. Her range is more in the area of her speaking voice, and her tone should communicate beauty, romance, and pathos. Her roles tend to be about women for whom we develop deep feeling, as opposed to the pert soubrettes or the coloraturas, who often are insane or in some way forbidding. The lyric soprano, by comparison, is usually the woman we fall in love with.

The next category of soprano is the *lyric-dramatic.* If we were to use the analogy of boxing, we have already looked at featherweights, bantamweights, and middleweights. The lyric-dramatic is a light heavyweight and the *dramatic* (or *heroic*) is the heavyweight of sopranos. This has nothing to do with physical size. Gwyneth Jones, the Welsh soprano, is of average weight and stature, yet she sings all the great heroic roles.

The lyric-dramatic soprano, as the name implies, combines the vocal characteristics of two different categories. These include the pure tonal beauty of the lyric and the sheer power of the dramatic soprano. In Italian opera, this singer is often called a *lirico spinto*. *Spinto* comes from the verb *spingere* ("to push"). This pushing should not imply discomfort (although poorly trained spintos do overtax themselves) but, rather, the pushing outwards of the customary boundaries of the lyric-soprano style. Higher and lower notes must be sung, and often with more volume than a regular lyric would employ.

In theatrical terms, lyric soprano roles are often women who engage our sympathies even if we don't fall in love with them. Many lyric-dramatic soprano roles are women who love a man but in some way suffer indignities as a result. It may be that he spurns her, but just as often the problem is that someone else stands in the way of happiness for the lovers.

Many of the most famous lyric-dramatic soprano parts are by Verdi: Elisabetta di Valois in *Don Carlo,* the Leonoras of *Il Trovatore* and *La Forza del Destino,* Aïda, Amelia in *Un Ballo in Maschera,* and Lady Macbeth. There are many spintos in Puccini and in the verismo and late-nineteenth-century Italian repertory, including Tosca, Madama Butterfly, Maddalena in *Andrea Chénier,* and the title characters of Ponchielli's *La Gioconda,* Giordano's *Fedora,* and Catalani's *La Wally.* Sieglinde in Wagner's *Die Walküre* is a prime example of this voice in the German repertory, which has relatively few spintos. Three in the Strauss canon are the Empress *(Die Frau ohne Schatten),* Chrysothemis *(Elektra),* and the title character in *Ariadne auf Naxos.* Callas, Caballé, and, especially, Tebaldi concentrated much of their efforts in the Italian lyric-dramatic repertory. The recordings of Tebaldi and Zinka Milanov are wonderful documents of these roles, not only because the sopranos were so well suited to the music but because the conductors and casts they worked with all understood the repertory so well. The great Verdi soprano of recent times was Leontyne Price, whose ravishing sound made the music glorious and thrilling. There is a new generation of spintos, including Aprile Millo, Susan Dunn, Deborah Voigt, Alessandra Marc, Sharon Sweet, Cheryl Studer, and Carol Vaness. These last two sing roles in the lyric, spinto and coloratura repertories.

The dramatic/heroic sopranos sing some of the most challenging roles of all. It is a gross oversimplification to call these roles loud, but when you see opera parodies of fat women blowing roofs off buildings through the sheer power of their voices, it is usually a dramatic soprano doing the blowing. The volume is necessary to sail over the the sound of the large orchestras of Wagner and Strauss. But volume without beauty of tone would result in a poor performance indeed. The great dramatic sopranos make audiences sit up and listen not only because of volume—although that can be thrilling—but because they make the passions and tribulations of great heroines so compelling. This happens through vocal beauty, expressive use of language, and impassioned acting. And the sheer stamina required to sing these roles inspires awe in us mortals.

Richard Wagner provided many of the major roles in the heroic repertory: Brünnhilde in three *Ring* operas *(Die Walküre, Siegfried,* and *Götterdämmerung),* Isolde in *Tristan und Isolde,* and Kundry in *Parsifal* all use dramatic sopranos, although Kundry can be performed by a mezzo-soprano capable of singing high notes. The title roles of *Salome* and *Elektra* may be as taxing as the Wagnerian roles, even though these Strauss operas are less than two hours long. Dramatic sopranos also sing Beethoven's Leonore, Mozart's Donna Anna in *Don Giovanni* (which can also be sung by a coloratura or a lyric-dramatic) and occasionally the Queen of the Night from *Die Zauberflöte* (which can also be sung by a coloratura). Also, Weber's Rezia in *Oberon* and Agathe in *Der Freischütz,* Verdi's Abigaille in *Nabucco,* Berg's Marie in *Wozzeck,* and, one of the most daunting parts in all of opera, the title character in *Turandot.* Even though she does not sing in the first act of Puccini's three-act opera, the music is so full of loud high notes that by the end of the performance, the soprano who successfully negotiates the score has proved herself truly heroic. Birgit Nilsson and Dame Eva Turner were the leading Turandots of the twentieth century, and now the role rests in the throats of Eva Marton, Ghena Dimitrova, Gwyneth Jones, and Linda Kelm. Callas and Caballé also sang the role, and Joan Sutherland made a remarkable recording of *Turandot,* although she did not include it in her onstage repertory. Another role that requires the fortitude of a dramatic soprano, even though it is essentially a coloratura part, is Bellini's *Norma*. Callas, Sutherland, and Caballé, who combined power with flexibility, were particularly suited to that part.

A name from the past that must be included in the description of heroic sopranos is Kirsten Flagstad (1895–1962). This Norwegian artist is synonomous with the Wagnerian heroines thanks to her luminous, powerful voice and her inspired phrasing. Her most frequent partner was the Danish tenor Lauritz Melchior (1890–1973). Although the old recordings don't do justice to their power, they are still valuable documents of peerless Wagnerian singing.

While the five major vocal categories used for sopranos can also be applied to other voices, there seems to be more specificity for the soprano voice than any other. For example, mezzo-sopranos are usually divided into two groups: lyric and dramatic. *Mezzo* in Italian means "half," but it also means "between," which is the sense in which it is applied to the voice. Steane describes the mezzo-soprano as "the voice of common sense, the happy medium between high and low."

Some audiences undervalue the mezzo-soprano in opera because she is often a supporting player or "the bad guy" in contrast to the more sympathetic soprano character. But mezzos often get the meatier dramatic parts. Carmen is a mezzo, and so are Amneris and Eboli, the nemeses of the heroines in *Aida* and *Don Carlo*. Rosina, the comic heroine in Rossini's *Il Barbiere di Siviglia,* was written for a mezzo, although the part is so juicy that it has also been performed by soubrette sopranos who sing much of the music in a higher transposition.

Lyric mezzo roles may have soubrette characteristics (Rosina, or the dizzily endearing Dorabella in *Così fan tutte*) or may fill the traditional girlfriend characteristics of the lyric-soprano repertory in roles such as Charlotte in Massenet's *Werther* or the title character of Thomas's *Mignon*. There is a separate category within the lyric mezzo range: the coloratura mezzo. The singing style is just like that of a coloratura soprano, though in a lower register. Yet the best coloratura mezzos, such as Marilyn Horne, can easily reach into the heart of the soprano range. When a coloratura mezzo sings with a coloratura soprano, as Adalgisa does with Norma (in *Norma*), the combination can be exquisite. (Adalgisa was composed for soprano, but is often sung by mezzos.)

Most of the great coloratura mezzo music is found in Rossini, whose colors and style are perfectly suited to the mezzo sound. While a few of these characters are women, usually in comedies (Rosina, Cenerentola, and Isabella in *L'Italiana in Algeri*), many of them are heroic young men in dramas and tragedies. This operatic type is known as a "pants" or "trouser" or *travesti* (cross-dressed) role. Why didn't Rossini use men for these roles? Maybe because the hearty richness of the mezzo voice may have sounded more virile to him than the slender tenor sound. Another possibility is that the castrati, who had become a rare commodity by the start of the nine-teenth century, had played these heroic roles and Rossini felt that the mezzo, with the same vocal range, would be the next best thing. Whatever the reason, coloratura mezzo-sopranos sing such meaty parts as Arsace in *Semiramide,* Malcolm in *La Donna del Lago,* and the title role in *Tancredi.*

Mozart also created great trouser parts such as Idamante in *Ido-meneo* (originally written for castrato) and Sesto in *La Clemenza di Tito,* both coloratura parts, and the wonderful, lyric Cherubino, the scene stealer in *Le Nozze di Figaro.* Octavian, the title character in Strauss's *Der Rosenkavalier,* is clearly an homage to Cherubino. In one scene, imitating the model of Cherubino, Octavian cross-dresses as a girl to deceive a man—so we have a woman playing a man playing a woman! In other operas, Hansel is usually a mezzo opposite a soubrette Gretel. Count Orlofsky, who throws the great Act II party in *Die Fledermaus,* is a mezzo. Nicklausse, sung by a mezzo, is the male friend of the title character in *Les Contes d'Hoff-mann,* but returns at the end of the opera as a woman, the Muse of Poetry.

Since castrati are hard to come by nowadays, the roles written for them in the first two centuries of opera are now usually played by mezzos, which means there is rich mezzo coloratura repertory in Handel and Vivaldi. Gluck's Orfeo is perhaps the most famous role inherited from castrati.

The other major mezzo category is the dramatic mezzo. These are usually women with something very deliberate in mind—most often to wrench a man from the clutches of a soprano rival. Carmen, Eboli, and Amneris are cornerstones of this repertory. So is Santuzza in the hormone-drenched *Cavalleria Rusticana*. Conversely, the mezzo Laura has the man in *La Gioconda* and must endure the heroine's wrath. At other times, dramatic mezzos are eager to lure a man sexually but with other purposes in mind (Dalila, Marina in *Boris Godunov*, Giulietta in *Les Contes d'Hoffmann*, and Maddalena in *Rigoletto*). There are mezzos who seem like evil incarnate, except when we learn that they have complicated, tormented souls: Ortrud in *Lohengrin*, Kostelnička in *Jenůfa*, and Klytämnestra in *Elektra* are good examples. Then there are mezzos who bring either caution or comfort to other characters (Azucena in *Il Trovatore*, Cassandre in *Les Troyens*, Venus in *Tannhäuser*, Fricka in *Die Walküre*, Waltraute in *Götterdämmerung*, and Brangäne in *Tristan und Isolde*). Smaller mezzo roles, such as Emilia in *Otello*, the Witch in *Hansel und Gretel*, and the nurse in Strauss's *Die Frau ohne Schatten*, are often as dramatically charged and memorable as the larger roles. It is the rare mezzo, aside from the serving maidens and grandmothers, who is not a colorful lady with something on her mind.

Some mezzos play both lyric and dramatic parts, such as Risë Stevens (a great Carmen, Octavian, Orlofsky, and Dalila), Giulietta Simionato, Tatiana Troyanos (a great Sesto, Venus, and Eboli), Maria Ewing (Dorabella and Carmen), and Marilyn Horne (the Rossini expert, but also admirable as Carmen, Eboli, Amneris, Orfeo, and Handel's Rinaldo). Specialists in the German roles, such as Christa Ludwig, Brigitte Fassbänder, and Waltraud Meier, have also sung many of the Italian and French parts. Frederica von Stade is much loved in lyric roles such as Charlotte, Rosina, Cherubino, Octavian, Hansel, and Cenerentola, while Janet Baker had a great following for her portrayals of classical characters *en travesti* such as Orfeo, Sesto, and Handel's Giulio Cesare. Cecilia Bartoli, Jennifer Larmore, Suzanne Mentzer and Theodora Hanslowe are now assuming many of the lyric and coloratura mezzo roles.

The leading dramatic mezzos of recent years have all been women with great flair who seem to have their pilot lights permanently lit, onstage and off. They include Ebe Stignani, Fedora Barbieri, Fiorenza Cossotto, Shirley Verrett, Grace Bumbry, and

Dolora Zajick. Verrett and Bumbry are leading examples, along with Maria Ewing, of mezzo-sopranos who have attempted to cross over into the spinto and dramatic soprano repertory. The results have been mixed. Verrett is an effective Lady Macbeth, Ewing is a provocative Salome, and all three have been interesting Toscas, yet many observers feel that they have paid a price in tonal quality by reaching beyond their original *Fach*. In fact, these three mezzos tend to choose the most theatrical soprano parts, so maybe they are not being entirely unfaithful to their origins. Conversely, many sopranos, including Regina Resnik and Helga Dernesch, have successfully shifted to the mezzo repertory as their voices darkened with age.

The *contralto* is the lowest female voice, a sort of vocal equivalent of melted dark chocolate. Notable contralto roles in opera are few; they appear more frequently in Handel oratorios. Perhaps the most famous contralto part is Erda, the earth goddess in *Das Rheingold* and *Siegfried*. Erda is earthiness incarnate, and her brief appearances in these two *Ring* operas bring a shiver of delighted recognition to many audience members. The astute Anna Russell described Erda as a green-faced torso who rises from the earth to caution Wotan, the chief god, about what will come—"Weiche, Wotan, weiche!" (Be careful, Wotan, be careful!)—before giving birth to nine daughters (the Valkyries)! Many Erdas are endearingly heavy—who wouldn't be if she were bearing nine children?

The other major dramatic contralto role is Ulrica, the fortuneteller in Verdi's *Un Ballo in Maschera*. This role was the occasion for the belated Metropolitan Opera debut in 1955 of the great Marian Anderson, the first African-American to sing a major role at the Met. Florence Quivar is a current Ulrica of note. Another great part for contralto, though often sung by a mezzo, is the heroic Marfa in Mussorgsky's *Khovanshchina*. A bel canto part often assumed by a contralto is Romeo in Bellini's *I Capuleti e i Montecchi*. There are also the small roles of La Cieca, the blind mother of the title character in *La Gioconda,* and *Andrea Chénier's* Madelon, the brief but moving part of a mother who gives up her last boy to fight in the French Revolution. Certain contraltos also essay *Elektra's* Klytämnestra.

Contraltos appear in comic guises in various Gilbert and Sullivan pieces, but the great comic part is Mistress Quickly in Verdi's *Falstaff*. This is one of the funniest roles in all of opera, and many contraltos (and mezzos with good low notes) have stolen the show from the title character.

Some of the best recorded singing by contralto is that of Kathleen Ferrier (1912–1953), the superb British artist who sang Gluck's Orfeo, created the title role in Britten's *The Rape of Lucretia,* and was outstanding in music by Handel, Bach, and Mahler. Ferrier's recordings are worth hearing to understand how beautifully soulful a plummy contralto sound can be.

Many are the *tenors* who can sing higher notes than contraltos. Actually, the highest adult male voice is the *alto,* or *countertenor,* which lies even higher than the customary tenor. The alto is like the unchanged voice of a boy, but with a fuller sound than the reedy piping that issues from the mouths of most boys. Under rare circumstances a boy's voice does not change significantly as he goes through puberty, so that we find a natural alto sound in an adult male. This kind of voice is usually called a countertenor. Some people do not consider these voices to be a "natural" sound, but rather a well-trained falsetto, a manufactured sound. Although countertenors can appear in any operatic country, the British have put them to the best use. Britten wrote Oberon in *A Midsummer Night's Dream* and Apollo in *Death in Venice* for countertenors, who also sing certain Handel roles, such as Giulio Cesare, that were once sung by castrati and are now usually played by mezzos. The leading countertenor in the twentieth century was Alfred Deller, who was succeeded by singers such as James Bowman and the American Drew Minter.

It is worth knowing that there exist a few rudimentary recordings by one of the very last castrati, Alessandro Moreschi. They indicate, through the scratchy sound, the emphasis given to the emotional aspect of vocal interpretation, and this—along with solid technique—is the artistic goal of the countertenors of our century. Once you get over the strange sound of the countertenor voice, you will appreciate the passion with which the best ones sing.

In the traditional tenor category, the subgroups mirror those found among sopranos. The light-voiced *tenore di grazia* is the male version of the soprano leggiero. There are *coloratura tenors, lyric tenors, spinto tenors,* the *tenore robusto,* who would be the equal of the dramatic soprano in Italian roles, and the *heldentenor* (heroic tenor), who sings the taxing German repertory, particularly Wagner.

The tenor voice, for many fans, is the most thrilling. In most singers, the voice is characterized either by suave, melting beauty or highly charged sound beams with a special "ping" that gives listeners goose flesh. A great tenor is hard to find, so when one comes along he is usually showered with attention and burdened with expectations: will he hit those high Cs as he did on his recording or as the tenor of our dreams did twenty years ago? Tenors are often characterized as nervous types who squeeze, pinch, and contort themselves to deliver the vocal goods. There have always been stories—usually apocryphal—about long sexual abstinence among tenors, based on the dubious theory that amorous exertions would cost them valuable energy and muscle tension when they needed it onstage. In fact, most tenors I've known lead very busy sex lives, probably because it provides relief from the stresses of their work. As with all singing, the keys are the natural gift of a voice combined with discipline and a superb technique.

The tenore di grazia is the suave romantic lead who spins out beautiful sound in roles such as Don Ottavio in *Don Giovanni* (a bore as a character, but endowed with two gorgeous arias) and the tenor leads in *La Traviata, Rigoletto, La Fille du Régiment, Lucia di Lammermoor, I Puritani, L'Elisir d'Amore, Don Pasquale, Martha, La Muette de Portici, Lakmé, Mignon, Manon,* and *Falstaff.* In the early part of this century, Tito Schipa was the chief exponent of this repertory, while in our time Alfredo Kraus has set an enviable standard that will be hard to top. Many are the opera lovers who when asked if their favorite tenor is Domingo, Pavarotti, or Carreras, will promptly answer "Alfredo Kraus." The versatile Pavarotti ably sings tenore di grazia roles, a couple of which are also essayed by Domingo, although both men have tended toward more dramatic roles as they have gotten older and the bloom in their voice has darkened.

In Mozart, aside from Don Ottavio, there are the noble, soulful tenors such as Tamino *(Die Zauberflöte),* Ferrando *(Così fan tutte),* and the slightly weightier title roles of *Idomeneo* and *La Clemenza di Tito.* Some tenori di grazia sing these roles, as do clear-voiced lyric tenors. Two great Mozart tenors from the middle of the twentieth century were Richard Tauber and Fritz Wunderlich, whose recordings attest to their great style and vocal beauty. More recently, the Swede Gösta Winbergh and the British David Rendall and Anthony Rolfe Johnson have assumed these roles.

Coloratura tenor roles are found where you might expect them, in Rossini and Handel. In the postwar era, Americans such as Chris Merritt, Rockwell Blake, Frank Lopardo, and Stanford Olsen have all sung them with varying degrees of success. Coloratura tenor roles require a tenore di grazia tone and flawless breath control. The Rossini roles include Almaviva in *Il Barbiere di Siviglia,* Lindoro in *L'Italiana in Algeri,* Idreno in *Semiramide,* and the title character in *Otello,* which you should not confuse with Verdi's opera.

Just as the lyric soprano is often the girlfriend, the lyric tenor is often the boyfriend. He is Rodolfo in *La Bohème,* the caddish Pinkerton in *Madama Butterfly,* Rodolfo in *Luisa Miller,* the doomed Lensky in *Eugene Onegin,* Maurizio in *Adriana Lecouvreur,* and Hoffmann in *Les Contes d'Hoffmann.* The lyric-spinto roles have a little more thrust and dramatic imperative, and include Verdi parts such as Ernani, Don Carlo, Manrico in *Il Trovatore,* Alvaro in *La Forza del Destino,* and Riccardo in *Un Ballo in Maschera.* There are Puccini's Cavaradossi *(Tosca),* Des Grieux *(Manon Lescaut),* and Dick Johnson *(La Fanciulla del West).* Add to these Enzo in *La Gioconda,* Andrea Chénier, Gounod's Faust, and Don José in *Carmen.*

The list of tenors in our century who have sung the great lyric and lyric-spinto roles begins with the legendary Enrico Caruso (1873–1921), who along with Maria Callas remains the most mythical operatic figure in our century. Caruso's gorgeous sound and virile singing set the standard by which all other tenors are compared. His career coincided with the advent of the phonograph, and his stardom extended far beyond the world of opera. His immediate heirs were Beniamino Gigli and Giovanni Martinelli, who were followed by many others after World War II, including Giuseppe di Stefano,

Carlo Bergonzi, Franco Corelli, and the Americans Jan Peerce and Richard Tucker.

Two Swedes deserve special mention. Jussi Björling's art was characterized by radiant sound and ardent singing, and his performances rank among the finest on record. Nicolai Gedda, who began in 1952 and only recently retired, sang many of the Italian lyric roles well but also essayed many parts in French, German, Russian, and English. He combined a beautiful voice with excellent acting and superb language skills and phrasing.

In recent times, Luciano Pavarotti and Plácido Domingo have set the standard for lyric and spinto tenor singing. Pavarotti, who probably ranks behind only Caruso and Callas in terms of impact on opera in this century, follows in the Björling mode, while Domingo, with his broad repertory and artistic intelligence, is the heir to Gedda's repertory and has also been an outstanding interpreter of the heavier dramatic repertoire. José Carreras brings beauty and ardor to certain lyric roles, though there was a period when he taxed his resources by aiming at dramatic parts that were too challenging for him. Neil Shicoff is an American who sings many of the lyric roles, especially Hoffmann, Rodolfo, and Don José.

Every tenor seems to have "calling card" roles that show him off to best advantage. For Pavarotti, they include Rodolfo, Nemorino in *L'Elisir d'Amore,* and Riccardo in *Un Ballo in Maschera.* For Carreras they are Don José and Andrea Chénier. For Domingo, they are Hoffmann, Cavaradossi, and Verdi's Otello.

Otello is one of the most difficult challenges in the tenor repertory because of the length of the role and the powerful singing it requires. Otello is a tenore robusto, whose meaning should be self-explanatory. The tenore robusto must have great stamina and breath control but must guard against his sound becoming ugly as he gives forth the volume. Other robusto roles include Aeneas in *Les Troyens,* Samson in *Samson et Dalila,* Radames in *Aïda,* and Canio in *Pagliacci* (a calling-card role for Caruso). One of the most challenging roles in this repertory is Calaf in *Turandot,* which has been attempted most successfully, perhaps, by Franco Corelli. This tenor, who was nicknamed *Coscie d'Oro* (Golden Thighs), was an object of adoration for many women and a substantial number of men; his sensuous singing and nervous energy in most roles—but particularly his Calaf opposite Birgit Nilsson—set an erotic standard in the tenor repertory that most singers since then have sought to match. One who has come close is José Carreras, whose sensitivity has made him a man many women want to marry or mother.

Radames, Otello, Samson, Aeneas, and Canio all were part of the unique *Fach* of the Canadian Jon Vickers, as were Peter Grimes and Laca in *Jenůfa*. Yet Vickers was equally acclaimed as a heldentenor in much of that repertory. These German-speaking dramatic heroes range from Florestan in *Fidelio* to Weber's Max in *Der Freischütz* and Huon in *Oberon* to all the major Wagnerian roles—Tannhäuser, Lohengrin, Siegmund, Siegfried, Tristan, Parsifal—and on to Strauss's Aegisth *(Elektra)* and Emperor *(Die Frau ohne Schatten)*.

Lauritz Melchior is probably the most acclaimed heldentenor of the twentieth century. He sang all of the tough Wagner parts with amazing ease but could probably be counted among the "stand and sing" group rather than the Vickers type, which endows its characters with great psychological subtext. In recent times, heldentenors have come and gone, with only a few (Vickers, of course, plus Wolfgang Windgassen, Sándor Kónya, James King, Siegfried Jerusalem, and a few others) making a lasting impact. At this writing, the great hopes in the heldentenor repertoire are Gary Lakes and Ben Heppner.

Baritones, of course, are the male correlate of the mezzosoprano. By this I don't simply mean that they are the middle voice, the one that most closely resembles the speaking voice. Like mezzos, baritones get to play a wider range of roles than are usually given to sopranos and tenors. While the higher voices are usually assigned to lovers and heroes, baritones can be dashing romantic types (Don Giovanni; Eugene Onegin; Escamillo, the toreador in *Carmen*), complicated father figures who love their children dearly but have some tragic problem in that relationship (Rigoletto, Simon Boccanegra, Amonasro in *Aïda,* Germont in *La Traviata*), friends of the tenor hero (Renato in *Un Ballo in Maschera,* Rodrigo in *Don Carlo,* Marcello in *La Bohème,* Wolfram in *Tannhäuser*), clever leading men (Figaro in *Le Nozze di Figaro* and *Il Barbiere di Siviglia*), comic relief (Papageno in *Die Zauberflöte*), "bad guys" (Iago, Scarpia in *Tosca,* Don Carlo in *La Forza del Destino,* Jack Rance in *La Fanciulla del West,* Barnaba in *La Gioconda,* Telramund in *Lohengrin*), tragic heroes (Macbeth, Wozzeck, Porgy, and Hamlet in Ambroise Thomas's opera) or the endearing old man who is the foil for humor (Falstaff). Richard Strauss also created the singular characters of Jokanaan in *Salome* and Orest in *Elektra.* These are but a few of the many roles baritones can assume. As you might expect, the best baritones not only possess a fluid, beautiful sound but are accomplished actors.

There are two basic categories of baritone: lyric and dramatic. These follow closely the parameters described in other voice categories. While some of the best baritones cross over from one category to the other, they tend to specialize more in one group or the other. Many young lyric baritones, as they mature, grow into the dramatic repertory.

A particular subgroup is known as the Verdi baritone. The great Italian composer wrote some of his finest roles for baritone, including Simon Boccanegra, Rodrigo, Amonasro, Don Carlo in *Forza del Destino,* Macbeth, Germont, Nabucco, Miller (father of Luisa), Iago, Riccardo, Falstaff, and (perhaps the most difficult and rewarding of all) Rigoletto. Whether noble or evil, Verdi baritone roles command attention. Verdi understood well how the juxtaposition of the baritone voice with those of tenor and soprano (who are usually in love) could create real drama. Verdi baritones provide the vocal and dramatic counterpoint to the two higher voices. Typically, it is the baritone who brings news or takes actions that affect the fate of the two romantic leads. When the Verdi baritone is the leading character (Nabucco, Macbeth, Rigoletto, Boccanegra, Falstaff), he is a person of great musical and dramatic complexity. We empathize with his tragic circumstances despite his flaws, and in the case of Falstaff, we laugh with him rather than at him. Verdi's genius for endowing his characters with great humanity is particularly evident in the baritone repertory. Antonio Scotti (1866–1936), in almost thirty-five years as the principal Italian baritone at the Metropolitan Opera, helped introduce this style to American ears. More recent Verdi baritones included Ettore Bastianini (1922–67), Gino

Bechi (1913–93), who also sang Rossini's Figaro more than six hundred times, and, most importantly, Tito Gobbi (1913–84), the consummate singing and acting Italian baritone. Gobbi was a frequent recording partner of Maria Callas and probably the only singer who could match her all-around artistic level. After retiring as a singer, he coached young artists and stage directors in his opera workshop, and produced many well-respected opera stagings. He appeared in more than twenty films, many as an actor. He had a much greater range of roles than most other Italians, appearing as Wozzeck and in many other German parts as well as all the great Italian characters. To name his Figaro in *Barbiere,* Rigoletto, Iago, Simon Boccanegra, Scarpia, and Gianni Schicchi is to only mention the names of his most famous parts.

Gobbi's heirs are a mixed lot. Renato Bruson, Piero Cappuccilli, and Matteo Manuguerra, all near the end of their careers, have shown some awareness of the great tradition and have left us with fine memories of solid performances. But the younger group, including Leo Nucci, Paolo Coni, Giorgio Zancanaro, and Roberto Frontale, will not be remembered as a golden age. It is common among opera lovers to complain that the true Italian baritone is a dying breed. It is fortunate that we have recordings to teach us what the great ones sounded like and, it is hoped, to influence a new generation.

There are many fine baritones from other parts of the world. America produced Lawrence Tibbett, Leonard Warren, Robert Merrill, Sherrill Milnes, and Cornell MacNeil. Milnes in particular is thought to possess an ideal voice for Verdi, although his acting tends to be "stand and deliver." Louis Quilico, from Quebec, brought solid performances to most of the repertory for many years, and now his son, Gino, has begun to carve a niche in lyric roles. Germany has given us fine artists such as Dietrich Fischer-Dieskau (one of the finest singers of song ever as well as an important opera singer), Hermann Prey, and Bernd Weikl. There have also been Ingvar Wixell from Sweden and Wales's Geraint Evans, a great Falstaff and Wozzeck.

The new breed of baritone is an internationalist, no less gifted than his brothers of a generation ago, but not anchored in a particular style. The American Thomas Hampson, who excels in Mozart and French roles, shares the world's stages with Russians Sergei Leiferkus, Dmitri Hvorostovsky, and Vladimir Chernov, the Finn Jorma Hynninen, and the versatile Briton Thomas Allen. Then there is the Swede Håkan Hagegård, whom you may have seen as Papageno in Ingmar Bergman's film of *Die Zauberflöte.* Hagegård sings and acts with great style, wit, and beauty and has become a superb recitalist to boot. This group proudly upholds the baritone tradition. If there is an outstanding Rigoletto or Simon Boccanegra among them, it will probably be Chernov.

There is an intermediate male vocal category that does not fully correspond with anything on the women's side: the *bass-baritone.* This category nowadays is blessed with some of the world's best singers, so operas that are congenial for them are being produced with great frequency. Any era that includes the Americans Samuel Ramey and James Morris, the Italian Ruggero Raimondi, and the Belgian José van Dam is rich indeed, and this group definitely qualifies for golden-age status. And Simon Estes has provided valuable performances in Wagner.

The bass-baritone manages to sing lower notes than the pure baritone but can also extend upwards to sing many traditional baritone parts. Much of the standard repertory of bass-baritone roles come from Wagner: the Dutchman in *Der Fliegende Holländer,* Hans Sachs in *Die Meistersinger von Nürnberg,* Amfortas in *Parsifal,* and, above all, Wotan in the *Ring* cycle, one of the most towering roles in all of opera.

Our century has had many fine bass-baritones whose recorded legacy is worth exploring. In the 1930s there were Rudolf Bockelmann and, especially, Friedrich Schorr (1888–1953), the great Wotan of his era. They were followed by Hans Hotter, born in 1909 and, as of 1994, still performing. Hotter is Wotan in *Die Walküre* and *Siegfried* in the historic *Ring* cycle recording led by Georg Solti. Norman Bailey, Walter Berry, Thomas Stewart, Donald McIntyre, and the great George London all held the bass-baritone standard high following Hotter's peak years, and it is on their shoulders that Morris and van Dam now stand.

Ramey is distinctive because of his superb coloratura skills. Just as Gobbi was the artistic challenge who brought the best out of Callas, Ramey has helped lead the Rossini revival by admirably singing opposite Marilyn Horne, Montserrat Caballé, and June Anderson in landmark productions and recordings. Ramey is also a provocative actor in roles such as the four villains in *Les Contes d' Hoffmann* (which also suit Morris and van Dam beautifully). He also plays both Don Giovanni and the Don's servant, Leporello.

Morris, after starting in French and Italian roles, which he still performs admirably, has become the great Wotan of our day. When two recordings of the *Ring* cycle were being made in the late 1980s, Morris appeared in both at the same time, a true testament to his pre-eminence in the role. He also sings the Dutchman and is a memorable Claggart in Britten's *Billy Budd*.

Raimondi has inherited Gobbi's wonderful phrasing, stage presence, and acting skills. He too has made films as an actor, and you certainly should view videos of his Don Giovanni (the soundtrack of which we will study in chapter 8) and his Escamillo in Francesco Rosi's film of *Carmen*. He is also an excellent Figaro, Scarpia, and Boris Godunov.

Van Dam is exemplary in French-language roles such as the *Hoffmann* villains, Escamillo, and Golaud in *Pelléas et Mélisande*. Of course, he has also appeared in works by Wagner and Verdi.

The *bass* is the male equivalent of the contralto, although he gets a lot more work than his female counterpart. The greatest bass role is probably Boris Godunov, but other memorable serious bass parts include Khovansky and Dosifei in *Khovanshchina;* the Commendatore in *Don Giovanni;* Sarastro in *Die Zauberflöte;* Rocco in *Fidelio;* King Philip II and the Grand Inquisitor, who share the most powerful scene in Verdi's *Don Carlo;* Procida in *I Vespri Siciliani;* Silva in *Ernani;* Ramfis and the King of Egypt in *Aïda;* Méphistophélès in *Faust;* the title character in *Mefistofele;* King Marke in *Tristan und Isolde;* Fafner and Fasolt in *Das Rheingold;* Hagen in *Götterdämmerung;* Arkel in *Pelléas et Mélisande;* Colline in *La Bohème,* and Crown in *Porgy and Bess.*

There is also the famous subgroup of comic basses often called the *basso buffo*. Classic basso buffo roles include Osmin in Mozart's *Die Entführung aus dem Serail,* Leporello in *Don Giovanni,*

Mustafà in *L'Italiana in Algeri,* Bartolo and Basilio in *Il Barbiere di Siviglia,* and Baron Ochs in *Der Rosenkavalier.* Puccini created small but vivid roles for basso buffo in *La Bohème* (Alcindoro) and *Tosca* (the Sacristan).

If you ever hear the term *basso profondo,* it implies a rolling bass that is the deepest of the deep voices. It should suggest a bottomless pit. It is important for basses to concentrate on vocal beauty, because sloppy singing makes them sound like foghorns. Many dramatic bass parts, especially Russian ones, are best served by a basso profondo.

The two greatest basses of the first half of this century were the Russian Feodor Chaliapin (1873–1938) and the Italian Ezio Pinza (1892–1957). History records Chaliapin as one of the greatest actors in opera as well as a superb singer; his Boris Godunov is the stuff of legend. Pinza was a handsome heartthrob whose Don Giovanni made women onstage and in the audience swoon. Both men covered a wide range of repertory. Many of the great basses have come from Bulgaria (Boris Christoff and Nicolai Ghiaurov) and Finland (Martti Talvela, probably the finest modern Boris, and Matti Salminen, a magnificent Hagen). Aage Haugland of Denmark and Kurt Moll and Hans Sotin of Germany also sing many important bass roles.

5. OPERA ONSTAGE: FANTASY MEETS REALITY

Now that we have come to know a little about every type of voice, let's look at what happens onstage.

In listening to recordings and radio broadcasts of operas and in reading libretti, you have created mental images of what these works might look like. So it may be a surprise—perhaps even a disappointment—when you finally see an opera onstage. You are likely to be farther away from the stage than you would be in a regular theater. You may not be used to unamplified sound (though it eventually may make amplified sound abhorrent to you). And you may wonder at the operatic style of acting.

Nonetheless, it is important, in your preparation for seeing an opera, to engage in fantasy. The music and the libretto will inspire colors, images, or stage pictures in your imagination that give the opera particular meaning for you. For example, you might envision the great hall in the second act of *Tannhäuser* as a dark vaulted chamber with blazing torches. If, when you go to the performance, you find that the designer has created a square room with beige walls and large windows, you will be forced to compare your image with the one created by the designer. This is not an issue of right and wrong but simply one of vision. What that designer saw and heard in the music and libretto and discovered in any study of art or history resulted in his or her vision of the great hall. Yours is just as valid. You can grow as an opera lover by comparing those visions, attempting to understand the choices and perceptions of the designer and contrasting them with your own. This will give you insights into the opera and foster your creative thinking. Then, when you see your next production of *Tannhäuser,* you can bring to it your original vision, that of the first designer, and any revised thinking you may have had since. All of these may be compared with the production now before you. As you continue to see performances of *Tannhäuser* throughout your operagoing career, your views of how that opera should look and sound will deepen. As you come to know the opera better, new meanings will emerge that you did not recognize when you were younger. This is why opera is a lifelong love affair for so many people.

At first you will probably fantasize about the look of an opera in essentially realistic, tangible terms. Sunlight will only be sunlight, and a crown on a king's head will be a rather conventional-looking crown. You will probably identify with the characters and issues that are closest to your own experience. Dramas with realistic stories, such as *Cavalleria Rusticana,* will seem more accessible than an epic event set in a remote time and place, such as *Les Troyens.*

Even the most realistic dramas in spoken theater require a suspension of disbelief. The lives of onstage characters must be charged with a certain dramatic imperative to keep our interest. While the events that befall theatrical characters often happen in real life, they seldom occur with the same pacing and dramatic buildup that make a drama riveting. The time frame in theater is different. In a three-hour play it is seldom the case that the characters we are looking at have gotten just three hours older by the end. Time moves forward in hours, days, months, years. In some plays, time moves backward, then forward, then back again. In certain surreal plays, time is frozen or has no meaning. All of this is true in opera as well. Apart from one-act works, there are not many operas I can think of that take place in the course of a day and a night: *Fidelio, Pagliacci, Tosca, Turandot,* a few others. Conversely, many opera stories take place over months and years, and some, such as the *Ring* operas, are almost completely lacking in time definition.

And then there is the subject of action onstage. While we can understand on the most literal level what is happening by reading the libretto, seeing it enacted is altogether different. If it is some great calamity, such as the collapse of the temple at the end of *Samson et Dalila,* the magic of stagecraft will make that happen. Cast members will not be hurt by tumbling pillars, which are made of painted Styrofoam. But if you, as an audience member, focus on the potential harm to the singers in that scene rather than what is happening to the characters in the opera, than you have not sufficiently allowed fantasy to take over your perception of the performance. Your goal should be to feel what the characters feel, not to wonder "How did they do that?"

The enactment of a more mundane event—a declaration of love or a fatal stabbing—will feel real only if you give over to fantasy. Realism as we think of it is best left for the evening news (which often seems surreal as well), while fantasy, emotion and transcendence are the province of the opera house. You used your fantasy when you listened to the recording, so why should you abandon it when you go to the theater? Let us assume, for example, that you pictured Riccardo and Amelia, the two lovers in Verdi's *Un Ballo in Maschera,* as handsome and beautiful, young and firm of flesh. Instead, when the curtain rises at a performance, you find a heavy man and woman in their fifties who have trouble getting close enough to embrace. If you find it hard to accept the sight of two obese people declaring and making passionate love, then you are permitting yourself to be bound by convention and the prejudice of a society that says that only young, thin, beautiful people can be heroic and in love. Opera, as I've said, is that giant reflecting mirror of the human experience, and what it reflects is you and all of your fellow audience members, who come in all shapes, sizes, colors, and ages.

And here we arrive at an essential secret that opera lovers know and those on the outside never suspect: the chief undercurrent in most operas is raw sex. Those who pooh-pooh opera think of it as a collection of loud, fat people with too much makeup who overact in front of an audience of overfed, sleepy people. But this is a cliché used by people who don't know what's going on. We who go to the opera often respond viscerally to the actions depicted onstage, many of which are far more erotic than a cheap film, a pulpy novel, or the latest rock video. Perhaps because in opera these sensations are deepened by glorious music, sung in a foreign language, and are not as frankly smutty as some popular entertainment, we do not think of it as something that the self-appointed guardians of morals in our society would target. A night at the opera is often thought of as participation in an elitist event that is sanctioned by the social and moral establishment. But don't forget how the censors were outraged by the first performances of *Rigoletto, La Traviata,* and many other operas. Some of the greatest masterpieces of the operatic literature include such prurient subjects as partner-swapping *(Così fan tutte),* incest *(Die Walküre),* teenage sex *(Salome, Roméo et Juliette),* prostitution *(La Traviata, Manon Lescaut),* adults having sex with adolescents *(Der Rosenkavalier),* rape *(Rigoletto, Tosca, Porgy and Bess),* extramarital sex (too many to mention), male homosexuality (indicated or implied in many of the works of Benjamin Britten), lesbian sex *(Lulu),* nuns having children *(Suor Angelica),* and plain old promiscuity (*Don Giovanni,* whose conquests are catalogued in a famous aria). Mozart's *Le Nozze di Figaro,* which is usually thought of as a comic romp that delights children and adults alike, is not only the story of revolt against the upper classes but that of a count who assumes it is his right, his droit du seigneur, to have sex with any woman in his employ whom he desires.

Are all of these activities bad? Certainly rape is a heinous crime, but as regards all the others, one can take a live-and-let-live attitude as long as no one is being harmed or forced to submit unwillingly. Yet whatever one's views, opera has for centuries been a forum for erotic exploration. You should not assume that only the young and the restless in the audience pick up that message. That octogenarian sitting next to you feels the current just as powerfully as someone younger, and perhaps with more comprehension. A wise and worldly person knows that there are many aspects of love, all of which are addressed in opera at one time or another. In opera, too, unrequited love gets at least as much coverage as consummated love—but isn't that also the case in life?

While the older, fleshy couple onstage may enchant us with the way they sing and what their characters are experiencing, the days of the hand placed over one's breast or the fist pressed to the forehead are gradually disappearing. Still, in a heavy costume, while singing difficult music, most singers will not roll about and cavort like gymnasts. Yet many singers are quite nimble and move about convincingly during a performance. Also, they act with their voices and their hands, making carefully planned gestures that are suggested by something in the text or the music. When a singer must be seen from the last row of the uppermost balcony, some of these gestures must be bigger than you would ever see in a stage play. That is why some singers are thought to be overacting. But remember my earlier caveat: we should not look for opera characters to recreate what we *see* in life. It is more important that they touch what we *feel*. The smart operatic actor uses a mixed repertoire of vocal inflections, thoughtful phrasing of sound, volume, and words, plus gestures large and small, preferably ones that have specific meaning in a specific moment rather than being generic stock poses.

Here again your comfort with fantasy should prevail. One of the reasons it is interesting to present opera to children who have been prepared for the experience is that youngsters are much more comfortable with fantasy than their hidebound elders. Of course, many of the racier aspects of certain operatic stories need not be dwelled upon in explaining an opera to a child. Operas with less complicated stories but more visual color will probably appeal to a child most. It also helps if an opera is relatively short, since even the most rapt young audience member can take only so much at once. *La Traviata* is probably a good opera for children who are ready to learn that not all stories in life end happily. The story is easy:

> Boy meets girl at party; they fall in love. Boy's father objects to this match, asks girl to let boy go. She does. Boy and girl meet at another party. He gets mad at her for leaving (not knowing that his father had arranged the breakup). Girl, who has been coughing, cries and faints. Time passes, girl is very sick, boy learns truth about breakup, and returns to girl. They make up. Girl dies.

You do not need to explain that the girl is a courtesan. But a performance of *La Traviata* has much to enthrall a child: beautiful music, two parties, ball gowns, dancing, pretty scenery, love, straightforward moral issues that can later be discussed. An afternoon at such a performance will be meaningful for some children. In our era, in which information is electronically spoon-fed and young people's social skills are often less fully developed than their computer skills, exposure to moral and emotional situations in a theatrical setting may spark parts of a child's imagination that were previously dormant. If you, as an adult, endeavor to rediscover your childhood sense of fantasy as you approach opera (and other art forms), you will be more richly rewarded by the performances you hear and see.

6. OPERA IN DIFFERENT MEDIA

When the Camerata Fiorentina first shaped opera, it was as a piece of musical theater. In later years, opera also appeared in concert form and as puppet theater. The twentieth century, with its technological innovations, made opera an art form that becomes valid, if different, when it appears in other media.

Opera in concert draws upon your powers of fantasy to envision the stage action. Customarily, lights in the auditorium are kept on so that audience members read the libretto as they hear the music. Opera companies may stage concert performances of lesser-known works—perhaps done to gratify a particular star who takes an interest in a congenial role—because the cost of a full production would be prohibitive. Symphony orchestras often stage operas in concert in an effort to depart from strictly orchestral repertory and to attract a different audience. Certain groups, such as the Opera Orchestra of New York, only present opera in concert. Since many operas in concert are rare works featuring great stars, often they are recorded live and then released commercially. While errors and missed notes will be captured in the recording (unless cosmetic changes are made later in a studio), the added excitement of a live performance often makes these recordings particularly memorable.

Recorded opera has brought the art form to people who otherwise would never know this music. In the early days of recording, each record side could only hold four minutes or so of music. As the technology improved, more sound could be contained on each record; and in the late 1940s long-playing records—LPs—were introduced, which eventually could hold thirty to forty minutes of music per side. While recordings of complete operas were expensive and ungainly at the dawn of the phonograph era, by the mid-1950s it was possible to collect boxed sets of most of the standard-repertory operas. These sets usually included libretto booklets and full-length recorded performances; like stage performances these were sometimes cut slightly—or heavily—in accordance with the custom of the times. (Today, it would be almost heretical to cut music from an opera score for a recording; some recordings even offer music that composers deleted from performance scores.)

Of course, these early complete performances were recorded in monaural sound, which presents a combination of all the sounds present, with no spatial distinction between different parts of the stage and the orchestra pit. Nonetheless these "mono" performances are not necessarily inferior, just different; and there is something very forward, very present about the sound of the leading singers that is quite gripping. The *Tosca* that we will study is a 1953 performance in mono that stands decades later as one of the greatest opera sets ever made.

By 1960, stereophonic sound had come into general use. Stereo gives a sense of space that mono lacks—the aural sense that the performers and the instruments are in different places, much as you would hear them in a theater. With the advent of stereo, some record producers attempted to introduce sounds that are part of the theatrical rather than the musical aspects of an opera: for example, face slaps or gunshots. A major breakthrough in the recording of opera came in the late 1950s through mid-1960s, when Decca Records (called London in the United States) made its historic set of Wagner's *Der Ring des Nibelungen,* with Georg Solti leading the Vienna Philharmonic and perhaps the finest cast that could have been assembled at the time. Producing this first complete *Ring* cycle on records was a daunting challenge, equal to scaling Mount Everest for a mountain climber. John Culshaw, the producer, wrote an important chronicle of the tribulations of this massive endeavor, called *Ring Resounding,* probably the finest document about how opera performances are recorded. One result of the Decca/London *Ring* cycle was that subsequent opera recordings were held to a much higher technical standard.

Many of the best opera recordings are made following a run of live performances in a theater, when the assembled cast, orchestra, and conductor have worked together intensively, know one another's styles and perceptions, and have become accustomed to listening and responding to one another. A few of the best Maria Callas recordings from the 1950s followed a series of performances at La Scala. At the other end of the quality spectrum one finds recordings in which international superstars have recorded their roles individually, to be edited into a final "performance" via fancy equipment. (A duet may showcase a soprano and a tenor who recorded their music months apart.) The best of these recordings can be quite impressive, but I can often sense a lack of cohesion and artistic vision. Sooner or later you will be able to note the difference as well.

The 1980s saw the introduction of digital recording, in which all of the sounds are recorded as bits of information that are then encoded in the small, shiny, beautiful compact disks that are now state-of-the-art. A CD can hold up to 80 minutes of sound, so that a six-LP recording can fit on three or four CDs. (I often wonder what Wagner would have thought of his monumental *Ring* cycle, a product of twenty-five years of labor, being reduced to fifteen small CDs.) Many fans of LPs feel that CDs sound colder and more technological, while LPs have a warmer, more natural tone.

Record companies with archives of great recordings from the past are now issuing these on CD format. Distant voices from the start of the twentieth century, such as Enrico Caruso and the Australian diva Nellie Melba, have been preserved for posterity in CD format. Remasterings of great older performances will often give more listening satisfaction than technologically superior new recordings. For example, Leontyne Price's performance in Verdi's *La Forza del Destino* from the mid-1960s is infinitely more exciting than anything being produced today.

Because recording technology permits retakes and cosmetic touch-ups of notes that are less than perfect as performed, it is unfair to compare studio recordings with live performances. The goal of most recordings is to give the best musical rendering of a particular opera. Live performances in a theater will seldom be perfect: a singer may be enduring a stuffy nose, or may have argued with a spouse or a colleague before going onstage. But a live performance is unique. It will reside in your memory for what made it distinctive, whether gratifying or disappointing.

The lesson here is that it is a big mistake to compare your recording—a document frozen in time that is reinforced in your ears with each hearing—with a singular live performance. If you hear Luciano Pavarotti perform live in a role he recorded twenty years ago, he will sound different. In all likelihood, his tonal quality will have changed, and he might also bring more insight to a character he has lived with for two decades. Some of the best live performances occur when a singer has developed insights into a character and made interesting acting choices, yet is still in good enough vocal condition to give a legitimate musical performance, too. The same idea applies to recordings as well.

In this book, we will use recordings to learn eleven operas. I think I have selected recordings that represent a fair cross section of voices, conductors, and singing styles. These recordings were made between 1953 *(Tosca)* and 1988 *(Eugene Onegin, Die Walküre)*, in mono, stereo, and digital sound, and feature eight conductors leading nine different orchestras. These selections are intended to give you a sense of recorded opera history so you can learn the differences it is possible to hear.

There exists a special category of recordings known as "pirates."

These are drawn from radio broadcasts, illegal tapings made by audience members or sometimes by a person connected with a production. Backstage employees at some theaters keep large archives of tapes that occasionally are sold to release as a pirate recording. Pirate recordings are illegal because the musicians involved do not receive payments or royalties for their performances. While many records stores stock CD versions of pirate recordings, I tend not to purchase them, since the recording quality is iffy and I object to the artists' being deprived of monies they are rightfully due. Yet I know singers who cherish pirates of their live performances, claiming that these otherwise would have vanished into the mists of memory.

I do confess to owning a few pirates, such as a 1979 *Andrea Chénier* from Barcelona starring Montserrat Caballé and José Carreras. Although the recording quality is poor, what with audience members coughing and unwrapping candies, the performance is electrically charged, and these artists are at their considerable best in front of the hometown crowd. Since Caballé was a wonderful Maddalena and Carreras a superb Chénier, and since they never made a recording of the opera together, this pirate is a valuable document that makes the heart of a real opera lover skip a beat or two.

Another type of recording is the official issuance of an old radio broadcast. Many opera companies, including the Metropolitan Opera, own the rights to their large archives of broadcast performances. The finest of these are occasionally released on CD, with the proceeds going to support the opera companies that own them. These are often worthy purchases because they tend to feature top casts at their artistic peaks who may never have made studio recordings together of particular operas.

Radio broadcasts are an excellent means for you to learn opera. They usually include descriptions of story and details about the composer and the librettist. Because you can listen to these broadcasts in your car, at the gym, in bed, or in many other locales, it is a comfortable, easy, and free way to get a grounding in repertory. Even if you don't take it all in the first time you hear an opera, it will, like a first coat of paint on a wall, give you a foundation on which to build. Since most opera broadcasts are advertised in advance in publications and on the air, you can plan to use these performances to study a particular opera seriously. You need only purchase a libretto or borrow one from the library and read along during the broadcast. Check with your local public or classical music station to find out which weekly time slots are allocated for opera broadcasts.

Opera has appeared on television almost since the invention of the medium. In the early days, one or two stationary cameras would capture whatever action passed in front of the lens. As cameras became lighter and more mobile, the action that could be captured for television became more varied. In essence, the telecasting of an opera performance is a report on that particular event, not unlike coverage of a football game or a political convention. Occasionally, outtakes from earlier tapings will be edited into the final version that is telecast.

But opera on TV is a different art form from opera in the theater. The sound will never be as good as live sound, no matter how sophisticated the audio equipment. Even a large-screen television cannot communicate the grandeur of a live opera performance. One of the few advantages of television is that you can see singers close up. This may be interesting for observing how they work, but it may also ruin the enchantment that distance can lend in a theater. The major difference between televised and live opera, though, is that when you are an audience member in an opera house, your eyes go to what draws them and you focus on the details that intrigue you. In televised opera, the television director (usually a different person than the stage director) decides on your behalf what you should be focusing on, thus depriving you of one of the most significant aspects of operagoing. Also, the framing aspect of a television screen may lead you to expect the kind of realism customary in this medium, and so opera singers and television directors are often encouraged to attempt to make even the most unreal operas realistic. They often pay a huge artistic price in the process, subverting the ideas and intentions of composer, librettist, stage designer, and stage director. Since many of the crucial elements of live performances are neutralized by TV, it is important that television broadcasts include subtitles that more or less translate what the singer is saying. My view is that televised opera is a good learning tool for the real thing but cannot be fairly called a replacement for live opera. Of course, for persons who are unable to go to the opera, television provides an important function that should not be underestimated.

The advent of the videocassette recorder has introduced another form of technology to opera. In terms of their ability to bring opera to those who otherwise would not see it, opera videos have the same advantages and disadvantages as television broadcasts. While television broadcasts come and go, on tape they can be used for repeated viewing and more intensive study.

Opera videos fall into three categories: (1) tapes of live telecasts; (2) specially made videos using singers and opera scenery, but not necessarily taped before an audience; and (3) opera movies that have been transferred to video format. Each type of video reflects a different aesthetic.

Telecasts of live performances are acted so that they can be appreciated by both the television audience and the live one in the opera house, so they do not seem the same as performances given for live audiences only, which would probably feature gestures designed to reach the back row of the uppermost balcony. In live telecasts, of course, if a singer makes a mistake or even loses his voice, this will appear in the video version unless it is dubbed later on. Such imperfections add to the drama of the live performance and offer compensations to those viewers who find perfection suspect.

Specially made videos—those not played before a live audience—require that acting and scenic design be scaled down to a dimension more suited to the small screen. In these, it is possible to do retakes if all does not go right the first time. Opera on film, which we will discuss below, requires acting for the big screen, a style that can seem ludicrous when transferred to the small screen.

There are dusty archives in film libraries containing silent versions of operas such as *Carmen*. An opera film without sound may seem absurd, but the piano accompaniment contributed some of the music and the audience filled in the rest from memory. When sound movies came along in the late 1920s, operas were filmed. Some of them, such as Weill's *Threepenny Opera* with Lotte Lenya, seem like films of stage performances rather than cinematic interpretations of the opera at hand. In Europe, especially in Italy, many films starring famous opera singers were made that seem to have an intentionally artificial air about them. The scenery looks like stage scenery rather than movie scenery designed to make the viewer think he is seeing a real place or scene. Instead, the viewer sees actual sets from opera productions. Performers such as Tito Gobbi and Gino Bechi had film careers almost as famous as their stage careers.

Cinema is an art form that mixes fantasy and realism. In a musical film it often seems strange when a character suddenly bursts into song. This contrivance must be expertly done to be plausible. A few filmmakers have managed to combine cinematic language and the basic elements of opera to transcend the problem of artificiality. One example is Joseph Losey's version of Mozart's *Don Giovanni*, starring Kiri Te Kanawa, Ruggero Raimondi, and José van Dam. Although the opera is set in Spain, Losey filmed it in the Palladian villas of northeastern Italy. The visual setting suits the sound and style of the music, and the singers were costumed as they might have been in Mozart's time.

When an opera is made into a movie, there is an important role reversal as to who is in charge. While at a live performance the conductor would certainly run things in terms of keeping all the forces together, in film the musical performances are taped in a recording studio and are then dubbed into the film. So opera singers acting in a film must lip-synch to their own prerecorded voices. They cannot keep their mouths wide open, as they might in a theater, because in a movie that would look strange. They must learn film acting, using more economical gestures and facial expressions than they would need onstage.

The film director takes the place of the stage director and adds the special advantages of film. For example, a special effect such as the vanishing of a character or the collapse of a building can be staged in film in a way that would be impossible onstage. If a director wants to film *La Gioconda* in Venice, using the actual sites depicted in the opera, that would be possible. Herein lies the blend of fantasy and realism. The Venice filmed would be the Venice of today, but the opera takes places in the seventeenth century. To present these sites as they are now would not serve the story; it would be necessary, through lighting, makeup, costuming, and perhaps film editing, to create a sensation that we are looking back almost four hundred years. How do we know what this place looked like back then? Research can be of some help, but the rest comes in the fantasy of the director and the designers of the film.

Most directors who film an opera ignore theatrical conventions such as stage curtains and intermissions. At the opening of Franco Zeffirelli's film of *La Traviata,* we hear the musical prelude that foretells Violetta's doom as we see a young moving man clearing her few possessions from the empty rooms in which she has just died. This does not take place in Verdi's opera. What Zeffirelli has done is to take the subject matter of the prelude and add pictures. Verdi intended that we hear this music without seeing anything so that our mood would be set for what is to follow. Zeffirelli probably felt that a dark screen during the music would be boring in cinematic terms, so he made adjustments based on what he felt a film version of *La Traviata* would require. Whether he is right or wrong is up to you. Since certain film directors go so far as to cut arias and scenes from operas, such a film cannot claim to represent the opera fairly.

While operas in concert, in recording, and in radio broadcasts give a good sense of the music, when these works are presented on video, film, or in puppetry, the operas merely serve as a springboard for translation to another medium that sets its own distinct aesthetic requirements. The use of marionettes or puppets to enact human situations is an old theatrical form, dating back at least to the Middle Ages. Puppets often served as alter egos or truth tellers, who were permitted their candor because they were inanimate. Court jesters (such as Rigoletto) were the satirists of their day, able to make fun of a king and his court by speaking through the puppet.

In Central Europe in the eighteenth century, puppet theaters that performed plays using marionettes added comic opera to their repertories. Initially, these puppet theaters used singers with harpsichord accompaniment; in the nineteenth and twentieth centuries, a piano often replaced the harpsichord. With the advent of recorded music, it became more popular and less expensive to do puppet operas to recordings.

Just as many adults mistakenly discount Disney-style animated films as an art form for children, most grown-ups think puppet theater and puppet opera are suitable only for youngsters. This is a mistake, as a visit to any of the marionette theaters of Salzburg or Munich will prove. The skill and craft of animating puppets is quite impressive, and making these figures take on operatic roles can be high art indeed. As with audio recording, video, and film, opera changes significantly when it goes into puppet form. It is no less valid, and in some cases it can illuminate aspects of a work that would be missed if a viewer focused on the scenery or the exploits of a human singer in a real opera production. For example, if a singer is particularly handsome or heavy or walking with a limp, we might focus on that singer and not on the character he is playing. In puppet theater, the marionettes are pure characters once we have suspended disbelief and forgotten that there are unseen human hands at work. This makes puppet opera an intriguing form for adults and an engaging way to introduce children to opera.

We have now examined the history of opera, the ideas and components that make an opera, and the various ways that the form has been adapted to other media. Now it's time to discuss what going to an opera is all about.

3.

GOING TO THE OPERA

I n the first chapter you gained a solid grounding in the history and development of opera. Next you learned about the individual components that make up an opera. In the chapters following this one you will use this knowledge to study eleven operas that will acquaint you, one by one, with most of the musical and dramatic elements you will ever encounter in an opera house. After learning your first three operas *(Rigoletto, Tosca, Lucia di Lammermoor),* you will be able to attend a performance of many standard repertory Italian language operas and find it to be a meaningful experience. After learning your fourth and fifth operas *(Il Barbiere di Siviglia, Don Giovanni),* your skills will cover an even broader range, and your ability to perceive and enjoy much of the standard repertory will equal that of most casual operagoers, who are interested mainly in the most famous works of the Italian and Mozart repertory. With the remaining six operas *(Les Contes d' Hoffmann, Eugene Onegin, Don Carlo, Tannhäuser, Die Walküre, Elektra),* you will significantly deepen your knowledge and abilities as an opera lover. By the time you have learned *Elektra,* you will be able to encounter any opera written in the last four centuries and have the skills to understand and appreciate it.

There is, however, one other thing you need to know about to complete your operatic education: how to go to the opera. For many novices and a fair number of more experienced people, operagoing provokes a certain degree of anxiety and insecurity. For the uninitiated, a night at the opera is a forbidding prospect. You may have spent a lot of money for your ticket (although this is not necessary), so the stakes seem high. This is unfortunate, because if you judge your night at the opera from the perspective of "Did I get my money's worth?" you are missing the point. The idea of opera is to be challenged, moved, spiritually or intellectually awakened. If you have allowed that to happen, or if you have been delighted by gorgeous music that has been sung and played beautifully, then your money has been well spent. So don't walk out of the theater asking yourself if the performance was worth twenty or fifty or a hundred dollars; wonder instead how you were touched and affected by what you just heard and saw.

Your first night at the opera, especially if you are attending a performance full of subscribers, can be a bit intimidating. Everyone but you, it seems, knows where he is going and what he is doing. This is only because they have been there before. Each time I attend a performance at an opera house I have never set foot in previously, I make a point of observing how people behave, how they are dressed, what they talk about, and how they respond to the performance. As I mentioned earlier, audiences in the *same* theater differ from night to night, so they certainly differ from one opera house to another. For me, observing the rituals in each opera house adds to my knowledge in meaningful ways. I learn about the citizens of this or that town, I discover the depth of their appreciation of things that perhaps I overlook. If I am in a famous place, such as Vienna or La Scala or the Metropolitan, there is a great thrill in wrapping myself in its history and thinking of the voices that have echoed there. When you are in an historic opera house such as La Fenice in Venice, the Maryinsky in St. Petersburg, or the Festspielhaus in Bayreuth, you can't help feeling the presence of Rossini, Verdi, Tchaikovsky, or Wagner, composers who were in these theaters supervising the world premieres of their operas.

PURCHASING TICKETS AND
SUBSCRIPTIONS

The first thing you must do, of course, to attend an opera is to buy a ticket. Since the likelihood is that you will initially purchase a ticket to one performance rather than a subscription to a series, let us talk about single-ticket purchases. In many theaters, sales can be done over the phone or by mail, but it is important that you have a sense of the layout of the auditorium. If you can spend, let's say, $35 for this ticket, you probably have a choice of one or two sections. Many theaters also have partial-view seats in these sections that cost somewhat less. So if you see that tickets in the third tier of a theater cost $35 and $30, it is important to inquire whether those at $30 are full-view seats. If you live in a city with an opera house, it is probably a good idea to acquire a seating plan of the theater from the subscription office to use for reference at home. Typically, when you purchase by mail or telephone there is a service charge. When you ask about seat locations in your price range, you are told you will receive the best seat available. In general this is true, although certain prime seats are held back to sell to patrons, donors, and regular subscribers to the opera. Don't forget that opera companies, especially in the United States, depend heavily upon support from corporations and individuals in the form of donations and subscriptions to keep the opera solvent. When you become a subscriber, you will enjoy the benefit of access to more desirable seats.

Whether you are a subscriber or a single-ticket purchaser, if you have any special needs, you must inform the box office of them. By "special needs" I am referring to any personal circumstances that might affect your night at the opera. For example, most theaters now have full access for ticketholders in wheelchairs. Many theaters even have special locations that are held specifically for wheelchair purchasers. If you have a cast on your leg, tell the box office which leg it is on. In this way, you will be sold a seat from which you can extend the cast into the aisle. If you are particularly tall, you may want a seat with extra leg room (an aisle or certain boxes), or if you're short, you may want an unobstructed view (such as the front row of an upper tier). If you are hearing impaired, ask whether the theater has an infrared hearing set that you can rent. If you are blind and travel with a guide dog, let the management of the theater know this and you will be provided with special assistance. In addition to helping people with special needs enjoy the performance, there is another key reason why the management should know where these people are. In the rare circumstance that the theater needs to be evacuated, the house manager can be certain that people requiring assistance will receive it. Fear of heights can figure in the "special needs" category. If this is you, let the box office know before you buy a ticket. I have seen numerous white-faced ticketholders creep down from upper levels of an opera house after discovering that their inexpensive tickets brought them closer to heaven than they had hoped. It may seem obvious to you, my intelligent reader, but many people do buy cheap seats without imagining that they might be located far upstairs.

The best option for purchasing tickets, especially the first time you attend an opera, is to go to the box office yourself. That way, you can choose from the tickets available, consult the seating chart, and ask any questions that might come to mind. You will know precisely where you will sit. Tell the box office person that this is your first opera and that you want it to be a memorable experience. Mention, too, that you are studying opera and you plan to attend on a regular basis. The box office staff will be motivated to help you because you represent return business. However, there are often very few tickets at the box office for major performances, so if you are aching to see a major star, you should plan ahead, purchase by mail or phone, and specify that you must have a full-view seat. When you become a more experienced operagoer, the full-view seat at your local opera company might not have as much importance. Assume, for example, that a new soprano has come to town to sing Lucia di Lammermoor. You have seen your company's *Lucia* production twice already, and you feel you know it well enough that you can buy a partial-view seat to hear the new soprano. But you should absolutely purchase a full-view seat each time you attend a performance you have never seen before.

You must bear in mind that the public has many misconceptions about ticket availability even at the box office. There are not a lot of seats available for many performances. Nor is there always a pair of "house seats" at the box office five minutes before curtain. Theaters hold house seats until forty-eight hours before a performance for sale to friends and relations of the performers. Since opera companies must sell tickets to keep their doors open, they are not likely to hold any seats back from sale.

There is another factor: people plan far ahead to go to the opera, and the closer to the date of the performance, the fewer tickets there are available. It is unlikely that you will be able to walk up to the window forty-eight hours before a performance by Te Kanawa, Domingo, or Pavarotti and come up with a ticket. Why? Let us assume that a particular opera house has 2,500 seats. If 70 percent of these are sold on subscription, that means that only 750 seats are left for public sale. These tickets are first sold to patrons and subscribers who attend on other nights of the week. Let us assume that 400 more are sold this way. The remaining 350 will go on sale by phone and mail order. Most theaters announce the date of this public sale well in advance. At the Metropolitan Opera, for example, it is usually six weeks before the week in which that performance will take place. So if 300 of these seats are sold to the general public by mail or phone, the remaining 50 are placed in the box office six weeks before the performance. In the 40 days before you might appear 48 hours before curtain, it is very likely that these 50 seats will be sold. The lesson here is to plan ahead. Contact your local opera company (or the one in the city you are traveling to) as far in advance as possible to receive a schedule and to find out about the dates established for advance purchases. (In many European opera houses, "booking" is the term used for what Americans call advance purchases.)

Once you receive your ticket (whether by mail or at a box office window), examine it immediately—even the most capable ticket personnel make errors. With the advent of computerized ticketing, some errors have been eliminated, but others still pop up. Check that the date and price correspond to what you wanted. It happens occasionally, particularly in February and March, that you receive tickets for the wrong month. The reason this happens in those two winter months is that February has twenty-eight days, so (except in leap years) the fifth of February and the fifth of March will fall on the same day of the week.

Also, as you check the date, check the starting time of the performance. Some theaters have both matinee and evening performances on certain days of the week. You don't want a ticket to the 1:30 P.M. *Carmen* if you planned to see the 8:00 P.M. *Aïda*. Another reason to check the starting time is that it varies from theater to theater. *Lohengrin* might start at 6:30 P.M. in Munich, 7:00 in London, 7:30 in San Francisco, and 9:00 in Milan or Barcelona. Even if you go to all of your operas at the same theater, starting times vary according to the length of the opera you are seeing.

Look at the seating chart at or near the box office window. This should give you a good idea of where your location is. In American theaters it is usually the practice to stamp the words "partial view" or "restricted view" on tickets for seats with less than optimal sight-lines. If this is stamped on your ticket, consider it fair warning. If this is a problem, resolve it before leaving the box office.

You will notice that your ticket says that latecomers will not be seated until the appropriate interval and that casting is subject to change without notice. It will also say that no refunds or exchanges are permitted. All of these rules are adhered to, so you should not expect to complain after the fact. Latecoming at the opera is an important topic that I will discuss later on. Regarding casting: singers are human beings, and they do get sick. When you buy a ticket to a performance of *Tosca* starring Caballé and Luciano Pavarotti and one of them (or even both) gets sick and cancels, this does not mean you will get your money back. You bought a ticket to *Tosca,* not to Caballé or Pavarotti. While the greatest stars have few equals, theaters generally will put on a qualified substitute (called a "cover") to handle the role. Sometimes you will even be present at an historic debut: Kiri Te Kanawa and Aprile Millo both made their first appearances at the Metropolitan Opera when they replaced ailing colleagues at the last minute. So, please do not yell at the box-office staff or the house manager about cast changes. Try to absorb your disappointment about not hearing your beloved star and focus on this performance as an opportunity to hear and learn something new.

Refunds and exchanges are exceedingly rare. If you bought a ticket to *Tosca,* for example, and at the last minute the opera company cancels that opera and replaces it with *La Traviata,* you may be justified in asking for a refund. This once happened at La Scala, but for the many people who traveled a great distance to attend a performance there, the *Traviata* gave satisfaction as well. Exchanges usually happen only if it is clear that an error was made by the box office. Many theaters will exchange tickets for subscribers under certain special circumstances: for example, the Metropolitan makes exchanges (not necessarily for another performance of the same opera) if a blizzard hits the New York region and people cannot reach the theater (the show does go on, however). Similarly, the Met will exchange tickets for subscribers whose series falls on a date when there is a major religious holiday. Subscribers know this and make their exchanges weeks and months in advance.

One final warning: as soon as you have examined your ticket, memorize the location, or at least write the information down on a separate piece of paper. If you leave your ticket at home or lose it, or it is stolen, you will be more persuasive if you can tell the house manager as much about your ticket as possible. This is a good habit to get into whenever you purchase a ticket to any performance or event. If you have purchased your ticket by credit card, keep the receipt and write the seat locations on it. I write my seat locations and starting times in my appointment book.

In summation, here is a brief checklist for purchasing tickets:

- Make sure that your locations meet any of the special needs I described.
- Check the price.
- Check the date of the performance.
- Check the starting time.
- Examine the ticket to see if it is marked "restricted view" or "partial view."
- Memorize your seat location or write it down to keep separately.

Where should you sit? Price, of course, is a determining factor, although you do not need to spend $100 to enjoy an opera. Many subscribers at the Metropolitan sit in the Balcony for $25 to $30 a seat. This price (which is significantly cheaper than tickets to Broadway shows) gives them a full view and superb acoustics. Some of them bring binoculars (politely called "opera glasses") to focus on details of the stage production. At the Met there is also the Family Circle, a section behind the Balcony, where tickets are cheaper still. This is rather high up, but the view is full and the sound is great.

If money is less of a problem, you may choose among several parts of a theater. People who like to sit very close to the stage and watch the singers perspire and the conductor work should specify that they want seats as close to the stage as possible. Many other audience members like to sit farther back on the ground floor (in America this area is called the Orchestra; in England it is called the Stalls). This way, they get a fuller stage picture, taking in scenic elements that might be lost on someone sitting very close. By sitting farther back, these audience members are also closer to the exits, the rest rooms, and the bar at intermission. Other audience members like to sit in the first or second tier up from the ground floor. This creates a different, more balanced stage picture, provides a view of the conductor and the orchestra musicians, and in many theaters it offers better acoustics.

The first tier often consists of private boxes. These are usually the most expensive seats in the house. Box seats can be moved about, as opposed to seats elsewhere, which are anchored to the ground. Boxes often contain anterooms, which provide three important benefits. The greatest is that if you come late to the performance, you can enter the box through the anteroom without providing undue disturbance. The second is that this is a place to hang your coat. The third is that if you want to take a brief break from watching the opera—a trip to the telephone or the rest room—you can re-enter during the course of the performance. In other areas of an opera house, once you leave the auditorium you must remain outside until the next scheduled seating, which usually occurs at the start of the next act.

In selecting seats the first time you purchase a ticket to an opera house, rely on your pocketbook and your instinct—or seek the advice of friends who already know the theater. Explore the theater during intermission, and if you find another section more appealing, purchase a ticket in that area for your next performance.

There is also the possibility of purchasing standing-room places. If money is really tight or if the performance is sold out, you might choose to slip on a pair of comfortable shoes and stand for a performance. Each theater has its own policy about standing-room tickets. In some, they go on sale the day all the seats are sold out. In other theaters standing places are sold on a designated day of the week for all performances in the following week. Other theaters sell standing places on the day of the performance only. You need to learn the routine at your local opera house.

Heed my warning (how operatic that sounds!): when you purchase a standing-room ticket, you have purchased the right to *stand* in a designated area. This does not entitle you to make a mad dash for an empty seat. Just because it is vacant does not mean it belongs to you. Its proper owner might arrive late, and there will be embarrassment and annoyance when you have to be removed from a seat. I once attended a performance of *Parsifal* in which I arrived moments before the six o'clock curtain. A standee had occupied my seat in the middle of a section and, knowing the lights were about to go down, pretended not to see the usher who was trying to attract his attention. I had to stand for the two-hour first act while someone illegally occupied my seat. This is not to suggest that you would do such a rude thing, but it is presented as an example of the kind of situation that can arise when people wrongfully occupy seats. Even if you surrender the seat to its rightful occupant, you are disturbing all of the people in the row as you climb over them to do so.

Standees should not slip ushers money in exchange for an empty seat. It is not the usher's seat to sell, and if such a transaction is discovered, it might cost the usher his job. This practice occurs more often in Europe, in the guise of a tip, but it is still unsavory. If you choose to tip an usher, it should be for his courtesy or assistance (for example, if you need help walking to your seat), but not for the purchase of a seat. There is only one circumstance in which a standee should sit. If the back rows of a theater are completely empty and the house manager authorizes that the standees may be seated in these seats, then the standees should occupy them. But this is not a license to run down the aisle and occupy seats that someone might have purchased.

If you arrive at a theater the day of a sold-out performance, you have two options: one legal, the other illegal. Many theaters set up a line near the box office to sell cancellations and returns. If a subscriber is ill or there is particularly bad weather, he or she might choose to donate the subscription tickets to the theater. This is not a refund; it is a monetary donation that can be used as a tax deduction. These locations are then resold to people waiting in line. If you are patient and lucky, you may come up with a seat.

The other means of buying tickets, from scalpers who make a living selling tickets at inflated prices outside a theater, is highly illegal. Here is another admonition: do not buy tickets from scalpers or other people outside an opera house. The tickets they are selling are often ones that were lost by or stolen from subscribers. Opera houses have complete lists of subscriber locations and issue identification cards to subscribers. If a subscriber has lost a ticket, he may contact the opera house and get a pass or replacement ticket for his location. If you innocently purchase the lost or stolen ticket from the kindly-looking old man outside the theater, you are out of luck. Scalpers often stand outside a theater announcing that a performance is sold out, which increases the anxiety for ticket seekers and raises the prices of the tickets being sold illegally.

There is only one circumstance in which you might consider purchasing a ticket outside the theater, and this too is risky. If a seemingly honest person says that his or her spouse or date could not make it for illness or work reasons and therefore one of the two tickets is available, you might consider this option. You will probably be seated next to the person selling you the ticket. Examine the ticket carefully (date, time, price), and never pay more than the price stamped on the ticket. You should then, upon making the purchase, say, "Let's go inside." If the ticket seller hesitates, this might be a scalper, and you should consider stopping the transaction immediately. Use your instinct and judgment. If this person is honest, you have possibly made a friend and someone you can purchase tickets from again in the future.

I don't want to encourage this practice; buying tickets outside a theater is very risky, and you may lose money. You might also wind up in an embarrassing situation if you are ejected from a seat—and maybe from the theater—to make way for the subscriber. The rule is simple: buy tickets from the company presenting the opera, not from someone unrelated to the theater.

Once you have been bitten by the opera bug, you may want to become a subscriber. Most companies announce their schedules in the winter or spring for seasons that begin the following autumn. The decision on which subscription to take is usually based on one of two priorities: schedule and repertory. If you decide, for example, that Tuesday is your opera night, you will select the most appealing series available on Tuesday. If, on the other hand, you are more interested in particular operas, you will probably pick the series that has the most operas and performers that appeal to you, regardless of the night of the week the series is given.

After selecting the series and the part of the theater you want to sit in, you should contact the opera house to get a sense of the availability of tickets. You might be able to place your order by phone, making payment with a credit card, or you might be instructed to make these arrangements by mail.

Subscribing to the opera has many advantages and few disadvantages. You do receive the best seats available. Since you will have the same seats throughout the season, you never have to worry about finding your seat upon arriving at the theater. You will know your neighbors, who might even become friends. This is the beginning of your social interaction at the theater, which is a big part of the operagoing experience. Subscribers receive advance offers to purchase tickets for galas and opening nights and have first crack at tickets to performances that are not on their series. For example, if *Don Giovanni* is not on your schedule but is on another, you as a subscriber will be able to buy tickets to it before they go on sale to the general public. Some opera houses offer exchange privileges to subscribers. A few opera companies offer discounts if you purchase full subscriptions. In general, the cost of a subscription is the face value of one ticket multiplied by the number of performances in the series. Many opera houses will ask for a charitable donation beyond the cost of the series. You are not required to give this, but if you are able to, it will help the opera company and become a tax deduction for you. Even the most fiscally responsible companies, such as the Chicago Lyric Opera and the Metropolitan, cannot pay their bills solely on the income derived from ticket sales.

There are three disadvantages to being a subscriber, but these can generally be overcome. The first is that when you buy a series of eight operas, there might be one or two that do not appeal to you. This more often happens when you have kept a subscription for several years. You like your night, your seats, and your neighbors, so you are not motivated to change your series if there are a couple of operas that do not entice you. You might give or sell those tickets to your opera house neighbors, or to friends, family, business associates, or clients. You might even elect to attend the performance. If it is an opera you have already seen and did not care for, give it another chance. Maybe you saw a bad performance and will be pleasantly surprised the second time around. Or perhaps you were not yet advanced enough in your opera knowledge to appreciate the work the first time you saw it. For example, it took me a long time to recognize the brilliance of *Elektra* and *Parsifal,* but I now love both of these works. If I had given up on them after one try, it would have been my great loss. On the other hand, there are a couple of very popular operas that I simply don't care for. If either of these works turns up on my subscription, I usually give away my tickets to someone who will enjoy it.

The second disadvantage to a subscription is that you are locked into certain dates, and sometimes events or emergencies arise that will prevent you from going. As a serious opera lover, I tend to schedule my other activities around my opera nights. In selecting your series, you should look carefully at the ebb and flow of your life. If your work requires you to rise at six A.M., a weeknight subscription is probably not for you. If, however, you live near your opera house, you can be a lot more flexible.

The third disadvantage in subscribing is that if you do not like your neighbors, you are stuck with them. This should not be a real problem, since most people are civil, but if you sit next to a flirt or a snorer or someone who wears heavy perfume, it may cause you discomfort. If you can politely rectify the situation, that is the best option. Failing that, you might discreetly seek the help of the house manager or the subscription department. Generally, these problems can be resolved with minimal discomfort.

This said, it must be restated that the advantages of subscribing to opera far outweigh the disadvantages.

PREPARING FOR
YOUR NIGHT AT THE OPERA

After purchasing your ticket, you should prepare for the performance. If you buy your ticket at the last minute, you should make these preparations before. The first is to study the opera you will see. The method for this is the same one you are using to learn the operas in this book. Purchase, rent, or borrow a recording of the opera you will hear. (Beginning on page 405, you will find a list of my recommendations for recordings of just about every opera you will ever come in contact with.) Read the synopsis in the booklet. While listening to the music, read the libretto and become acquainted with the characters and the key musical passages in the opera. If you have friends who know this particular opera well, ask them for advice and opinions. As you will discover, everyone in and around opera has an opinion on everything.

Try to have a good night's sleep the night before you go to the opera or even a quick nap that day. Memorize your seat location in case you lose or forget your ticket.

Your attire should be attractive and comfortable. Too many people dress for the opera as if they were going to a ball or a wedding. Since you will be sitting for a long time, you should wear loose-fitting clothes. Tight collars, bustlines, waistlines, or shoes will make you miserable and distract you from enjoying the performance. As a general rule, comfortable business attire is suitable for the opera. There are special circumstances—such as galas, opening nights, or festivals such as Salzburg and Bayreuth—in which formal attire is required. Again, however, these clothes should be comfortable. A woman in a billowing ball gown will not sit happily through five hours of *Die Walküre*. Ladies should not wear large hats or tall hairstyles that will obstruct the view of the person seated behind them. Similarly, men and women who wear too much cologne or perfume can ruin an evening for everyone nearby, especially those with allergies and asthma. This happens more than you realize and is not said in jest.

You should make every effort to have a light meal before the performance. If you do not eat you will become hungry and distracted during the performance. If you are someone who becomes weak with hunger, you might faint, especially if you are wearing tight clothing or a high collar. Some people arrive at an opera house after happy hour, full of liquor and peanuts. It is not possible to appreciate an opera if you are befogged. Other people arrange to have a big meal full of cream sauces and red wine. I love such meals, but they are not appropriate before an opera—you will be overstuffed and the wine will make you drowsy. Many overeaters also develop gastric problems during a performance and must leave the auditorium. They are awfully disappointed when they cannot re-enter the auditorium until intermission. House doctors in opera houses see more patients who have had too much or too little food along with excessive alcohol than people with any other complaint. If you have spent money on a ticket and a lot of time preparing to see the opera, you don't want to miss the performance because you are sick from over- or underconsumption.

ARRIVING AT THE OPERA HOUSE

Most opera houses open their doors to the public thirty minutes before the start of the performance. You should aim to be in the auditorium twenty minutes before the scheduled curtain time. Do not tell yourself that "these things never start on time." They do. Even if an opera starts five minutes late, this does not mean that you should run in at the last minute. If you are driving to the theater, allow enough time for finding a parking space. If you are using public transportation, be sure to allow enough time so that you do not have to race to the performance. If you are dining nearby, be sure to get the check, pay the bill, and use the rest room with plenty of time to spare.

Hang on to your ticket stub throughout the performance. This is your document of entry and proof that your seat is indeed yours.

You might choose to check your coat. If it is wintertime and you have a heavy coat, it will act like a blanket in your lap and lull you to sleep if you are at all tired; on rainy nights, you do not want a wet coat on your lap. It is an unfortunate fact that coats left unattended on seats during intermissions are occasionally stolen. If you do choose to take your coat to your seat, it would be wise to carry it with you when you get up.

After checking your coat, go to your seat even if you have other things you want to do first. This is particularly important if you have purchased a single-sale ticket (as opposed to a subscription) or are using a pass or a replacement ticket: you will have located your seat and you will know that it is yours. It often happens that a person will hold a ticket for, let's say, seat G2, but will not pay attention to which part of the theater. And so he or she wanders from level to level, all of which have a seat labeled G2. Once you know where your seat is, get a copy of the program from an usher. In Europe these are often sold; in America and Canada they are almost always free.

Use the rest room, perhaps have a coffee or a soft drink (if the first act is not too long), and then return to your seat. Read the cast page in the program; reacquaint yourself with the characters and see who's singing what. Look at who is conducting, who did the scenery, lighting, and stage direction. You might also read any notes that give background on the opera. You should then read the synopsis for the first act, even if you prepared at home. There might be differences in this production from the version you learned at home. By now it should be near curtain time. If you need anything from your pockets or your handbag, get them now. Unwrap any candies and lozenges you expect to use. Have tissues in hand for runny noses or emotional tears if you think you will need them. Take spectacles and opera glasses out of their cases. Close your purse definitively and do not touch that zipper until intermission. Put down your program. Start letting thoughts of the day drift out of your head. Focus on the story, the characters, on the music you are about to hear. Ignore conversations going on about you and concentrate on the opera at hand.

Soon the lights will dim, the maestro will enter the orchestra pit, and the performance will begin. If you had arrived two minutes before curtain, raced to your seat before the doors shut, climbed over (and disturbed) a row full of patrons, and were unable to mentally and physically prepare for Act I, you would not be able to enjoy the performance to the fullest.

You will notice, as you watch an opera in most theaters, that you are not being distracted by the arrival of latecomers. This is one of the beauties of operagoing. Theaters respect your right to concentrate on the performance without having to stand up to let people pass to their seats. There are other reasons why latecomers are not admitted. If thirty latecomers (not an unusual figure) arrive during the first act of an opera, the noise they would cause entering the theater would prove a real distraction not just to the audience but to the performers. In addition, light flooding into the auditorium each time the door opens might spoil carefully planned scenic effects onstage.

I mention this because one day, through no fault of your own, you will arrive late for an opera and will feel frustrated and helpless. Many theaters now have television monitors that carry the sound and picture from the stage. This will not be television technology of the type you have on your set at home, because the theater is not full of television cameras, but you will have some idea of what is happening onstage. If you are angry about being kept out of the auditorium, think of all the times you have sat undisturbed in an opera auditorium, free to focus completely on the performance.

The policy of when to seat latecomers varies from opera house to opera house and production to production. A general rule is that a seating may take place only if there is a complete stop in music and action. This really occurs only when there is a major scenic change between two scenes in an act and the composer has not provided music for this change. In some productions of Verdi's *Il Trovatore* or *Don Carlo,* for example, these pauses occur, but in others the scenery either moves quickly or is so abstract that the music never comes to more than a minor halt. In Wagner, Mozart, Strauss, and Puccini these pauses seldom happen. In general, latecomers must wait until the first intermission to be seated.

WATCHING THE OPERA

It may sound to you as if I am being rather pedantic about these instructions I have offered. Most people who go to the opera are civil and well-behaved. Yet by developing certain routines, you will get more out of the experience. By listing various disturbing behaviors of a few audience members, I am encouraging you to become part of the majority of well-mannered operagoers. You will be able to gently encourage other audience members to follow your example.

It is sad but true that television has turned many people into bad audience members at performances of opera, concerts, ballet, theater, and at the movies. Television is about rapidly changing images, short attention spans, frequent breaks, and behaving exactly as you wish, because you are in your own home. If you talk during a TV program, not too many people will care. If you open packages of food, blow your nose loudly, verbalize a sneeze ("ah-choo!"), or give sound and volume to a yawn, so what? I believe that at home anyone should be allowed to do as he or she pleases. But in an opera house, you are part of a group. In fact, one of the great thrills at a memorable evening at the opera is the electricity that courses through an involved audience. I love the group dynamic that permits four thousand people to get goose bumps at the same moment and then to give a roaring ovation during the curtain calls. There is a great sense of community and simultaneous release that is exhilarating.

So what follow are a few behavioral observations about what other people do that you might not care to imitate.

- It is absolutely rude to talk or sing during a performance. If something must be expressed, it can wait until the intermission.
- Coughs and sneezes are often unavoidable, but they can be anticipated and their noise can be muffled.
- Playing with your program or pulling out a flashlight to read is annoying to patrons seated nearby.
- Conducting should be left to the maestro, even if the music is thrilling.

- Beeping watches should be turned off. In a theater of twenty-five hundred seats, even twenty such watches can create two minutes of ruined concentration every hour and half hour. Why two minutes? If my watch is a minute fast and yours is a minute slow, there will be two minutes of beeping.
- Physicians carrying beepers that cannot be silenced should leave their beepers and their seat locations at the chief usher's office. In the event that the doctor is beeped, he or she can be notified.
- Sometimes sleepiness cannot be avoided. However, if a person dozes off and begins to snore, a gentle nudge from a neighbor will gratify anyone seated nearby.
- If you know that you must leave a performance in the middle of an act, notify the people in your row that this will occur and ask if they prefer that you stand in the back of the auditorium. If you are courteous enough to raise this topic, it would be thoughtful of the person on the aisle to offer to change seats so that you can quietly slip out.

And now, what *should* you do at a performance? This is much easier. You have prepared for the opera you are seeing, so you should permit yourself to use your senses to their fullest to appreciate the performance. If you know, from your preparation, that special effects will occur or that certain music announces a grand entrance, you should make a point to look for these. Otherwise, sit back and enjoy. You need not analyze as you watch unless some novel realization strikes you. You need simply perceive and allow your heart to take over. Permit yourself to be moved by the beauty of the music or the pathos of the drama. Revel in the glorious sound of a singer or the skill with which he or she sings. Let the scenic effects and subtle lighting changes fire your imagination.

If the view from your seat permits, also watch the interaction between the conductor and the instrumentalists. Observe how the maestro paces the production, speeding things up here, slowing things down there. At some point he may dampen the volume so a singer's voice can shine through. At other times, the orchestra will blossom forth and capture our imagination. Notice how the singers interact with one another, with the conductor, and occasionally with a person you do not even see: the prompter.

Remember: attending an opera is not about the literal comprehension of every word that is spoken. Rather, it is about allowing several communicative means to reach you in whatever way they do. There are orchestral and choral music. There are the solo vocal lines. There are the words in the libretto. There are scenery, lighting, costumes, and choreography. The sum of these is the experience of seeing an opera. This leads me to discuss a topic that has become highly controversial in recent years: supertitles.

This technology—projected titles above a proscenium arch that offer general translations of what is being sung—was introduced at the Canadian Opera Company in Toronto in the early 1980s. Supertitles soon became very popular at many opera houses in North America. Opera managers believed that these translations would make the text, and therefore the opera, more accessible to audiences. Many companies even project titles in English when the opera is being sung in English. More than anything else, this is a terrible indictment of the diction of the artists onstage.

A few theaters have resisted the trend, including the Metropolitan Opera, the Opera Theatre of Saint Louis, and the Santa Fe Opera. At this writing, the Met is experimenting with a system that would display titles on the backs of seats. In Europe, the Royal Opera at Covent Garden, London, and several theaters on the continent now use titles.

It must be acknowledged that many audience members have responded with great enthusiasm to supertitles. It is also possible that new audiences have come to opera as a result of these titles. In spite of this, I count myself among those who oppose supertitles. As I have emphasized throughout this book, opera is a composite art form in which words are but one of the elements. While it was the text that gave inspiration to the composer, this inspiration came in the original language. Mozart, Verdi, Strauss, and Puccini responded to the poetry and musicality in the language of the libretto. A generalized English reduction of much of the language only serves to cheapen the opera. We do not feel the inspiration and follow the opera in all of its forms. Rather, our eyes continually flick up to the titles and down to the stage action. We lose focus on the details of the action onstage and pay attention instead to the literal aspects of the translation. For many audience members following the titles, their attention to the music wanes as well. All of this completely subverts the operatic aesthetic.

Some singers believe that titles help audience members understand humor when opera is sung in languages they don't know. Other singers and many audience members are disturbed when laughter comes at the wrong time. If a title appears too soon or too late, this throws off the timing of the laugh. Titles that do not faithfully translate the subtlety of a moment sometimes result in unexpected laughter that breaks singers' concentration. Eva Marton once walked out of a performance of *Tosca* in San Francisco when a poorly translated title caused a ripple of laughter at a moment of great drama.

The main problem, I believe, is that in asking audience members to focus on this literal aspect, supertitles distance them from all of the other components of an opera. One might argue that translators of supertitles will eventually become more sensitive to the literary value of a libretto, but this is not enough. By making the story so plain, supertitles only tell us what one character says to another. But we diminish our awareness of the music—it becomes background music, as in a film. The sound of the voice is the prime component of opera. It precedes all of the other elements. If the focus shifts to literal storytelling, then you don't have an opera. You have a printed text with musical accompaniment.

You might say that supertitles are good for those who choose to read them and can be ignored by those who don't. But even those who try to ignore them inevitably look upward and become involved with them. If more operagoers devoted even a small amount of time to preparation before a performance, they would not require the titles. If, as has been suggested, titles attract newcomers to opera, then these people are being attracted to a cheapened, diminished version of the art form. If we continue to encourage literalness at the expense of imagination and fantasy, an essential component of the appreciation of opera will be destroyed. If we can follow the story but we cannot *feel* it, what have we accomplished?

There you have it. You know how I feel on the subject of supertitles. You will undoubtedly encounter them as you become a regular operagoer, and you should approach them with caution. I hope you realize, as you develop the habit of preparing for opera performances, that titles offer you only a small amount of what you need to know about an opera. Study the libretto, or at least the synopsis, in advance so that all of the other aspects of the opera can reach you during the performance. If you allow yourself to get lazy, opera will become less meaningful.

APPLAUSE

One of the questions I am most frequently asked is when it is appropriate to applaud during an operatic performance. This inquiry rises in part from the American penchant to applaud frequently and the desire to give a standing ovation at the end of a show. In truth, standing ovations are now accorded much too commonly and indiscriminately, as if the audience needed to do this to convince itself it got its money's worth.

During the course of an act of an opera, my advice would be: *if in doubt, do not applaud.* The impulse to show appreciation is a nice one, but it often interrupts the flow of the performance. Under no circumstances should you applaud the scenery: it cannot hear you. The scenic designers might be gratified at the sound, but they know that their job is to serve the artistic vision of the production. On the opening night of a production the creative team takes a curtain call, and you can show your appreciation then. On other nights the designers are probably not even in the opera house.

As a general rule (there will always be exceptions) do not applaud during an act of a German opera. (In fact, Wagner gave specific instructions that there be no applause *after* the first act of *Parsifal,* which he pompously referred to as a "stage-consecrating festival play in three acts" rather than as an opera or even a music drama. You are allowed to applaud after the second and third acts.) The reason for this is that most German operas created after Beethoven's *Fidelio,* are through-composed. That is, there is an uninterrupted flow of music that applause would only interrupt, shattering the mood. The one famous exception in German opera is Zerbinetta's

aria in Strauss's *Ariadne auf Naxos.* Almost at the end of this difficult tour-de-force, the aria seems to end in a flourish and audiences
start to cheer. But the aria goes on; this was Strauss's playful send-
up of coloratura arias.

With Italian and French opera the rules are more variable. Certainly after the big solo arias and great bel canto mad scenes the
orchestra comes to a complete halt to allow for applause. The great
divas expected this and still do. In Verdi, you occasionally can hear
a halt in the music that he built in for applause—after Radames's
"Celeste Aïda" at the beginning of *Aïda,* for example. Sometimes,
Verdi placed a very brief pause between the first and second parts of
a big aria. In this pause the character might change mood and the
singer would have a moment to collect herself before finishing the
aria. This occurs in Violetta's "Ah, fors'è lui . . . Sempre libera" in
La Traviata. Enthusiastic audiences often jump on this pause as a
cue to applaud, with the result that we cannot hear the singer who
has already begun to sing the rest of her aria.

There are certain moments in opera that invariably provoke applause during music. These are so well-known that the applause is
no longer an intrusion. One of these is the moment when Musetta
and Marcello reunite in Act II of Puccini's *La Bohème.* As you attend opera more frequently, you will develop the skill to know when
to applaud. I have one other suggestion on this subject. Whether at
the end of the aria or the end of an act, wait until the orchestra has
played the very last note, take a breath, and then applaud. The composer wrote those notes for you to hear. Do not, in your enthusiasm,
applaud through them. Let them sink in before you start pounding
your hands together.

Do not think I am against applause. When the time is right, I am
just as enthusiastic as the next man. I love showing my appreciation.
If an artist has been quite wonderful, I will happily cry "Bravo!"
when he appears for his curtain call.

Let me explain about "bravo." This term of endearment and
gratitude should be reserved only for those who have really moved
you. "Bravo," by the way, is the masculine singular form of this
adjective and should be shouted at a male singer or conductor.
"Brava" is reserved for divas and for female conductors. If you are

cheering more than one person and there is at least one man in the group, you shout "Bravi." If there are only women in the group you are cheering, you cry "Brave" (pronounced "bra-vay").

Two other observations about applause and cheering. I have never understood why when audiences cry "Brava" for a woman, they shout in the upper registers of their voices, while "Bravo" for the men is uttered a full octave lower. Make note of this phenomenon. It is as if the audience must in some way reflect the gender of the person standing before them.

The other observation is that applause in Europe tends to last longer than in America. The Viennese, in particular, love to count how many curtain calls a popular artist is accorded; they will stay for forty minutes to cheer a great performance. In America, by contrast, curtain calls exceed five to eight minutes only in rare circumstances. There are two reasons for this. The first is that union contract agreements for certain opera house employees stipulate that their workday is over when the applause has ended, not when the performance has ended. If the applause lasts a very long time, it costs the company more money. The other reason is that Americans often live farther from their opera houses than do Europeans. When the curtain comes down, many Americans rush to their cars for the drive home. It makes me sad to think that after artists have given a brilliant performance, they see the backs of half the audience as they step forward for their curtain calls.

You will notice that some people enjoy booing. This is a practice I would discourage. Singing is a human endeavor, and there are nights when each one of us is less than perfect physically or emotionally. I know of a very famous singer who was having severe crises in his personal life. His health was precarious, one of his children was suffering from a possibly fatal illness, and he had been a target of criticism in the press. He did everything possible to keep his child's medical problem out of the news, but the stress weighed on him. He sang a performance of a very difficult role very well but cracked on one note. Some audience members, evidently feeling that the one cracked note in a three-hour opera justified abuse, heaped boos and catcalls on this great artist. Even the most beloved artists, such as Leonie Rysanek, have been subjected to merciless booing when they had an off-night. One night in the 1960s, a tearful Rysanek came before the crowd and asked their forgiveness!

Although the two examples I cited occurred in the United States, this pack mentality of booing, jeering, and occasionally rioting is at least as prevalent in Europe. Paris has a famous history of audience unrest, as do Milan and Parma. In Italy, people express their disapproval by whistling. This may sound strange to an American, who hears whistling as a sign of approval. My rule about booing: don't do it. If you did not like what you have heard or seen, do not applaud. If enough people do not applaud, the silence will be deafening and the message will get through.

INTERMISSIONS

After the applause for the first act of the opera you are attending, it is time for intermission. While the scenery is being moved, the singers change costumes and take a break before the next act. The length of an intermission in the United States is usually between fifteen and twenty-five minutes, depending on how much scenery must be moved. In Europe intermissions are sometimes longer as audience members have light meals or stretch their legs.

Intermissions in many opera houses are highly social. Friends meet for drinks, coffee, or pastries and compare impressions about what they have just seen and heard and what they anticipate for the next act. Occasionally, spirited arguments break out as one person declares, "No one ever sang that aria better than Gigli in 1937!" and someone else remarks, "No one else here was alive in 1937!" Opera fans love to debate and evoke their own golden ages, and they can be very entertaining to listen to.

Even if you are alone at intermission, audience members tend to be open, friendly, and willing to talk. This is a great place to meet people: you share at least one interest and probably others. These are people you can have as operagoing friends. If the passion for opera really kicks in, you will find yourself coming up with all sorts of things to ask your friends about. They will insist they have heard it all, whether or not they actually have. This kind of bragging has sometimes intimidated newcomers to opera, but consider it part of the fun.

At a certain point during the intermission you will hear bells or gongs encouraging you to return to your seat. You should pay any bill and take care of any needs before going back into the auditorium. Then, quietly read the synopsis for Act II and begin to focus on the act to come. If there is a second or even a third intermission (as in Puccini's *Manon Lescaut*), you will repeat the process. The general rule, though, is to read the synopsis only for the act you are about to hear. Otherwise, you will unnecessarily retain too much information and think too far ahead in the story.

After the performance, try to keep it in your head for a while before reverting to thought of other things. Talk about it with your friends. When you get home, go back to your recording to rehear passages that impressed you. Compare the singer on the recording with the one you heard in the theater, bearing in mind that you heard a live performance. A recording can be edited and adulterated. You heard the real thing: a human voice, unadulterated by microphones and technology, making direct contact with you while singing music as a great composer wrote it. If you sit in La Scala in Milan and hear a woman sing the title role in *Norma*, you are doing what people have done since that opera had its premiere there in 1831. Wherever you are, nothing can beat a performance of live opera—not a recording, not a video, not a film.

You might want to keep the cast pages and the notes from your program. Years from now you might discover that you heard that world-famous soprano when she was a struggling unknown.

There is also immense joy to be derived from hearing opera in other theaters, whether in your home country or abroad. Part of this comes in observing how different audiences behave. The Germans, for example, are quiet, good listeners. At the intermission, many of them stand quietly, while others may join a large group walking around the lobby. This is an odd sight for a newcomer. The audience members form a circle or an oval and all walk in the same direction around the perimeter of the lobby. You would never see such a thing in Italy. At the end of a great performance, Germans cheer lustily and pound their feet. The English are similarly quiet during performances, wonderfully entertaining during intermission (which they call the interval), and very appreciative at curtain calls. The Spaniards and the Italians dress elegantly, and there is a lot of eye contact and flirtation going on at intermissions. At intermissions in Italy I often feel like a guest in the party scene of *Don Giovanni*. The French run hot and cold but can be very opinionated. When they love an artist (Jessye Norman, for example), that person is practically adopted as a national hero and treated as a treasure. This may seem excessive, but it is quite commendable. The French, to their everlasting credit, have always placed culture at the center of national life. The Viennese are as opinionated as the French, but also as protective of culture. They love to give awards and commendations to singers. If an artist has given a great performance in Vienna, fans will gather at the stage door after and, when the singer exits, will carry him (or her) back to the hotel and then stand under the artist's window serenading him. If, however, an artist gets on the wrong side of the Viennese public, he or she will have to scrape and cower and seek forgiveness before being absolved.

Opera audiences in Europe are dressier than those in America, but formal clothes appear only at galas and certain festivals. There is also a lot of postperformance socializing in restaurants, bars, and cafés as the happy celebration following a great performance (or the vigorous debate following a controversial one) continues until the wee hours. This does not happen much in England, however, since public transport shuts down at midnight and the pubs close slightly before. So, after the opera in Britain, it's a quick nightcap and then home to bed.

Operagoing in Europe is a wonderful way to meet interesting local people and perhaps make new friendships. Some of the great adventures of my life began in the boxes and lobbies of some of the great opera houses in Europe. Appendix C at the end of this book is probably the most complete list you will ever find of the names, addresses, and telephone and fax numbers of every significant opera house in North and South America, Europe, Africa, Asia, Australia, and New Zealand. Consult this whenever you have plans to travel.

It is now time to study your first opera, Giuseppe Verdi's *Rigoletto*. Your great operatic adventure is beginning. With any luck—and a little effort on your part—this will be the start of a lifelong love affair with an art form that always bewitches, occasionally frustrates, but will surely enrich you in innumerable ways.

DISCOGRAPHY
FOR OPERA 101

Here is a list of recommended recordings of the eleven operas you will study in this book. While most operas have more than one worthy recording, I believe these constitute a fair cross section of conductors and singers representing different styles and tastes.

To learn the operas addressed in the forthcoming chapters most effectively, you should use the compact disks I recommend. This is because I make specific comments about the performers you will be listening to and the libretto booklet you will be reading. With certain operas, including *Les Contes d'Hoffmann, Don Carlo,* and *Tannhäuser,* there is a significant difference in the scores or even the languages used in various recorded versions of these works.

Compact disks can be costly, but there are three ways this problem can be addressed:

• Start studying opera with a friend or a group of friends. Learning opera as a group is a wonderful way to develop knowledge and also to discuss various views about a particular work. Also, if you are studying opera with a group, you can choose to purchase the recordings collectively and pass them around, or one of you can purchase the first recording, another of you the second, and so forth.

• If you are using this book for a course in school, it is possible that your teacher or the school has already made arrangements for the music, although it will be necessary for you to acquire a copy of the libretto for each opera so that you can study the text as you listen to the music. Libretti seldom cost more than $5 each.

• More and more stores now sell used copies of compact disks. Be sure, when you purchase a used recording, that the libretto book is included. Also, examine the disks to check for any serious scratches or blemishes.

• If the expense of the recordings is too great, there is always the library. Many public libraries in major cities have these recordings on compact disk.

Listed below each recording is a suggestion for an alternate opera, which I include for two reasons. First, very dedicated readers may wish to deepen their knowledge of each area we explore. Second, almost all of these operas are popular works that are frequently performed. If one of the alternates is being produced at your opera house, you should learn it too (*after* studying the recommended opera) in preparation for seeing a performance.

Recordings are listed by the name of the opera, followed by the name of its composer in parentheses. Then you will see the name of the conductor, followed by principal cast members. Be sure to look at the entire cast carefully before purchasing a recording, since many artists record roles more than once. And check the name of the record company and the catalog number of the recording, which usually is printed at the bottom of the spine of a CD box.

CHAPTER 4. *RIGOLETTO:* LEARNING YOUR FIRST OPERA

Rigoletto (Verdi). Bonynge; Sutherland, Pavarotti, Milnes. London/Decca 414 269-2

Alternate: *La Traviata* (Verdi). Bonynge; Sutherland, Pavarotti, Manuguerra. London/Decca 410 154-2

CHAPTER 5. *TOSCA:* OPERA AS DRAMA

Tosca (Puccini). De Sabata; Callas, di Stefano, Gobbi. EMI 47174
Alternate: *Pagliacci* (Leoncavallo). Ghione; Gigli, Pacetti, Basi-
ola. EMI 7 63309 2

CHAPTER 6. *LUCIA DI LAMMERMOOR:* DRAMA EXPRESSED THROUGH
MUSIC

Lucia di Lammermoor (Donizetti). Bonynge; Sutherland, Pavarotti,
Milnes. London/Decca 410 193-2
Alternate: *I Puritani* (Bellini). Muti; Caballé, Kraus, Manu-
guerra. EMI CMS 7 69663 2

CHAPTER 7. *IL BARBIERE DI SIVIGLIA:* OPERA AND COMEDY

Il Barbiere di Siviglia (Rossini). Chailly; Horne, Nucci, Barbacini,
Ramey, Dara. Sony S3K 37 862
Alternate: *L'Italiana in Algeri* (Rossini). Scimone; Horne, Battle,
Palacio, Ramey. Erato 2292-45404-2

CHAPTER 8. *DON GIOVANNI:* CLASSICAL OPERA

Don Giovanni (Mozart). Maazel; Te Kanawa, Moser, Berganza,
Raimondi, van Dam. Sony M3K 35192
Alternate: *Le Nozze di Figaro* (Mozart). Levine; Te Kanawa, Up-
shaw, von Otter, Furlanetto, Hampson. DG 431 619-2

CHAPTER 9. *LES CONTES D'HOFFMANN:* FRENCH OPERA

Les Contes d'Hoffmann (Offenbach). Cluytens; Gedda, d'Angelo,
Schwarzkopf, de los Angeles, Blanc, London. EMI CMS 7 63222 2
Alternate: *Carmen* (Bizet). Abbado; Berganza, Domingo, Co-
trubas, Milnes. DG 419 636-2

CHAPTER 10. *EUGENE ONEGIN:* ROMANTIC OPERA

Eugene Onegin (Tchaikovsky). Levine; Freni, Allen, Shicoff, Bur-
chaladze. DG 423 959-2
Alternate: *La Bohème* (Puccini). Karajan; Freni, Pavarotti, Har-
wood, Panerai, Ghiaurov. London/Decca 421 049-2

CHAPTER 11. *DON CARLO:* GRAND OPERA

Don Carlo (Verdi). Giulini; Caballé, Domingo, Raimondi, Verrett, Milnes. EMI 7 47701 8
    Alternate: *Aïda* (Verdi). Muti; Caballé, Domingo, Cossotto, Cappuccilli. EMI 47271
    Second alternate: *Boris Godunov* (Mussorgsky). Fedoseyev; Vedernikov, Arkhipova, Piavko, Sokolov. Philips 412 281-2

CHAPTER 12. *TANNHÄUSER:* OPERA AND IDEAS

Tannhäuser (Wagner). Solti; Dernesch, Ludwig, Kollo, Braun. London/Decca 414 581-2
    Alternate: *Fidelio* (Beethoven). Karajan; Dernesch, Vickers, Kélénén, Donath, Ridderbusch. EMI CMS 7 69290 2

CHAPTER 13. *DIE WALKÜRE:* EPIC OPERA

Die Walküre (Wagner). Levine; Behrens, Norman, Ludwig, Morris, Lakes, Moll. DG 423 389-2
    Alternate: *Les Troyens* (Berlioz). C. Davis; Veasey, Lindholm, Vickers. Philips 416 432-2

CHAPTER 14. *ELEKTRA:* PSYCHOLOGICAL OPERA

Elektra (R. Strauss). Solti; Nilsson, Collier, Resnik, Stolze, Krause. London/Decca 417 345-2
    Alternate: *Così fan tutte* (Mozart). Levine; Te Kanawa, Murray, Blochwitz, Hampson. DG 423 897-2

4.

RIGOLETTO

LEARNING YOUR FIRST OPERA

As far as dramatic effectiveness is concerned, it seems to me that the best material I have yet put to music (I'm not speaking of literary or poetic worth) is Rigoletto. *It has the most powerful dramatic situations, it has variety, vitality, pathos; all the dramatic developments result from the frivolous, licentious character of the Duke. Hence Rigoletto's fears, Gilda's passion, etc., which give rise to the many dramatic situations, including the scene of the quartet which, so far as effect is concerned, will always be one of the finest our theaters can boast.*

These words were written by Giuseppe Verdi in 1853, two years after the premiere of his *Rigoletto*. He may sound a little immodest, but I think he was simply acknowledging a fact that many observers had recognized before him. This opera has often been considered as nearly perfect as can be imagined. While other operas, such as *Le Nozze di Figaro*, have also been given this distinction, *Rigoletto* seems to be a textbook example of everything an opera should contain: instantly memorable, highly dramatic music, characters and situations we care about, and action that lunges forward, taking us on an emotional ride that is heightened by the music's power.

With a playing time, including intermissions, of approximately two hours and forty-five minutes, *Rigoletto* is also remarkable for its conciseness. Some people think that one of the highest compliments that can be paid to an opera is that "there is not an extra note in it." This means that every word and every note have meaning in the opera and that the work would be less than perfect without them. An opera does not have to be short to merit this accolade. The same has been said of Wagner's five-and-a-half-hour *Götterdämmerung,* and, with only the slightest hesitation, I would agree. But the fact that Verdi can pack an equal musical and dramatic punch in half that time is in itself quite an achievement.

Verdi wrote the music for *Rigoletto* in forty days. Though other composers, such as Rossini and Donizetti, took as little as two weeks to write the music for fine operas, when you realize what a towering achievement *Rigoletto* is, you will know how remarkable it is that this music could be written in less than six weeks. Other composers, such as Wagner and Beethoven, often spent years completing a work. Verdi himself devoted more time to the composition of most of his operas than he did to *Rigoletto.*

This, then, is a prime example of what artists call inspiration. This phenomenon, which is probably inexplicable in practical terms, occurs in creative people in all fields at one time or another. Inspiration is an artistic imperative in which the need to express and create, when combined with talent, results in a singular work of art. Most great artists experience several periods of inspiration in their lives, but they may also endure periods of creative infertility, which can be a source of great torment for them. When we think of the suffering artist, we usually imagine a person who is creatively fallow. This factor makes the achievements of the greatest artists that much more impressive. Looking at the canon of work of a Michelangelo, a Mozart, or a Dickens, one realizes the degree to which they were blessed with inspiration.

By the time Verdi wrote *Rigoletto,* he was the leading operatic composer in Italy. Bellini and Donizetti were dead; Rossini was long retired and living the life of a bon vivant in Paris. Yet even if these other composers had still been active, Verdi probably would have been the one on top. He had already had notable successes, such as *Nabucco* (1842), *Ernani* (1844), and *Macbeth* (1847), among the sixteen operas he wrote before *Rigoletto.*

After *Ernani,* Verdi entered what he called his *anni di galera,* or galley years—a period of intensive work in which he struggled to forge his personal vision and style of musical drama in order to achieve primacy among Italy's opera composers (Donizetti died in 1848). Part of his effort was devoted to finding expressivity in his orchestrations to give more dramatic punch to his story and his characters. His advances in this area are notable, starting with *Attila* (1846) and continuing with greater sophistication with most of the succeeding operas of the *anni di galera: Macbeth, Il Corsaro* (1848), *La Battaglia di Legnano* and *Luisa Miller* (1849), and *Stiffelio* (1850).

During these years Verdi was attracted to characters who were individuals who stood in contrast to the morals and standards of their societies. As we have discussed earlier, Verdi was a great patriot who was one of the leaders of the movement called the *risorgimento,* the resurgence of the Italian city-states that struggled to throw out foreign powers in the middle of the nineteenth century and form the Republic of Italy. Therefore, Verdi's characters often challenged authority or were tyrannical heroes with tragic flaws (such as the Macbeths) who are ultimately brought down.

It was through his work depicting these various individuals and their passions that Verdi became so adept at character delineation. This skill first showed its fullest range in *Rigoletto,* but it would reappear and often deepen with most of the operas that came later: *Il Trovatore* (1853), *La Traviata* (1853), *I Vespri Siciliani* (1855), *Simon Boccanegra* (1857), *Un Ballo in Maschera* (1859), *La Forza del Destino* (1862), *Don Carlo* (1867), *Aïda* (1871), *Otello* (1887), and *Falstaff* (1893).

So the opera we have chosen as our first, *Rigoletto,* stands at an important nexus in the art of Giuseppe Verdi, arguably the most important opera composer of all. While Wagner exerted a greater influence on other composers and in intellectual circles, Verdi's work has claimed the favor of larger audiences around the world. *Rigoletto, Il Trovatore, La Traviata, Un Ballo in Maschera,* and *Aïda* are staples at every major opera house, and most of Verdi's other works probably appear onstage somewhere in the world almost every night of the year. Mozart and Puccini probably have four operas each that are part of the standard repertory, and the popular works of Donizetti, Wagner and Strauss are produced with relative frequency. Other composers, such as Rossini, Bellini, Mussorgsky, Offenbach, Tchaikovsky, and Bizet, have one or two works that are part of the standard repertory. But for many new operagoers and some experienced ones, opera is first and foremost Giuseppe Verdi.

Rigoletto was the first work after the *anni di galera*. Some observers say that this work is so accomplished because he devoted more time to it than he had given to his previous works. But as we know, although he had time to think about the ideas in the story, he actually produced the music in forty days. What I think is more likely is that the *anni di galera* allowed Verdi to achieve a total mastery of his abilities and that *Rigoletto* is the first product of this struggle. From this opera on, his expressive means seldom failed him.

Because *Rigoletto* is our first opera, we will devote more painstaking coverage and detail to this work than to those that follow. This is simply because this will be your first encounter with many of the basic operatic components, which you will rediscover in the next operas you learn. *Rigoletto* contains almost every element that one can find in an opera: arias, duets, trios, a quartet (perhaps the most famous in all of opera), orchestral and choral passages, dance, a compelling story, and brilliant music. All that is missing is an overture, which is not essential to an opera's success. Verdi chose instead a concise and dramatically effective prelude that is less than two and a half minutes long.

The recording of *Rigoletto* we will use is the London/Decca version led by Richard Bonynge and starring his wife, Joan Sutherland, as Gilda, Luciano Pavarotti as the Duke of Mantua, and Sherrill Milnes as Rigoletto. The recording was made in 1971, when all of the artists were at the peak of their vocal splendor, yet were also experienced enough in their roles to bring great meaning to their characterizations. In the small role of the Countess Ceprano is a very young Kiri Te Kanawa. By this time, Bonynge and Sutherland had worked closely for about seventeen years, so each was attuned to the other's style and instincts. However, as you will hear, this does not compromise the performances by the other artists. Bonynge leads a very tight, dramatic performance that gives the listener a feel for the drama as well as the music.

Let's begin. A compact disk recording of an opera almost always includes a libretto in the box that contains the disks. This is where you should look first when learning an opera, since it often offers a great deal of information that is useful for appreciating the opera.

This booklet is representative of what you should expect to find. Typically, for an opera in Italian, there will be translations in English, French, and German of the cast list and the entire text. When a libretto is in French there will almost always be translations in English and German, and usually in Italian. A German libretto will contain English, French, and, most of the time, Italian translations. Libretti in other languages will usually contain English and German or French.

Open your *Rigoletto* libretto to pages 2 and 3. This is the cast list. By reading a cast list you learn the names of the major characters, their relationships to one another, and the artists performing them. Sometimes the cast list will tell you the vocal category of the singer or role, such as "Joan Sutherland, soprano" or "Martti Talvela, bass." While you may think it is insignificant to read this list, doing so will be your first acquaintance with the characters. This will enable you to start developing mental pictures of them, and if you already know some of the singers' voices, you will more easily recognize their characters when you hear them. By knowing who is singing at any given moment, you can envision the action onstage. The cast page will also tell you which chorus and orchestra were used and who led them. In recordings it is not uncommon to find orchestras and choruses that are not part of a particular opera company. As you know, sometimes an opera recording is the document of a series of performances in a major opera house, in which the conductor, orchestra, chorus (if applicable), and soloists created a production together. Yet, as often as not, an opera recording is a studio performance that contains artists who may have never sung these roles together onstage. The most successful studio performances, such as this *Rigoletto,* are those that give a sense of live theater.

Page 4 gives you basic details about the length of the recording and those who were involved in its creation. This performance was originally created for LP records and was transferred from the master tape to compact disk. One advantage of CDs over vinyl is that you can pinpoint an exact spot on a recording. Thanks to this I am able to indicate for you the exact spot on a CD that I want you to pay attention to. With vinyl records, you may recall, you had to take the arm holding the needle and skip about to find a specific moment. In the process you could easily scratch the record.

Page 5 is very important, and you should look at it closely. Each act is divided into a series of cues and tracks. The cue is a given line from the text; the track is the entire segment that begins with the cue. The first cue on this recording is the prelude, which has no words, so that the page indicated is the place in the libretto where the prelude is played. In every case, the page indicated relates to the original language of the libretto—here, Italian. In this booklet, the Italian text appears on the even-numbered pages; the English translation, in a column to the right of the Italian, appears on the odd-numbered pages. This way, as you hear the Italian, you can look across to find what those words mean in English.

In cue 2, the sung part of the opera begins. "Della mia bella incognita borghese" indicates the first words sung in this cue. The numbers in parentheses (1:44) indicate the length, in minutes and seconds, of this track. The name in parentheses is the character singing these words, in this case "Duca"—the Duke of Mantua. If you have questions about the name of the character, refer back to the cast list.

In some cases, cues begin at a change in the action, such as when a new character speaks. In other cases, such as numbers 3, 7, and 12 in Act I, they mark the beginnings of solo arias or of the preceding recitatives. Track 8, as you can see, is a duet with Rigoletto and Gilda. When you see ellipses (. . .) such as in cue 12 on the first CD and cue 6 on the second, this means that the first words you see are the first words the singer sings, while the words after the ellipses are the name of the aria being sung. Gilda's famous Act I aria is called "Caro nome," so few people would know what you are talking about if you were to say that you heard Joan Sutherland sing a great "Gualtier Maldè."

Now take a look at the right-hand column of this page. CD 2 contains the music for Acts II and III, yet the cues run from 1 to 15. The lesson here is that cues are assigned by CD and not by act.

Pages 6 and 7 contain an essay by William Weaver about *Rigoletto*. Most opera recordings include at least one such essay to give the listener more knowledge about the particular opera, or perhaps about the recording you are about to listen to. For some recordings, the essay will be translated into the other languages in the libretto. That is the case here. For other recordings, there will be a different essay in each language: a German expert on the opera writes an essay for German readers, and so on. By the way, William Weaver is one of the men I most admire—at least from afar, since I have never had the pleasure of getting to know him. He is an American who lives in Tuscany and writes extensively on Italian opera and other topics as well as working as a translator.

Page 8 is a vintage photograph of Amelita Galli-Curci, an Italian soprano who was a leading interpreter of Gilda in the early twentieth century. It is not unusual for libretti on recordings to contain photographs or drawings that evoke singers or costumes or scenery. These are intended to give your imagination more to work with as you listen to the opera.

Pages 9, 10, 12, and 13 contain a detailed synopsis of the opera. You should do with this what you do in the opera house: read Act I, then listen to it. Then read the second act and listen to it. Do not read ahead to find out what happens later. It is more important that you retain as much of the action of the scene you are listening to as you can before going on to the next. You will see that pages 13 through 31 contain French and German translations of the essay and synopsis you read in English, along with other drawings and photographs. With each libretto that accompanies a recording, you should take a couple of moments to look through the pages with the foreign languages, if only to see the pictures you might have otherwise overlooked.

Turn to pages 32 and 33. You will see that the prelude is indicated before the first scene of Act I. You should begin to envision yourself in a theater and imagine what the music you are hearing might look like. In other words, is the curtain down while the prelude is playing? Probably, but not necessarily. You can decide for yourself and then, when you go to the performance, see what the stage director chose to do. His or her choice may be no more valid than yours, but if it is different, you might give thought to why it was made.

Listen to the prelude. The very first notes denote the curse that will be cast upon Rigoletto in the first scene. As you know from Weaver's essay, the opera was previously entitled *La Maledizione* (The Curse), and this word, along with *maledetto* (cursed), is one you will hear at key moments in this and other Italian operas. While we with our modern points of view may consider curses insignificant, they have always played a significant role in literature. A curse advances or colors a plot. In modern terms, think of someone who is cursed as a person who suffers from extreme bad luck or must endure a painful fate. Fate, I expect, is a more palpable concept for the contemporary mind.

After the curse music (which lasts about forty-five seconds), you will suddenly hear music that suggests a galloping, mounting tension. This represents the anxiety of the character of Rigoletto and to me sounds like a racing heart. What do you hear? What follows (at around one minute, fifteen seconds, or 1:15) is a pleading or imploring. The music then settles into a mysterious rumble before suddenly building up volume and tension again to jolt you into a heightened awareness for what is to follow. You need not always approach music in the literal terms I have just used, but composers often write specific passages in operas to denote specific characters, actions, or phenomena (such as the curse). In this very short prelude, Verdi has already taken us on a short emotional roller coaster, and he launches us immediately into the action that follows.

Whenever reading a libretto, be sure also to read the production and staging notes that are interspersed throughout the text. This libretto was written by one of Verdi's favorite librettists, Francesco Maria Piave, who also wrote *Ernani, I Due Foscari, Macbeth, Il Corsaro, Stiffelio, La Traviata, Simon Boccanegra,* and *La Forza del Destino.* As you can see, Piave was relatively specific in his description of settings and has placed various stage directions throughout the text. Verdi also had a hand in these indications.

The action for the first scene of Act I takes place in the ducal palace of Mantua. Since this is a real building, it is possible now for designers to go to Mantua to explore it. In their stage productions, they can reproduce what they have seen or design scenery that evokes it. In Verdi's day it was less likely that a production of *Rigoletto* in Germany, England, or the United States would be so literal, since scenic designers relied as much on their own imaginations as on drawings they might have seen of the ducal palace of Mantua. Nowadays, too, designers may also choose to design a palace that is more generic than specific. Of course, it is essential that whatever scenery is created be useful in theatrical terms. It would be of no use to have a literal presentation of a room in the ducal palace if you cannot see and hear the characters because of any obstruction that scenery might create. For purposes of listening and seeing *Rigoletto* in your mind's eye, you should "view" the action in this recording in whatever room your imagination creates.

The music at the start of track 2 clearly indicates that the festivities are at their height. I'm certain you can envision a party at full tilt in which the Duke of Mantua, as master of the party, boldly walks about the room, admiring women while talking to the courtier Borsa. This is the Renaissance, during which intrigues at court were a key part of life in a duchy. Borsa plays up to the libertine Duke by encouraging conversation about women. Notice how the topic of conversation changes from the unknown woman at church (who happens to be Gilda) to other women, while ladies and gentlemen pass by. The dialogue between the two men—a recitativo to full orchestra—briefly stops as the ladies go by. Clearly the Duke cannot be truly obsessed with the woman at church if his fancy can be captured by the women before him. In fact, he has already cast his eye on the Countess Ceprano.

This leads us, in track 3, to the first of the opera's three great tenor arias: "Questa o quella." This is not merely an aria but a means to move the action forward to the next part of the scene, the dance sequence during which a lot of crucial action takes place. Listen to the aria in purely musical terms and you can hear the way Verdi, in about ninety seconds, creates a deft portrait of the frivolous, self-gratifying Duke. Reading Piave's lyrics will make the psyche and the intentions of the Duke even clearer.

I have mentioned elsewhere in this book that I consider Luciano Pavarotti one of the most able singers in terms of the use of language as a mode of expression. Even if you do not speak Italian, you probably were able to understand every word you read in the libretto as Pavarotti sang. You may want to replay this brief aria to experience his diction again. Every syllable is clear, and he colors certain words with his voice to give them more meaning. In the sixth line, in which he says "Di che il fato ne infiora la vita," notice the bloom in his voice as he says "infiora." While it is translated as "gladdens," the word actually means "adorns with flowers." "Gladdens" is a useful translation in terms of the length of the sentence, but it does not have the floral meaning of "infiora." I'm sure the bloom that Pavarotti imparts to this word was intentional.

Four lines later, notice the slight roll in his *r*'s in "morbo crudele." He does not roll every *r* in this aria to the same extent; he does so here to give emphasis to the words "bitter ill." After the brief minuet, in which he encounters the Countess Ceprano, the same roll of the *r* reappears when he ironically says "Crudele" to the Countess as he tries to coax her to stay.

On page 38, the broken vertical lines in the exchange between the Duke and the Countess indicate that they will repeat the words that they have sung. (For future reference, when you see an unbroken bracket or line next to the lyrics for more than one character, that means that they are singing together, often in the form of a dialogue in which both sing at once.) Listen again to how seductive Verdi's music for the Duke is and how sensuously Pavarotti sings it.

This erotic moment is quickly broken by the penetrating laugh of Rigoletto, the Duke's hunchbacked court jester, who makes his first appearance. The character of Rigoletto is richly complex; we are able at some times to learn his private thoughts and feelings while at others we can observe his public behavior. He also mirrors the feelings of other characters, much as sad-faced clowns do in the circus. So this first burst of laughter is a sort of forced gaiety. To please the Duke, Rigoletto mocks Ceprano, who is humiliated by the Duke's open wooing of the Countess. This little interruption by Rigoletto ends quickly, and he falls silent.

In track 4 the action continues to hurtle forward at a dizzying pace. Although the music is festive and buoyant, more serious things are happening just beneath the mirth. We learn not only of the courtiers' spiteful allegation that Rigoletto has a mistress (who is actually not a mistress but his beloved daughter, Gilda) but also that each courtier despises Rigoletto for one reason or another. As Rigoletto, in attempting to please his master, suggests brutal or severe ways to get Ceprano out of the picture so that the Duke can seduce the Countess, we see the jester's capacity for cruelty and will better comprehend some of the wrongdoing he later engages in. (Let me digress to remind you that I am being unusually analytical here. When you read a libretto and listen to music, simply endeavor to follow what is going on and be open to the feelings that the music and story arouse in you.)

With track 5 the mood changes radically. The levity of the previous music is shattered as the Count of Monterone enters the scene, seeking revenge for the Duke's having seduced his daughter and bringing dishonor on the family of Monterone. Rigoletto, ever eager to remain in favor with the Duke, mocks and further enrages Monterone. Listen (at 1:40) to the violins as Monterone sings "Ah sì, a turbare." Instead of putting a booming orchestra underneath this booming bass voice, Verdi chose the color of the violins to indicate the heightened nervousness of the situation, especially regarding the fate of Rigoletto. As Monterone delivers his curse ("sii maledetto," top of page 54), listen also to the assembled courtiers. Verdi's music slowly builds up the horror of the moment. Imagine the sound of the chorus as a realization dawning inside the head of Rigoletto. (And don't forget, curses are taken seriously in opera.)

Press the pause button on your CD player and go back to page 9 to read the details of the plot of Act I, scene 2. Then read the very specific stage directions that are italicized on page 55.

Track 6 begins with music that creates an eerie, foreboding atmosphere. Listen to how the music suggests the darkness of night. The sinister Sparafucile is here to present his credentials to Rigoletto. In the process he plants an idea in the jester's head that Rigoletto will explore in the great monologue "Pari siamo" (track 7). Listen to the chilling low note as Sparafucile repeats his name for Rigoletto as he exits. Would you forget such a man?

Now to "Pari siamo." This is a wonderful example of what we shall call an internal monologue. In opera, characters muse out loud about their fate or their plans. Even though they are singing in a loud voice, we must assume that no one can hear them except all of us in the audience. Notice how, in under four minutes, Verdi and his librettist take Rigoletto through an endless stream of thoughts. You must imagine that in his anxiety, Rigoletto's restless mind jumps from idea to idea. This is a brilliant monologue because it not only presents the character's thoughts but also, through Verdi's orchestral scoring, gives us an excellent sense of Rigoletto's emotional state.

At the start, we see that Rigoletto is troubled by the irony of his being similar to an assassin. He then worries about Monterone's curse. Then he bemoans his fate at being in the employ of the selfish, libertine Duke of Mantua. Then his thoughts go toward the members of the court, most of whom despise him for being ugly, hunchbacked, and insulting. Rigoletto blames the courtiers for his abusive behavior. Suddenly, at 2:46, the pounding orchestra stops and we hear the single "voice" of the flute penetrating Rigoletto's thought. As we will soon discover, this flute is associated with Gilda. This is a prime example of how opera composers use a particular instrument or melody to bring a character or idea into the head of the person singing and into the mind of the audience. The flute appears as Rigoletto says "But here I become another person!" Just as quickly, his thoughts turn back to Monterone's curse; then he decides that his worries are all foolish. As the music becomes festive, his beloved Gilda rushes in. You might want to play this track again to discover what a brilliant creation this fairly brief monologue is.

In the father-daughter duet in track 8 and part of track 9, we discover (through words and music) how much Rigoletto loves Gilda. Their intertwining voices suggest this and also imply how obsessive Rigoletto is about sheltering his daughter from the dangers he fears surrounds her. Listen to the music well as you read the libretto and you will see how deeply Verdi understood this situation and was able to express it in music. The duet covers a great range of emotions, including the recollection of Gilda's dead mother, which is a defining factor in the behavior of both characters. Rigoletto attempts, in his limited way, to be a caring parent, but the result is that he is overbearing and smothering in his love for his daughter. He cannot fully trust anyone (listen to how he interrogates the maid, Giovanna, about whether she is telling the truth). As you can tell even without reading ahead, Gilda will rebel, and because of the naïveté born of her sheltered life she is destined for tragedy.

After Rigoletto's departure, the next part of the scene is the secret arrival of the Duke to woo Gilda. While to him she is merely another prospective conquest (and a virgin at that), the innocent Gilda is smitten and infatuated with this mysterious, handsome young man who says he is merely a student. Notice how his seductive words and music can be heard in two ways: as sincere wooing in the ears of Gilda, but as insincere sweet talk in our ears. The fact that Gilda is Rigoletto's daughter only makes the prospective conquest more tantalizing to the selfish Duke, who will delight in causing grief to his jester. Listen to the intertwining of the voices of Gilda and the Duke and notice how different this sound is from that of her duet with Rigoletto. You can hear how the Duke insinuates himself into Gilda's heart and thoughts. You have just heard the difference, in purely musical terms, between filial love and romantic love. This is yet another of the succinct masterstrokes that came cascading from Verdi's pen during the composition of this opera.

During track 11 we realize that while this wooing is going on within Rigoletto's house, there is also action in the street below. As you hear the voices of Ceprano and Borsa, begin to imagine the scene. The noise outside finally interrupts the Duke's plan, and he angrily must slip out without completing his conquest. He begins to leave, telling Gilda his name is Gualtier Maldè. But it takes him a long time to exit. In life we would say good-bye just once ("addio"). One thing that many newcomers to opera complain about is that singers repeat themselves. Imagine, though, that young lovers have to say good-bye but do not want to. This part of the scene is the musical equivalent of the two characters' smothering each other with little kisses as a way of not saying good-bye until they absolutely have to. And that powerful last note, sung in unison, is the musical equivalent of the big erotic kiss that seals the good-bye.

Track 12 is the aria "Caro nome." This is a famous showpiece for coloratura soprano, and Sutherland sings it gloriously. Imagine that Gilda has just had her first romantic kiss and her lips are still burning and she is feeling tingling in parts of her body that she never noticed before. This is the departure point for this aria, a long, dreamy monologue in which she fantasizes about this young man who has just (dishonestly) declared his faithful, undying love for her. As you listen to this, think back to your first crush.

In "Caro nome" many singers introduce their own variations on the composer's music in order to put a personal imprint on the character they are creating. You can hear this starting around 2:50, and you should note Sutherland's amazing agility and dexterity. As you can see in the libretto, while Gilda is singing to herself in the house, there is a lot of action on the other side of the wall in the street below. The men are planning to kidnap Gilda, thinking she is Rigoletto's mistress. Because she is so wrapped up in her thoughts, she doesn't hear what is going on.

In track 13 you are hearing four male voices: the blindfolded Rigoletto, Ceprano, Marullo, and Borsa. Onstage, of course, it is easy to pick out who is singing. On disk, though, you need to introduce your imagination to envision the scene. This happens to be a good opportunity to create a dramatic situation in your head based on words and sounds. After all, this is exactly what Verdi did when he composed this scene. For that matter, it is what every composer needs to do; so take this moment to reflect on that.

In track 14 you can hear the mirth of the courtiers as they excitedly set about abducting Gilda and tricking Rigoletto. Listen, starting at 1:21, to the racing sound of the orchestra and imagine it to be the heart and mind of Rigoletto as he discovers what has happened. This emotion is ratcheted up further at 1:48 as the full horror sinks in. This music is amazingly evocative of Rigoletto's panic and realization that he has been deceived. At the last moment of Act I, he cries out against the curse, which he blames for what has happened. Everything we have learned about Rigoletto, Gilda, the Duke, Monterone, Sparafucile, and the courtiers is summed up in this one powerful moment, and as we are sent to intermission, our mind already is fixed on what will happen in Act II. Verdi, like many great composers, believed in creating powerful closing moments to opera acts as a way of placing an exclamation point in the audience's imagination.

Read the synopsis for Act II on page 10 before listening to any more music. Act II is on the second CD, so we will start with track 1 of that disk. Here is the second famous tenor aria, "Ella mi fu rapita." Some people interpret the words in this aria to suggest that the Duke genuinely cares about Gilda; other people think that he is more upset at the fact that someone has kidnapped her before he has had the chance to have her. He muses about her innocence and purity. Do you think that he actually loves her for these qualities, or particularly desires her because she is a virgin? It is up to you to decide if the Duke is a vain libertine or if he actually experiences genuine human feelings for Gilda. This is what I refer to when I talk about singers' giving different interpretations to a character. One tenor might play the Duke as a complete cad; others may make him more ambiguously romantic. Still others may believe that the Duke is genuinely in love with Gilda and will give up his libertine ways. In the beautiful passage at 2:25 ("Parmi veder le lagrime"), is the Duke being sincere in his feelings, or is he deceiving himself into thinking he's in love just because his conquest was incomplete? For another clue, listen to how quickly his mood changes to delight in track 2 when he learns from the courtiers that they have kidnapped the girl they think is Rigoletto's mistress. Yet in track 3 he reverts to the ardor of a man who might actually be in love. We will have to stay tuned to figure out the Duke's real feelings.

At the start of track 4 is another brilliant musical stroke. The weeping sound of the violin and Rigoletto's simple singing of "la-ra, la-ra" in place of words indicate his complete absorption in his grief. He occasionally focuses on what others say to him but then returns to his grief.

After the courtiers discover that the girl they abducted was Rigoletto's daughter rather than his mistress, the jester launches into his condemnation of the members of the court. "Cortigiani, vil razza" is one of the most powerful parts of this opera that is so full of powerful moments. This is one of the great baritone arias in all of opera. Listen to the surging strings at the start of the aria and imagine their sound as Rigoletto's tense, high-strung state. The jester has now revealed the side of his character that is the obsessively loving father. His pleading and begging ("My lords, I beg you, have pity, have mercy . . .") present to the court a very different face than that of the mischievous jester.

Track 6: We now have Gilda's sad confession ("Tutte le feste al tempio"), with its mournful oboe introduction replacing the virginal flute that accompanied Gilda in Act I. Does Gilda's vocal line sound like sobbing to you?

Track 7 has the thunderous chords of Monterone followed by the thrilling duet of Rigoletto and Gilda. While he plots revenge against the Duke, Gilda implores her father to spare the man she still loves. The rousing music usually brings goose bumps to the audience, which often bursts into cheers even before the orchestra has played its last note. This music is the last sound of optimism for Rigoletto before the tragedy that we feel will come in Act III.

Now read the synopsis of Act III on page 12 before listening to more music. As exciting as the first two acts have been, the third act of *Rigoletto* is one of the most perfectly constructed, musically and dramatically, in all of opera. It opens at the house of Sparafucile and his sister, Maddalena, an inn on the banks of the Mincio River outside of Mantua. The subject matter is exactly the same as at the end of the last act, although the music this time is somber. Gilda still is determined to save the life of the Duke, whom she loves and who she is convinced loves her.

The act begins with track 8, where we hear the Duke ask for wine and a room for his intended assignation with Maddelena. Track 9 is the world-famous "La donna è mobile," the opera's third tenor aria. In it the Duke gives even fuller expression to his cavalier attitudes about women. This is all the more striking because Gilda (and many audience members) actually believed his declarations of love for her. Instead, she is already forgotten and he is preparing for his next conquest, the voluptuous Maddalena. Here the brilliance of the scene comes forth. Outside, we have a soprano (Gilda) and a baritone (Rigoletto); inside are a mezzo-soprano (Maddalena), and a tenor (the Duke). Because the vocal types and the personalities are so distinct, we are able to grasp the drama inherent in the conflicting interests of these individuals as each describes his or her feelings. Just as in Act I, scene 2, the characters are separated by a wall. The Duke wants to bed down Maddalena (track 11: "Bella figlia dell'amore"). She, in turn, playfully resists him, even though she is attracted to him. Gilda is horrified to discover she has been betrayed. When Rigoletto's voice enters, joining the other three voices, the result is the famous quartet. In it, each character—Gilda, Maddalena, the Duke, Rigoletto—maintains his or her individual personality and actions while integrating musically with the others. In group singing in many operas, you will find that characters often lose their identities during certain musical passages. This happens when composers create passages that unite the characters in common music, forcing them to abandon the drama. Here, the music and the drama remain distinct because each person is singing something distinct.

Track 12: As the deal is cut, Rigoletto does not refer to the Duke by name, instead calling him "Delitto" ("Crime") and calling himself "Punizion" ("Punishment"). As these words are spoken, the sound of strings and a flute in the orchestra suggest a coming storm. Listen to the clarinet evoke the Duke's seduction music as the sound of the impending storm returns in the orchestra. Then listen to how Verdi paints the sound of a storm by using a humming chorus offstage. This is a pure sound effect: there are no chorus members in view of the audience.

As the storm continues to build in the orchestra and chorus, the Duke goes for a nap. The last sound we hear of him is his familiar refrain of "La donna è mobile" before he drifts off to sleep. A powerful scene follows as Maddalena argues to save the Duke's life. Sparafucile agrees to kill someone else in his place if such a person appears. Track 13: Gilda, still hopelessly in love, decides that she will die in the Duke's place. As you listen to this section, note the sounds of the storm in the orchestra and chorus. The storm abates slightly before raging again, just as there is a lull before the dramatic climax that is about to come. As Gilda pounds on the door to the inn, the storm reaches full throttle. Suddenly the door flies open and, as you can hear, Gilda is stabbed by Sparafucile. Listen, then, as the storm slowly dies down and tranquility returns.

Track 14: Rigoletto returns as the last rumblings of the storm are heard. As Sparafucile hands him the sack containing the corpse of the Duke (or so thinks Rigoletto), the jester rejoices that he has his revenge. Suddenly, the voice of the Duke is heard from the inn. Ironically, he is still singing about the fickle behavior of women. This moment chills Rigoletto, as it does many audience members.

Then comes the horrible discovery that the body in the bag is none other than Rigoletto's own daughter. After Gilda recognizes him, they sing. Again, realists might dispute the ability of this fatally wounded girl to sing so long before expiring. In fact, it is a very brief period of time. Just as we had the prolonged erotic farewell of Gilda and the Duke in Act I, we now have a prolonged father-daughter farewell at the end of the opera. Notice, though, that Gilda expires quietly rather than singing out at full volume. This is more in keeping with a realistic death.

At the end, crushed by the curse and by his own foolishness, Rigoletto gives out an anguished cry that rings in the audience's ears and hearts long after the curtain has come down. Notice that the ending of the opera echoes the last moments of Act I. This reminds us of the inescapable force of the curse.

You are now well on your way to learning your first opera. Inherent in it are many of the elements you will see again and again in many other operas. We have heard solo arias, duets, a trio, a quartet, the use of chorus as dramatic characters (the courtiers) and for special effects (the storm). Various instruments in the orchestra have been employed to give particular dramatic structure or flavor to key moments. The orchestra itself has provided a detailed running commentary on the action onstage. There are powerful dramatic situations, characters we can empathize with, and music that is instantly memorable.

These features are all present in your alternate first opera, *La Traviata*. Verdi wrote *La Traviata* two years after *Rigoletto*. Censors had objected to *Rigoletto* because of the idea of plotting to murder a king (later demoted to a duke). *La Traviata,* with its story of a prostitute with consumption who is loved by a man from a bourgeois family, alarmed censors with its sympathetic portrayal of a courtesan. It had a disastrous debut (because of a poor performance) before becoming an acknowledged classic later on. Unlike *Rigoletto,* with three important leading characters, *La Traviata* is unquestionably a vehicle for the soprano playing Violetta, while the tenor (her lover, Alfredo) and the baritone (his father, who objects to this relationship) are really supporting players. The recording on

London/Decca, conducted by Richard Bonynge and starring two of our *Rigoletto* singers, Joan Sutherland and Luciano Pavarotti, will be an excellent introduction to this opera.

With this and every other recording you listen to, follow the same procedure: Read the cast pages and the introductory essays. Then read the synopsis for Act I prior to listening to it. Then read Act II, listen, and so forth. If you liked *Rigoletto,* you are very likely to enjoy *La Traviata.*

5.

TOSCA

OPERA AS DRAMA

Floria Tosca, the title character of Giacomo Puccini's masterful creation, is one of the great roles in all of opera. While the glorious, stirring music of *Tosca* is shared equally by its three main characters, the title role stands apart as being one of the most challenging, detailed dramatic parts in the operatic repertory. The musical challenges are also forbidding: while there is a great deal of lyricism in the part, a true Tosca must also summon the power and volume required of a dramatic soprano.

In *Rigoletto* we studied an opera that has three major characters who all attract our attention and our sympathies at various moments, but in *Tosca* there is no question who is the object of our fascination. Even when she is not onstage, the men are usually thinking and talking about her. Tosca is also an unusual character because she is an opera singer. The only performance she gives as a diva occurs offstage; when she is onstage (that is, when we audience members see her), we see an opera singer away from work. Confused? Think of her as you would an actress playing the role of an actress in a play. It is singularly fascinating to observe how an opera singer plays the role of a diva.

Tosca the opera is based on an 1887 play, *La Tosca*, by Victorien Sardou, which was a popular vehicle for actress Sarah Bernhardt. The play has five acts and considerably more subplots than one finds in the opera. This is an important point to note. Many famous plays, when adapted for opera, are cut, telescoped, or in some way rearranged to suit the different requirements of opera. Yet it can be argued that some of these plays—including *Le Mariage de Figaro* and *La Tosca*—were actually improved upon in their operatic incarnations. Although Boito and Verdi discarded an entire act of Shakespeare's *Othello* to produce the opera *Otello,* the opera is just as compelling as the play.

Tosca has a running time of about three hours (including intermissions) and makes an excellent first opera if *Rigoletto* is not playing at a theater near you. Because the orchestral music and the story are so riveting, it is possible to enjoy even a mediocre performance. But if you have good singing actors in the roles of Floria Tosca, her lover, Mario Cavaradossi, and their nemesis, Baron Scarpia, then you are in for a treat.

As you will soon realize, Puccini created music that clearly indicates very specific dramatic moments or actions. You will recognize them when you listen to the recording we will study, and you will notice them again when you see a live performance of *Tosca.* With every *Tosca* performance you attend, you will likely pay special attention to how that evening's diva enacts each familiar moment. For example, in Act II, soon after Tosca reluctantly consents to submitting to sexual relations with Scarpia in order to save Mario's life, she suddenly chances upon the knife (next to a basket of fruit) with which she will abruptly kill Scarpia as he approaches her. As the music signals the moment of the discovery of the knife, every singer playing Tosca responds differently. Most, I believe, err by adopting a wide-eyed silent-movie gesture that overplays the moment and would surely attract the attention of the nearby Scarpia. The best version of this moment I have witnessed was by Montserrat Caballé, not a singer known for her acting skills. Caballé's Tosca had resigned herself to the fact that she must have sex with the repulsive Scarpia. As any woman of a certain style might do, Caballé's Tosca removed her earrings before the encounter and, as she slowly placed them on the table, discovered the knife near her hands. Instead of rearing back in shock to indicate the knife, Caballé simply placed her hand on it, ready then to spin around and plunge it into Scarpia's chest.

Tosca is filled with cherished moments such as this, and we go to performances to see how they are enacted. I have surely seen at least thirty different singers in the title role, starting with Maria Callas in 1965, and each woman, in one way or another, made the part her own. Three of these—Grace Bumbry, Shirley Verrett, and Maria Ewing—are mezzo-sopranos who ventured into soprano repertory. Each created a vivid portrayal because of her heightened sense of drama, though they were slightly lacking musically. Yet their stage Toscas are often thrilling: a Bumbry *Tosca* I saw in Vienna in 1976 (with Plácido Domingo and Sherrill Milnes) is one of my most unforgettable nights at the opera. And while Kiri Te Kanawa's creamy, lyrical voice might be considered too sweet for the high-strung Roman diva, it brought particular beauty to the portions of the role that require romance or pathos.

So why did I select a monaural recording, more than forty years old, as the performance of *Tosca* we should study? Because the 1953 *Tosca* starring Maria Callas, with Giuseppe di Stefano as Mario and the unbeatable Tito Gobbi as Scarpia, is one of the greatest opera recordings ever made. One of the contributing factors to this is that the opera had its premiere in 1900 and Puccini lived until 1924. This means that many of the members of the La Scala orchestra and chorus in 1953 may have had direct contact with Puccini or those who knew him. The conductor, Victor de Sabata, and the singers certainly knew coaches and colleagues who worked with Puccini. The result is a performance that has a powerful sense of authenticity that is unmistakable. Hearing a La Scala performance of *Tosca* from that era is not unlike being able to watch the 1927 Yankees with Babe Ruth and Lou Gehrig playing in Yankee Stadium. The links to history and classicism are irreplaceable.

But the main reason I selected this recording is Maria Callas. While Enrico Caruso was the dominant opera star at the start of the twentieth century and Luciano Pavarotti towers over the opera scene as the century draws to a close, Callas was a mythic figure from the early 1950s until her death in 1977, even though she had basically stopped singing twelve years before. She was the consummate diva: she lived for her art and had a difficult personal life. She frequently quarreled with opera managements, had rivalries with Renata Tebaldi and other artists, and had as many detractors as admirers. Hers was not the most beautiful voice: it often failed her, despite her excellent technique and musicianship. Yet she had few rivals in her ability to plumb the musical and textual meanings of a character she played. And she was a superb actress.

Callas's 1953 Tosca found her in good vocal shape and with enough maturity in the role. She had deeply thought about every moment of the opera and could give her performance many layers of meaning and feeling. Since *Tosca* draws heavily on the play that is its source, the words take on much more importance than in most other operas. When you listen to this performance, pay close attention to how Callas and Gobbi use the Italian language to maximum effect. Read the libretto closely as you follow the performance. You do not need to speak Italian to appreciate the artistry that Callas and Gobbi possessed. After two or three hearings, you will be able to repeat many of the Italian passages yourself. Lines such as "Muori dannato," "E avanti a lui tremava tutta Roma," and "Presto! su, Mario!" are embedded in the mind of every opera lover.

Maestro de Sabata leads a wonderfully vibrant, balanced performance that achieves great dramatic effect by bringing forth all of the famous (and many of the less famous) masterstrokes in the score. As you listen to this performance, always try to picture precisely what is happening onstage. The librettists give you the context and Puccini's music offers many more details. If you can envision what the characters are doing at any given moment, you will be able to appreciate this perennially popular opera.

Let's begin. As you did with *Rigoletto* (and as you should do with every opera you study), take the libretto booklet that comes with the recording and read page 1: this way you will become familiar with the names of the characters and the artists playing them. Then read John Steane's brief, excellent essay about Callas and Tosca on page 5 and then the notes on pages 6 and 7. Now read the plot synopsis for Act I *only* on pages 7 and 8. Take a quick look at the photographs of the principal artists on pages 22–25 to put yourself in the mood for a historic performance. You are now ready to learn *Tosca*, starting with the first CD and the text on page 26.

Tosca is an unusual opera for several reasons. I have already mentioned the fact that we have a diva playing a diva. In addition, as I noted, this opera draws very heavily on the play it is based on. The words in *Tosca* are of the utmost importance not only for the performers but for the composer. Listen carefully as you read the text and you will notice how well Puccini paints with his music all of the great actions and emotions of the story. *Tosca* is also unusual in that it takes place in real locations that anyone familiar with Rome would recognize. The first is the church of Sant'Andrea della Valle, which sits on the Corso Vittorio Emanuele in the old center of Rome, not far from the Pantheon. The second act is set in the Palazzo Farnese, near the church of Act I. While this palace is no longer open to the public (it is the French embassy), it is a landmark familiar to most Romans. The third act occurs within and on the roof of the Castel Sant'Angelo, a building on the banks of the Tiber River that dates back to ancient times. From the Castel Sant'Angelo there is an excellent view of the Vatican and the dome of St. Peter's. When a work of art is so anchored in reality, it creates different rules for how it is perceived by its creators and its audiences. Since the locations are so familiar (especially to the Italian audiences for whom the opera was created), anyone watching *Tosca* will pay attention to how the settings are recreated onstage. Then, because the audience's imagination is not used to envision a particular time and place, viewers go more rapidly to the story and the action in the opera. *Tosca* is also distinctive because it is set in a very tight and specific time frame. All of the action occurs in less than twenty-four hours. Act I happens in the bright, optimistic light of morning. Act II takes place in the waning, more dangerous light of evening. The final act occurs at dawn, a moment that might be ripe with future hope but also, as we know, a time when people are executed. The realism in *Tosca* is due in part to the popularity of the verismo movement (see pages 40–41), which swept through Italian opera at the end of the nineteenth century.

One of the hallmarks of *Tosca,* as with *Rigoletto,* is its conciseness. This observation also applies to the stage directions, which are explicit and to the point. Pay special attention to them as you follow the libretto. In this way, you will powerfully envision what is happening onstage. If necessary, use the pause button on your CD player to give yourself enough time to read all of the stage directions and notes. Unfortunately, the individual tracks are listed only on pages 2–4 of the booklet and are not indicated in the libretto; and so throughout this chapter I will list page numbers in addition to track numbers to give you more guidance.

The opera begins quickly with the ominous chords that we will associate with the evil Scarpia. These last only a few seconds before the surge of music that suggests the rushed entry of Angelotti, who is seeking refuge in the church of Sant'Andrea della Valle. Within moments, we meet the other key characters in the first scene of the opera. The Sacristan, as you will discover, will pop up occasionally to provide comic relief just as the dramatic knot tightens. The role of comic relief in tragedy goes back to ancient times. By letting the audience exhale and laugh periodically, the dramatist can then reintroduce the dramatic elements at a higher level of tension.

Immediately after the Sacristan, we meet Mario Cavaradossi. Unlike the Duke of Mantua in *Rigoletto,* Cavaradossi is a genuine hero. He is a sympathizer of those fighting against the Bourbon domination of Rome. He is in love with Tosca, our heroine, and he is faithful to her, even if he paints portraits of other women. He also has two of the finest tenor arias Puccini ever wrote; and before we know it, in track 2 (page 30), he sings the first one, "Recondita armonia," in which he declares his love for Tosca. The importance of this is to set the stage for the dramatic events to follow. The fact that we know that Mario and Tosca truly love one another (despite her jealousy and insecurity) will make their rather extreme actions later on more plausible.

After the short aria, the opera speeds along as we quickly discover who Angelotti is and then have our first view of Tosca. Her insistent cries of "Mario!" are the first sounds we hear from her (pages 36–38) and will also be among the last. Notice how Maria Callas gives each recitation of the name a different meaning. Our immediate impression of Tosca is a woman who is vain, imperious, superstitious, and jealous. At first this may not seem like someone we should care about, but in short order we do as she reveals her feelings. As you read along while Callas sings, look at the words and listen to how—with her voice—she gives meaning to the ideas and emotions the words represent. The quicksilver changes in Tosca's mood are all captured in Callas's detailed performance. For example, on page 42 she sings of love, and immediately after (page 44) she flies into a rage of jealousy over the portrait of a woman she believes to be a rival. There follows (on page 46, beginning with Mario's "Quale occhio al mondo") a rapturous love duet as Tosca yet again changes mood. A lesser singer and actress could not make these shifts believable, but Callas is convincing.

No sooner has Tosca exited than the music suddenly takes a dramatic turn, as Puccini jolts us back to harsh reality. In track 6 (page 50), Mario again turns his attention to the hidden Angelotti. We learn many plot details in this sequence. Angelotti must escape the hands of the evil Scarpia; on page 52, as Angelotti talks of "Scarpia scellerato," the orchestra chimes in with the chords we heard at the start of the opera that identify the evil character. To aid in Angelotti's escape, Mario offers the key to his villa. Notice, as the cannon is fired and the men run for cover, how the music in the orchestra sounds more joyous than menacing. We are witnessing the transition from one dramatic state to another. After the tension of the scene with the two men plotting the escape, we see the return of the comic Sacristan, to be followed by a bunch of rambunctious choirboys. Puccini's orchestra leads us from the tense drama to the more lighthearted scene with the Sacristan and his acolytes. Listen to the flutes and triangles during this transition. The Sacristan also mentions that Tosca will be singing later at the Palazzo Farnese, a fact we will bear in mind.

Suddenly (track 7, page 58) Scarpia enters and chastises the Sacristan for all the commotion: "Un tal baccano in chiesa! Bel rispetto!" This is one of the most powerful entrances—musically and dramatically—in the entire operatic repertory. Play it again, if you wish, to get its full impact, and imagine what it looks like onstage. Also, remember to pay close attention to Tito Gobbi's diction and vocal acting—he is the equal of Callas in his ability to get the most out of every word and moment.

What follows is Scarpia's interrogation of the terrified Sacristan, who lets slip several key facts that lead Scarpia to believe that Mario (*Tosca's lover,* he reminds himself) is aiding the cause of the revolutionary Angelotti. (Remember that Scarpia is an enforcer for the

Bourbons who dominate Rome, while Angelotti and Mario are on the side of Napoleon, who they hope will free Rome.) On page 66, as Scarpia speaks Tosca's name, we hear strains of music we associate with her. This not only suggests her presence in Scarpia's thoughts but indicates to us that she is soon to return. Suddenly, we hear the familiar "Mario, Mario!," which Callas delivers differently here—compare them to the first "Mario"s she sang at the start of the opera.

Scarpia plays on Tosca's jealousy (using a fan as a prop) much as Iago plays on the jealousy of Othello when he brandishes Desdemona's handkerchief. Notice how, at the start of track 9 (page 70), with the words "Ed io venivo a lui tutta dogliosa," an incredibly mournful sadness overtakes Callas's sound and speech. Tosca becomes convinced that Mario has run off with the Marchesa Attavanti and goes to break them up. Scarpia, who has succeeded in unnerving Tosca, also realizes he desires her. After Tosca leaves (with the great "God will pardon me. He sees me weeping"), Scarpia gloats in his sinister aria "Va, Tosca!" (page 74). The evilness of his sound comes in stark contrast to the Te Deum that is being sung in the church as Act I comes to a monumental close with a stage full of churchgoers attending mass. The juxtaposition of sacred and profane could not be clearer or more striking. The last line—"Tosca, you make me forget God!"—says it all.

The second act of *Tosca* is one of the most famous and powerfully dramatic in all of opera. The performance of this act that you are about to hear is, I believe, the best one ever recorded. In fact, there are few recordings of any opera that more vividly convey the sense of theater that is so much a part of opera. I would like you to listen to the act the first time while reading the libretto and my comments. Then, with this added knowledge of what the scene is about, listen to it again straight through, preferably with your eyes shut, so you can envision what is happening onstage based on what the music is telling you. This exercise is crucial in developing your skills for studying and learning opera. That is one of the reasons I selected *Tosca* as your second opera. In the future, as you study new operas in this book and on your own, remember the powers you used to hear drama in music that you developed in Act II of *Tosca*.

The curtain rises to reveal Scarpia's candlelit office in the Palazzo Farnese. This being 1800, there was not yet electricity. The candlelight adds a lot to the mood of the scene, and, as you will discover, the candelabra play an important part in the stage action. As Scarpia muses to himself at the start of the scene, he observes that "for myself the violent conquest has stronger relish than the soft surrender," and goes on to explain in great detail how much he enjoys the conquest of women he will then cast aside. In most productions, Scarpia is dressed up in a shiny black outfit that connotes evil, and is usually given a gray or white wig to wear as well. Nonetheless, the best Scarpias often project a genuine sexual attractiveness (or at least energy) that enables them to charge the scene in a way that a lecherous dirty-old-man type would not. It is an unhappy truth that certain evil people are often sexually alluring. Without adding the mental image of the black clothes and the wig, listen to Tito Gobbi and try to decide if he sounds in any way alluring. The key to this is that if a Tosca finds a Scarpia attractive on one level even as she despises him, her interaction with him will be quite different than if she finds him repulsive in every way.

In the third track (page 82) we learn that Spoletta, the oily spy, has arrested Mario after searching Cavaradossi's villa for Angelotti. Later in this act, Mario's cries while being tortured will punctuate the action (he will, however, be offstage, so we must imagine what is happening rather than witnessing it). But in the first interrogation scene, it is Tosca's offstage voice we hear. She is singing a cantata for the Queen of Naples, who is a Bourbon and therefore of the family against which Angelotti and Mario are struggling. You will notice that Callas's voice is very strident in this passage, but don't forget how stressed Tosca is: she knows that Mario is harboring a fugitive, and she wants to protect him from the very oppressors for whom she is singing. At the moment that Mario angrily denies Scarpia's charges by crying "Menzogna!" ("Lies!"; page 84), Tosca is practically screaming. In your mind's eye, you should envision Mario facing Scarpia and his henchmen, with Tosca nowhere to be seen.

At track 4 (page 88), Tosca enters and discovers Mario being interrogated. The tension in the scene tightens as Mario is dragged off to the torture chamber. His cries will now be heard as Scarpia brings psychological pressure on Tosca. Scarpia gets straight to the point: "What about the fan?," referring to Mario's alleged (and untrue) infidelity with the Marchesa Attavanti. Tosca rebuffs him. You should bear in mind in the coming moments that Tosca is summoning all of her skills as an actress in her scene with Scarpia. She repeatedly (and in differing ways) insists that Mario was alone at his villa. Scarpia knows she is lying, she knows she is lying—but does she know that Scarpia knows she is lying? That is your decision.

Presently, the torture begins. The tension mounts in the orchestra, then in Scarpia's voice, and then the scene's first big climax comes as Tosca cries "Non è ver!" (page 94). This moment is bloodcurdling for the character of Tosca and, when done by a great artist, for the audience as well. From here, the scene will build as the torture of Mario begins. Tosca is torn between Mario's pleas that she not divulge any secrets and her desire to tell all in order to stop Mario's torture. Throughout the rest of this act are lines so famous that any opera lover can recite them. Most of them are Tosca's: "Non so nulla" ("I know nothing"), "Non posso più" ("I can stand no more"), "Assassino!," and "Quanto? . . . Il prezzo!" ("How much? . . . What is your price [for Mario's freedom]?"). (Catty operagoers often exclaim "Non posso più" when they don't like the way a singer is singing. Opera fans are very adept at quoting opera dialogue in other contexts, and Tosca is full of such quotables.)

By track 7 (page 102), Tosca can no longer tolerate the torture of Mario and reveals that Angelotti is hiding in a garden well. Listen then to the orchestral passage that accompanies the dragging on-stage of the tortured Mario. What do you see? The music tells all, including the moment Mario sees Tosca. This is the sound of love, which quickly turns to anger as Mario feels that Tosca has betrayed him ("Hai tradito!"). When word comes that Napoleon's armies have defeated the Bourbons at Marengo (page 108), Mario cries victory ("Vittoria!")—an act that seals his fate. He rejects Tosca as he is dragged away to await execution.

And now (page 110) comes the most famous part of this famous act, in which Scarpia informs Tosca that she must consent to sex with him in order to save Mario's life. How mean and cold he is when he remarks that his poor little supper was interrupted! His subsequent false courtesy is quickly curtailed by her direct question: "Quanto?" The scene escalates again as Scarpia reveals his wishes (which, of course, Tosca already must have sensed). He cruelly grasps for her, crying "Mia . . . mia!"—"Mine . . . mine!" as Tosca cries "No!" and "Vile!" Finally the drumroll of the condemned brings the scene to a halt as Scarpia tells Tosca that Mario has but an hour to live.

Why did Puccini stop the action here, only to have to start it up again later? Shouldn't the scene propel toward its inevitable conclusion? You may have noticed that Tosca, our title character and the object of our concerns, has not yet had a solo aria and the opera is half over. It is often said that while Puccini did not want to slow down the opera here, he (and perhaps Ericlea Darclée, who created the role at its premiere in Rome in January 1900) felt that Tosca should have an aria to herself. So the action pauses as Tosca reflects on the meaning of her life in a very famous aria, "Vissi d'arte, vissi d'amore" ("I lived for art, I lived for love"). This is indeed a beautiful aria, which many singers perform in concert, but do we really believe that Scarpia would cool off and back away to allow Tosca to muse about her life for a few minutes? It is at moments like these that people who are critical of opera complain that opera is not real. Well, opera *is* real: it is a real art form with conventions that we who love it understand. Tosca is reflecting on her life in a thought process that takes three minutes of opera time but might actually take only seconds in her head. We audience members understand this and do not bother to question the realism of a rapist (which, after all, is what Scarpia essentially is) waiting a few minutes before attacking. Listen to Callas sing "Vissi d'arte" (track 10, page 116) and enjoy it for the music and the emotion it powerfully conveys. The words also remind us that this religious woman would have to be driven to the brink to kill someone ("Never did I harm a living creature!"). Yet kill she does.

Just as we are about to learn whether she will give in (page 118), the news arrives that Angelotti has killed himself rather than be arrested. Yet Scarpia is still intent on hanging Cavaradossi. When Scarpia again asks for her decision, we hear her answer not in words but in music (track 11, at 2:00). But she quickly wants to arrange for Mario's release. Scarpia agrees that Mario will face a mock ("simulata") execution. He instructs that the simulated execution be done as it was with Count Palmieri (page 120). What does this mean? Maybe the music will tell you. Tosca then asks Scarpia to sign a document granting her and Mario safe passage from the country. Listen to the music as he writes. Tosca has gone to take a glass of wine to calm her nerves and notices a knife on the table. Do you know at what point she sees it? The music tells you. (The moment comes on track 12 at 1:04, but try to hear it without looking at the timer on your CD player.) She takes the knife discreetly in hand. Forty-three seconds later, as Scarpia reaches out for his prize, you can hear exactly what Tosca does with the knife. "Muori dannato! Muori, muori!"—"Die accursed! Die, die!"—she urges Scarpia, and the passion and the hatred flood forth in Callas's inimitable delivery. Listen to the music as it sinks in that she has killed Scarpia. Then she utters the famous, ironic line "E avanti a lui tremava tutta Roma!" Other divas have dragged this line out endlessly, but Callas realized that the impact was in the words even more than in her delivery.

Listen then to the music that Puccini composed to accompany Tosca's actions. She cleans her hands, then looks for the note of safe conduct. To her disgust, she realizes that it is in Scarpia's clenched fist. As she is about to leave, her religious side takes over: she places a candelabra on either side of Scarpia's head and then a crucifix on his chest. You can hear each of these moments in the music (at 5:02 and 5:18 for the candles, 5:40 through 5:44 for the cross), and then the sound of Tosca's terrified exit as she leaves the room.

As you probably have noticed, one of the leading characters in *Tosca* is dead and there is still one more act to go. If you were watching this performance in an opera house, Tito Gobbi would come out for his solo bow at the end of the second act. It is somewhat unusual that one of the leads does not appear throughout an opera, but Scarpia's influence will be felt throughout the last act, musically and dramatically.

After all of the emotion of the second act, we begin the third one differently. The first notes echo a duet of freedom Tosca and Mario will sing later on. Then, quickly, the music becomes sweet and lilting. It is dawn. In the distance we hear the innocent voice of a shepherd boy singing in Roman dialect. The bells of nearby churches chime in the distance. Onstage, a jailer is dozing until Mario is led to the scene. This sequence lasts five minutes—quite a long time given the rapid pacing of the rest of the opera. After Mario has convinced the jailer to permit him to write to Tosca, he writes her a farewell. As he writes, he thinks of her (as snatches of music from Act I flood his head—this music, of course, represents his thoughts). His famous aria, "E lucevan le stelle," is sung by a man who is convinced he is about to die without ever again seeing his beloved. Listen to the beauty of the words and music of this gorgeous lament (track 15).

Suddenly, Tosca appears, and in their joyous reunion she tells Mario he is free. She explains how she killed Scarpia, and Mario sings tenderly about the sweet hands that justice put to such bloody use. Tosca explains that Mario need only pretend to die in a mock execution before they will be free to flee the country together. They rejoice in a tender duet. While all of this music and action may seem extraneous, it makes our minds and hearts consider other ideas. If we believe Mario and Tosca will survive, we are gladdened by their happiness. If we feel that they are doomed, then we are saddened that their ignorance is in no way blissful.

At track 18, Tosca explains how Mario should fake death before the firing squad (they will, she assumes, be firing blanks). Then the firing squad enters. From the side, Tosca coaches him on how to enact his death. (A better translation of "Così?" on page 142 is "Like so?" rather than just "So?")

Track 19: Tosca becomes anxious as they wait for the firing squad to do its work. In a brilliant piece of theater, Puccini has Tosca narrate the execution as she sees it. Of course, she assumes that the soldiers are firing blank bullets and that she and Mario will leave together in a matter of minutes. It is ironic that Tosca cries "Muori!" to her beloved, the same word she used with Scarpia. As the firing squad retires, she counsels Mario not to move, to stay still and continue his act until everyone has gone. Does the music suggest the triumph or the tragedy of Tosca's plan? When they are alone, she calls to him: "Presto! su, Mario! Andiamo! Andiamo! Su!" You don't need to speak Italian to know that Mario is indeed dead. The terror and horror in Callas's voice fill this moment memorably. As it turns out, the "mock" execution of Palmieri that Scarpia and Spoletta spoke of was in fact a real killing. Scarpia intended to have sex with Tosca at night and then to execute Mario at dawn.

Spoletta has discovered the dead Scarpia and comes to capture Tosca. Rather than being caught, Tosca, with Mario dead and her own life doomed, climbs to the ramparts of the Castel Sant'Angelo and cries "O Scarpia, avanti a Dio!," vowing that they will meet before God. She then jumps to her death in the Tiber River below as Spoletta and we watch in horror. And the curtain comes down.

You may be hard-pressed to think of any piece of spoken theater that has the same emotional and dramatic power as Puccini's *Tosca*. This is not to belittle the legitimate theater, of which I am a great fan; but I think you have just learned how a highly dramatic opera, with words, music, and powerful staging, can pack a theatrical punch the likes of which you are unlikely to come across elsewhere. *Rigoletto* and especially *Tosca* are prime examples of this. In the other operas we will study in this book, we will see how various composers sought to explore comedy and drama in music. Our next opera, *Lucia di Lammermoor,* is equally dramatic, but there the drama happens in the voice rather than in the words. We will see how a composer can describe drama through sound.

The alternate opera for learning more about verismo and high drama is *Pagliacci.* We all know the famous aria "Vesti la giubba," in which a sad clown dresses for his performance while lamenting his betrayal by his wife. This 75-minute work is usually shown on a double bill with *Cavalleria Rusticana,* another powerful verismo opera. The pair is collectively referred to as *Cav/Pag.* A very good performance of *Pagliacci* appears on EMI, starring Victoria de los Angeles, Jussi Björling, and Leonard Warren. A great historical recording from 1934 features Beniamino Gigli, one of the century's great tenors, and the orchestra and chorus of La Scala.

6.

LUCIA DI LAMMERMOOR

DRAMA EXPRESSED
THROUGH MUSIC

Beauty is a subjective thing. What one person finds arresting or aesthetically pleasing may have no effect on someone else. This applies not only to the visual arts but also to music. When we think of bel canto opera, of which *Lucia di Lammermoor* is a leading exponent, the emphasis on beauty plays a crucial role in our perception of the opera. We may walk out of a performance of *Rigoletto* and exclaim how moving it was or leave a performance of *Tosca* reeling from its dramatic impact. But one of the first comments you will likely hear after a great performance of *Lucia di Lammermoor* is how beautiful it was.

Most of the effort that goes into a production of *Lucia* centers on how its different elements—singers, orchestra, stage direction, scenery, costumes, lights—can be brought together to give this opera maximum beauty. This goal is good and bad at once. While for most people *Lucia* is a work of undeniable beauty, if beauty remains the focus of a production, many other aspects of this opera will be ignored. This story is as moving as *Rigoletto*'s and has elements of drama that rival those in *Tosca*. But where in *Tosca* the drama is palpable in the action as well as the music, in *Lucia* we experience the emotions and events of the opera almost entirely in musical terms. When the music is as beautiful as that of *Lucia*, it becomes incumbent upon the performers to convey its inherent drama while bringing out the beauty of the music with loving care. It is also necessary for audience members to pay attention to the drama instead of merely sitting back and bathing in glorious sound.

The only time an opera company (or a recording company) should consider producing *Lucia di Lammermoor* is when it has a first-rate singer on hand to perform the title role. Without her, there is no point in doing this opera. The problem with this assumption, though, is that *too* much attention can be paid to the diva, at the expense of the other singers and the total production. I am always amazed at how many audience members leave the opera house after Lucia's mad scene even though there is still great tenor music to come. *Lucia di Lammermoor,* even more than *Tosca,* is a diva's opera. At other points in this book I have discussed diva worship. Although many audience members, particularly women, get a special charge out of glorious tenor singing, the diva, particularly the soprano, is the primary object of our attentions. In operas in which the diva shines, it is difficult for any other singer to compete. This is particularly true in the bel canto repertory, which is full of great soprano roles. So while I do not discourage you from plunging headlong into diva worship, remember that she is part of a larger production, all of whose elements should be observed and enjoyed. (For an amusing view of diva worship in small-town Italy at the start of the twentieth century, I commend to you a 1992 British film called *Where Angels Fear to Tread.* In it, an entire town in Tuscany turns out to hear a hefty diva sing Lucia. At the conclusion of the mad scene, she is showered with bouquets and garlands, bringing the performance to a complete halt even though the tenor's big scene is still to come.)

As we study this recording of *Lucia,* which stars Joan Sutherland in one of her signature roles and also features excellent performances by Luciano Pavarotti and Sherrill Milnes, you might want to notice how these three singers, whom we first heard in *Rigoletto,* sound by comparison in this opera. The reason I selected two operas with the same casts was so you will see how singers embody different roles differently. Take some time to make comparisons. Gilda's aria, "Caro nome," sounds like some of the music in *Lucia,* but much of the rest of the role has the characteristic drive and imperative that we find in so much of Verdi's music. Gilda and Lucia are both women in love who, each in her own way, make huge sacrifices for the men they love. We feel for Gilda because she is making a mistake that leads to her tragic end. Yet Lucia, who is routinely portrayed as a victim, does, in fact, assert herself rather startlingly. That she is insane in the latter part of the opera is typically used as an excuse for her behavior, but a modern view might have it that her extreme actions are reasonable. As you get to know Lucia, ask yourself how her behavior would be perceived if she were not insane. Her stabbing of the man she was forced to marry would then make her seem more like a sister of the gutsy Tosca than a weak, vulnerable innocent. Sutherland's voice may sound similar in both roles, but notice how she suggests innocence, a too-trusting nature, and sexual awakening as Gilda, while projecting idealized love, mental collapse, and raving insanity as Lucia. These distinctions occur not only in the way the music is written but in how it is sung as well.

While Pavarotti plays the Duke of Mantua as a ruthless libertine, in *Lucia* he is an ardent lover and a romantic hero. When Edgardo burns with love, it *is* love, not lust. Pavarotti sings scrupulously in both roles, yet notice how as the Duke he sounds seductive and lecherous while as Edgardo he is loving and noble. Find moments in his performance that speak to you in those terms.

Sherrill Milnes, the baritone, has a different task. As the title character in *Rigoletto,* he commanded our attention with the drama and pathos of his portrayal. In this opera, he assumes a role that is more typical in the baritone repertory: the bad guy who comes between the soprano and the tenor. In *Tosca,* we met one of the most extreme examples of the evil baritone. In other operas, the baritone often interrupts the romance for other reasons: family honor, duty to country, or perhaps because he too loves the soprano. In this case, Enrico is Lucia's brother. He wants her to marry Arturo, the man he has selected, because Arturo's wealth is needed to prop up the sagging financial conditions of Lammermoor, home of Lucia and Enrico Ashton. So Milnes must portray Enrico not as evil but, rather, as a man whose agenda has made him completely insensitive to his sister's feelings.

Many of the recitatives in *Lucia* (which are accompanied by orchestra) sound conversational rather than singsong; the characters express their feelings as the orchestra comments. The arias, duets, and ensemble pieces are, by contrast, masterpieces of musical invention. Here, much more than in the first two operas we studied, you should listen to the music as an abstract form and then explore what feelings it provokes in you. Then, as you look at the words to which the music is set, ask yourself whether the sound communicates what the words express. It is here that you will find one of the keys to bel canto. While, as a style, it is full of sublime beauty, it is also remarkably straightforward. Characters say what they feel and speak of what they want. Singers with superb diction (such as Pavarotti) can make this music more vivid by giving beauty and meaning to the words as well as the music. Yet where bel canto differs from verismo and other styles is that the distinctive quality of each singer's voice plays a much bigger part in the creation of a character. So the Lucias of Joan Sutherland, Maria Callas, Montserrat Caballé, and June Anderson, to name four leading exponents, are all distinctive because each woman brings a different sound to the character. While we compare Toscas based on their acting and speech as well as their musical qualities, Lucias ultimately rise and fall based on their ability to create a memorable vocal personality.

But what is it that we listen for? Lucia is sad almost from the moment we meet her. She is having difficulty recovering from the death of her mother. She is tormented by visions of ghosts and spirits. Her brother wants her to marry a man she does not love. The man she does love, Edgardo, is unavailable to her. After her forced wedding Lucia, in a fit of madness, murders her groom and then undergoes a series of hallucinations before collapsing and dying of a broken heart. Lest you believe that these are musty old stage conventions with little relevance today, think of any contact you have had with persons who are emotionally disturbed. There is a raw edge to their feelings, an immediacy and a tangible sense of chaos that one does not so readily find in someone more in control of his or her faculties and behavior. So we listen to each singer's Lucia to experience how she creates—in strictly musical terms—the girl's wide range of passions.

In listening to Donizetti's music, try to envision the mood he is responding to in his subject matter. This story, set in seventeenth-century Scotland, has elements of both *Romeo and Juliet* (the story of young lovers from feuding families who are prevented from marriage but are joined in death) and *Macbeth* (the somber mood of mist-shrouded Scottish castles and the references to ghosts and spirits of the dead). Yet *Lucia* is based on *The Bride of Lammermoor* (1819), a novel by Sir Walter Scott that is a typical example of nineteenth-century Romanticism. So Donizetti drew upon contemporary as well as historical inspirations. In addition, he wrote the opera for two very popular singers, Fanny Persiani and Gilbert-Louis Duprez, tailoring the music to their talents. The arias we treasure today were written with specific voices in mind. Donizetti was thinking of his opening night in Naples and not about future interpreters of Lucia and Edgardo.

As you listen to the music, note how different instruments provide accents in the orchestra. The harp, in early passages of the opera, suggests the innocence and vulnerability of Lucia. Later on, the harp returns as a sad and ironic reminder of how Lucia's innocence and vulnerability have been shattered. French horns (popular with Rossini, who had used them in *La Donna del Lago* and *Guillaume Tell* to suggest the mysteries of the forest) are effective at various moments in *Lucia* as characters wander in the woods. Drums and cymbals provide an urgent counterpoint to fervent emotions in the famous sextet.

Above all, the flute is the most important instrument in the orchestration of *Lucia di Lammermoor*. In the mad scene the flute is put to brilliant use as a single voice that we hear in counterpoint to the voice of Lucia. The voice of the flute, in fact, is the voice she hears in her head. This dazzling effect is one of the most accomplished efforts in all opera and theater in communicating the workings of an insane mind. At most productions of *Lucia* you attend, you will find the name of the solo flutist listed on the cast page right there with the singers and the conductor. It is interesting to note that Donizetti himself went mad toward the end of his life. One wonders whether his particular insights into insanity were in any way revealed in his music.

The issue of psychology brings me to another crucial point. It has become faddish in recent years for stage directors to retell the story of *Lucia* in contemporary psychological terms. When Sigmund Freud gave a vocabulary and a structure to his understanding of the functioning of the human mind at the beginning of the twentieth century, he completely changed the way scientists and artists looked at human behavior. We must remember, though, that humans did not behave differently as a result of Freud's observations; they only perceived this behavior differently. Feelings and conditions such as passion and insanity have existed since the beginning of human history, and we find them represented in the theater of ancient Greece as much as in the art of today. But it is dangerous, in most cases, for a stage director to impose twentieth-century psychoanalytical perceptions on a nineteenth-century character. It is more important to understand the conditions from which the character sprang rather than impose our own perspective on her.

In a similar vein, there is something else to observe about the characters in *Lucia* that they share with many others in opera, theater, and literature. In some of the operas we will study, particularly those by Verdi and Wagner, many characters exist not only on their own terms but to embody the beliefs and ideals of their composers. Verdi and Wagner were both revolutionaries who used their art to promote ideas and challenge conventions. In contrast, the characters in *Lucia di Lammermoor* are the opposite of the ideological surrogates of Verdi and Wagner. In *Lucia,* the sociohistorical conditions and attitudes that produced the characters are a constant that go unquestioned and unchallenged; they function simply as a context in which the characters exist. We do not expect that Lucia, Edgardo, and Enrico will rise out of these circumstances and change their world. Rather, they must abide by the rules and mores of their society. It is for this reason that so many operatic characters, including Lucia and Edgardo, assume they will find peace, love, and happiness only in death. What would Freud have to say about that?

Let's begin. As always, start by reading the notes at the beginning of the libretto. On page 21 you will find the English-language section. There is a good essay by Christopher Raeburn, the producer of this and many classic recordings for London/Decca Records, that explains some of the historical significance of recording a legendary performance such as Sutherland's Lucia. Raeburn tells us that this is the second Sutherland *Lucia* on disk. Why do more than one? Ideally, an artist grows and deepens her understanding of a role and perhaps her ability to sing it; therefore, she imparts different values in each performance. Also, if she works with different costars and a new conductor, the results will vary. The first Sutherland *Lucia,* recorded not too long after her historic Covent Garden performances of 1959, contains all the freshness of youth (a virtue) and would be the envy of most other singers. Yet she surpasses that performance with this one. (I should note that her 1982 performance at the Metropolitan Opera, captured on video in the autumn of her career, is in many ways more astonishing: while still displaying almost all of her unmatched vocal powers, she also brings great drama and pathos to the role.)

Following Raeburn's essay is a worthy commentary by the excellent William Weaver. But I must challenge one point he raises when he rhetorically asks, "But who reads librettos carefully?" My answer is that you do, because you understand that the words are a key to initial comprehension of an opera. By the time you attend a performance, you will have read the libretto and will be ready to perceive the opera primarily in musical and visual terms. In fact, all operagoers who believe in proper preparation attempt to read a libretto before attending a performance. Mr. Weaver is addressing his query to other than the likes of you, dear reader.

The need to read the libretto is reinforced by the wretched synopsis that begins on page 25 of the booklet that accompanies this recording. While Salvatore Cammarano's libretto is straightforward and tightly structured, the jumble that passes for a synopsis here will help you understand why the uninitiated make fun of many opera plots. You should still read about each scene before listening to it (as you would on any other recording), but do not become overwhelmed trying to decipher what this synopsis says. You will understand the essentials of the plot from reading the libretto and the comments I make in this chapter.

Lucia di Lammermoor begins with a prelude that is less than three minutes long. While the terms "prelude" and "overture" are often used interchangeably, there is something of a difference. A prelude is typically a brief orchestral passage that serves to introduce an opera, setting the mood in a concise manner. It does not necessarily draw from music used elsewhere in the opera, but there is no hard-and-fast rule about this. Preludes often (as here) lead immediately into the action, while overtures, which are more symphonic in scale, are played as freestanding pieces before the opera begins. Wagner, ever different, wrote preludes that are longer than some overtures. His preludes appear not only at the start of an opera but at the start of later acts as well. In *La Traviata* and *Don Carlo,* Verdi placed short preludes before later acts. (We will examine the overture in the next chapter when we study Rossini and *Il Barbiere di Siviglia*.) Donizetti's prelude to *Lucia di Lammermoor* very effectively captures the atmosphere and moods of this opera. By turns somber, mournful, and emotionally charged, it will quickly focus your mind on the story at hand.

In listening to the first few minutes of singing in the opera, you will realize that it is largely conversational recitative that sets the action for the audience. Within this context, however, Donizetti has created orchestral "commentary" that is varied and incisive. As you read the words that are being sung, pay special attention to the orchestral voices that accompany them. It is not until 7:40 minutes into the opera that we first encounter an aria, Enrico's "Cruda, funesta smania." This aria, slightly more than two minutes long, really fits into the larger framework of the scene, which sets the stage for all the action that is to follow. Here Enrico asserts and vows his intentions, as will Lucia and Edgardo in the next scene. Pay attention as well to the chorus, here and throughout the opera, as it underscores, agrees, or disagrees with the statements made by the principals. Notice that the chorus's commentary is defined not only in verbal but also in musical terms. When its music contrasts or clashes with that of a principal, it often suggests disagreement. When the choristers sing in unison with a principal, they more than likely agree. Opera is not always this simplistic, and the role of the chorus is not always so basic. It is important, when you attend operas in which the chorus plays a prominent role, to give some thought to what character or characters the chorus represents. Are the choristers supposed to represent "the people" in general, or are they a collection of individual characters in supporting roles? In the mad scene of this opera, some members of the chorus are sympathetic to Lucia's plight; others are more shocked and horrified. When you attend a performance of *Lucia* or any other opera, look occasionally at what the chorus members are doing.

The introductory sounds of scene 2 are different from those of the first scene. The harp, as I noted earlier, signals the ethereal, otherworldly character of the dreamy and distracted Lucia. Although the music sounds feathery, the notes tell you that in fact Lucia is quite agitated as she impatiently waits for Edgardo. This harp solo underscores what I mean when I say that this opera is both beautiful and dramatic. If you hear only the beauty and ignore the drama, you will miss a lot.

The character of Alisa is of a kind that you see in many operas: the maid or companion, usually sung by a mezzo-soprano to provide a lower voice and musical contrast to the leading lady. There are many famous mezzos who refused to sing these roles at the start of their careers, fearing that they would never graduate to the major parts—to paraphrase Grace Bumbry, she didn't study singing for years to come onstage to announce "La cena è pronta" ("Dinner is ready"). Yet other artists will tell you that there are no small roles, only small performers.

Lucia's first aria, "Regnava nel silenzio" (track 6), sounds so beautiful and buoyant that you must recall that at first she is singing of tragic events. Only later does she change mood to sing of her beloved Edgardo ("Quando, rapito in estasi"). Listen to this music closely and carefully. Sutherland extracts great drama from it by flawlessly negotiating its tricky roulades (rapid successions of "rolling" notes) that suggest her fluttering heart. In addition, this music (and the music from her upcoming duet with Edgardo, "Verranno a te sull'aure," track 10), will return prominently in the mad scene.

Edgardo and Lucia's scene is essentially a conversation in which vows are expressed which, as we know, will come into conflict with those sworn by Enrico in the first scene. Read the italicized note on page 79 about the importance of vows in the context of the time and place in which the story is set. The old-fashioned operatic convention of vows and oaths may be easy to make fun of, but, as I said above, Lucia, Edgardo, and Enrico are products of their society. They are also full-blooded people with strong, conflicting emotions and loyalties, and herein lies the drama.

Scene 2 ends with great swells of passion and romance. After hearing this hunk of glorious music, there is no doubt that our sympathies will be sworn to Lucia and Edgardo.

On to the second disk, which contains Act I, scene 3. In some productions this scene and the next are referred to as Act II. Different productions of an opera often divide the acts and scenes differently; sometimes this is the choice of the director or conductor, or the composer himself may have changed his mind in revising an opera. But for our purposes, in *Lucia* and every other opera we study, the way we break down acts and scenes will follow the dictates of the recording we are studying.

Act I, scene 3 takes place a year after scene 2. We learn that Edgardo's letters to Lucia have been intercepted, and when she enters, "the strangeness of her glances indicate[s] . . . the first signs of madness." Listen to her sing "Il pallor funesto" (track 2) without reading the words. Try simply to perceive from the music what the character is feeling. Yes, the music sounds beautiful and is exquisitely sung, but is this person happy? Again, beauty and drama collide in unexpected ways. Then listen to the passage again, this time reading the libretto, and see how you react to the combination of music and words. She speaks of deathly, awful pallor, of suffering, grief, and inhuman harshness. But the glimmerings of insanity come not in the words but in the sound.

The anguish continues. Enrico lies to Lucia by showing her a forged letter indicating that Edgardo has given himself to another woman (thus breaking his sacred vow to Lucia). Listen to track 3 ("Soffriva nel pianto") as a different mood overtakes Lucia. You have already seen a character of quicksilver moods in Tosca. Lucia's mood changes are more subtle, since almost all of the colors come from the palette of sadness and grief. Again, it is the music that describes and delineates the range of her feelings. The uninitiated listener would surely remark at how beautiful the duet of Lucia and Enrico is without understanding the context, but you know better.

At track 5 there is something worth noting. Enrico sings of how

Lucia could betray him ("Se tradirmi tu potrai"), and she answers by singing essentially the same music. But her words are radically different; this, in effect, is an argument rather than a situation of agreement. You have found that when two characters are singing the same music, they typically agree. So this circumstance is something new. This is why, as I have stated, you cannot assume that certain conventions always have the same meaning.

After Enrico exits, the more sympathetic Raimondo attempts, for the good of the family and in memory of Lucia's mother, to convince the girl to forget Edgardo and make the sacrifice of marrying Arturo. Listen carefully to Raimondo's music of sacrifice, for it too will return in the mad scene later on.

Act I, scene 4 (track 9) is a ceremonial scene in which the private dramas will now be played out in public. What has until now been a series of dialogues explodes onto the larger canvas of "the public" in the form of the relatives, courtiers, pages, guards, and servants who people Lammermoor Castle. As might be expected, the crowd is pleased at the news of the wedding of Lucia to Arturo. It seems like a good match; of course, they have no idea of the private conflicts that have been taking place. Arturo is alarmed to learn of Edgardo's love for Lucia, but Enrico insists that the source of Lucia's misery is her deceased mother. Notice how, after Enrico says these words (bottom of page 105, track 10 at 2:00), suddenly the orchestral music changes. This is the entry of Lucia, and you need only listen to know exactly how she looks. Read the stage directions carefully as you listen to the music. Donizetti was every bit as incisive as Puccini in *Tosca* (though less obvious) in describing actions in musical terms.

The surprise entrance of Edgardo leads to the famous sextet (track 11). Notice how every character comes forth to sing of his or her feelings about this fine mess they are in. Throughout the sextet there is a sublime blending of voices, some coming forth briefly for a solo line, others carrying the discussion along for several lines. Imagine, as you listen, six people who are all thinking aloud. (This is indicated in the libretto by parentheses: whenever you see a passage surrounded by parentheses in a libretto, it means that the character is musing to himself.)

First we have Edgardo noting Lucia's apparent remorse while Enrico expresses *his* remorse for Lucia's wretched state. She then joins in, bemoaning her fate. Raimondo, Arturo, and Alisa each add their feelings of compassion for Lucia. At its conclusion, Enrico and Arturo rush at Edgardo with drawn swords, but Raimondo intervenes and convinces Edgardo that Lucia has willingly consented to marry Arturo. Edgardo returns her ring and then strips his ring from her hand. You can hear, in the music that follows, as all parties quarrel around her, Lucia's mental collapse. Her last high note is one of true madness, and she faints dead away at its conclusion. This should not be treated lightly. Such was Sutherland's vocal power that audiences would thrill to the note and cheer her virtuosity, but she also brought to it a heart-stopping theatricality. Many singers can produce the note, but few can charge the moment with as much drama. If you hear other Lucias (on recordings or in the theater), they will be hard-pressed to match the musical and dramatic impact of Sutherland at this moment.

(A parenthetical observation before we continue: the conducting of Richard Bonynge on this recording is full of drive, drama, lyricism, and precision. I have asked you frequently to listen to what the orchestra is "saying" at given moments. The conductor, in effect, is its interpreter. Because Bonynge is Sutherland's husband, he has often been accused of favoring her, or at least of being more sympathetic to her. I challenge you to decide if these assertions are true. I think you will find great beauty and drama throughout the orchestra's performance, no matter who is singing. It was Bonynge who first heard in his wife's voice the makings of a matchless bel canto artist. Many other conductors, who saw Sutherland's large physical size and heard the size of her voice, tried to push her into dramatic rather than coloratura roles. Because Bonynge worked so closely with Sutherland to help her develop her astounding gifts, he was frequently—and unfairly—accused of being a sort of Svengali who got work only because his wife insisted that he be her conductor. This underestimates his own formidable talent, to which this recording and the *Rigoletto* surely attest.)

Let us now proceed to Act II, which is on the third disk. The first scene, starting with loud claps of thunder, consists of glorious music for two male voices, as Edgardo and Enrico vow revenge against each other. This scene serves two purposes. While audience members are roused by the grandeur of the music and revel in the sound of two great voices, the soprano can collect her thoughts and resources before the scene to come: the mad scene, one of the greatest summits in all of opera.

The mad scene is a set piece—that is, a piece of music in which all action surrounding the singer stops and all attention focuses on the solo performer. There are other set pieces (such as the "letter scene" in *Eugene Onegin,* which we will learn later) that have a performer alone onstage. But part of what makes the mad scene in *Lucia* so memorable is that the girl's delirious rantings and hallucinations are enacted in front of a stunned group of people of whom she is entirely oblivious. They are celebrating the marriage of Lucia and Arturo when Raimondo arrives with the appalling news that Lucia has murdered her bridegroom. The tone of the chorus (track 5) has changed from joy to immense sadness.

Listen to the music of Lucia's entrance (described at the bottom of page 135) and you can envision the scene: she is dressed in white clothes that are covered in Arturo's blood. She floats into the room as would a ghost. The flute and Lucia's airy voice are all we hear. At the beginning of her scene, fragments of memory dart in and out of Lucia's raving mind. You can hear this as she changes thoughts: the music starts, stops, changes direction. Suddenly, the flute intones the music of her love duet with Edgardo ("Verranno a te"). Then Lucia starts hearing what she calls "celestial harmonies" and enacts the wedding to Edgardo that never took place. Other music enters her head (through the flute) as she mimes the ceremony before an imaginary priest. In track 7, at 7:00, there begins the extraordinary call-and-response of Lucia and the flute. Sutherland, through sheer musical and technical brilliance, makes this moment of insanity extraordinarily poignant and gripping. (Too often nowadays, unknowledgeable audience members break the magic of this moment by bursting into applause. The scene is not yet over, and the concentration of artist and audience should not be disrupted.)

The wedding guests are watching all of this in shocked disbelief. When Enrico, ever insensitive to his sister, enters ("S'avanza Enrico"), he is restrained by the crowd and by Raimondo. Lucia states aloud that it was her brother who was the source of all of her unhappiness. At the start of track 9, we again hear music from earlier in the opera ("Spargi d'amaro pianto"). The roulades and trills (the rapid-fire alternation of two adjacent notes) are further musical evidence of a complete mental collapse. With one last plaintive cry, Lucia's body fails her and she crumbles to the floor in a senseless heap. (While the stage directions indicate that Lucia is led away, almost every production you will ever witness has Lucia collapse onstage.)

You may want to listen to this scene again without the libretto. Simply close your eyes and picture the scene: the great hall, the costumed crowds, the festivity, the sudden appearance of Raimondo with bad news, and then the ghostlike Lucia, perhaps with a dagger still in her bloodied hand, breaking into the scene and wildly hallucinating as if no one were watching. Your imagination will be highly effective in staging this scene.

As I mentioned earlier, many people think *Lucia di Lammermoor* is over with the heroine's climactic high note. In fact, Enrico, Raimondo, and Normanno still have a few words to say in this scene. And then comes the final scene, which is basically an extended solo for the tenor. Why did Donizetti add this scene? It was not in Scott's novel. We know that while Fanny Persiani, the first Lucia, was still a rising artist when she played the role, Gilbert-Louis Duprez was one of the foremost singers in Europe. Perhaps Donizetti felt—or the tenor demanded—that the last music go to him. But Lucia and Edgardo need to be joined in death to share the bond they could not have in life. Edgardo's two great arias, "Fra poco a me ricovero" (track 12) and "Tu che a Dio spiegasti l'ali" (track 14), are separated by the appearance of the chorus, which mourns the dying Lucia, and then of Raimondo, who announces Lucia's death. In having Edgardo describe his grief to them (rather than thinking aloud to himself) Donizetti heightens his hero's sense of urgency about his desire to die and join Lucia. As with so much of the music in this opera, these solos of Edgardo's are so beautiful (and have such graceful orchestral accompaniment) that it is easy to ignore their great dramatic urgency. They do not sound like music tacked on to gratify a famous tenor but seem, rather, the logical conclusion to this tragic love story.

Lucia di Lammermoor is such a popular opera that it receives more productions than any opera that I could propose as an alternative for this chapter. My goal here was to have you learn how music can be the primary way of depicting drama in an opera. This is a constant in most of the bel canto repertory. Donizetti's *Anna Bolena*, based on the story of Anne Boleyn, Jane Seymour, and King Henry VIII, has many of the same elements as *Lucia*, but it is not produced nearly as often. I am a great fan of Bellini's *I Puritani*, which has a terrific mad scene (from which the heroine actually recovers), a beautiful tenor aria, and a magnificent duet ("Suoni la tromba") for baritone and bass. There are three superb recordings of this opera, each featuring a major diva. Joan Sutherland and Maria Callas were memorable as Elvira, but I also commend to you the version with Montserrat Caballé and Alfredo Kraus, both in sublime voice and singing exquisitely.

7.

IL BARBIERE
DI SIVIGLIA
OPERA AND COMEDY

If beauty is a subjective thing, the notion of what is funny is even more so. What makes one person laugh may leave someone else cold. If you think about the things you laugh at, you will discover a good deal about your outlook on many aspects of life. Most of us find humor in certain jokes, puns, and wordplay, because language is a common denominator that brings the communicator and the listener closer. We also laugh at visual humor: mime, funny movements and gestures, and, in many cases, the misfortune of others. To paraphrase the character of the 2,000-Year-Old Man portrayed by Mel Brooks: "What is funny? If I cut my finger, that's not funny. If some other guy gets his head bitten off by a tiger, now that's funny!" The ability to find humor in one's own frailties and misfortunes is not a universal trait, yet most of us manage to laugh at those of someone else.

The concept of humor in music is much more subtle and, like most forms of humor, effectively resists analysis. Basically, if it's funny, you know it. Communicating fun in musical terms is a task at least as difficult as expressing drama, love, and tragedy. Nonetheless, certain composers have managed to communicate humor and wit. Among these are Haydn (in his "Surprise" Symphony), Mozart (in his sublime serious comedies *Le Nozze di Figaro, Don Giovanni, Così fan tutte,* and *Die Zauberflöte*), Donizetti (in *La Fille du Régi-*

ment, Don Pasquale, L'Elisir d'Amore), Verdi (in *Falstaff*), Puccini (in *Gianni Schicchi*), Richard Strauss (in portions of *Arabella, Der Rosenkavalier,* and *Ariadne auf Naxos*), and even Wagner (in parts of *Die Meistersinger von Nürnberg*).

Yet I defy anyone to disagree that the composer who most ably captured the spirit of humor in music was Gioacchino Rossini. So adept was Rossini at expressing comedy in sound that many august scholars and music lovers have discounted his serious work in comparison. One of the first to make this observation, in 1822, was Beethoven. Upon meeting the thirty-year-old Rossini, Beethoven told him that attempting anything but comedy would be pressing his luck. This oft-repeated comment, which was also meant as praise for *Il Barbiere di Siviglia,* has left an unfair critical legacy. Why do we accept that Donizetti could have written *La Fille du Régiment* as well as *Lucia di Lammermoor,* yet we can't admire *Guillaume Tell* and *Semiramide* because they are by the greatest composer of comic operas? As I mentioned elsewhere, it has only been in recent times that Rossini has been given the consideration he is due. This is a result of dedicated scholarship and the availability of singers—especially Marilyn Horne—who have mastered the fiendishly difficult technique and style that proper Rossini singing requires.

What is it that gives Rossini his special brand of humor? I commend to you the fine essay by Volker Scherliess on page 10 of the booklet accompanying the recording we will be studying, on Sony Classical. Scherliess makes the point that Rossini's melodic writing "aims from the outset at technical brilliance" that inspires feelings of joy and wit in the listener. I find when I listen to Rossini's comedies that a big smile breaks across my face in short order. This pleasure comes from the frothy verve of the orchestral writing and the buoyancy of the vocal line. Yet the music really soars only when a conductor and orchestra play it with great attention to the dynamics (volume) that Rossini called for. Too many sloppy musicians play Rossini in a way that makes all of it sound the same. Similarly, if a singer does not (or cannot) sing the notes as written, observing which is an eighth and which is a sixteenth note, the music will lose its polish and verve. The particular excitement in hearing a Rossini opera is not unlike what we experience in *Lucia di Lammermoor* and in other bel canto; the music is beautiful, but it requires a great singer to make it meaningful. In the show-stopping arias in *Il Barbiere di Siviglia* (Figaro's "Largo al factotum" and Rosina's "Una voce poco fa") we thrill not only to the music but to the singer's ability to perform it. We had contact with this phenomenon in the mad scene in *Lucia* and, to a lesser extent, in "Caro nome" in *Rigoletto*.

A combination of a sensitive conductor and a capable cast are hard to come by for Rossini operas. Through the years, an evolving performance practice has changed the nature of these operas. "Performance practice" refers to the customs and traditions that have accrued during the many years that an opera has been staged. These changes usually happen for one of two reasons. In the more felicitous case, there might have been a singer on hand with special talents who could add an extra note here or an unusual passage there. Fans would delight in hearing these variations by a talented vocalist, who would often add them to a performance over the protestations of a conductor and, in recent years, a stage director. In Rossini's time (and for much of opera history before him), operas were produced as entertainments for the audience at hand rather than with regard for the future. If a particularly demanding singer insisted on singing an aria in a way that showed him or her in a favorable light, the composer usually acquiesced. In *Il Barbiere di Siviglia,* singers made a habit of adding their special touches. The result of this phenomenon is that we have a legacy of written transcriptions and recordings of dozens of major singers' versions of Rossini's music. But with all of these versions floating around, it is often difficult to know what the composer's original intention was. Rossini was not helpful in this regard because he enjoyed writing alternative arias for singers who did not care to sing the one originally written for an opera. For example, in the music lesson scene in Act II of *Il Barbiere di Siviglia,* many Rosinas sing arias that are particularly suitable to their voices. This tradition began in 1819, when a singer named Giuseppina Ronzi de Begnis substituted a barcarolle called "La biondina in gondoleta," which was more flattering to her voice and skills. (Most singers, in fact, chose arias that Rossini did not write.) When she still performed Rosina onstage, Marilyn Horne often sang arias from other Rossini operas: "Di tanti palpiti" from *Tancredi* or "Tanti affetti" from *La Donna del Lago*.

The other circumstance in which the music is altered is less happy: sometimes a singer just cannot handle the music as written, so adjustments are made to make it easier. This does not apply only to Rossini. As you become a more practiced listener, you will realize that certain famous artists who are losing some of their high notes now sing portions of certain roles in a lower key to make them easier. Sometimes these lowered versions become so familiar that we forget what the role was really supposed to sound like.

I confess that there are recordings of *Il Barbiere di Siviglia* with slightly stronger casts than the one I selected. Though many people (myself included) consider Marilyn Horne an unbeatable Rosina, there are certainly other good interpreters of the role, whom you will want to listen to for comparison—Teresa Berganza, for example. (Although Rossini wrote the role for mezzo-soprano, it is so desirable that many sopranos appropriate it, singing it in a higher key. Beverly Sills's performance is among the many you will find on disk, and Kathleen Battle has made Rosina a staple of her repertory.) Samuel Ramey is an excellent Basilio, and Enzo Dara is a master of the buffo repertory. Riccardo Chailly has a natural feeling for this music, as do the orchestra and chorus of La Scala. Less strong are Leo Nucci as Figaro and Paolo Barbacini as Almaviva. Nucci frequently barks music that he should sing more suavely, though his use of language is quite good. Barbacini is often overwhelmed by the rigorous demands of the role. This is most evident in certain solo passages, where there is no ensemble around him to cover some of his most exposed notes.

Why, then, did I pick this recording? Horne, Ramey, Dara, Chailly, and the Scala forces are all superb Rossinians worth learning this opera from. In addition, the recording uses the critical edition of the score prepared by Alberto Zedda. Maestro Zedda is actively involved in the work of the Rossini Foundation in Pesaro (the composer's birthplace). A critical (or revised) edition of an opera is one in which a great deal of musicological detective work has been done to restore a work so that it resembles as closely as possible the one actually written by the composer. In other words, performance practice has been scraped away, so that what you hear in this recording is much closer to the music as Rossini wrote it than the way it has been interpreted through the years. You will hear many adulterated *Barbieri* in your life, so I want you to learn the opera as its creator might have presented it to you.

You will quickly discover that the music in *Il Barbiere di Siviglia* sounds quite distinct from that of *Rigoletto, Tosca,* and even *Lucia di Lammermoor.* For one thing, in *Barbiere* the recitative, or narrative line, is accompanied by harpsichord (or a fortepiano), while in our first three operas there is orchestral accompaniment. In this regard, *Barbiere* looks back to an older, eighteenth-century style.

Although *Barbiere* and *Lucia* are both bel canto operas, they were written to achieve different theatrical results. In *Lucia,* the principal character is mournful and gradually goes insane. Her music is characterized by a languid, beautiful line of melody joined with roulades of rapid-fire notes that suggest her disintegrating mind. Enrico's music is forceful and aggressive; Edgardo's music has lyricism and passion. By comparison, the vocal requirements in *Il Barbiere di Siviglia* are amazing agility, breath control, sensitivity to the words, verve, and timing.

If you think about what the keys are to success in humor, timing is foremost among them. As you listen to Rossini's score, you will find that much of the humor is the result of clever timing. During the recitatives, we are in real time—that is, characters speak to one another conversationally, if somewhat rapidly. During the arias, duets, and ensembles, time is compressed, accelerated, bent, or frozen. The possibilities for humor come in this altered state of time. Time freezes when a character explains what he is thinking about or what he is about to do. In duets and ensembles, as characters sing back and forth at one another, often repeating the same words or musical lines, the repetition implies humorous friction and conflict. In the text, as you will discover, there are many references to tempo and dynamics. When a character says "Let's move quickly" or "Shhhh! Be quiet!" it is often the setup for a comic moment to follow.

A famous signature element in Rossini is the crescendo, which often is called the "Rossini crescendo" because it is so instantly recognizable as being by this composer. A crescendo is a gradual increase in volume, which tends to provoke a quickening of the heartbeat of the listener, who will probably, without realizing it, move closer to the edge of his seat. The Rossini crescendo was often used to suggest a complexity of feelings or the confusing aspects of a story. Mind you, it is not the audience that it confused but the characters. At some of his big crescendi Rossini characters often turn and directly address the audience as they explain their bewilderment at the events happening around them.

Rossini's crescendi are characterized by a repetition of a principal theme, with new instruments entering the orchestral line with each repetition. Often the newest instrument will offer a slightly different way of expressing the theme that will show off the special characteristics of that instrument. For example, violins may play the theme the first time, then cellos will chime in with a lower-voiced version. Then we might hear flutes playing the theme, making one envision birds floating and bobbing above the music. Then, perhaps, an oboe will play the theme more slowly while the strings and flute will play it at their original tempo. Then they might all be joined by the boom of a drum—all of which will be followed by a clarinet that will take a middle voice in the by now many-voiced choir of instruments playing the theme.

The Rossini crescendo can also work with human voices. For example, if you listen to the quintet in Act II (disk 2, track 8), you can choose to hear the five voices as musical instruments rather than human voices. You will find that Rossini was very creative in getting sonic effects from voices as well as instruments. He did an even better job at this in *L'Italiana in Algeri* (1813, three years before *Barbiere*), where, in the thrilling septet that closes the first act, the singers eventually abandon words and only make sounds that approximate particular instruments. No matter how many times I hear a well-executed Rossini crescendo, it is still full of freshness and vigor. This vitality at each rehearing indicates how deeply one can respond to music that many snobs disparage as superficial.

We encounter many of the pleasurable qualities of Rossini's music (and some great crescendi) in the overture to *Il Barbiere di Siviglia*. Rossini wrote many marvelous operatic overtures that have taken their place in the repertories of most symphony orchestras. Until recent years and the great Rossini revival, we knew the names of many Rossini operas only through their overtures. *La Gazza Ladra, Torvaldo e Dorliska,* and *La Scala di Seta* were entirely forgotten, but their overtures survived.

Rossini was not the only outstanding composer of operatic overtures. Mozart wrote brilliant ones, and, as you know, Beethoven created four overtures for *Fidelio* before he felt he got it right. Verdi and, especially, Wagner wrote magnificent overtures that brim with drama. What all of these overtures have in common is that they help the audience prepare for a great night at the opera. When you sit in a theater and listen to an overture, thoughts of the outside drift away and you start to focus on the opera you are about to see. Once upon a time, operagoers arriving late could march to their seats during an overture, although now most major opera companies shut their doors tight once the maestro has entered the orchestra pit. Some theaters will seat latecomers after the overture, but you should not expect this. When you attend a performance of an opera with an overture, remember that it is part of the opera and not background music to your thoughts on some other subject. An overture is your scrumptious appetizer before the meal.

Rossini, ever different from other composers, took a distinct approach to overtures. In most operas by other composers, the overture relates to the music you hear later in the opera. In some cases, such as Wagner's *Der Fliegende Holländer* and Verdi's *La Forza del Destino,* the overture seems like a summation of the opera, because it introduces many of the major musical themes and dramatic motifs. The overture also sets a specific mood for the story we will be seeing and hearing. Mozart's overtures, which have some of the verve and brilliance that Rossini would later specialize in, effectively capture the mood of the story that will follow. By contrast, Rossini wrote an overture to entertain his audience, and if he liked it well enough, he might use it again in other operas. For example, the overture to *Il Barbiere di Siviglia* is one of the greatest ever written. Audiences love the mirth and excitement it creates and usually are put in the mood for a sparkling evening of comedy when they hear it. So it will probably surprise you to learn that this overture was written not for *Il Barbiere di Siviglia* but for an early opera seria,

Aureliano in Palmira (1813), a seldom-heard work whose title figure is a third-century Roman emperor. Rossini used it again in 1815 for *Elisabetta, Regina d'Inghilterra,* about Queen Elizabeth I of England, a good work that is only now attracting attention. It may seem strange that this bubbly overture once preceded two serious operas, since it sounds so perfect for comedy. But for most of Rossini's career, the overture was simply the music that got the audience into their seats. It was only with *Semiramide* and later *Guillaume Tell* that Rossini sought to create an overture that foreshadowed the music and temperament of the opera that would follow. Self-appointed serious music lovers and experts have often found Rossini's recycling of overtures and other music to be objectionable, but Rossini was a practical man of the theater, and if he knew something would work particularly well in a new setting, he made sure to use it.

The libretto of *Il Barbiere di Siviglia* was based on the 1775 play *Le Barbier de Séville* by Beaumarchais, who also wrote *Le Mariage de Figaro* (1781), the basis for Mozart's immensely popular *Le Nozze di Figaro* (1786). The three principal characters in *Barbier*—Figaro, Rosine, and the Count Almaviva—returned in *Mariage*. In the first play, Figaro was a clever barber who managed to arrange everyone else's affairs and make a little money in the process; Rosine was a charming young woman attracted by the advances of the love-struck Count. In the later play, Figaro is in the service of the Count and is chafing at being brighter and more capable than the man he works for; Rosine is a sad, neglected woman who has creature comforts but wonders where all of her moments of sweetness and pleasure have gone, and the Count is a foolish, self-absorbed womanizer lacking any of the charms he had in *Barbier*.

On December 15, 1815, Rossini signed a contract to write an opera for Rome's Teatro Argentina. The opera was to be staged in February, and the subject had not even been selected. It is generally assumed that the subject of Figaro was picked because it was already popular and could quickly be set to words and then music. Cesare Sterbini was engaged to write the libretto, and Rossini then wrote the music in less than two weeks. Is it any wonder that he borrowed some music here and there?

Rossini was aware that audiences knew these characters from

Beaumarchais's plays, from Mozart's opera, and from six other operatic versions of *Barbier* by other composers. The most famous of these, by Giovanni Paisiello, was written in 1782 in St. Petersburg, where the composer was working at the invitation of Catherine the Great; it was immediately a great audience favorite and remained so for the next thirty-four years. The premiere of Rossini's version on February 20, 1816, was one of the great fiascos in opera history. The seventy-five-year-old Paisiello was the grand old man of Italian music, and his *Barbiere* was widely loved. Rossini had acknowledged this by naming his own opera *Almaviva, o L'Inutile Precauzione* (Almaviva, or The Useless Precaution). Many in the audience came prepared to hate Rossini's opera and did everything they could to sabotage the performance. Rossini fled the Teatro Argentina fearing for his life. At the opera's second performance, out of the glare of the Paisiello partisans, Rossini's opera, now called *Il Barbiere di Siviglia,* was well received, and by its third performance it was such a hit that Paisiello's version soon slipped into obscurity. (It is still performed occasionally and is worth seeing.) Rossini's opera quickly became the model against which every opera buffa is compared. (By the way, the Teatro Argentina, near the church of Sant'Andrea della Valle and the Palazzo Farnese (from *Tosca*), is still one of the leading theaters in Rome, although it is used primarily for spoken theater nowadays. Visit it if you ever go to the Eternal City.)

Let's begin. As always, review the names of the characters and the cast (page 2 of the libretto) and then read the essay on page 10 and the synopsis of Act I (pages 14–15). This is a rather complete description of the action, because there is a lot of stage business, but you will follow it better as you read the libretto and hear the music.

Track 1 of the first disk is the overture. Close your eyes as you listen to it and see where your mind wanders. Now that you have read the synopsis for Act I you have some context for imagining what the setting and the characters look like. Despite its origins, this overture does capture the spirit of *Il Barbiere di Siviglia*. (It is remarkable, though, that one can listen to it and recognize, too, its usefulness for an opera about the Virgin Queen of England. Is that because the music is generic or so vividly dramatic?)

As you listen to the overture, imagine that you are in the Teatro Argentina at the fourth performance of the opera in 1816. By now it is a huge hit, and you have come to the theater with eager anticipation. Does the overture heighten your expectation and put you in the mood to see and hear more? That is what should happen.

Track 2: As always, read the italicized stage directions. Notice that the very first words uttered in the opera, by Almaviva's servant Fiorello, set the tone for what follows: "Quietly, very quietly, without talking." This is the setup for the first series of jokes involving volume and timing, both of which play crucial roles in propelling comic situations. From this point forward, as we listen to the performance, I am going to resist telling you where the funny moments are (the opera is full of them) and will instead let you find your own. Occasionally, though, I will try to make you understand how the humor works.

Track 3 begins with sudden loud music, disrupting all efforts at silence. The Count's aria, "Ecco ridente in cielo," is a love song to Rosina. It is also, if you read the lyrics, rather pompous and self-important in tone. You should really think of this as a parody of this type of ardent love song. It also happens to be very challenging musically. These are among the first notes the tenor sings in this opera, and he must already negotiate runs and roulades when his voice is not fully warmed up. Our tenor in this performance, Paolo Barbacini, does a decent job, but he sounds strained and choked toward the end. Rossini wrote music that is difficult for most artists, which is why we are grateful when a Horne, a Sutherland, or a Ramey comes along who can handle its demands.

As the story progresses in track 4, you hear your first Rossini crescendo, this one including orchestra, chorus, and solo singers. Listen to how it works and compare it with others that come later in the opera. People who don't understand Rossini will claim that all of his crescendi are the same, but you will discover otherwise. The track ends with the musicians bursting into raucous song, ruining any effort by Fiorello and Almaviva to maintain silence.

In track 5 we find harpsichord accompaniment to the recitatives. Do you like this sound? Some people think it wispy, others evocative in that the musical commentary comes from an old-fashioned instrument that makes them feel they've gone back to another time and place. What is important too about this recitative is that, with only the lightest instrumental commentary, it is incumbent on the singer to give more meaning and variety to what he is saying.

At the end of this track, another disruption brings the arrival of Figaro. The barber arrives with great flourish (track 6) with his aria "Largo al factotum." This is one of those arias, like "La donna è mobile" in *Rigoletto,* that are well known to nearly everyone, whether or not they have any interest in opera. You have heard it many times, and you have seen parodies of it in cartoons and commercials. You probably are interested in seeing how it fits into the context for which it was created. Here we have a character who thinks a lot of himself and wants everybody to know it. Figaro views himself as indispensable and proceeds to catalog all of his clients, skills, and accomplishments. (In our next opera, Mozart's *Don Giovanni,* you will hear another famous catalog aria and you may make a comparison.) "Largo al factotum" is a musical ego trip. We do not learn about Figaro; we learn what he thinks of himself. The music suggests all of the leaps and backflips the barber says he can do to please his clients. Notice that at a certain point he stops using words and simply sings "la-la-la-la-la" in rapid fire. Compare the use of this repeated syllable to suggest joy and brio to Rigoletto's sadder "la-ra, la-ra"s. Figaro's great aria, which spills over with words and activity (as he mimes every client who requires his attention), is a showpiece of singing, acting, and breath control that Leo Nucci handles with skill, although he is not as silken as such other contemporary Figaros as Håkan Hagegård and Thomas Hampson. Nucci does have excellent diction in his native language and gives meaning to the recitatives that follow.

At the top of page 56 is a line that loses something in the translation. When Figaro tells the Count, "Siete ben fortunato; sui maccheroni il cacio v'è cascato," our translation says, "You are very fortunate, it couldn't be better." What the librettist wrote is, "You are very fortunate; the cheese has landed on the macaroni." This farinaceous equivalent of what Americans call "landing buttered side up" made perfect sense to any pasta-loving member of an Italian audience. Rossini was the greatest gourmand of any composer and could tell the difference between Genoese and Neapolitan pasta simply by tasting it. I make this digression simply to remind you that local flavor in any opera is often hard to translate, but we must bear in mind that most composers and librettists wrote operas for an audience of native speakers and had no idea that their work would be performed a century later in North America.

On page 58 (track 7, 2:22), we first hear the voice of Rosina, the love interest and the only major female character in this opera full of male voices. How does Marilyn Horne's darker, more womanly voice sound to you in the role of a young woman no older than Gilda or Lucia? Our standard for these young, virginal women has been the high voice of Joan Sutherland, yet here we have a rich, mellow sound to depict the same type of character. Rosina is like Gilda in that a man has kept her locked away, presumably "for her own good," as the sexist thinking of that time would have it. Unlike Gilda, who is naive and trusting, Rosina has a certain amount of innate intelligence and wit that helps her survive in ways that the vulnerable Gilda cannot. Also, since we know that a comic opera will result in a happy ending for our heroine, there is none of the foreboding and doom that we sense in *Rigoletto*. We enjoy the plot twists and the cunning ways of Figaro, Rosina, and Almaviva even though we have a good idea how things will turn out. Do you think that the warm sound of Horne's voice suits Rosina's temperament and intelligence, or would you prefer a higher, more girlish sound in the role? Think about this as you hear the performance. Also, make note of Horne's superb facility with the music and her impeccable diction that gives the character and the opera so much more meaning.

We also meet Bartolo, Rosina's guardian. It is customary to think of him—and there are many such characters in the opera buffa repertory—as a bumbling "dirty old man," and if he is portrayed as a stereotype, that is how we will perceive him. But try to find in Bartolo's words and music other keys to his persona. Does he want Rosina for her money alone? Does he have any feelings for her? You can see Bartolo as a foolish character with likable traits or as a total buffoon who is the butt of every joke. Think too, as you listen, about the vocal acting done by the very expert Enzo Dara.

Continue listening (track 8) to the wooing of Rosina by Almaviva (using the assumed name of Lindoro), and notice how Rossini creates amorous charm in his liquid melody. Rosina reveals her similar feelings by imitating Almaviva's song until she is abruptly interrupted. This turning point, which in theater is known as a beat, requires us to focus on a new direction in the music and the story. This beat is very clearly delineated by the sound of a window being slammed shut.

After Figaro deftly makes himself indispensable to Almaviva in his efforts to win Rosina (track 9), they hatch a plot (track 10) in a brilliant duet. Here, in words and music, we can see the measure of each man and understand his thoughts. Figaro is clever and eager for gold. Almaviva is fixed on winning Rosina and will do anything to achieve that—even dressing up as a drunken soldier to crash into Bartolo's house. The scene ends with the Count singing of the flame of love while Figaro hears the clink of money in his pocket. Listen to the vocal lines and the orchestral crescendo. Here is the sound of contrasting ambitions in two different men from different stations in life.

Immediately on the heels of this duet we have a recitative by Fiorello (track 11) about the indignities of serving Almaviva. This recitative may seem like a throwaway, but it serves an important function. In addition to providing ironic commentary on the behavior of Almaviva and Figaro, it gives the audience and the orchestra the chance to catch their breath after the duet and before the opera's other great showstopping aria, Rosina's "Una voce poco fa." Just as tragedy has moments of comic relief to shift gears before proceeding to an inevitably tragic denouement, comedy has pauses and beats that are strategically placed to disrupt what otherwise would be a singular comic trajectory.

Now it is Rosina's turn to explore her feelings (track 12). You will notice that the libretto calls this aria a *cavatina*. This is a term that denotes an aria (usually short) that comes in one or two sections. A cavatina is often used to reveal the vocal and psychological characteristics of a character. Lucia's "Regnava nel silenzio" in Act I of Donizetti's opera is an example of a cavatina you have already learned. That aria has an entirely different flavor from the vivacity of "Una voce poco fa" or "Largo al factotum," which is also a cavatina.

Rosina's is a catalog aria as much as Figaro's. After declaring that she will have Almaviva at any cost, she lists all of her skills and talents. In the music we hear the craftiness and determination of this woman, but we are not put off by her ambition: she is indeed charming, and we want her to win. She also makes it very clear that no man will dominate her ("I let myself be ruled, I let myself be guided. But if they touch me on my weak spot I'll be a viper"). It is therefore touching to remember that in *Le Nozze di Figaro* Rosina—now the Countess Almaviva—is a sad, defeated woman for much of the time. But we are now in Act I of *Il Barbiere di Siviglia* and should focus on the story at hand. Listen to Marilyn Horne's dazzling mezzo coloratura in this treasurable rendition of the cavatina. There is no doubt, as the aria ends, that Rosina will eventually have her way.

Disk 2, track 1 begins with the recitative that immediately follows the inevitable applause that greets Rosina's aria. In it, she repeats her resolve and decides that Figaro would be useful to her. So who should appear? Indeed, Figaro is everywhere at once, as he informed us earlier. We now have a series of conversations: first Figaro and Rosina, then Rosina and Bartolo, who are subsequently joined by the servants Ambrogio and Berta. These conversations are all recitative, and they constitute a sort of witty repartee that moves the action forward. With Ambrogio and Berta, we also have the comic element of his yawning and her sneezing. Notice how the words of Rosina and Bartolo combine with the sneezes and yawns as the conversation moves forward—another way that Rossini uses sound and timing for comic effect.

Scene 8 (page 98) is a classic. We now meet the last principal character in this opera, the music teacher Don Basilio. This devious and oily fellow has a lot of juicy comic moments in this opera, which probably explains why great basses are happy to assume this relatively small role. In Basilio's aria, "La calunnia" (track 2), notice how the music very closely follows the message and meaning of the words. With every word such as *piano* (softly), *scorrendo* (spreading), *tuono* (lightning), or *colpo di cannone* (shot of a cannon), the music and Samuel Ramey's pronunciation give you a full sense of what is being described. The aria is also notable for its crescendi, different from others we've heard because of the slow speed at which they develop.

At the start of scene 9 Figaro tells Rosina of Bartolo's plan to draw up a marriage contract for himself and Rosina. This conversation between the equally wily Figaro and Rosina leads to the wonderful duet "Dunque io son" (track 4). It turns out that Rosina has already written a note to "Lindoro" (Almaviva) indicating her interest, and the duet concludes with Figaro observing that Rosina "could deliver a lecture on cunning." Listening to this duet, one senses that these are two characters with a lot in common. Yet it is interesting that they never seem to show any romantic interest in one another. For that matter, the Figaro of *Barbiere* is a character with very little private life to speak of (although Rosina suggests, in lying to Bartolo, that he has a daughter). Figaro exists purely as a clever businessman.

As Figaro exits and Bartolo arrives, the old man grills Rosina about the comings and goings in the house. This leads to Bartolo's solo aria (track 6), in which he informs Rosina that he will not be deceived or defeated by her plans. The music gives you a good sense of Bartolo's petty, finicky, suspicious personality. Of course, Rosina is not discouraged, as she very succinctly announces in her brief recitative (track 7). I am sure that by now you have noticed how these brief recitatives serve the dual purpose of commenting on what has just been said and functioning as the transition to the next scene. The first act of this opera is more than ninety minutes long and has sixteen scenes, most of them quite brief, so the transitions are much more important than in the other operas we've learned. (A "scene" in this sense usually implies the arrival or departure of a character, though not necessarily a change of scenery. You can see changes of settings indicated in the libretto.)

We then have another brief comment from the still-sneezing Berta before advancing to a big scene of conflict: the arrival of Almaviva disguised as a drunken soldier. He meets Bartolo, whom he proceeds to irritate by mispronouncing the doctor's name in increasingly insulting and humorous ways. Rosina slips into the room (unnoticed by Bartolo) and Almaviva quietly reveals to her that he is "Lindoro." Notice how subtly Rosina enters in musical terms. Her voice joins a duet already in progress, and we only casually make note of her entry. Eventually, as you will hear, Bartolo notes her presence.

Throughout this scene there is a lot of stage business going on: drunken embraces, Rosina's attempts to avoid being noticed, the passing of a note from Almaviva to Rosina, Rosina's sleight of hand as she switches Almaviva's note with a laundry list, and so on. You need to read the stage directions carefully and also to listen for the moments in the music when these pieces of business are taking place. Rossini makes this wonderfully clear. He was a great man of the theater and knew that audience members in the back of the auditorium also had to know what was happening, so he used the music as well as the words to indicate these actions. For example, there is Rosina's extended, exaggerated "Grazie, grazie" (bottom of page 134) as she switches the two pieces of paper.

With the entry of Berta (still expressing bewilderment) and Basilio (absorbed in notes for a music lesson) we have the beginning of what will build to a midsized Rossini crescendo, with all of the characters expressing their ideas to themselves, occasionally to each other, and occasionally to us. The ensuing confusion, as depicted musically, is a palpable example of Rossini's comic genius. Despite the chaos, we in the audience know what is going on and we savor every moment of it. Notice how the mounting fury of the crescendo slows at key points, only to pick up again. The scene takes on an added dimension as Figaro enters and breaks up the confusion. His is the hand behind most of these events, and he has arrived to stir the pot some more. Notice that the stage direction calls for him to arrive with the shaving sink under his arm. What could this be for? Is it simply a prop that we associate with a barber? Is it supposed to suggest that his work was interrupted when he had to come break up a fight heard by half the town? The answer is for you to decide.

As the insults continue to fly, the music and the speed of the scene pick up again, until there is another interruption: a pounding at the door. I mention this and all of the other such instances throughout this act to show you how carefully crafted this opera is in musical and dramatic terms. You must realize by now that our ability to perceive humor has been carefully calibrated and manipulated by the creators of *Il Barbiere di Siviglia*.

As everyone is silenced by the knocking, we catch our breath (as do the singers) before we plunge into what we think will be the wild finale to the first act. Yet there is another halt: as Almaviva reveals his true identity to the officer (track 9), the pause of "general astonishment," which is broken up only by strings and a flute, brings everyone to a halt. Each character then reveals his or her view of the proceedings ("Fredda ed immobile") in a very slow buildup to the huge crescendo of the finale. Note how Figaro stands apart to comment about what is happening, and listen to how Rossini uses voices to pick up the pace. Finally, in track 10, we have the effect of a musical roller coaster as the great concluding series of crescendi arrives. Notice how the words tell us that each character senses a great din in his or her head, like the pounding of anvils. In fact, in reading this thirteen-line passage, you realize that Rossini evoked every word carefully and brilliantly in this music that raucously concludes Act I.

Read the synopsis for Act II, then begin listening (disk 3, track 1). Notice how, after all the commotion at the end of Act I, the first sounds we hear in Act II are the hesitant strains of the harpsichord. After Bartolo's brief comments, we are set for the next clash between Almaviva and Bartolo. This time Almaviva gains entry dressed as a music teacher named "Don Alonso," ostensibly to give Rosina her singing lesson. "Alonso" is there to replace the allegedly ailing Don Basilio. Notice how "Don Alonso," though a tenor, adopts the unctuous tones of Don Basilio. The hypocritical niceties exchanged by Don Alonso and Bartolo, of course, are insults. Finally, "Don Alonso" convinces Bartolo to bring forth Rosina by presenting what is allegedly a love letter she wrote.

You may wonder why Rosina can recognize the disguised Almaviva while Bartolo cannot. This is a theatrical convention: we must assume that a woman in love would sense her beloved while a distracted old man would not notice. (Mozart played with this convention of lovers recognizing or not recognizing one another in *Così fan tutte*, a sophisticated psychological comedy that is too often presented merely as a sex farce.)

In Rosina's aria (track 4), she sings long enough for old Bartolo to doze off before she quickly tells Almaviva of her confinement. The humor in this scene comes as Bartolo stirs and Rosina must go back to her "music lesson." Bartolo then sings his ridiculous arietta (little aria) as Figaro arrives, basin again under his arm, to give Bartolo a shave. More stage business happens as Figaro manages to get the keys from Bartolo that later will be used to liberate Rosina. In the meantime, Rosina tells Almaviva (who she thinks is "Lindoro") that she will be his.

The shaving scene (track 8) is another priceless musical segment. This quintet begins with the surprise arrival of Don Basilio, who is not ill after all, and continues with Figaro shaving Bartolo to distract the old man from all that is happening in the room. Finally, a purse of money convinces Basilio that he really is sick ("Go and take some medicine") and he is told to go straight to bed ("Presto a letto"). What follows is a humorously prolonged scene of farewells ("Buona sera") as Basilio is shoved out the door. Rosina and Almaviva plan for her midnight escape, and then Bartolo suddenly realizes that "Don Alonso" was someone else in disguise. In a transitional recitative (track 10) Bartolo laments his foolishness and the way he is being taken advantage of.

We now have a solo aria by Berta, the maid (track 11). In many productions this aria is omitted for reasons of time. This is a shame, because it is a delightful interlude that comments on the frailties of the other characters and the peculiar nature of love, which, after all, is the motor behind much of this story. The aria also gives the other singers needed rest before the next big scene. Clearly, Rossini would not have included this aria if it was not important. Too often, opera houses and conductors cut music from operas for reasons of economics. If an opera runs long, overtime has to be paid to stagehands, ushers, and orchestra and chorus members.

Basilio returns after being summoned by Bartolo and reveals that "Don Alonso" may be the Count. Bartolo then tells Rosina that her beloved (whom she still calls "Lindoro") has been unfaithful. To get even with "Lindoro," she agrees to marry Bartolo that evening. All of these plot twists are devices to lead up to a confused finale and its ultimate resolution.

We then have a thunderstorm (track 13), which includes the arrival of Figaro and Almaviva to fetch Rosina. Notice how the sound of this storm is different from the one in *Rigoletto* and, for that matter, the brief storm in *Lucia di Lammermoor;* each is intended to serve the action occurring in the opera at that moment. The *Rigoletto* storm is menacing (suggesting to us Gilda's impending demise), while this storm, though at least as full of precipitation, is in a more comic vein. Notice how it approaches, builds, rages, and then dies down.

During this storm Figaro and Almaviva climb into Bartolo's house. Rosina repulses "Lindoro" until he reveals his true identity. When the Count discovers that Rosina loved him as a man and not because of his station in life, he is filled with joy. Rosina, once she learns the truth, is also overjoyed. Now that this part of the plot confusion is resolved (and following a lovely trio in which Figaro joins in), we move one step closer to the finale.

When Figaro suddenly discovers that the ladder—their means of escape—is gone, all seems doomed. As you continue to follow the recitative, including the arrival of Don Basilio and the notary, notice how quickly a gold ring and a pistol can turn Basilio into a witness to the marriage of Almaviva and Rosina. Bartolo arrives with soldiers to arrest the men who broke into his house. Almaviva again reveals his identity, and Bartolo is defeated. In the aria "Cessa di più resistere" (track 18) the Count asserts his authority and attempts to restore order. He will marry Rosina, love will triumph over greed, and Bartolo will be forced to accept the circumstances. This is made easier in the finale when Almaviva allows Bartolo to keep Rosina's dowry. Love may have indeed triumphed over greed, but that is only because Almaviva is wealthy enough to have paid Figaro and Basilio. But this opera is not about the class struggle in quite the explicit way that *Le Nozze di Figaro* is. *Il Barbiere di Siviglia* was meant to be comic entertainment, and its creators succeeded handsomely.

While the finale seems to have come with Almaviva's aria, the resolution of the issue of the dowry occurs in a brief recitative before the opera concludes in a finaletto, a second small finale, in which the characters come forward to tell the audience about the power of love to vanquish evil intentions. This moralizing coda is typical of eighteenth-century classical opera. Since *Barbiere* was based on an eighteenth-century play, Rossini honored the convention. When you study the operas of Mozart (beginning with *Don Giovanni* in the next chapter), you will see the moralizing coda as an efficient and pleasing means of sending the audience home.

Now that the opera is over, you will probably wonder if you got every joke. When you see a performance, you will find that much more humor is added onstage as singers show off their acting skills. If, on the other hand, you happen to attend a performance with a boring Rosina, Bartolo, and Figaro, you are in for a long night even if they are wonderful singers. Your goal in learning any comic opera is to decide where the librettist and composer placed the humor and then to see how conductor, stage director, and singers can heighten it.

As an alternative to *Il Barbiere di Siviglia,* I commend to you another comic masterpiece by Rossini: *L'Italiana in Algeri.* There is a superb recording on Erato conducted by Claudio Scimone and starring Horne, Ramey, and Kathleen Battle. In addition to the splendid septet that closes Act I, there are many wonderful comic scenes throughout. One particularly priceless scene, which runs on the same premise as the shaving scene in *Il Barbiere,* occurs when Isabella (a character at least as clever as Rosina) silences and humiliates Mustafà to distract him from what is going on around him. This is the "Pappataci" scene. Use the skills you have developed in reading and hearing your first four operas (and particularly *Il Barbiere di Siviglia*) to appreciate the brilliant *L'Italiana in Algeri.*

We will now go on to Mozart's *Don Giovanni,* which many opera lovers consider the greatest opera ever written. I would never venture an opinion as to which opera is the greatest, but *Don Giovanni* would certainly appear on my short list. It is an opera of enormous complexity, but I believe you are now ready to approach it.

8.

DON GIOVANNI

CLASSICAL OPERA

There are three things in the world I love most—the sea, Hamlet, *and* Don Giovanni.

—Gustave Flaubert

ozart's *Don Giovanni* is among the most exalted of all operas. I would argue that other works, including *Le Nozze di Figaro* and *Rigoletto,* are more perfect in their construction. The shifting scenes and action in *Don Giovanni* make it a real challenge to stage directors. The story is not quite realistic: although many of the characters have emotions and responses like those of everyday people, the magical and supernatural elements, which might have been plausible in 1787, strain credulity in the late twentieth century. The title character, an old-fashioned male chauvinist rake, is certainly not any modern person's idea of politically correct; to many, in fact, he is a glorified rapist. Yet the writer and composer E. T. A. Hoffmann called *Don Giovanni* "the opera of all operas," and many other leading musical and artistic figures in the past two hundred years have concurred. It seems that the themes and ideas in *Don Giovanni* touch listeners in each generation in some way, if not necessarily the same way.

Part of the greatness of this opera, as in all of the most towering works of art and nature, is that it does not offer easy answers. The sea, *Hamlet,* and *Don Giovanni* are all mysterious, universal, and have multiple meanings to each person who encounters them. In fact, when the same person comes to the sea, *Hamlet,* or *Don Giovanni* at different points in life or in different frames of mind, new meanings and insights can be gained.

We can appreciate *Don Giovanni* for its indisputably sublime music. We can argue and speculate endlessly about the moral choices of its leading characters. We can debate the implications suggested by its dramatic situations: Do we pay for our sins? Can sex without love be meaningful? Do the morals and values of Mozart's time still apply to us two hundred years later?

In addition to its many other virtues, this is an opera of ideas. We will explore this concept further when we study Wagner's *Tannhäuser,* but this is your first exposure to a work that was born in a strong philosophical context and provokes debate based on how each one of us perceives its meaning. *Don Giovanni* is a product of the end of the eighteenth century, a period of political upheaval and social revolution. The old aristocracy was confronted with the values of individualism and the rights of man that were being promoted in France and America. Scientific advances also made people think differently about the earth and the universe. All of this new thinking was part of the environment in which Mozart and Lorenzo da Ponte, his librettist, were working. One of their great contributions to opera was the introduction of political and philosophical ferment to the operatic stage.

One of the many ways this opera can be interpreted is as an assertion of the value of man in the face of God. In fact, *Don Giovanni* can be viewed as a challenge to the very existence of both God and Satan. The subtitle of this opera is *Il Dissoluto Punito* (The Dissolute Punished): the title character dies at the end and presumably goes to Hell. But was Don Giovanni punished by a higher being, or was he simply paying the wages of sin? In other words, is there a divine hand in our actions and our fate, or are we our own masters? It can certainly be argued that Don Giovanni led a contented life and had no regrets when his time was up (as you will discover, he never repents). Mozart and da Ponte elected to present these characters and issues to us, but they do not offer an opinion about them.

I do not wish to suggest that our first four operas are inferior to *Don Giovanni*—they are all masterpieces—only that the goals of their creators were different, as were the eras when they were created. *Rigoletto, Tosca, Lucia,* and *Barbiere* all deal in marginal ways with politics and social issues, but they are not works that cause us to explore deeply the philosophical and moral implications of the characters' actions and statements. Rigoletto, for example, is a complex character with good and bad sides, but we empathize with his situation rather than question his actions. Of your first four operas, the one that is closest to *Don Giovanni* is *Il Barbiere di Siviglia,* both musically and in the strong presence of eighteenth-century values. Also, both operas take place in Seville, the Spanish city that has served as the locale for such disparate operas as *Le Nozze di Figaro, Fidelio,* and *Carmen.*

You might ask why *Don Giovanni* was not the first opera we studied. I think that a mistake many newcomers to opera make (or are encouraged to make) is believing that the works of Mozart are good for absolute beginners. Mozart's music is so beautiful that the assumption is often made that neophytes will enjoy listening to it no matter what is happening onstage. But his music is also quite complex and challenging to opera newcomers. In addition, the drama in Mozart's works is often baffling or seemingly inconsequential. The stories and emotions are quite subtle and require much preparation to be fully appreciated. The Classical era is quite removed from our own. Most of our social and philosophical values (not counting those that derive from religion) come from the nineteenth and twentieth centuries. Similarly, much of the "classical" music we listen to comes from the nineteenth-century Romantic tradition: Beethoven (a transitional figure from the Classical era to Romanticism), Schubert, Schumann, Chopin, Mendelssohn, Berlioz, Brahms, Wagner, Verdi, Tchaikovsky, Bruckner, Liszt, Grieg, and early Mahler, to name a few. Somehow, the music of Mozart, Haydn, Handel, Bach, Vivaldi, and most of the other great composers from before 1800 is consigned to a different form of appreciation. Too many people listen to these composers while eating brunch or pursuing hobbies—in other words, as background music. This is profoundly unfair, since theirs are the shoulders on which the nineteenth-century composers stand. In addition, the music from the Baroque and Classical eras is often performed in conjunction with Christian religious observances, so that some listeners think it to be a different kind of music from that heard in the concert hall or the opera house. Yet, as you know from reading the first chapter of this book, one of the main sources of opera was religion, whether in church ritual or morality plays.

Yet Mozart is a singular figure in musical history. His music—at least his most famous achievements—is immensely popular. Many of his symphonies and concerti and a few operas have remained in the standard repertory since their creation. This is not only due to their inherent beauty but because Mozart had great champions and admirers (especially Mendelssohn, Tchaikovsky, and Richard Strauss) who played and promoted his music. Festivals featuring his music are routinely held around the world, including Mostly Mozart at New York's Lincoln Center and the Salzburg Festival in the Austrian city that was his birthplace. Nonetheless, as time goes on and the eighteenth century becomes more distant, we become more removed from the values that shaped the art and morals of that time. So it is my conviction that a newcomer to opera needs to understand some of the operas that followed those of Mozart before moving back to his time.

Many of the characters you came to know in *Rigoletto, Tosca, Lucia di Lammermoor,* and *Il Barbiere di Siviglia* have temperamental and dramatic links to characters in *Don Giovanni.* The title character is as licentious as the Duke of Mantua and as charming as Figaro. Donna Anna has the pathos and rage of Lucia. Donna Elvira has the passion and jealousy of Tosca. Zerlina is clever and resourceful like Rosina. Leporello, Don Giovanni's servant, has some of the jester in him, à la Rigoletto, combined with Figaro's insouciant attitude toward authority. His is the voice of the common man. Don Ottavio has some of the uprightness and nobility of *Lucia*'s Edgardo, although many people nowadays think him to be a wimp. The Commendatore will make you think of *Rigoletto*'s Monterone, whose purpose is to avenge a wrong that has been done to a loved one.

We have seen elements of *Don Giovanni* in each of the operas we have studied. There is the impending sense of doom coupled with festivity that one finds in *Rigoletto*. There is sexual blackmail and ferocious drama, as in *Tosca*. There is hysteria and the presence of ghosts and apparitions, as in *Lucia di Lammermoor*. And there is brilliant comedy as well as harpsichord-accompanied recitative, as in *Il Barbiere di Siviglia*. Coincidentally, there is a storm in this opera too, although I must tell you that I did not require that the operas selected for your instruction have a meteorological episode.

Don Giovanni himself is one of the most challenging and prismatic characters in all of opera. We all see different things in him. To some he is a hero, to others he is an antihero, to others he is despicable. Every great artist who portrays him brings special personal characteristics to the role. The two great Dons in the middle of the twentieth century were Ezio Pinza and Cesare Siepi. Their recordings are classics, and as you come to love this opera, you should seek out these performances. In our day we have several fine Dons, including Thomas Allen, Thomas Hampson, James Morris, Ruggero Raimondi, and Samuel Ramey. We will be hearing Raimondi, who, I believe, brings more facets to the role than his contemporaries. His Don Giovanni is elegant, aristocratic, seductive, cynical, dangerous, and always very musical. With his superior diction in his native Italian he caresses, growls, barks, and sweetens words to make each one meaningful.

Raimondi starred in a film version of *Don Giovanni* that is the source of the recording we are using. Each artist on the recording appeared in the film, which was directed by Joseph Losey and is one of the best opera films ever made. The conductor is Lorin Maazel and the singers include Kiri Te Kanawa, Edda Moser, Teresa Berganza, and José van Dam. There is only one weak link: Kenneth Riegel as Don Ottavio. It is crucial to have a cast as strong as this one. While this opera could not succeed without a great artist in the title role, there are several important characters in *Don Giovanni*.

There are three women in the opera, each of whom responds to the Don in her own way and brings out different aspects of him. Donna Anna is a noblewoman whose father, the Commendatore, is killed after initiating a duel with Don Giovanni at the start of the opera. Prior to that, she had experienced her first sexual awakening thanks to the Don. By "awakening" I do not necessarily mean actual sexual intercourse (that is up to you to determine) but, rather, the unleashing of erotic feelings that were previously suppressed or undiscovered. That Donna Anna's most powerful sexual feelings are connected to the man who kills her father makes her life complicated, to say the least. Donna Anna is engaged to Don Ottavio, who is solid, loyal, coolheaded, and rather dull. What we have is the old story of a woman torn between the boyfriend type and the husband type. In the end, Anna puts off her wedding to Ottavio. The vocal type for Donna Anna is unusual for Mozart. It has been sung by dramatic sopranos such as Birgit Nilsson and Hildegard Behrens, who generally specialize in Wagner heroines. Powerful coloraturas such as Joan Sutherland have also sung the role, as have lyric-dramatic sopranos such as Carol Vaness. Our Anna is Edda Moser, who has disappeared from the opera scene in recent years. She brings power, a decent coloratura technique, nobility, and passion to this difficult role.

Donna Elvira is a different sort of character. In Mozart's day she was viewed as the woman seduced and then abandoned. Yet her anger and her efforts at revenge often seemed funny to eighteenth-century audiences and provided a degree of comic relief from the high stakes of Donna Anna's dilemma. In our times, we often see Elvira as a person who grows in understanding and tolerance as the opera progresses. While Anna is on a downward spiral to inevitable unhappiness, Elvira becomes stronger and more insightful. Toward the end of the opera she says that she feels pity for the Don. This can be interpreted to mean that she is a foolish pushover who doesn't learn from her own mistakes, or that her sophistication has grown to the point where her anger has subsided and her ability to accept her circumstances and others' weaknesses has grown. As Elvira, we will hear Kiri Te Kanawa in one of her finest roles. She has often been called the best Mozart soprano of her generation. Certainly her Elvira, Countess Almaviva *(Le Nozze di Figaro),* and Fiordiligi *(Così fan tutte)* are exquisite creations that make reviewers compare her singing to honey, cream, and silk. For operagoers who think of Te Kanawa as a beautiful, placid woman with an artistic temperament to match, her Elvira comes as quite a shock. She burns with fire and passion that is a combination of lust and jealousy.

The third woman is Zerlina, a peasant girl Don Giovanni meets and woos on her wedding day. Zerlina is not a lady of high standing like Anna and Elvira, but she is also unencumbered by the social constraints that afflict women in upper-class Seville. When the Don woos her, she flirts back. Unlike Anna and Elvira, who fly into great rages, Zerlina remains in control of her fate. She enjoys playing with the emotions of Masetto, her jealous fiancé; she provokes him to stand up to the Don and enjoys kissing his wounds when he is badly beaten. Zerlina is often played by a soubrette soprano of the Roberta Peters–Kathleen Battle type. This recording has a piece of unusual casting that succeeds brilliantly. Teresa Berganza, one of the great mezzos of the postwar era, is a very sensuous Zerlina. Although hers is a voice that shares a lot with Marilyn Horne's in texture and tone, Berganza lightens it somewhat to sing Zerlina.

Leporello, Don Giovanni's servant, is continually beaten and abused by the Don and frequently complains of his lot, yet he has his own great brand of charm and humanity. In some productions Leporello is wrongly presented as a superficial buffo type, but he is not a Dr. Bartolo. In the best performances, Leporello is a fully developed character who participates in all of the actions of the opera and has a broad range of feelings. He must also be able to impersonate Don Giovanni in one crucial scene. In this recording our Leporello is the superb José van Dam.

The final character is the Commendatore, Donna Anna's father and an imposing figure in life as well as death. In one of the surreal elements of this opera, the statue of the Commendatore that stands atop the old man's grave speaks. Don Giovanni invites the statue to dinner, the statue accepts. I will not tell you any more about this confrontation between Don Giovanni and his stone dinner guest. The durable bass John Macurdy was in fine voice when this recording was made.

You have probably noticed that Mozart's palette of voices is rather unusual. We have four low male voices (Giovanni, Leporello, the Commendatore, and the baritone Masetto) and only one tenor (the stiff, awkward Don Ottavio). Anna is a powerful soprano, Elvira is usually sung by a lyric soprano or, occasionally, a high mezzo. Zerlina is often a soubrette, and sometimes a mezzo. So *Don Giovanni,* with the exception of Don Ottavio, is an opera featuring low male voices and high females. As you listen to the music, note how Mozart creates great musical variety among the voices. We always know who is Don Giovanni, who is Leporello, and who is the Commendatore, even when they are singing together.

You would expect that the creators of an opera that is so universally admired spent long months and years to produce it, but another amazing thing about *Don Giovanni* is the speed with which it was created. The commission came from the Royal Theatre in Prague early in 1787 to create an opera that would star the twenty-one-year-old Italian baritone Luigi Bassi, who had a smashing success as the Count in the Prague premiere of *Le Nozze di Figaro* a few months earlier. Mozart and da Ponte were attracted to the story of Don Juan, and the librettist set to work. Da Ponte was particularly eager to create a brilliant libretto to outdo a treatment of the Don Juan story earlier that year in Venice. The character originally had appeared in *El Burlador de Sevilla,* a 1630 play by Tirso de Molina. Don Juan appeared again in plays by Molière and Goldoni and in several operatic settings. Da Ponte drew from all of these sources, discarded some characters and scenes, created a couple of new situations, and produced a libretto that was very attuned to contemporary thought in 1787. He and Mozart referred to *Don Giovanni* as a "dramma giocoso," or humorous drama. It is true that there are moments of high comedy in this opera, but you can hear from the very first notes that the opera is full of strong emotions, profound thought and great tragedy. How could an opera so full of violence and cruelty be otherwise?

Mozart still had not composed much of the music by September 1787, and the opening night was set for October 29. He worked quickly (and obviously with great inspiration) almost up to opening night. It is said that he wrote the overture less than forty-eight hours before the curtain went up. The reception at the first night was the greatest of Mozart's career. The opera was less warmly received at its Vienna premiere in 1788. Emperor Joseph II is reported to have remarked that "the opera is heavenly, even more beautiful than *Figaro,* but not food for the teeth of my Viennese." Mozart is said to have responded (under his breath), "Well, then give them time to chew on it!"

Let us now begin to study *Don Giovanni*. Read the cast list on page 3 of the libretto booklet and then read the essay on page 11. What this booklet sorely lacks—this was a real oversight by the company that released it—is a synopsis. By now, however, you are up to the challenge of going straight to the libretto. When the text is as vibrant and as beautifully constructed as this one is, you will have few problems. This is now the time for you to rise to intermediate status as an opera cognoscente. You have learned more than you realize and you will be able to use this background to approach *Don Giovanni* under your own power. Nonetheless, I will still give you guidance along the way. But, starting with this recording, you will be bringing more of yourself to learning an opera.

The overture to *Don Giovanni* sweeps us right into the action and the story. As I mentioned, Mozart wrote this overture just before the opera's premiere, but the haste with which it was written does not in any way diminish its impact. Unlike Rossini's overture to *Il Barbiere di Siviglia*, the overture to *Don Giovanni* is very specific to this opera. In fact, much of the music in the overture is drawn from the opera. The famous surging chords that start the overture foreshadow the great encounter between Don Giovanni and the Commendatore in the penultimate scene of the opera. Gradually though, the powerful drama metamorphoses into a buoyant sweetness, and by the overture's end the chill we felt from the opening chords has been warmed. Notice how the overture leads directly to the action rather than being a Rossini-style symphonic overture that we applaud before the action begins.

In the first scene, Leporello is already grousing about having to serve Don Giovanni. We know that this is hardly the first time he has complained this way. This aria is a typical dramatic device that goes back to the Greeks and is used today: one character talks about the leading character. In this way, we learn about two people at once and will also be able to compare Leporello's views of Don Giovanni with our own.

The mood created by this amusing introduction is shattered by the entry of Donna Anna and Don Giovanni, who is wearing a mask. After their furious quarrel (Is he trying to rape her? Although it is not stated, it is a fair assumption), Anna runs into her house. Her cries have summoned her father, the Commendatore, who challenges Giovanni to a duel. The Commendatore is killed. Anna returns with her fiancé, Don Ottavio, and they discover her dead father. Anna makes Ottavio vow to avenge the death of the Commendatore (track 5: "Fuggi, crudele.") Notice one important line uttered by Ottavio to Anna: "You have in me both betrothed and father." This may be noble, but is it what Anna wants?

What is so remarkable in this opening sequence is the speed with which so many events have set up actions and relationships that affect the course of the story. Although they were introduced quickly, they are by no means superficial. We have already learned much about Leporello, Giovanni, Anna, the Commendatore, and Ottavio. Note specifically that Giovanni has shown no remorse for his actions toward Anna or his murder of her father. If anything, he is frustrated that his seduction of Anna was foiled. Leporello, ever the ironic reporter of things as they are, puts it best: "Well done! Two pretty exploits: to ravish the girl and butcher her father."

We now switch to a street in Seville for scene 4 (track 6). It is early in the morning after the night of the murder of the Commendatore (do not be misled when Leporello refers to it as "this hour of night"—it is at the clear light of dawn). Despite the events of last night, all Giovanni is thinking about is another sexual conquest. He is so intent on this that he can perceive the scent of a woman before he can see her. The woman who appears, Donna Elvira, is barreling down the street complaining aloud about having recently been seduced and abandoned. Giovanni, not yet aware that he is the seducer in question, tells Leporello that he intends to console the lady. (The same way he has consoled eighteen hundred other women, Leporello remarks as an aside.) Once recognized, the Don makes a halfhearted attempt to placate Elvira, who thought he really loved her, and Leporello must come forward to make excuses for his master. What follows (track 9) is Leporello's famous catalog aria ("Madamina! Il catalogo è questo"). Leporello tells us that the Don cares little about what kind of woman he has sex with, although he prefers inexperienced girls. José van Dam does a brilliant job with this classic number, which is the prototype of catalog arias.

Do you think Leporello is proud of his master's accomplishments, or is he highly cynical? This is a good example of a phenomenon that occurs throughout the opera: depending on the interpretations of the singers, the conductor, and the stage director, many of the actions, ideas, and intentions of each character can be interpreted differently. The results vary depending upon the combinations that occur. A loyal Leporello with a seductive Don Giovanni will give off different sparks than a cynical Leporello with a seductive Don; and if the Don is more evil than alluring, the effect will be different again. With the addition of every character, the variables for dramatic variety increase exponentially. A vengeful Elvira will interact differently with a cynical Leporello than a woman who is highly aroused sexually. An angry Anna will interact differently than a repressed one. I have seen more than fifty performances of *Don Giovanni,* and one of the enduring fascinations of this great work is to note the interpretive choices made by each performer and to observe how they merge in ways that I have not previously seen.

You will notice in the libretto (page 66) that the brief scene in which Elvira vows revenge has been omitted. It is probable that it was removed because Joseph Losey, the director of the film, believed that her desire for revenge was obvious. Making excisions in operas has been customary for centuries. For example, as I mentioned in the previous chapter, Berta's aria in *Il Barbiere di Siviglia* is often omitted. Excisions and omissions in opera are, in general, a regrettable practice that has diminished somewhat in recent years. This is due in part to the efforts of conductors such as Claudio Abbado, Sir Charles Mackerras, James Levine and Riccardo Muti, who have often emphasized the importance of fidelity to the intentions of composers and librettists.

The next scene (page 68, track 10) takes place in a wooded glade near Giovanni's palace where peasants are celebrating the marriage of Zerlina and Masetto. Giovanni, glad to be rid of Elvira, enters and espies the pretty Zerlina. He decides to pursue her and sends Masetto and all of the other peasants to his palace, where wine, music, and food will be in abundance. Although Masetto resists, he cannot as a peasant challenge the orders of the upper-class Don Giovanni. Zerlina, it must be said, is flattered by the attention of the Don and enjoys making Masetto jealous. When Don Giovanni courts her in the famous duet "Là ci darem la mano" (track 14, page 84), Zerlina delights in being wooed, but we are not certain if she will submit to Giovanni's advances.

As it turns out, Elvira, angrier than before, arrives and warns Zerlina not to be deceived, encouraging her to leave before she gets hurt ("Ah! Fuggi il traditor!" page 88, track 16). She leads Zerlina away. As Giovanni again observes that lately all of his plans seem to go awry, Ottavio and Anna interrupt his musings. They tell Giovanni that they need his friendship (don't forget, in scene 1 it was nighttime and Giovanni was concealing his identity), but the furious Elvira bursts in before they can tell him why. Elvira thinks that Giovanni is now trying to seduce Anna. This was a moment of humor for eighteenth-century audiences: we now take it seriously because we find Elvira more sympathetic and less ridiculous than people did in Mozart's time. By the end of this beautiful quartet, in which each voice reveals the particular feelings of the character, Anna and Ottavio do not know whom to believe: is Giovanni lying or is Elvira insane?

This question is brilliantly answered in the music that immediately follows Giovanni's hurried departure (track 20). In the pounding chords of the orchestra we hear Anna's sudden realization that the voice of the man they were seeking help from was that of the killer of her father. In the highly dramatic scene that follows, Anna recalls how Giovanni forced himself upon her and subsequently murdered her father. Listen, in Anna's aria "Or sai chi l'onore" (page 106, track 21), to the unusual contrast of her rather strident vocal line and the orchestral comment that accompanies it. Do the milling strings and lilting oboe sound incongruous given the subject matter and the way it is being described in the voice? There are many ways to interpret this choice. I think the orchestra is reminding us of the noble underpinnings of this well-bred lady who is temporarily losing her composure and showing real flashes of fire.

Following this flaming aria is one of Mozart's most exquisite creations, Don Ottavio's "Dalla sua pace." In an opening recitative he wonders how a nobleman such as Don Giovanni could be so dastardly and then vows to do all that he can to avenge the suffering of Anna. In fact, Ottavio has two beautiful arias in this opera, the other being "Il mio tesoro" in Act II. It is frequently remarked that Mozart did not much care for the tenor voice and chose to give better roles to lower male voices (Giovanni and Leporello here, Figaro and Almaviva in *Le Nozze di Figaro*). This may be true, but he surely did not shortchange tenors with roles such as Tamino in *Die Zauberflöte*, the title characters in *Idomeneo* and *La Clemenza di Tito*, Belmonte in *Die Entführung aus dem Serail*, Ferrando in *Così fan tutte*, and Don Ottavio.

Ottavio, unfortunately, has become something of a laughable character in modern times. He is a sort of Sevillian Dudley Doright, who has good intentions but is so stiff and uncharismatic that many women (including Donna Anna) ultimately question why they would want to be with this nice bore. You just know he is a poor conversationalist and an uninspired lover and that life spent with him would be comfortable drudgery. The way most tenors who sing Ottavio become persuasive is in their performance of the two arias. Ottavio's solo music is so meltingly beautiful that a tenor who understands it and has the technique to perform it can almost walk away with the vocal honors at a performance of *Don Giovanni*. While Kenneth Riegel is a good, solid performer, he does not capture the sweet lyricism of Ottavio's music. It could be that he decided (or was encouraged) to emphasize the Dudley Doright aspects of the role, which certainly helps us understand why Anna may harbor a deep-down attraction for Giovanni despite the Don's awful deeds: at least he sets her hormones coursing. If you can find CD reissues of recordings of Ottavio's arias by John McCormack, Richard Tauber, or Jussi Björling, you will have a better idea of how gorgeous these arias can be.

We are now at the start of the second disk and have reached the fifteenth scene of the opera. Librettists and composers all have different notions of what constitutes a scene. In fast-moving operas such as *Don Giovanni* and *Il Barbiere di Siviglia*, scenes are short and flow directly into one another. In *Lucia* the scenes are longer and more distinguishable. As often as not in operas such as *Lucia* there will be changes of scenery to indicate the new locales. Performances may come to a complete stop while the scenery changes. In other operas, particularly those of Wagner, there is music in between the scenes so that if scenery is being changed the audience's concentration on the drama is maintained by the music. In Wagner's operas the scenery is sometimes changed as the audience watches, at other times either with darkened lights or a lowered curtain.

Scenic designers for operas such as *Don Giovanni* and *Il Barbiere di Siviglia* face a different and more difficult task. With so many scene changes (*Don Giovanni* has thirty-six scenes), scenery must be able to move to suggest new locales. For example, it is possible to design a production of this opera in which the large pieces of scenery are stationary and suggest a Sevillian ambience; then smaller pieces of scenery, costumes, lighting, and props can serve to make each scene specific. This is where better-equipped theaters have an advantage. The area above the proscenium arch (in other words, high above the singers' heads and out of view of the audience) is called the fly space. It is here that horizontal metal rods called *battens* hang. Pieces of scenery can be attached to the battens and the battens can be made to "fly"—that is, they can be raised and lowered to effect changes of scene. In this way, for example, battens with scenery suggesting Donna Anna's house can fly out (up) at the end of scene 3 as other battens with scenery suggesting a street in Seville can be flown in (down) for scene 4. This change can happen in seconds as characters walk on and off the stage. The Metropolitan Opera House has more than one hundred battens in the fly space, of which thirty can be used in a single production.

With the start of scene 15 (disk 2, track 1), we are at Don Giovanni's palace. Leporello has been getting the peasants drunk and muttering to himself about leaving the service of the self-gratifying Giovanni. Presently the Don arrives. You would expect him to be a bit rattled by his encounters with Elvira, Anna, and Ottavio, but all he can think about is eating, drinking, dancing, and sex with a dozen "country wenches" ("Fin ch'han dal vino," track 2).

The scene shifts to a garden outside, where Zerlina begs Masetto to forgive her seeming infidelity on their wedding day. Her music is coquettish, but the words are rather forceful ("beat me . . . pull out my eyes"). At the sound of Giovanni's voice, Zerlina is frightened and Masetto is again suspicious. He hides as Giovanni arrives. After sending the peasants away for more revelry, the Don resumes his wooing of Zerlina, who is more reluctant than before. She is fearful of what the jealous Masetto may do to Don Giovanni, who, it must be remembered, is an aristocrat. Masetto's anger cools enough so that, at the Don's invitation, the three of them return to the party as the distant sound of dancing music is heard.

Donna Elvira, Donna Anna, and Don Ottavio arrive, all wearing masks. They are trying to muster the courage to confront Giovanni for his evil doings. They are interrupted by the sound of a minuet (track 9, 1:04). This agreeable music gives us a brief pause before the anxiety heightens. Leporello then invites the masked guests inside (cynically observing that here are two more potential conquests for Giovanni). Anna, Elvira, and Ottavio pray for strength in a gorgeous trio ("Protegga il giusto cielo," track 10).

The lights of the ballroom illuminate the final scene of Act I. This scene is full of action. Leporello attempts to distract Masetto so that the Don can dance with Zerlina, finally bringing her to an adjoining room where he attempts to have sex with her. She cries for help, breaks free, and runs back into the ballroom. Giovanni pins the blame for Zerlina's seduction on Leporello, although no one believes that story. Anna, Elvira, and Ottavio denounce Don Giovanni, Zerlina and Masetto join in with their contempt, and poor Leporello has even more reason to be angry with his master.

Read the lyrics carefully and listen to the music that goes with each line. In this way, you will have a fair sense of the action even though you are sitting at home. This music is quite evocative. Note certain lyrics as well. On page 142, when all the characters sing "Viva la libertà" ("Let freedom reign!"), we understand that "freedom" has a different meaning for each one of them. This is a brilliant coup de théâtre on the part of da Ponte and Mozart. It is ironic, revealing, intensely political, and crystallizes in an instant the emotional and social state of each character.

As you listen to the music of track 12, Anna and Ottavio nervously dance the minuet (in 3/4 time), Giovanni and Zerlina dance the contredanse (usually done in 2/4 or 6/8 time, the latter being twice the speed of the minuet), and the unlikely couple of Masetto and Leporello dance an allemande (in 4/4 time). Even if you don't read music, you can understand that each couple is dancing at a different speed to different music played simultaneously. This makes the scene both comic and indicative of how out of sync each character is with everyone else in this tense situation. Nonetheless, the music proceeds in a genteel fashion until we hear Zerlina's sudden cry from the adjoining room "Gente! . . . Aiuto!" (page 146, track 12, 3:30). Notice how the strings in the orchestra, which were playing the polite dance music, begin to whirl as the action picks up. After Giovanni unsuccessfully blames Leporello, the others tell Giovanni that they know about all his guilt.

The close to Act I (page 152, track 14) is a perfect ensemble that is the musical and dramatic summation of the action and a foreshadowing of Act II. Zerlina, Masetto, Anna, Elvira, and Ottavio all swear vengeance against Giovanni. The Don is angry at the storm of emotions and problems caused by the day's events and bothered that things have not been going his way lately, yet he insists that he is not afraid of his accusers or anything else. Leporello, for once, actually echoes the Don's sentiments: he may not like his master, but he realizes that even the wrath of God will not frighten Don Giovanni. In this piece we again encounter storm music, though much more subtly than before. Notice the roll of thunder that goes through the orchestra as Zerlina, Masetto, Anna, Elvira, and Ottavio sing "Odi il tuon della vendetta" ("Hear the thunder of vengeance" while Don Giovanni and Leporello sing "E un'orribile tempesta minacciando" ("A fearful storm threatens").

While Rossini, in his concluding music to acts, took more time and often used more variation and invention, Mozart's Act I finale is two minutes long and gets straight to the point with great power. The last notes of the orchestra in Act I send us out to intermission buzzing with anticipation, while Rossini's music sends us out with a big grin. Both states are enjoyable, but you should be aware of the difference. I emphasize this because too many casual listeners of Mozart's music think of it as pleasant rather than incisive, dramatic, and thrilling.

Act II opens on a street in Seville. Leporello is angry at Giovanni and threatens to resign. Four gold pieces from Giovanni convince him to change his mind. Surely this is not the first time such a trans-action has taken place between servant and master. Leporello tries to change his master's ways, but women, says Giovanni, are more important for him than food or air. He offers a strange view of fidelity: "To be faithful to one is to be cruel to the others." To which Leporello sarcastically remarks: "I've never seen a heart so all-embracing." No sooner has Giovanni bought Leporello's loyalty again than he plots to seduce another woman—in this case, the servant of Donna Elvira. Since the girl is from Leporello's class, the Don intends to impersonate Leporello to complete the seduction. Servant and master exchange cloaks, with Leporello expected to carry Elvira away so that her servant will be available for Giovanni. They go and stand under Elvira's window.

Elvira again falls for the seductive voice of the Don, who calls to her from the darkness below her window (page 162, track 17). Although hesitant, she agrees to come downstairs. When she arrives, she does not realize that the man in Giovanni's cape is Leporello. She tells him how she has missed him, and Leporello enjoys "making up" with her as if he were Giovanni. Listen to van Dam effectively imitate Raimondi. When the Don makes sudden noises, Elvira and Leporello flee and Giovanni is free to woo the maid. Nowadays we may consider this a cruel trick against Elvira; in Mozart's time it was a comic scene as the woman some audiences considered foolish and gullible is deceived again.

What follows (page 176, track 20) is the famous seduction aria, "Deh, vieni alla finestra," which became the "hit single" from the opera. Throughout Europe, baritones sang this in concerts and amateur singers in cafés and taverns sang it after a few drinks. Young men sang it as they courted young women. When performed by a singer of Raimondi's talent, with the mandolin accompaniment from the orchestra pit (the singer playing the Don holds a mandolin that he pretends to play), this aria is the epitome of seductiveness. Listen to it twice. The first time, simply close your eyes and envision the scene. On second hearing, read the words and see how Mozart found the musical means to express da Ponte's sentiments.

But this seduction, too, is not meant to happen. Masetto arrives with a search party to beat up Giovanni. Since he is disguised as

Leporello, Giovanni is able to divide up the group and send them in all directions. When only Masetto remains, he beats the young man up and steals away. Zerlina arrives and tries to heal Masetto's wounds with kisses and tenderness ("Vedrai, carino," page 190, track 25). The scene ends as she places his hand on her heart (and breast), telling him that that is where the cure to his problems resides.

In the next scene (page 192, track 26), we are at the courtyard outside Anna's house. Notice that da Ponte and Mozart specifically tell us that it is a *dark* courtyard with *three* doors. They must have a reason for being so precise, so you should bear these details in mind as you hear and read this scene. Listen to Te Kanawa as Elvira here; she is much different from the angry woman we knew. Here is someone radiating romantic contentment—the marriage of Mozart's music and her voice make that abundantly clear. Leporello is nervous that he will be found out and does everything he can to (literally) keep Elvira in the dark. Ottavio, Anna, Zerlina, and Masetto arrive and denounce Leporello, who they presume to be Giovanni. Elvira protests their denunciations until she and everyone else discover that the man they thought to be Giovanni is indeed Leporello. We have seen instances in other operas of people dressing in disguise—Gilda in *Rigoletto;* Almaviva (twice) in *Il Barbiere di Siviglia*—so we know that these scenes can have different flavors depending on the action. Never do we think to laugh in *Rigoletto,* but in *Barbiere* the intention is that we laugh heartily. In *Don Giovanni,* there is humor in this scene but also serious elements. We do not admire Giovanni for his deception; we have mixed feelings about how Leporello is misleading Elvira. While we laugh, we do it with a degree of restraint, partly because the entrance of the serious-minded Anna and Ottavio has altered the scene's tone.

When Leporello reveals himself, Anna runs away in shock and horror. Ottavio, Elvira, Zerlina, and Masetto all want to beat Leporello up; he pleads for mercy, places all the blame on Don Giovanni, and manages to escape. It is here that the three doors come into play: only one is for escaping and there is a brief moment of humorous confusion as he attempts to flee.

Tracks 32–33: Ottavio asks the others to stay in the house to console Anna while he goes out to avenge them all. He vows to return only "as the messenger of punishment and death." This is the famous aria "Il mio tesoro."

We now go to the third disk. The aria you are about to hear, Elvira's "Mi tradì quell'alma ingrata," immediately follows Ottavio's in the same scene. Envision that Ottavio walks offstage through one door as Elvira enters through another. This great aria, which reveals Elvira's contradictory feelings, was not heard by the opera's first-night audience in Prague. It was added a year later in Vienna because it suited the woman playing Elvira. Imagine how the scene ended in Prague, with Ottavio's aria rather than this one: the lasting impression was one of sweetness rather than the unusual blend of fire and compassion in Elvira's aria. This aria is really the first moment in the opera when many eighteenth-century audiences took Elvira seriously. Note that Elvira foresees a deadly thunderbolt poised above Giovanni's head and a fatal abyss open before him. Despite her anger and betrayal, what she feels for him is pity. Is this foolish or insightful? One could spend hours thinking about Elvira's attitudes and behaviors. Do they reflect the eighteenth-century view on matters of the heart and on crime and punishment, or is she a very unusual woman who stood apart from the norm? As I mentioned earlier, what makes this opera so extraordinary is that one can look at so many of the behaviors and attitudes of the characters in different ways.

We now come to a crucial scene in the opera. We are in a cemetery that includes several equestrian statues, including one bearing a likeness of the Commendatore. (Most productions have only one statue—the Commendatore's.) Read the scene (page 208, track 3) as you listen. Clearly, Giovanni is gloating about his self-serving behavior, showing little regard for the feelings of Leporello as he brags about seducing a woman who mistook him for his servant. Leporello, the servant, becomes ever more angry and resentful. Suddenly, astonishingly, their argument is interrupted by a booming voice. The voice comes from the statue of the Commendatore. Until now, every scene in every opera we have studied dealt in the realm of realism, even if occasionally we were asked to stretch our willingness to believe. All of the characters in *Rigoletto* and *Tosca* are real people with weaknesses and conceits that are part of their nature. Lucia may hear voices and see ghosts, but that is a product of her insanity. Of course, there are plenty of insane people in the real world (you may even run into one or two in an opera audience). The characters in *Il Barbiere di Siviglia* may seem like caricatures, but their behavior is drawn from real life. Until this point in *Don Giovanni,* the characters have been wonderfully rich and complex—and real. So it may come as a bit of a shock when a voice comes from a statue of a dead man. And here we take an important step forward in your operatic education.

In our modern world, where film and television create a certain degree of realism even when the situations and characters they present are unreal, audiences at theater and opera performances often seem confused when they are presented with a different form of reality. Yet great storytelling of all types sometimes requires us to give ourselves over to the assumptions of the story. In other words, its world does not have to be ours. When we read *Alice's Adventures in Wonderland,* an indisputably great work, we cannot appreciate it if we expect it to conform to our assumptions. Many films are set in contexts that do not relate to our daily lives, yet we allow ourselves to go where they go. One of the things that is so thrilling about opera is that it can take our minds and feelings to extraordinary places. The very unreality of certain characters and situations is what is often so compelling. You will discover this in some of the operas we have yet to study: to a large extent in *Les Contes d'Hoffmann,* less so in *Don Carlo, Tannhäuser,* and *Die Walküre.* As you go to more operas, you will find that unreality (or a different reality) forms the basis for many great works. You should embrace this aspect of opera and allow your fantasy to take you to places beyond the scope of your daily life. To be transported not only by the music, the singing, the sets, and the costumes but also by the power of your own imagination is one of the joys of operagoing.

So in track 3 at 2:10, we hear the voice of the Commendatore (or is it the voice of the *statue* of the Commendatore?) tell Don Giovanni that his laughter will be silenced by morning. After being slightly alarmed, Giovanni regains his courage and tells the trembling Leporello to invite the statue to dinner that evening ("O statua gentilissima," page 222, track 4). The statue accepts the invitation by nodding its head. Aside from the drama of the moment, you might note that this is a beautiful duet for two deep male voices that are briefly joined by a third.

In the short scene that follows, we are back at Donna Anna's house. She informs Ottavio that she wants to delay their wedding until her father's death is avenged because her grief is too great. Could this be the only reason? Might she also be tiring of Ottavio, whose actions do not speak as loudly as his words? Anna's wonderful, introspective recitative and aria (tracks 6 and 7)—the longest solo passage by any character in the opera—bring us completely into her thoughts and feelings. This scene also serves the very important function of separating the cemetery scene from the climactic dinner scene that follows. If those scenes were consecutive, we might not feel their impact as powerfully as we do. The cemetery scene is impressive but would diminish the great dinner scene if one followed the other. Also, Donna Anna's rejection of Ottavio includes the proviso that she will not marry him until Don Giovanni is killed. If, in the next scene, Giovanni dies, will Anna then marry Ottavio?

The last scene takes place in the banquet hall of Don Giovanni's palace (page 230, track 9). While Giovanni puts on festive airs, there is a sense of uneasiness as the arrival of the stone guest is awaited. This anticipation is tempered a bit (for us in the audience) by the repartee about how hungry Leporello is and how much Giovanni is eating. But the fact that both men are ravenous (each in his own way) is another clue to the state of agitation that underlies this scene.

Mozart periodically has the onstage orchestra break in with some music on which the Don and Leporello comment. The first of these, at 1:04 on track 9, is a quotation from the 1786 opera that was the masterpiece of Vicente Martin y Soler (1754–1806), *Una Cosa Rara*, the "rare thing" of the title being female constancy. When Giovanni asks Leporello how he likes the music, the servant responds, "It's just the thing for you." The second musical interruption, at 2:25, quotes a 1782 opera by Giuseppe Sarti (1729–1802), *Fra i Due Litiganti il Terzo Gode* (Between Two Combatants It Is the Third Who Enjoys). These two references are obscure today, but the third, at 3:09, may be familiar to you: it comes from *Le Nozze di Figaro,* Mozart's big hit of the previous year (1786). The joke here, which was understood by most audience members in 1787 and many today, is that the music quoted is Figaro's aria "Non più andrai," in which he tells the young Cherubino that he will have to forget chasing girls now that he is going into the military: "No more, you amorous butterfly, will you go fluttering round by night and day, disturbing the peace of every maid, you pocket Narcissus, you Adonis of love." Upon hearing this music, Leporello says, "Now, that tune I know only too well!" By introducing a laugh here, Mozart unwinds our tension a notch before the inevitable confrontation.

In track 10 (page 236) Elvira arrives to implore Giovanni one last time to change his ways. Giovanni ignores her, cynically raising a glass to toast wine and women. She leaves, and suddenly we hear her scream. Leporello goes to see what the problem is and he too screams. The stone guest has arrived for dinner. Notice, as Leporello recounts the tramping sound of the statue's feet ("ta, ta, ta, ta"), how this sound is not imitated but rather reconfigured in the music as the stone guest pounds on the door. An imitation would have been too obvious. By throwing us off guard musically, Mozart disarms us and we listen more carefully to what follows.

At track 11 (page 246), the statue of the Commendatore enters the room, accompanied by the chilling chords that opened the opera. Listen to him as he claims the dinner to which he was invited. For the first time, Don Giovanni is really caught off guard; he too cannot comprehend that a stone statue could step down from its pedestal and walk to his house. The Commendatore tells Giovanni that he wants to return the courtesy by inviting him to dinner. Although Leporello pleads with his master not to go, Giovanni says he has no fear. To seal the agreement, the statue asks Giovanni to shake his hand. You can hear in the music (track 11, 5:09) the very moment when the Commendatore's stone cold grip overtakes Giovanni. But even with the threat of hell and damnation, Giovanni refuses to repent. Soon flames and voices rise from below; Giovanni is dragged down to hell as the statue of the Commendatore leaves.

Notice the brilliant drama of Mozart's music in this part of the opera. The trio of low voices—Don Giovanni, Leporello, and the Commendatore—is thrilling and at the same time connotes the netherworld. The strings in the orchestra toss and swirl like waves in a raging sea. Suddenly there is the sound of inevitability with the roar of trombones. This is an unusual instrument for an opera orchestra, especially in Mozart's time. To me, as they growl louder each time they speak, there is the sense of a widening chasm as the mouth of hell opens up to swallow Don Giovanni. This is one of the greatest scenes in all of opera.

You might think that a scene like this would be a fitting end to this opera—at this point, what could one possibly add? As a matter of fact, in the very last years of the eighteenth century, as the tide of the Enlightenment ebbed while that of Romanticism began to crest, it became the practice in most theaters to end the opera with Giovanni's descent to hell as the last image audience members saw before going home. The idea was to impart a certain "fear of God" that was probably not part of da Ponte and Mozart's original intentions. As I have suggested, the creators of *Don Giovanni* presented us with characters and situations for us to consider; they did not attempt to push an agenda down our throats.

So Giovanni's descent to hell is followed by a scene in which we see how the other characters respond to his demise. Anna asks Ottavio to wait a year before marriage. (What might she do in that year?) Elvira vows to enter a convent, which was a refuge in Spain for troubled women with no place else to turn; occasionally, it was where unwed pregnant women went. (Could it be . . . ?) Masetto and Zerlina have less momentous plans: they are going home for dinner. And Leporello is going job hunting: he will find another, better master. All the characters, in a quick moralizing coda, tell us that the death of sinners will always match their life.

We leave this opera, if we have heard a good performance, with more questions about morals and human nature than we had when we entered the theater. Are the bad always punished? Are the virtuous always rewarded? Are we better off living in fear than living an exciting life? Virtue for virtue's sake, or achievement at any cost? Is fidelity desirable, or even possible? Were Giovanni's pride and bravery laudable? How is it possible that we can love and admire a despicable person?

Mozart and da Ponte, men of the Enlightenment, pondered these and other questions in an era when vistas were opened and topics that were not previously discussed suddenly burst forth in the salons of Europe. With *Don Giovanni,* Mozart and da Ponte created a work that has encouraged generations of audiences for more than two centuries to ask themselves what meaning they get from their lives. There are few questions more important, yet how many of us know the answer? Its universal relevance, along with its sublime beauty and thrilling drama, is why *Don Giovanni* is such a towering work of art.

If, as you are studying *Don Giovanni,* you have the opportunity to see or hear *Le Nozze di Figaro,* this would be a good opportunity to learn an opera that is as beloved as (perhaps even more so than) *Don Giovanni.* You will learn more about the work of Mozart and da Ponte and experience what many people consider the most erotic opera ever written. I don't agree with that assertion, but *Figaro* does have a healthy sexuality about it that has somehow diminished in our times. It is not because we do not engage in sex but because we have become so clinical and analytical about it, finding it necessary to name every action, declare every preference, and attach a statement to each act, that we have trouble remembering that sex is about love and pleasure. We should all be allowed to enjoy it (safely). *Figaro* (written in 1786) is, as you know, also about rebellion against the upper classes and helped stoke the fires that led to the French Revolution. It too has exquisite music, although with intermissions it is considerably longer than *Don Giovanni,* which is one of the many reasons why I did not select it to teach you about Mozart, da Ponte, and opera from the Classical era. My recommended recording, led by James Levine and starring Kiri Te Kanawa, Dawn Upshaw, Ferruccio Furlanetto, and Thomas Hampson, is on the DG label.

We have now reached an important turning point. The five operas we have learned so far are in Italian, the first language of opera. Next will come *Les Contes d'Hoffmann,* in French, followed by the

Russian *Eugene Onegin*. After a return to Italian for Verdi's *Don Carlo*, we will learn three operas in German. Right now you have the skills to approach most operas in Italian. By the end of this book you will be able to approach any opera in any language and gain a meaningful appreciation of it.

9.

LES CONTES
D'HOFFMANN

FRENCH OPERA

ome might consider it heretical that I chose *Les Contes d'Hoffmann* to be our exemplar of French opera. It is the one famous opera by Jacques Offenbach, who was otherwise known for his operettas, a form that is often considered inferior to opera. And when you realize that there are so many magnificent native-born composers to choose from, including Rameau, Auber, Berlioz, Halévy (Offenbach's teacher), Massenet, Bizet, Gounod, Delibes, Saint-Saëns, Charpentier, Debussy, Ravel, Satie, and Poulenc, why did I select an opera by a German-born composer?

As I suggested to you in chapter 1, one of the hallmarks of French opera and of French culture in general is the ability to absorb elements of other cultures and impart distinctly French characteristics to them. Remember also that two of the most important composers of French opera were foreigners: Lully, an Italian who was one of the great early creators of French opera, and Meyerbeer, the towering figure of French grand opera in the nineteenth century, who was actually born in Berlin.

Any opera in the French language will immediately impart a different flavor than anything we have heard in Italian. In chapter 2 we examined how each language creates a different atmosphere in an opera. Listen to the French, with its more restrained vowels, and notice how the effect is different than the open-throated sound that

Italian vowels produce. The storytelling in *Les Contes d'Hoffmann* is different from anything we have seen in Italian opera. While in Italian operas we saw a certain degree of naturalism, or at least behavior based in reality, in *Hoffmann* we have characters who have a very fictional feeling about them. In only a few of them (especially Antonia, Giulietta, and perhaps Hoffmann) do we find traits of people we might claim to know. This is not to suggest that all of French opera is more fictional than Italian opera, but it is noteworthy because *Les Contes d'Hoffmann* is deeply appreciated by the French people, who seem very in tune with its particular artistic sensibility. It is fair to say, therefore, that one of the things that makes *Hoffmann* a French work is that the French so proudly claim it as part of their national cultural heritage.

Although Offenbach (1819–80) was born in Cologne, he moved to France at the age of fourteen when his father, despite great financial hardship, sent the boy there to further his cello lessons. Young Jakob soon became Jacques, and his talent and likability brought him into the heady musical atmosphere of mid-nineteenth-century Paris, when the city was the opera capital of Europe. It was also the home of Rossini, who was a giant in Parisian musical and social circles. In many ways, Offenbach was like Rossini: he enjoyed life, had prodigious talent, and composed music that aimed to please. Also, because his greatest fame was in creating comic operettas and buoyant music, few people expected "serious" work from him. Rossini saw greater skill in Offenbach and nicknamed him "the Mozart of the Champs Elysées." Offenbach wrote his first operetta at the age of twenty.

Offenbach, whose health was precarious in the last decade of his life, was eager to leave an opera that would be more substantial than the operettas with which he made his fame. He had been intrigued by the story of E. T. A. Hoffmann much earlier in his life, and the idea for an opera about the famous German lawyer, composer, and author seemed promising. In fact, the opera is based on an 1851 play by Jules Barbier and Michel Carré that is a conflation of elements of Hoffmann's life and of three of his stories.

Offenbach was famous for being a fast and tireless worker, so it is notable that he devoted more than three years of his life—the last three years—to *Les Contes d'Hoffmann*. During this period his health declined precipitously. At the same time he also composed five operettas to meet pressing financial obligations. When you listen to the scene featuring Antonia, the singer who will die if she sings too much, it is hard not to think of Offenbach burning himself out by feverishly writing music in a race with the death that he knew would soon arrive. He was even at work on the score the day before he died.

In fact, Offenbach did not complete *Les Contes d'Hoffmann.* At his death on October 5, 1880, he had completed the entire piano score but had orchestrated only the Prologue and the first act (which we shall call the Olympia act after the woman who is Hoffmann's love interest in this act). Offenbach also left indications for the orchestration of the rest of the opera, which was completed by Ernest Guiraud (1837–92), who had composed the recitatives for *Carmen* following the death of Bizet in 1875.

When *Les Contes d'Hoffmann* had its premiere at the Opéra-Comique on February 10, 1881, it was not the work that Offenbach had envisioned. The first reason, of course, was that it was completed by Guiraud: no matter how faithful he might have been to Offenbach's intentions, it was still not the same as having the piece fully orchestrated by the composer. More significant, though, were the major changes made by the impresario at the Opéra-Comique, Léon Carvalho. The Giulietta act (set in Venice) was discarded and the Antonia act was relocated from Munich to Venice so that the famous Barcarolle (which you will recognize) could be included. An aria that was originally written for one character was carelessly given to another. Despite all of these changes, the opera was a great success and enjoyed a long run (101 performances) in its premiere production.

Subsequent productions in other cities further tampered with *Les Contes d'Hoffmann.* In Vienna, for example, the Giulietta act was restored, but with so much of its music and story missing that it bore little resemblance to the one created by Offenbach. Other productions were mere approximations of what Offenbach had created. The publishing house of Choudens brought forth numerous revised editions of the score that included music added by various singers, conductors, musicologists, and impresarios.

In 1887 a huge fire at the Opéra-Comique destroyed almost everything the theater owned from the score of *Les Contes d'Hoffmann* that was in Offenbach's own hand. The performance practice that developed after the fire was even more extreme than that which evolved for Rossini operas. By the turn of the century, there were efforts to create a standard performance edition of Offenbach's opera. Not surprisingly, these efforts still go on today. Conductors and musicologists study whatever might turn up in Offenbach's own hand for clues. An edition published in Berlin in 1907 included music that had been deleted from the Giulietta act. An edition created by Arthur Hammond in England in the 1940s was influential in restoring many of the most theatrical moments to the opera. A score in Offenbach's hand that was acquired by the Paris Opéra in the 1940s greatly enhanced the amount of material scholars could use to try to create a definitive version. A version prepared for a production at the Komische Oper, Berlin, in 1958 had currency for a while. In 1977 Fritz Oeser, a German musicologist, published a new edition that included a lot of seldom-heard music drawn from Offenbach's sketches. A major innovation of the Oeser edition was the inclusion of more music for the character of Nicklausse, making him/her (the role is sung by a mezzo-soprano) more prominent. More recently, an edition by Michael Kaye was published that uses still more recent discoveries as well as elements from many of the previous editions.

E. T. A. Hoffmann (1776–1822), as you know, was a real person. He was a Renaissance man, accomplished in law (he was a leading judge in Berlin), musical composition (he wrote eleven operas, a symphony, and a fair amount of choral music), conducting, and music criticism, but above all was a creator of stories and fables, many of which included fantastical and supernatural elements. Hoffmann was also supposed to have had a rather active sex life, his homely appearance notwithstanding. And as you know from the *Don Giovanni* chapter, Hoffmann was a great admirer of Mozart: so intense was this esteem that Hoffmann changed his name from Ernst Theodor Wilhelm to Ernst Theodor Amadeus in Mozart's honor.

When we meet Hoffmann (the opera's protagonist, not the man) in the Prologue of Offenbach's work, he is in a tavern in Nürnberg. Next door is a performance of *Don Giovanni* starring a prima donna named Stella (Italian for "star"). Stella is Hoffmann's ideal woman, and he is looking forward to being with her after the performance. We will learn that in Hoffmann's eyes Stella has characteristics of each of his beloved women: Olympia, Antonia, and Giulietta ("An artist, a young girl, and a courtesan").

You might notice some parallels in this opera to *Don Giovanni.* The most obvious reference is that Mozart's opera is being performed next door to the tavern that is the setting of the Prologue and the Epilogue. Also, we have a charismatic leading character who is defined in part by three prominent women. Both men are striving for ideals in their lives. We might consider the Don selfish and Hoffmann naive, but they do represent a yearning and a passion that make them great characters. Unlike the Don, however, Hoffmann inspires in us great compassion and pity. He is the other side of the Don Juan myth: he loves women who elude him; he idealizes them and cannot understand why he loses them. While Giovanni epitomizes the conflict between good and evil, Hoffmann is affected by these forces, but his struggle ultimately comes down to art versus love.

The very detailed story in *Les Contes d'Hoffmann* includes twenty-two characters, many more than in any of the operas you have learned so far. It was Offenbach's idea that all of the singers in the opera (except the one playing Hoffmann and the woman doing the voice of Antonia's mother) play several roles. In fact, all of the characters who appear in Hoffmann's three tales are drawn from persons we meet in the Prologue. In Offenbach's ideal version (seldom realized) the singer who plays Luther, the proprietor of the tavern, also plays Crespel. The man who plays Spalanzani also sings Nathanaël, a student in the tavern. Another student, Hermann, is sung by the man who plays Schlemil. Because the three main women in the opera all represent facets of Stella, Hoffmann's ideal woman, Offenbach hoped that one singer would portray Olympia, Giulietta, Antonia, and Stella. Similarly, one bass or baritone would ideally sing the roles of the four villains, Lindorf, Coppélius, Dapertutto, and Dr. Miracle. There are four roles for one comprimario tenor: Andrès (Stella's servant), Cochenille (Spalanzani's assistant, who winds the doll Olympia), Pitichinaccio (the dwarf), and Frantz (Crespel's nearly deaf butler, who provides comic relief in the dramatic Antonia act). Most notably, the mezzo-soprano who plays the Muse of Poetry also portrays the trouser role of Nicklausse. This character, the only one who is always on Hoffmann's side, is the key to our understanding our hero.

Hoffmann is a character who succeeds in art and fails in love. His true and most faithful love object, in fact, is his art. It is often observed that Offenbach, though popular and, from what we know, happily married, did not achieve great art—that is, his brilliant operettas were not great art because they were merely a diminished form of grand opera. Offenbach hoped that *Les Contes d'Hoffmann* would be his lasting artistic masterpiece. The resonance of Mozart (who produced great art but died impoverished), Don Giovanni (a great lover who did not know love), and Offenbach himself can all be felt in the music and story of the poet Hoffmann.

While we had some sense of the surreal and the supernatural in *Don Giovanni, Les Contes d'Hoffmann* relies on them heavily, especially in the conjurings by the villains. The loss of Hoffmann's reflection, the coming to life of the portrait of Antonia's mother, and the glasses that transform a mechanical doll into a human in Hoffmann's eyes are but three of many instances. Offenbach wanted this to be an *opéra fantastique,* an opera in which fantasy, spectral images, spells, and magic play a crucial part, since they are central to many of the stories of E. T. A. Hoffmann.

To mount a production that honors the intentions of Offenbach is difficult. Creative stagecraft is required to make all of the magical effects take place. In addition, a versatile cast of great singing actors is essential, particularly in the title role and for Hoffmann's four loves. There are few, if any, singers who can portray all of the heroines effectively: The music for Olympia requires a coloratura soprano; Giulietta is often sung by a mezzo-soprano or a soprano with a good lower register; Antonia requires a lyric soprano with a certain degree of power. (Stella is a spoken role, easily managed.) Most performances of *Hoffmann* cast different singers as Olympia, Giulietta, and Antonia. There are three wonderful Hoffmanns before the public as this book is being written. Plácido Domingo is justifiably famous. Neil Shicoff sings the part very well and gives Hoffmann a desperate edge that is very compelling. If you have the rare chance to hear Alfredo Kraus sing the role, you will marvel at the beauty he imparts to Offenbach's melancholy poet.

In most versions of this opera, Hoffmann first recounts his meeting Olympia, then Giulietta, then Antonia. Some productions and recordings nowadays rearrange the acts so that their order is Olympia, Antonia, and Giulietta. The thinking behind this is Nicklausse's observation that the three women ("an artist, a young girl, and a courtesan") who represent aspects of Stella are listed in an order different from the sequence usually performed. Several musicologists believe that this sequence was Offenbach's original intention. This revised version, which was staged at the Metropolitan Opera in 1992, is dramatically and intellectually provocative. It must be stated, then, that *Les Contes d'Hoffmann* does not yet have a definitive critical edition more than 113 years after its first performance. The opera that we see today, no matter which version is presented, does not—cannot—fairly represent Offenbach's intentions. But that may not be important. *Les Contes d'Hoffmann,* as we see it today, is a unique opera in that it combines what Offenbach gave us with what many hands have added to it since. Nonetheless, the story and the music thrill audiences because they make us care passionately about them.

With this confusion about so many versions of this opera, there is no ideal recording of *Les Contes d'Hoffmann.* There is a fine version from 1972 with Plácido Domingo in the title role, Joan Sutherland as the four women, and Gabriel Bacquier as the villains. It is conducted by Richard Bonynge, who did a scrupulous job of reconstructing much of the music available from various sources. Bonynge chose to use spoken dialogue instead of Guiraud's recitatives. I have chosen to forego this recording primarily because you are well acquainted with the work of Sutherland and Bonynge and I want you to hear other artists. You will hear Domingo in another of his signature roles, Verdi's *Don Carlo,* when we study that opera in chapter 10.

I have chosen instead an older (1964) performance of equally high artistic caliber. In it, three different women play Hoffmann's loves. With Gianna d'Angelo (Olympia), Elisabeth Schwarzkopf

(Giulietta), and Victoria de los Angeles (Antonia), you will hear how different vocal types sound in these roles. Nicolai Gedda, one of the finest tenors of the postwar era, sings the part beautifully and has excellent French diction that gives you much of the flavor of this language and makes you believe that he is indeed a poet. The villains are portrayed by three different singers: Nicola Ghiuselev (Lindorf), Ernest Blanc (Dapertutto), and George London (Coppélius and Dr. Miracle). London was a magnificent bass-baritone whose recordings you should seek when you look for great performances from the past. The cast is full of native French speakers, which is an advantage. The one questionable choice is the use of a baritone (Jean-Christophe Benoit) as Nicklausse. This creates a different dynamic because it is harder for us to believe that this loyal friend could perhaps be a different incarnation of the Muse of Poetry. But this casting choice makes those of us familiar with this opera's many versions look at the role afresh and we can come to our own conclusions. Another strength of this recording (on Angel/EMI) is the conductor André Cluytens. Born in Belgium and a naturalized French citizen, Maestro Cluytens was a superb interpreter of the French operatic repertory, and his presence on a recording of a French opera is almost a guarantee that it is worth purchasing.

It is now time to listen to the performance. I have already given you substantial background about the opera, its context and settings, and the nature of the roles. My goal is that with each new opera you learn, you will bring more of the skills of appreciation and comprehension that you have developed in using this book. Read the introductory essay in the libretto of our recording (pages 10–15). Then read, act by act, the synopsis in the libretto (pages 15–20). This libretto is keyed to the tracks of the recording, a good idea.

One note: This libretto refers to the Prologue as Act I, the Olympia act as Act II, the Giulietta act as Act III, the Antonia act as Act IV, scene 1, and the Epilogue as Act IV, scene 2. I, however, will refer to them as they most often appear in opera houses nowadays: Prologue, Act I (Olympia), Act II (Giulietta), Act III (Antonia), Epilogue.

In the first sequence of the Prologue, note how the sound of the

French words and Ghiuselev's low voice produce something you have not yet heard. Remember the sounds made by Sparafucile and the Commendatore and see whether the sound that the French language creates pleases you or displeases you when compared with the Italian sound you know. In fact, this is not so much an issue of good and bad as of being different. You will make similar observations when we learn operas in Russian and German.

The students' drinking song (track 6, page 48) is typical of so many that one sees in opera. Alcohol provides the convenient dramatic device of loosening a character's tension or altering his or her state. The drinking chorus in *Hoffmann* is also important because it introduces a melody that connotes frivolity—this will take an ironic turn during the Epilogue, and you should listen for it.

In track 7 (page 51) the students toast Stella's ability as a singer of Mozart. Offenbach does not make clear in this opera whether Stella is portraying Donna Anna, Donna Elvira, or Zerlina. However, other literary sources suggest that the real Hoffmann was partial to Donna Anna, so it is likely that our Stella is playing her. Does that make you think differently of Hoffmann's ideal woman than you might if she were portraying Donna Elvira or Zerlina? Notice too, at 2:16 of this track, how Nicklausse jokingly imitates Leporello, in effect declaring himself a "servant" to "master" Hoffmann. This again underscores the profound influence that Mozart had on Hoffmann and Offenbach. One thing to look for throughout the opera is these moments in which Offenbach reveals something of himself in the character of Hoffmann. Don't forget that Offenbach was very aware that this opera would be his last artistic statement.

Notice how, in the middle of his recounting of the legend of Kleinzach (track 8, page 55), Hoffmann's mind wanders to a woman he loves. Is it Stella or someone else—perhaps the Muse of Poetry? Throughout the opera you will see a tug-of-war in the character of Hoffmann between the creative mind of an artist and the aching heart of a lover.

Later in the Prologue we are introduced to another constant in the opera. Hoffmann recognizes Lindorf, and although the libretto *indicates* that their exchange of comments is gracious, we know this is a heated discussion between enemies. Hoffmann refers to Lindorf as an agent of Lucifer, while his rival calls him a fugitive from hell. Hoffmann remarks that whenever Lindorf is near, misfortune is seldom far behind (track 10, page 61). It is in this passage too (on page 63) that Stella is referred to as three women in one (artist, young girl, courtesan). Hoffmann denies that he is in love with Stella. He has been chastened, he says, by three disastrous experiences in love. The music of the second act of *Don Giovanni* fades into the background as Hoffmann starts to tell his stories.

The set of the tavern fades away, as you can hear in the music by the end of track 10, and soon Spalanzani's workshop comes into view (track 11, page 65). You can hear him busy at work as all sorts of objects and contraptions spin and turn in various parts of the room. Spalanzani, in his first speech (track 12, page 65) sets up for us the problems that will cause some of the drama in this scene. Hoffmann then appears. The tenor singing Hoffmann has made a quick makeup and costume change; he is now a much younger man than the one we saw in Luther's tavern. Notice how the music in Hoffmann's declaration of love for the doll, Olympia (track 13, page 66), tells us much about Hoffmann's blindness to reality although the words are those of a typical love song. We can hear him deceive himself. Hoffmann's blindness is a metaphor: the wicked Coppélius will give Hoffmann special glasses through which only he can see Olympia as a human being, but the glasses only complete a process that began in the heart and the mind of the poet. Notice the musical introduction for the entrance of Coppélius (track 15, page 69). It is possible, in listening to this opera, to hear and recognize a great deal of the action without seeing it. Listen to how Offenbach introduces Olympia and how the conflict among different characters is described in strictly orchestral terms. The musical motives (what we might jokingly call "signature tunes") of each character are quoted periodically in the orchestral score. When two or more characters are quoted at once, you can hear what interaction is taking place. The master of the technique of using orchestral motives was Wagner, who died three years after Offenbach. Although they were very different sorts of composers, Wagner cast such a giant shadow across musical Europe that other composers could not help being influenced by him. Whether by embracing or by rejecting him, almost all of them reacted to Wagner.

Olympia's aria (track 20, page 77) is a genuine tour de force for a great singer: she must not only sing this difficult coloratura aria but also act the part of a mechanical doll that breaks down periodically and has to be rewound. You will hear all of this in the music.

Tracks 21–24: Hoffmann is overwhelmed with love for this inanimate object. He, in fact, has invested some of his soul in her (the true sense of the word "animate" is to give a soul to something). When Hoffmann's spectacles break and Coppélius then destroys Olympia, we are seeing and hearing the destruction of a certain part of Hoffmann too. Notice how ambiguous the music is at the end of this act. It is very festive, despite the destruction of Olympia and Hoffmann's being made a fool of. We feel for our hero, and we are perhaps startled by the indifference and cruelty shown to him by the partygoers.

So ends the first story of Hoffmann's tragic loves. Now read the synopsis for Act II.

Act II in this recording (and in most productions you will see of *Les Contes d'Hoffmann*) is about Hoffmann's encounter with Giulietta. The act starts with the opera's most famous melody, the Barcarolle (track 25). This term comes from the Italian *barca* (boat) and suggests the slow, graceful movement of a boat over water. Notice how, even if you have never been to Venice, you can imagine a gondola gliding down the Grand Canal in the evening, its lantern creating glints of light in the water and in the glass of palace windows. Giulietta sings of this night of love along with Nicklausse (but not in this particular version, where Nicklausse is a baritone rather than a mezzo-soprano). Nicklausse, as we will learn at the end of the opera, is the alter ego of the Muse of Poetry, Hoffmann's most faithful love.

The action in this act is made very clear in the libretto and the music. Hoffmann declares ardent love for Giulietta. She, being a courtesan, lets him believe that she loves him too. The evil character in this act, Dapertutto, again represents the diabolical forces that conspire against love and art. Giulietta, working at the behest of Dapertutto, asks Hoffmann for his reflection "to disengage itself [from the mirror] and come and hide completely whole within my heart." This is another incidence of Hoffmann transferring his essence or his soul from himself to the woman he passionately, blindly loves. This is made even clearer when Giulietta tells Hoffmann she wants his heart, his soul, and his life (page 99).

Note that the first part of this act is on the end of the first disk and continues (page 93) on the second disk.

Act II ends (track 6, page 101) with what is called a septet, but this ensemble is really a sextet with the chorus as the seventh character. This splendid piece starts slowly and builds with great drama as each character joins in to voice his or her view of the events. Hoffmann again is a victim of his own blindness. He does not comprehend that Giulietta is a courtesan who will practice deception if she is paid to do so. As the chorus remarks, she sells her kisses. Dapertutto delights in causing this suffering, while Nicklausse despairs for his friend. As Hoffmann duels with Schlemil over Giulietta, the chorus offstage sings of love. As the duel continues, a gondola sails by with Giulietta laughing raucously in the arms of Pitichinaccio, the dwarf. Once again Hoffmann realizes too late that love has blinded him from the truth.

We now go on to Act III (Act IV, scene 1, in this libretto): track 8, page 106. The setting is the home of Crespel and his daughter, Antonia. Read the synopsis on pages 18–20 of the booklet and then proceed.

For most of this opera's admirers, Antonia is the most sympathetic of the three women Hoffmann loves. She is certainly the most accessible. Olympia is an automaton and Giulietta is won with money and jewels rather than love. Antonia loves Hoffmann and wants to be with him. It is her father, Crespel, who fears that her fragile health will be imperiled if she pursues her romance.

Once you hear this act, decide whether you think the sequence of Olympia, Giulietta, Antonia is the most effective one dramatically. Should we follow the clue given by Hoffmann in the Prologue ("artist, young girl, courtesan") and switch the Giulietta and Antonia scenes? Base your decision on the music as well as the story. Both sides can make strong cases. In the sequence most commonly used (Olympia, Giulietta, Antonia), we see Hoffmann go from the least plausible woman to the most and therefore feel his loss keenly when Antonia dies. On the other hand, if we accept the sequence that ends with Giulietta we can say that Hoffmann, after losing his beloved

Antonia, resorts to a courtesan because such a woman would invariably say yes to whatever he wants as long as the price is right.

The act opens with Antonia singing metaphorically about herself having fled Hoffmann but loving him still. Her timidness and her sweet feelings of first love are in some way reminiscent of Gilda. The charming song of Frantz, the nearly deaf servant, changes our mood from Antonia's languors and Crespel's fears (track 10, page 109). This is a sort of novelty number popular in French opera in which a supporting player is given a moment to shine. In this home of singers, Frantz remarks that while he can't sing, he is a very good dancer. This rickety old retainer then attempts to dance until he stubs his toe. Notice that the first line of this song, "Day and night I put myself out," is the second quotation in this opera of Leporello's complaint at the opening of *Don Giovanni*. Although French was not Offenbach's first language, he had great dexterity in it and loved plays on words. You may be surprised to discover that there is a similar novelty number sung by an old Frenchman in the next opera we learn, the Russian *Eugene Onegin*. You will understand why Tchaikovsky included it when we learn that opera.

Another detail is worth observing: while in the Olympia and Giulietta acts Hoffmann gives away his soul, there is a difference in the Antonia. On track 12, 0:51, page 112, Hoffmann and Antonia each state "My soul is filled with happiness" as they celebrate their reunion. For the first time Hoffmann experiences equal fulfillment with the woman he loves. Their duet (tracks 12–13, page 111) is one of great beauty. Notice how Antonia loses strength as she sings. What may sound like bad or harsh singing by Victoria de los Angeles is actually the sound of Antonia's wavering health.

But it seems that Hoffmann is doomed to fail tragically in love. Diabolical intervention—this time by Dr. Miracle—will again take away the woman he loves. The powerful closing scene of this act (tracks 17–18, page 123), in which Antonia sings herself to death in response to the voice of her dead mother as Dr. Miracle fiddles wildly, is frightening and horrifying. The insanity that overtakes Antonia is not of the Lucia variety; rather, it is a form of spell that she unsuccessfully struggles to break.

As Antonia expires, the orchestra swirls (track 19, page 131) as the scenery changes and we return to the tavern in Nürnberg for the Epilogue (in this recording, Act IV, scene 2). A drunk and depressed Hoffmann has now told his tales to the students. The performance of *Don Giovanni* concludes and the evil Lindorf (like the evil Coppélius, Dapertutto, and Dr. Miracle in the tales) intercepts Stella, Hoffmann's beloved, before the poet can have her. Nicklausse observes that Hoffmann's three women were all really parts of Stella. The misery these stories have provoked in Hoffmann have compelled him to drink even more heavily. Nicklausse has slipped out, and suddenly Hoffmann, in his drunken haze, sees the Muse of Poetry. She wills that Hoffmann the man be no more and that the poet be reborn. "I love thee," she says, "Hoffmann, be mine!" Hoffmann says that his soul is fired with ecstasy and says, "Beloved Muse, I am thine." Lindorf leaves the tavern with Stella, who cannot understand why the drunken Hoffmann ignores her.

Though diabolical forces have deprived Hoffmann of womanly love, he has gained the love of his Muse, whom he loves in return. Art, that thing of eternal beauty, has triumphed.

In terms of popularity, the only French opera that outstrips *Les Contes d'Hoffmann* is *Carmen,* which many people consider the most popular opera of all. The other candidates for the most popular opera are Verdi's *Aïda* and Puccini's *La Bohème.* These three operas are often referred to in opera houses as ABC *(Aïda, Bohème, Carmen),* also suggesting that they are the fundamental works for any company to have in its repertory. The second tier of classics in most theaters would probably include *Le Nozze di Figaro, Il Barbiere di Siviglia, La Traviata,* and *Tosca.*

Carmen has one of the great roles in all of opera, one that almost every mezzo tries to make a central part of her repertory. Carmen is defiant, independent, erotic, mysterious, jealous, passionate, superstitious, and ultimately doomed. Despite the presence of other good roles, this opera unquestionably belongs to her. What Tosca is for a dramatic soprano and Lucia is for a coloratura, Carmen is for a mezzo, though many sopranos have been tempted by the role as well. The Carmens of Regina Resnik, Risë Stevens, Marilyn Horne, and Teresa Berganza are particularly memorable. My recommended recording, on DG, stars Berganza, with vivid conducting by Claudio Abbado and a superb cast featuring Plácido Domingo as Don José, Ileana Cotrubas as Micaëla, and Sherrill Milnes as Escamillo, the toreador.

When music is as familiar as that of *Carmen* is (you know much of it already), it is sometimes difficult to recognize how ingenious and dramatically suitable it is. From the very first notes we are swept up in great drama and are carried along for much of the evening. I do think, however, that *Les Contes d'Hoffmann* is a more suitable introduction to French opera than *Carmen*. This is because *Carmen* is full of recitatives (spoken rather than sung in many modern productions) that can slow down proceedings if you do not speak French. Also, Act III, set in the snowy mountains where Carmen will learn her fate from her Tarot cards, can seem very long. A performance of *Carmen,* including intermissions, can last four hours, which is too long if you are still new to opera. But once you have become a more experienced operagoer, prepare well for *Carmen* and then go and enjoy it. *Hoffmann* is almost as long but, in my view, moves along more quickly.

In the next chapter we will directly address the most popular operatic topic of all: love. While we have explored this subject in every opera so far, we will take a step forward with *Eugene Onegin.*

10.

EUGENE ONEGIN

ROMANTIC OPERA

As you know, Romanticism was the great artistic movement of the nineteenth century. Two works that we have studied, *Lucia di Lammermoor* and *Les Contes d'Hoffmann,* are suffused with Romantic images and ideals. Whether in music, literature, or the visual arts, Romanticism emphasized a departure from the values of the Enlightenment in the eighteenth century, which favored reason in philosophy and classicism in literature, music, and the visual arts. With Romanticism, instinct became preferable to reason. Fantasy and sentiment became exalted virtues in the creative artist. Emotionalism replaced the sharpened wit that characterized the temperament of the eighteenth century. Country life and pastoral settings were a popular theme among the romantics, as were dreams and the supernatural.

One of the things that lay underneath the grand theories of Romanticism was a change in attitudes about the nature of love. Romanticism, for many people, represented a return to simpler times and more traditional ways of love. Many Romantics considered *Don Giovanni* one of the first works of their movement, insisting that it was a moral fable about loveless sexual excess. While Romanticism might be viewed as a fundamentally conservative movement, there were Romantics, such as Wagner, who were rebellious. To some artists and thinkers, a Romantic hero was a rebel and an outsider; he was an individual *against* society as compared with the Enlightenment hero, an individual who enjoyed freedom in society.

Love, the most universal human feeling, has been described by poets and artists since the beginning of time. Lovers may be in love, but they may not be able to understand or explain it. Through the centuries, love has been explained in political and religious terms, in erotic or Platonic, tragic or comic terms. In the middle of this century, prior to the so-called sexual revolution, much love was defined as forbidden love. Nowadays, artists, writers, and musicians often express love in terms of the inability of lovers to communicate; love, therefore, is diminished or denied because it cannot be expressed. In other circumstances some of us politicize love in search of the right to express it.

Love in the era of Romanticism was idealized and made noble in both its exalted and tragic contexts. *Lucia di Lammermoor* is a prime example of Romanticism's tragic view of love. *Tannhäuser,* which we will study later, uses the redemptive power of love to bring peace to tormented characters.

In our first six operas and most others you will ever encounter, love serves to color relationships between characters. There is paternal/filial love between Rigoletto and Gilda, who also has a virginal love for the licentious Duke. There is jealous, erotic love between Tosca and Mario and idealized, unrequited love between Lucia and Edgardo. Rosina and Almaviva have a playful, flirtatious love. Donna Anna and Don Ottavio have a sterile love; Donna Elvira is filled with wild, obsessive, hormonal love. Don Giovanni, the famous lover, is a narcissist who really only loves himself; his claim to love all women is actually a means to see his own reflection in them. Hoffmann's loves are blind, unrealistic, or doomed. Beethoven's *Fidelio* is a paean to marital love. In all of these operas, the love among various characters is part of a larger context in which the stories are built. Love is a given that then serves to push the story in other directions. For example, the fact that Gilda loves the Duke leads to the opera's inevitable tragic conclusion.

Tchaikovsky's *Eugene Onegin* is a rather special opera. In it, love is the theme, not a pretext for launching the action. Its characters and situations are all about the many aspects of love. In other words, love is the reason we care about these characters and what happens to them. *Eugene Onegin* was written by a composer who drank deeply at the well of Western European culture. Tchaikovsky (1840–1893) loved Italy and the music of Mozart and was exposed to most of the artistic currents of his time. Yet he never disregarded his profound Russian roots and the special, highly sentimental way that Russian literature and music could express love.

His opera was inspired by a poem by Alexander Pushkin (1799–1837), which was written in 1831, in the early years of the Romantic movement. Tchaikovsky first approached the subject forty-six years later. While Pushkin wrote the poem with cold, ironic detachment, making Onegin almost a Don Giovanni–type antihero, Tchaikovsky found different elements in the story and imbued it with warmth and pathos. Pushkin's writings come from deep in the Russian soul and are as well known to Russians as Shakespeare is to the British. Pushkin provided literary sources for many great Russian composers, including Glinka *(Ruslan and Ludmilla),* Tchaikovsky *(Mazeppa, The Queen of Spades),* Mussorgsky *(Boris Godunov,* probably the greatest Russian opera), and Rimsky-Korsakov *(The Golden Cockerel, Mozart and Salieri).*

Pushkin had a lot in common with Onegin; he was bright and dashing but became very jaded and cynical. Coincidentally, he died in a duel, as does the poet Lensky, Onegin's friend and rival in the story. Tchaikovsky identified less with Onegin than with Lensky and Tatyana, the heroine of the opera. She is someone who suffers from a yearning to love someone who rejects her. Lensky, who is a relatively ordinary person in the poem, in the opera is the incarnation of doomed creative talent. Tchaikovsky felt strongly about both characters and their longings. He was struck by the fact that important events in his life in the late 1870s coincided with incidents in the opera. He was receiving passionate love letters from a young woman, Antonina Milyukova, whom he scarcely knew. Onegin rejects Tatyana's declarations of love with tragic consequences. Tchaikovsky felt that if he rejected Milyukova, she would commit suicide (as she threatened to do in one of her letters). The composer, who was a homosexual, decided to marry the young woman in July

1877. The marriage quickly failed; Tchaikovsky suffered a nervous collapse and himself attempted suicide. Somehow, though, none of this turmoil impeded the composition of *Eugene Onegin.*

As with the echoes of Offenbach's life in *Les Contes d'Hoffmann* and the sad coincidence of Donizetti's going insane a few years after composing *Lucia,* there is a special poignancy when the tragic events in the life of a composer parallel those of an opera he has created. We cannot help wondering how much of his own life and feelings he brought to a role. Did his sufferings make for greater art? This is what we asked ourselves about the character of Hoffmann. And this is what Tosca reflects on when she sings "Vissi d'arte, vissi d'amore" ("I lived for art, I lived for love").

Tchaikovsky understood the anguish and the bliss of love even if he did not achieve much happiness in his own love life. This is why he could read the rather ironic language of Pushkin's poem and find passion and longing in it. So taken with it was he that he sat down in one feverish night after reading it and composed Tatyana's famous letter scene even though he had not yet sketched the form of the opera in musical and dramatic terms. It was this scene that struck a chord of recognition in the composer, who at the time was receiving missives from Antonina Milyukova.

Tchaikovsky realized that some of the language in the poem could provide the direct speech in key passages for the libretto, but the narrative voice of the poem had to be removed and replaced by dialogue among the various characters. The composer entrusted the job to Konstantin Shilovsky, although he later made substantial changes and additions to Shilovsky's text. He also realized that this would not be an opera in the traditional sense but a series of what he called "lyric scenes." In fact, the score refers to *Eugene Onegin* as "lyric scenes in three acts." Although there is a dramatic progression to the story, each of the "lyric scenes" is richly suffused with a distinct mood and flavor. It is the composer's great achievement that he manages to evoke in music the emotional feelings of longing and repressed desire that are central to the characters. Notice throughout the opera how the sounds from the orchestra and the voices are different than what you have heard before. The scale of this opera is very intimate and opens up only in the dance sequences.

Otherwise, we have characters who speak of their feelings or, in many instances, withhold them. The orchestral accompaniment is often very delicate.

Why is there so much repression of feelings among the characters? These characters imitate the social mores of provincial Russia of the 1820s. In other words, they role-play, adopting the behaviors they believe are expected of them. Only in their most private or vulnerable moments do we see how they really feel.

Romanticism pervades the opera. There are fantasy (if not the "fantastic" that we have in *Les Contes d'Hoffmann*), melancholy, dreamy bucolic settings, and glorification of the simple ways of peasants and gentry. Acts I and II are set in the countryside, which lends a flavor to the music and to the way we perceive the characters. In contrast, Act III takes place in the sophisticated and somewhat jaded ambience of upper-class St. Petersburg.

When the curtain rises, however, we are in the country. Madame Larina is surrounded by her devoted servant Filipyevna, who is also nanny to Larina's daughters, seventeen-year-old Tatyana and her younger sister, Olga. Olga is courted by the eighteen-year-old Lensky, an impetuous, slightly eccentric poet. His friend Onegin, a couple of years older, has been around a bit and seems worldly by comparison. He has a smooth, superficial charm and enjoys dalliances with women rather than the deep involvement that Lensky champions. Olga is vivacious and outgoing; Tatyana is sensitive, delicate, and painfully shy. She is also trusting and incapable of deceit. All of these characters are real and complex people, not the larger-than-life figures we see in many operas. Tosca, Lucia, Don Giovanni, and Hoffmann, for all their fascination, are not people we think of as being like us. But the awkwardness of young love, with its uncomfortable combination of exciting discoveries and broken dreams, is something all of us can identify with. So when we watch a performance of *Eugene Onegin* we are touched because we can feel the aching that the characters feel.

Tchaikovsky understood that his delicate exploration of love would be ruined if the roles of these young people were played by a matronly, middle-aged soprano and a portly, mature-looking tenor and baritone. At his insistence, the first production was done at the

Maly (Little) Theater at the Moscow Conservatory and mostly starred students at the school. Its premiere, on March 29, 1879, was a general success. (We might speculate that the talented young performers embodied the roles well and were able to experience the emotions of the characters even if they could not analyze them. What older artists bring to their roles is knowledge born of experience.) A couple of years after its premiere, *Eugene Onegin* had a very successful production at the Bolshoi Theater in Moscow. The title role was taken by the young baritone Pavel Khoklov, whom Tchaikovsky considered an ideal blend of vocalism, interpretation, appearance, and temperament. The opera soon traveled to the West, including an 1892 production in Hamburg, where Tchaikovsky met the young conductor Gustav Mahler. During this period, Mahler was at work on his highly emotional Second Symphony, and one wonders whether the deep sentiments of *Eugene Onegin* influenced its composition.

The recording we will use to learn this opera is very fine. Its one failing is that it has only one native Russian speaker in the cast— Paata Burchuladze in the small but crucial role of Prince Gremin. One of the beauties of *Eugene Onegin* is the distinct sound of the Russian language and the emotional coloring that it gives to the music. No matter how talented a foreign singer is, a native speaker has a distinct advantage in imparting its flavor and the subtext.

Nonetheless, this recording on DG, conducted by James Levine and starring Mirella Freni, Thomas Allen, and Neil Shicoff, has a collection of first-rate artists with a special sensitivity for this material. Temperamentally, each of these singers is ideally suited for his or her role. Maestro Levine lavishes great love and sensitivity in shaping the orchestral playing, creating the dreaminess and longing that perfume this score.

Although Freni is an Italian who is almost unrivaled in much of the Italian romantic repertory, her long marriage with the Bulgarian bass Nicolai Ghiaurov has given her a special window into the world of Russian opera in which her husband excels. He was instrumental in introducing Freni to congenial music in the Russian repertory, including the roles of Tatyana and Lisa in *The Queen of Spades*. Freni added this role when she was a grandmother in her early fifties. You would never know this to see her or hear her. It has always been her special skill to embody emotionally complex, sensitive yet strong and always lovable young women (Liù in *Turandot,* Micaëla in *Carmen,* Susanna in *Le Nozze di Figaro,* and especially Mimì in *La Bohème*). Freni's unique talent and skills, as well as the care with which she maintained the fresh bloom in her voice at an age when most sopranos have lost much of their abilities, make her one of the most beloved of all opera stars.

Thomas Allen is an excellent British baritone who is a superb vocal and physical actor. He understands the unlikability of characters such as Onegin and Don Giovanni yet manages to make audiences care about the people he is portraying. It is fair to say that Neil Shicoff, the tenor who plays Lensky, is a specialist in high-strung characters such as Don José in *Carmen,* Hoffmann, and the title role in *Don Carlo*—important and difficult roles that gain dimension when sung by artists with considerable emotional underpinnings. The orchestra, chorus, and all of the artists carefully imbue this music and story with emotional restraint, so that the rare bursts of passion that come forth take on even more meaning.

Let us begin. As always, acquaint yourself with the names and relationships of the characters (page 2 of the booklet) and then read the excellent essay by John Warrack (pages 23–30). This will give you a lot of valuable background on the opera, some of which I have already discussed. The photograph on page 24 shows Tchaikovsky and Antonina Milyukova, the woman to whom he was briefly married and who provided many of the elements of the character of Tatyana.

On page 23 there is a quotation from a letter Tchaikovsky wrote to his brother during the composition of *Eugene Onegin* in which he exalts the virtues of this story compared to those of other operas then popular. The "Pharaohs" and "Ethiopian princesses" refer to characters in Verdi's *Aïda.* The "poisoned cups" appeared in many operas, including Verdi's *Ernani.* The reference to "tales about automata," is not a reference to Olympia and other characters in *Les Contes d'Hoffmann* (which did not have its premiere until 1881, two years after the premiere of *Eugene Onegin*). Rather, "automata" describes the predictable and superficial characters Tchaikovsky saw in many other operas. Read the synopsis for Act I, scene 1 (page 32) before starting your CD player.

The sound of the introductory music (disk 1, track 1, page 67) may make you think that you somehow have dropped into the middle of the opera. Tchaikovsky deftly gives us the sense that the emotional climate we are about to discover has been going on for a while even if we are only now coming to it. Listen to how frankly and unabashedly emotional this music is.

We are now in the first scene of Act I. This opera has seven "lyric scenes," and I refer to acts only to make clear when the intermissions occur. Act I has three scenes, Acts II and III each have two. The curtain rises to show Madame Larina and Filipyevna making jam. Inside the house, Olga and Tatyana sing of love and sorrow, and soon the older women remark that they too knew those feelings once. Filipyevna reminds Larina that while her husband was courting her she was dreaming of another man who was unattainable. This quartet concludes to the melancholy strains of a cello.

Although you have been listening to this recording for little more than five minutes, it must already be clear to you that this opera probably sounds like nothing you have yet heard. The slight nasality of Russian is different from the nasality of French. There is something inescapably sentimental about the sound of this language that lends itself to the flavor of this opera. Notice, too, the sensitivity and restraint in the orchestral writing. Tchaikovsky uses the orchestra to create a range of emotional colors. There are very few bright colors in Tchaikovsky's palette, and most of those he saves for dance music. Instead, we have muted hues that are no less dramatic for the absence of splashiness and ostentation. You will need to adjust your ears to all of these new sounds if you are to feel the deep emotions in these "lyric scenes."

The focus expands with the arrival of peasants coming in from the harvest (track 3, page 77). It is typical in Russian operas to have prominent choral passages representing the Russian masses, the backbone of old Russian tradition. Tchaikovsky and many Russian composers introduced Russian folk melodies in their music (his "1812" Overture is full of them), and there are passages in this chorus celebrating the harvest that are as Russian as vodka and black bread. This is also the first dance sequence, and the peasants do traditional folk dances in a circle. It is important to note the style of dance in each scene, because the dance is indicative of the temperament of the moment.

Note the change in sound after the joyous dance. We hear only the melancholy voice of Tatyana (track 4, page 83), which provides startling contrast to the previous chorus. Note too that Mirella Freni sounds very much like a young girl, a remarkable achievement for an artist in her early fifties. What we have in Freni is that rare and happy circumstance of a singer who looks and sounds the part but also brings the wisdom of years that can be infused into the performance.

We discover that Olga is considerably more upbeat than her sister, who is swept up with the stories of love and suffering she is reading in her books. Her mother remarks (page 87), "It's only fiction. As the years went by, I came to see that there are no heroes in real life." This is a very telling line, straight from the ironic pen of Pushkin, that stands in stark contrast to the views of the dreamy Tatyana. Listen to the sudden orchestral outburst as Larina, Olga, Tatyana, and Filipyevna see Lensky and Onegin coming up to the walk. The bustle in the orchestra (track 5, 2:45) is tied not only to the actions onstage but to the stream of thoughts running through the minds of each of these women.

Track 6: Lensky and Onegin arrive. Onegin observes (page 95) that while Olga is more bubbly, surely Lensky the poet should have been attracted to the sorrowful Tatyana. She, on the other hand, experiences love at first sight. This may seem like a theatrical convention that doesn't occur in real life, but as some of us know firsthand, it can happen, although it is often accompanied by a certain degree of blindness and denial. We see what we want to love. We do not necessarily perceive the other's flaws.

Track 7 (page 99) contains several turning points in the opera. Lensky, in a beautiful arioso, declares his love for Olga. As his heart swells, she deflates it with teasing. The scene shifts back and forth between Lensky and Olga in one part of the garden and Onegin and Tatyana in the other. Onegin makes the blasé, general conversation of a bored city sophisticate ("It must be dreadfully boring to live here in the country, so far from everything"). The innocent, trusting Tatyana responds much more seriously ("I have my books, I have my dreams; dreams have been my companions since my earliest days"). Lensky and Olga return, and he tells her in no uncertain terms how deep his love is for her. We see an interesting parallel in this scene. Onegin's observation was correct: the deeply sentimental Lensky might be more suitable for Tatyana, while the more superficial Onegin would probably be a better match for the carefree Olga. Filipyevna sees that Tatyana is smitten with Onegin. Notice the slow, quiet ending and compare it with the endings of most opera scenes you know.

Read the synopsis for scene 2 (page 32) before continuing. We are now in Tatyana's bedroom. Just as the orchestral introduction to the opera made us think that we were entering a situation that was already in progress, here the first sounds of the strings in the orchestra signal an upsweep in emotion. We sense that Filipyevna and Tatyana have already been talking when we arrive (track 9, page 105). Filipyevna tells Tatyana the story of her arranged marriage—there was no question about falling in love. Tatyana, of course, is lost in her own thoughts about Onegin.

As her nanny leaves, Tatyana sits down to write a letter to Onegin describing all of her thoughts and feelings about this man of her dreams, a man she scarcely knows. The famous letter scene (track 10, page 115) shares something with other scenes you have learned: Lucia's mad scene, Tosca's "Vissi d'arte," Donna Elvira's "Mi tradì"; each is a reflection of the inner feelings of the character. What is different, though, is that while the other women are looking back with sadness, Tatyana is afire with hope and passion about the future. The fourteen-minute letter scene is a renowned showpiece for a singer. There are few circumstances in which audience members can devote so much time to one character and one singer. Although not much happens in the scene, this dreamy young girl's recitation of her feelings of first love overflows with emotion. A great artist, such as Freni, can captivate an audience here and produce an important result: although the opera is called *Eugene Onegin,* the most important character, the one we care about most, is Tatyana.

Read the words to the letter scene carefully as you listen to the music. This sudden burst of emotions reveals a side to this shy girl that she has not shown to others. Notice that in the course of this aria there are eight distinct changes in mood: these are indicated in the text and you can hear them in the music. This, in fact, is a wonderful object lesson in how a composer can read a text and then create music that evokes the feelings expressed in the words. The first passage, on page 115, starts with "Let me perish" and concludes with "Wherever I look, I see him!" The orchestra then takes over and changes our mood before Tatyana writes and then cries, "No, that's all wrong!" as she destroys this draft of her letter (page 117). Continue reading and listening and you will find the other transitions (or beats, to use a term you know).

Tatyana has stayed up till dawn writing her feverish declaration of love for Onegin. You can hear this realization that the morning light has arrived (track 11, page 123) in the music. Tatyana entrusts her letter to Filipyevna, whose grandson will take it to Onegin.

Now read the synopsis of scene 3 (page 33). This scene (track 12, page 129) takes place in another part of Madame Larina's garden. Servant girls sing about flirting with boys. The undercurrent of this innocent, rustic peasant folk song about boys and girls provides a touching contrast to the events that will transpire with Onegin and Tatyana. He tells her that he is not interested in marriage and can only offer her a brother's love. He speaks of being unable to recapture the soul of innocence, that he has become a free-roaming person who could not abide the confinement marriage would impose. Rather than having Tatyana respond to his words, Tchaikovsky reintroduces the singing servant girls. Read the concluding directions to the scene: "The voices of the servant girls die away. Onegin offers Tatyana his arm; after giving him a long, imploring look, she rises mechanically, accepts his arm and they leave slowly." Passion and feeling have now been put back under lock and key. These two characters resume the role playing that is expected of them.

Now read the synopsis (page 33) for the first scene of Act II, the fourth scene of the opera. The music begins on the second CD. Track 1: The first notes we hear, starting with a flute and then with the addition of strings, bring to mind the letter scene, although the flavor of the music is different, more anguished than ecstatic. It is several months since Onegin's rejection of Tatyana. We are inside the Larina house at a ball in honor of Tatyana's name day. Gradually (at 2:10) the music changes from a reminder of the letter to the buoyant dance music (a waltz) of the ball. Remember that Tchaikovsky was one of the greatest composers of dance music, if not the greatest of all. *Swan Lake, The Sleeping Beauty,* and *The Nutcracker* are three masterpieces. That is why the dance music in *Eugene Onegin* is more thrilling than that of most other operas. Also, note how the waltz gives a different flavor to this scene than the peasant dances did to the first scene of the opera. In the sixth scene of the opera, in St. Petersburg, the more sophisticated polonaise will evoke different feelings than did the other dance music of this opera. This is another effective way that Tchaikovsky gives emotional color and weight to different scenes in the opera.

During this waltz, Onegin and Tatyana dance. He is quite bored and contemptuous of these provincial people. Notice (page 141) how Tchaikovsky has created two groups of gossips to comment on the young couple. Group A thinks they make a lovely couple. Group B thinks Onegin is a cad who has been cruel to Tatyana. Then (page 143), both groups agree that Onegin is a character not to be trusted ("He won't kiss ladies' hands . . . he drinks only red wine—by the tumblerful!"). This annoys Onegin, who is now mad at his friend Lensky for insisting that he come along to the ball. To get back at Lensky, Onegin decides to flirt with Olga.

Track 2: Olga and Lensky quarrel. He is insanely jealous of Onegin, who has now danced many dances with Olga. She tells him he has nothing to be jealous of and ridicules him. This encounter is interrupted by Triquet (track 2, 3:40), a Frenchman who is a tutor for Tatyana. In the Russia of that time, knowledge of French language and culture was a symbol of proper education and status. Russian audiences briefly shared this sense of breeding and culture by enjoying Triquet's charming French song in the middle of a Russian opera. Triquet's song is in honor of Tatyana, for whom this party was organized. This little interruption may remind you of Frantz's song in the Antonia act of *Les Contes d'Hoffmann.* Compare them in terms of sound and style and their dramatic effect on their respective scenes.

Track 3, page 154: Dancing resumes. This time it is a mazurka. In between, the jealous Lensky exchanges taunts with Onegin. Soon the quarrel brings the dancing to a halt. Larina begs them not to argue in the house.

Track 4, page 163: The argument has gone too far. Lensky decides his friendship with Onegin is over. Onegin expresses a rare regret for his actions. Lensky will not hear this. He feels that both Onegin and Olga have hurt him. As custom dictates in this time and place, Lensky challenges his former friend to a duel. The choral music toward the end of this scene may sound curiously festive, but by the time the orchestra chimes in to conclude the scene, there is little doubt that the seeds of tragedy have been sown.

Now read the synopsis for Act II, scene 2 (page 33). Track 5, page 173: The scene opens at dawn on the banks of a stream near an old mill. This being Russia in January, it is likely that there is a lot of snow. The music for this scene begins with the sound of mournful cellos. Grave notes are then introduced from other parts of the orchestra. We find Lensky and his second, Zaretsky. The opening notes of the scene return as Lensky reflects on his short life. This aria has much of the flavor, if not the sound, of "E lucevan le stelle," Cavaradossi's aria in *Tosca* at dawn on the day he knows he will die.

Track 6, page 177: Onegin and his second, Guillot, arrive. As Lensky and Onegin turn their backs and take their paces, each man remarks that he does not think their quarrel merits a duel. But duty, honor, and convention require them to go through with it. In moments, these two men who loved one another as friends will turn and shoot. And Lensky will die.

By this point in the opera, social convention (or, in the case of Onegin and Tatyana, the lack thereof) has prevented all of the young characters from experiencing the gratification and joy that love can bring. The older characters, Larina and Filipyevna, seem world-weary on the subject. They do not believe in romantic love and choose instead to pursue their maternal instincts, loving and caring for Tatyana and Olga.

The final act shifts to St. Petersburg. It is several years since Onegin has killed Lensky. He is now twenty-six years old. Read the synopsis of Act III, scene 1 (the sixth "lyric scene") on page 34 before listening to the music.

Track 7, page 183: From the first notes the orchestra plays, we can tell that we have moved from the provinces to St. Petersburg, then the capital of Russia and its great artistic, economic, and social center. The music of the polonaise tells us this is a grand occasion in the mansion of a nobleman. At the end of the dance, we see Onegin standing alone. His first line (track 8) is revealing: "I am bored here too." Nothing in his life has yet aroused his passion, which is part of this character's tragedy. In his monologue, Onegin explains how a life of restless wandering has not given him anything meaningful. He has no roots, no attachments, no obligations.

Suddenly, he is interrupted by another dance. As it ends, Prince Gremin enters with an elegant woman of regal bearing and tasteful dress. Guests bow to them. Onegin soon realizes that it is none other than Tatyana. She recognizes him and briefly loses her composure.

Onegin asks Gremin who the woman is. "My wife," the prince replies. The prince is substantially older than Onegin and Tatyana. In a famous aria (track 9, page 191) Gremin explains how his life has changed since marrying Tatyana. After a life in the high society of St. Petersburg, Gremin tired of the pretense and vacuity of social relations. Suddenly this passionate, emotional, and genuine person came into his life, and he has experienced true love.

Track 10, page 193: Gremin presents Onegin to Tatyana, who acknowledges that they have already met. After polite conversation, Tatyana says she is tired and departs with her husband. Onegin, for the first time, explodes with feelings of love, jealousy, dreaminess, and passion. Could this be the same girl he rejected years before? How could he have been so presumptuous, so foolish? Notice the passion and pathos that have heretofore been absent from his music. As he sings his last words, "Wherever I look, I see her" (echoing Tatyana's sentiments in the first act), dance music swirls up and carries him away.

We have reached Act III, scene 2, the final scene in the opera. Read the synopsis on page 34 before listening to track 11 (page 197). The feelings of love for Onegin have returned to Tatyana. The orchestra tells us of the storm in her soul, which continues as Onegin appears and rushes to her feet. Onegin's cold heart has finally been warmed with love. He declares his love for Tatyana and she confesses that she still loves him. He insists that his love has nothing to do with her new station in life but with his recognition of feelings that he had always suppressed. Nonetheless, duty and convention step in. Tatyana says she must be faithful to her husband, although she does not experience the same sort of love for the prince that she does for Onegin. Tatyana rushes out. After a brief, stunned moment, Onegin, all alone, leaves in despair. The orchestra follows his footsteps and tells us of the ache in Onegin's heart.

Again, longing will replace love. We can only envision the sadness and emptiness ahead for Tatyana and Eugene Onegin and wonder at what might have been.

Eugene Onegin is now part of the standard repertory for most major opera companies, but the fact that it is in Russian means that it is not staged as often as operas in Italian, German, or French. Therefore, it may be some time before you get to see a performance. It is much more likely that Puccini's *La Bohème* will be playing somewhere near you. Many people who do not know much about opera think *La Bohème* is a great first opera. I do not agree. There is actually a lot of recitative and repartee that slows down the action. The arias are beautiful, but one has to wait for them. Therefore, I recommend that you consider *Rigoletto, La Traviata, Tosca,* or *Cavalleria Rusticana/Pagliacci* for your first night at the opera. *La Bohème* is more about young lovers than about love. The basic, rather predictable story is: boy meets girl, they fall in love, they quarrel, girl leaves boy, girl gets sick, they make up, girl dies. What this opera does have in common with *Eugene Onegin* is that both benefit from the fresh faces and voices of young singers, although those in *La Bohème* do not need the sophistication of those in Tchaikovsky's opera. Because this opera is so frequently presented, many productions of *La Bohème* are sloppy and underrehearsed, so that the delicate beauty of Puccini's opera is often obliterated.

When you study *La Bohème,* look for the recording on London/ Decca conducted by Herbert von Karajan and starring Mirella Freni and Luciano Pavarotti. Freni, as I suggested earlier, is the perfect

Mimì, and Rodolfo is one of Pavarotti's signature roles. For comparison, there is a treasurable recording on Angel/EMI from the 1950s conducted by Sir Thomas Beecham and starring Victoria de los Angeles and Jussi Björling. I am afraid that after hearing these two performances, though, you will find that few you will hear in an opera house will ever measure up.

After the intimacy and emotionalism of *Eugene Onegin*, we will go to the opposite end of the spectrum and learn about grand opera, the style that comes to mind when most people think of opera. We will study Verdi's *Don Carlo*, one of the most towering works in the repertory.

11.

DON CARLO

GRAND OPERA

For people interested in opera as an art form, the idea of grand opera either quickens the pulse or is profoundly off-putting. Many audience members who unquestioningly love grand opera generally believe that bigger is better and that they only are getting their money's worth if they hear a cast of hundreds and a booming orchestra accompanying singers draped in expensive costumes performing in front of opulent scenery as horses and elephants troop by. This sort of production is usually mounted for tourists during the European or North American summer. Audience members who claim to loathe grand opera tend to disdain these big production values, which, it must be admitted, do provide a certain kind of visceral thrill.

The problem with grand opera these days is that we really don't know what it is or how to produce it. As I mentioned earlier, grand opera is a form that was created to please the large moneyed classes in Paris in the nineteenth century who wanted to pay to see grandiose productions. These typically emphasized crowd scenes, long ballets, spectacular scenic effects, and general opulence. Stories often had cataclysmic endings, but there was not always the care in the musicodramatic plotting found in the best of classical opera, bel canto, and Verdi and Wagner.

The most popular composer of grand opera was Giacomo

Meyerbeer, who dominated the opera world in Paris from the premiere of his *Robert le Diable* in 1831 until his death in 1864. It is probably fair to say that his only rivals in Europe were Wagner and Verdi, neither of whom ever enjoyed the success in Paris that Meyerbeer did. Because Paris, more than Vienna, Milan, or any other city, was considered the operatic capital of Europe, Meyerbeer was the king of the biggest hill. His style and influence were once considered so great that it is almost inconceivable that today he has been reduced to a mere footnote in most general interest books about opera. Only three of his works—*Les Huguenots* (1836), *Le Prophète* (1849), and *L'Africaine* (1864)—seem to hold forth at all. While Meyerbeer's operas are performed occasionally in France, which has large government subsidies for the arts, they are seldom seen elsewhere. There are good reasons for this. Audiences have forgotten him and do not clamor for his works. Wagner once referred to Meyerbeerian spectacle as "effects without causes." It seems that mindless spectacle—which is a part, though not all, of Meyerbeer's art—no longer appeals to opera audiences, even if it does seem to have a lot of currency in the Broadway musical. For opera audiences nowadays the spectacle must usually mean something. Therefore, the triumphal march in *Aïda* succeeds these days only if it connects to the drama that surrounds it. Few singers seek training in Meyerbeer's style, in part because it is difficult and in part because there is little demand for vocalists who can sing it. Above all, the vast expense of mounting productions with large choruses and orchestras, massive scenery, and expensive special effects puts Meyerbeer out of reach for most opera companies, which are invariably strapped for cash.

We must remember that the taste for grandeur in opera had existed since the time of Lully in France, and perhaps even before that in some operatic productions in Venice. Certain composers, including Gluck and Mozart, did not have much need for that kind of opulence, but most composers and producers have always known that a little spectacle can go a long way toward making an opera a hit. Meyerbeer was not the only composer of nineteenth-century grand opera. He had several contemporaries in France whose works occasionally surface today. The form probably was at its most opulent among these French composers, but grand opera's influence reached elsewhere. Grandeur remained part of the operatic aesthetic long after French grand opera had begun to wither. Mussorgsky's *Boris Godunov* has most of the elements of grand opera, yet these elements are part of a huge dramatic and musical canvas in which they serve the story. To give but one example, the scene of Tsar Boris's coronation is one of the most spectacular in all opera, but it never seems excessive or gratuitous. In the twentieth century, Puccini included spectacles such as the Act I procession in *Tosca* and Act II, scene 2 of *Turandot* because he enjoyed the challenge of making them work as drama. He must have known, too, that they would be big crowd pleasers.

And then we have the cases of Verdi and Wagner. I explained at considerable length in chapter 1 that these two composers were the colossi of nineteenth-century opera and, by extension, opera for all times. When opera fans take sides, insisting that they are either Wagnerians or Verdians, I mourn the fact that they don't permit themselves to revel in the greatness of both composers. Each man took elements of grand opera and combined them with his own artistry to produce some of the greatest operas of all.

Both Wagner and Verdi were engaged in the social and political debates of their time and used opera to explore their ideas. Wagner's operas are usually large-scale and expansive. Verdi injected elements of grand opera in his works when he felt they were suitable. There are probably only two Verdi operas that can be fully called grand opera: *Don Carlo* (1867) and *Aïda* (1871). I know that many readers of this book will disagree with this assertion. Certainly many Verdi operas have crowd scenes, big choruses, opulent settings, and dance sequences. Passions run hot and heavy in many Verdi works, and they are often expressed in very loud voices singing over an orchestra that races and booms. But much of what makes grand opera grand is the scale of the composer's intentions and the extent to which they are realized. When Verdi put beautiful party scenes in *La Traviata* or crowds of Venetian nobility in *Otello* and Genoese political figures in *Simon Boccanegra,* these were not gratuitous choices intended to please audiences. Verdi put them there because they made dramatic sense.

Don Carlo and Aïda may be considered grand opera because the entire scale on which they were created was grand. One of Verdi's intentions with these works was to use the grandeur and opulence as a means to explore the dramatic content of these stories. Aïda takes place in ancient Egypt. There are pharaohs, impassioned princesses, oppressed slaves, and heaps of spectacle, but these all give color to the two-tiered story. We have Aïda, the Ethiopian princess who is captured and made a slave of Amneris, the Egyptian princess. There is also Radames, the great Egyptian soldier who leads the conquest of Ethiopia. Amneris loves Radames, but he loves Aïda, who must choose between love and duty to her country. Amneris is intensely jealous; how can Radames possibly prefer an Ethiopian slave to an Egyptian princess? There are other issues for Aïda. How can she love the man who conquered her country? How can she choose between her love and loyalty for her father, Amonasro, the Ethiopian king, and her passion for Radames? The dramatic issue of love vs. familial or political obligations is the same as in *Lucia di Lammermoor* and the many incarnations of *Romeo and Juliet*. Yet Verdi was interested in juxtaposing the private tragedies and tribulations of kings, princesses, and military heroes with the vast tableau of the masses in ancient times: victorious Egyptians and vanquished Ethiopians. In *Lucia* the crowd mirrors, echoes, and responds to events in the story. In *Aïda* it provides vivid contrast by representing mass populations affected by the actions of the protagonists. In the most carefully thought-out and produced stagings of *Aïda*, all of these elements are in proper balance. Unfortunately, most *Aïda* productions are more concerned with spectacle, and Verdi's interests are largely neglected. You are likely to see many performances of *Aïda* in your operagoing life, so you should devote time and thought to looking beyond the spectacle and into the story. Verdi's music is wonderfully dramatic and incisive if you hear a production that is well played and sung.

Let *Aïda* be your alternate work for learning about grand opera. There is a fine recording on EMI led by Riccardo Muti and starring Montserrat Caballé and Plácido Domingo, both of whom we will hear in our study of *Don Carlo*. Leontyne Price was a supreme interpreter of the role of Aïda, and there are two recordings featuring her in her prime. You should listen to these for her magnificent portrayal, but the Muti recording is a better all-around performance of the opera.

Aïda is justifiably famous, but *Don Carlo* is a more complex and accomplished work, and in recent years many critics have come to consider it Verdi's greatest achievement. I am not in the business of declaring bests, but I certainly think *Don Carlo* deserves to be grouped with *Rigoletto, La Traviata, Simon Boccanegra, Aïda, Otello,* and *Falstaff* on a list of great Verdi operas. Get to know them all and come to your own conclusions.

What makes Verdi's art so distinct is how palpably we feel the drama in his characters. He had a preference for vivid characters who often are forced by love, duty, or unavoidable circumstances to make painful choices. Some adhere to strong personal convictions at great sacrifice: Gilda, for example, or Radames, who would rather die than renounce Aïda. Others, such as Macbeth and Otello, have great flaws that inevitably bring tragedy down upon them.

Verdi's ultimate goal was the expression of human drama, and he put his art in service of that goal. His natural talents, which he worked hard to refine, were valuable tools that he used in its pursuit. Verdi's genius was that he understood how to make vocal and orchestral music suggest not only the issue of the drama but also the psychological underpinnings that accompany it. For example, when Rigoletto discovers that Gilda has been kidnapped, it is the orchestral music that tells us how his heart is racing and the thoughts that are running through his head.

Verdi emphasized direct, heartfelt expression as an ideal and kept symbolism to a minimum. Rather, his characters say what they feel, or, at the very least, the orchestra tells us what they feel if they themselves cannot verbalize it. But there is no question that Verdi's men and women care deeply about what they want and what they believe. There is a primal sense of humanity about even his most restrained and noble characters. While Elisabetta in *Don Carlo* always maintains the bearing of a queen, her private passions and sufferings are very clear.

The struggle against power and authority—and the exploration of how these forces should be used—are central to Verdian thought.

As you read earlier, Verdi was a prominent political figure who led the fight to free Italy from foreign domination. In his younger years, prior to the failed uprising against Austria in 1848, he was an idealist who embraced a philosophy of pure liberalism. Verdi was so frequently subjected to censorship in his work that it was logical that he should be attracted to the ideals of individual freedom and self-determination. After 1848, his operas became less explicitly political and more intimate. Yet *Rigoletto* and *La Traviata* were no less provocative or controversial in the eyes of authority figures and social arbiters. The Duke in *Rigoletto* represented corrupt, dissolute authority, and *La Traviata* was a sympathetic portrait of a prostitute.

As the cause of Italian freedom was rekindled in the mid-1850s, Verdi wrote a new kind of political opera. These include *I Vespri Siciliani* (1855), *Simon Boccanegra* (1857), *Un Ballo in Maschera* (1859), *La Forza del Destino* (1862), *Don Carlo* (1867), and *Aïda* (1871). In these works we see Verdi less as an idealist than as a realist and fatalist. These operas are much deeper explorations of the havoc and misery that unchecked authority and oppression can wreak. In some cases, including *Don Carlo,* these operas are incisive examinations of the limitations of power and of the solitude and sorrow that leaders often experience in private.

In all of Verdi's works, we clearly know and hear his political convictions. By contrast, in the operas of Mozart and Wagner, we have relied on thinkers and philosophers who brought—and continue to bring—their own interpretations to bear on these composers' intentions and ideology. Mozart and Wagner invite interpretation and speculation because their works are not always as pointed and straightforward as Verdi's. Mozart's characters typically live in the eighteenth-century moment in which we meet them. Politics forms a subtext to their actions and behavior rather than being what they focus on and speak about. Many of Wagner's characters live outside of any specific time or context, so we experience these people and their moral and political subtexts in an abstract way.

By comparison, in Verdi there is an immediacy about the moment in which we find his characters, yet we also see them in a well-defined political and historical context: in other words, the present and the past both have relevance and weight in determining what they do and feel. Many of Verdi's operas are set between the fourteenth and eighteenth centuries, the period that saw the rise of most major nations and states in Europe. The class structures and social conditions of these societies were well documented and provided specific environments in which Verdi's characters could live. Almost all of Verdi's operas take place on broad dramatic and musical canvases. These are the stories of kings and queens, princes and princesses, dukes, doges, military heroes, cardinals and other pillars of the church, conspirators and assassins. Their choices and their fate affect not only their personal lives but also the destiny of peoples and nations. The only major Verdi operas that are about ordinary people are *La Traviata* and *Falstaff*. *Stiffelio* (1850) is a fine, less-known work about the domestic problems of a Protestant minister in Salzburg.

The literary source of *Don Carlo* was the 1787 play *Don Carlos* by Friedrich von Schiller (1759–1805). This great German writer, whose idealism and hatred of tyranny provided the themes for much of his work, was one of the most important sources of inspiration for nineteenth-century composers. Those are Schiller's words you hear in the "Ode to Joy" in Beethoven's Ninth Symphony. Other Schiller works resulted in many important operas: Verdi's *Giovanna d'Arco, I Masnadieri, Luisa Miller,* and *Don Carlo,* Donizetti's *Maria Stuarda,* Rossini's *Guillaume Tell,* and Tchaikovsky's *Maid of Orleans.* His adaptation of Carlo Gozzi's *Turandot* became Puccini's source for his final opera.

Although Verdi was strongly drawn to the politics in Schiller's play, he was too smart an operatic dramatist to make *Don Carlo* a case study in liberal philosophy. He knew that for audiences to absorb the consequences of the secular liberalism and religious conservatism that compete in the play, he had to give more emphasis to the human dilemmas that these philosophies produce. In the opera, the idea of sacrificing romantic love for political and religious concerns becomes at least as important as those concerns themselves. For example, Verdi added a first scene, known as the Fontainebleau scene, that is simply referred to in passing in Schiller. This scene makes clearer to the audience the relationship between Don Carlos, the infante (son of the king) of Spain, and Elizabeth of Valois, daughter of King Henry II of France. They meet in the Fontaine-bleau forest in France, which underscores the fact that this opera is not only about personal conflicts but also about national sover-eignty (Schiller's play is set entirely in Spain). The two young people fall in love and declare their intentions to marry. Word then arrives that Elizabeth's father has arranged that she marry Philip II, King of Spain and father of Don Carlos. This marriage would bring peace and prosperity to France, which was suffering during an extended war with Spain. For the good of her people, Elizabeth must forgo her pledge to Carlos and marry his father. Verdi added other scenes and details throughout his opera to give a depth and a gravity to the characters and situations that one does not always find in the play. (In the Italian versions of the opera, Carlos, Elizabeth, and Philip are called Carlo, Elisabetta—sometimes Isabella—and Filippo. I will use "Carlo" and "Elisabetta" but stick to the more customary "Philip" for the king.)

The evolution of Verdi's opera is a long and interesting one that was conditioned by various factors. When Meyerbeer died in 1864, the Paris Opéra needed a composer of great stature to create a grand opera to coincide with the Universal Exposition held in Paris in 1867. The Paris premiere of Wagner's *Tannhäuser* in 1861 was one of the most notorious fiascoes in the history of opera, so Wagner was out of the question. But Verdi had already had some success in Paris in 1855 with *Les Vêpres Siciliennes* (later translated into Ital-ian as *I Vespri Siciliani*)—although it did not garner nearly the ac-claim that Meyerbeer and his French contemporaries enjoyed—so Verdi was selected to create the new grand opera for Paris.

Even for a composer of Verdi's stature this was a challenge. Such an opera, of course, would be in French. The producers wanted spectacle and grandeur, while Verdi cared most about finding meaning and inspiration in the story he would set to music. Various subjects were proposed, and Verdi warmed most to the Schiller play, with which he had been acquainted for more than fifteen years. The libretto was fashioned by Joseph Méry and Camille Du Locle. Méry died in 1866, and Verdi continued to work with Du Locle. The composer added various scenes from the play in order to sharpen the drama—he would keep spectacle to gratify French tastes, but it had to serve the drama. Verdi composed much of the music at his home near Parma but had to flee when some of the fiercest battles of the Austro-Prussian war (this part of Italy was under Austrian rule) raged near his house. He traveled to Genoa and then back to France, working all the time on his opera. During this period, his father died.

The Paris Opéra in the nineteenth century was different from other companies in several important ways. It was the richest opera house in Europe. Great singers were available because the fees were high. Financial rewards for composers were also quite substantial, which is one reason why the likes of Bellini, Donizetti, Rossini, Wagner, and Verdi could be lured to the Opéra and other theaters in Paris. For these composers, too, the presence of great singers and the most sophisticated stage equipment made Paris a desirable place to explore aspects of their artistic vision. No other theater offered such potential or such extensive rehearsal time as the Opéra. *Don Carlos,* as it is called in French, was in rehearsal for many months prior to its premiere in 1867. The opera had a large chorus and orchestra, stage bands, an extended ballet, and elaborate settings: forests, palaces, royal chambers, churches, monasteries, Spanish gardens, and public squares. There was a massive scene featuring an auto-da-fé, the public condemnation and burning of heretics at the behest of the Spanish Inquisition.

This opera was in every way big: aside from the physical grandeur and orchestral splendor, the passions and crises experienced by its characters were also on a grand scale. If *Eugene Onegin* is a series of precious miniatures, *Don Carlos* is a collection of vast canvases overflowing with details and complexity. But these would not merely be a series of eye-catching tableaux. Verdi wanted his opera to have the effect of "transforming our theaters," as he said. This would be a new form in which all of the elements of stagecraft would serve the dramatic ideal rather than provide mere spectacle.

But Verdi's ambitions ran into logistical problems, even at the Paris Opéra. When *Don Carlos* was completed, it was his longest opera. The running time of his five-act opera was five hours and twelve minutes. The management of the Opéra asked Verdi to make cuts so that the audience could get out of the theater before midnight, when public transport shut down for the night. Verdi authorized numerous cuts before opening night. The result was a rich, if flawed, work that did not fully realize Verdi's desire to use great theatrical resources in tandem with powerful music and drama to explore the power of the Church at odds with that of the State.

Don Carlos was neither a rousing success nor a failure. Verdi thought the long rehearsal period had robbed the drama of spontaneity and vitality. He was used to working in the compact time frame of Italian opera houses, where ingenuity and spontaneity often resulted in fresh, vital performances. Paris, he felt, had overrehearsed *Don Carlos,* creating a dry, uninspired result.

After the Paris premiere, Verdi continued to make cuts, revisions, and amendments. When the score was printed, much of the deleted music was not even included. Some of this music was presumed lost until the 1960s, when it was discovered by scholarly musicological detectives. In October 1867 the opera was staged in Bologna, in Italian, as *Don Carlo.* This was, in effect, a tightened version of the opera heard in Paris. For a production in Naples in 1872, Verdi added music to the duet between King Philip and Rodrigo, Marquis of Posa. In the succeeding years, many theaters made cuts and adjustments that suited their own needs or limitations. Until very recently, the opera has almost always been performed in Italian, except in France and Belgium.

In 1882–83 Verdi, who was frustrated at the way his opera was being treated, decided to rework the opera to make it manageable for theaters that didn't have the scenic and vocal resources of Paris. He completed a four-act version in Italian that left out Fontainebleau but incorporated the tenor aria from that scene into the opening act. This version was staged at La Scala the following year. This version was more cost-effective and has been used ever since by companies that could not afford the five-act version. In 1886, yet another version was staged in Modena (in Italian). This one contained the original Fontainebleau act (translated, of course) and the revised four acts that had appeared at La Scala, with the tenor aria back in its original setting.

As you might expect, there is no definitive performing version of

Don Carlo. It shares this trait with *Les Contes d'Hoffmann,* but there are important differences. Offenbach's opera was completed by others, and the many changes and revisions it has undergone all happened after the composer's death. In *Don Carlo,* Verdi wrote all the music and oversaw all the cuts and revisions in the various versions produced during his lifetime. Conductors and musical scholars argue about which is the best version. Many say that the Modena version (five acts in Italian) represents Verdi's most advanced thinking on the subject, combining as it does the original first act and the revised versions of the following acts. Some major companies still stage the four-act version, as the Chicago Lyric Opera did in the 1980s and as La Scala did in 1992.

In the past few years, a few companies have begun to stage a five-act version based on the original 1867 Paris production. Purists say that since Verdi wrote his music to a French text, the Paris version is the only one to use. Some French-language productions have even restored much of the music that Verdi cut before the opening night in Paris. This practice has raised objections as well. Many feel that if Verdi himself deemed the cuts necessary, it is not up to us to restore them.

Although I find the French version interesting and freely acknowledge that much of the music sounds better in that language, I favor the five-act Modena version. The drama is tighter, yet it contains the important Fontainebleau act, without which the opera seems sadly truncated. The Modena version represents the summit of the artistic evolution of *Don Carlo,* and I believe that musicologists err in second-guessing this particular composer's instincts.

For your information, there is a recording of *Don Carlos* in French conducted by Claudio Abbado and starring Plácido Domingo in the title role and Ruggero Raimondi as King Philip II. These three artists contribute magnificent work, but the rest of the cast is not up to their level. This opera should not be done unless there are five outstanding singers, and this recording has only two. Maestro Abbado also added (sometimes as appendices) as much music as could be located from the Paris production, whether or not it was cut before opening night. The result is interesting for those who know this opera intimately but confusing for everyone else.

We will learn the opera in Italian in the Modena version, the one that you are most likely to encounter in world opera houses. The recording I have selected was made in 1971 under the baton of the venerable Italian conductor Carlo Maria Giulini. His cast includes five great singers at the top of their form in roles that are especially suited to their talents. Plácido Domingo is Don Carlo, a very challenging role for a tenor, to which this singer brings great artistry. Carlo is a lightning rod whose actions arouse responses from all the other characters. His psychological makeup is quite complicated. He is unstable but not insane. He can be firm and assertive at times, weak and neurotic at others. Despite his being the title character, Carlo does not have a show-stopping aria as do the other characters. He does, however, have a great deal of difficult music that defeats most tenors. Domingo, however, is completely up to the task.

Montserrat Caballé sings Elisabetta with exquisite delicacy and compassion. Ruggero Raimondi, in the pivotal role of King Philip II, creates a vivid musical and psychological portrait of this ruler of a vast empire who must nonetheless accede to the demands of the Church. He has a loveless marriage and a son who despises him for marrying the woman that he (the son) loved. Like Elisabetta, Philip has sacrificed private happiness for the sake of his country. The Princess Eboli is another of Verdi's great creations. Eboli is the mistress of the king but actually loves Carlo; her intrigues set many of the tragic events of the opera in motion. This role, which calls for a powerful dramatic mezzo who is also a great actress, is given an authoritative performance by Shirley Verrett.

Then there is Rodrigo, the Marquis of Posa, sung by Sherrill Milnes. Rodrigo is one of the great Verdi baritone roles. He represents, in many ways, the liberal ideology of the young Verdi, while Philip is the model of Verdi's more mature, fatalistic world view. In Philip we have a character whom we see in terms of politics as well as personal relationships. Philip understands that compromise and submission are occasionally inevitable, even for a king. Rodrigo, on the other hand, is full of idealism and burns with the passion of his beliefs. He does not seem to have a sexual personality and even in his dying words he only talks politics, telling Carlo, "You were destined to reign and I to die for you."

The polar opposite of Rodrigo is the Grand Inquisitor. Although this character is onstage for only about ten minutes in the entire opera, he represents the power and the persecution that the Catholic Church in Spain was capable of in the sixteenth century. His private visit to King Philip in Act IV is the turning point of the opera. This scene is a tug-of-war between the authority of the monarchy and the power of the Church. The Grand Inquisitor is not a moral or spiritual figure nor is he, of course, a figure of sexual or romantic interest. Rather, he is the embodiment of cynical politics, an incarnation of lust for power and control. Verdi insisted that he be ninety years old and blind, but he never put into print why he made these specifications.

There is a brief, mysterious role called "il frate" (the friar), who represents, among other things, the spiritualism that is missing from the Grand Inquisitor. I will let you discover more about the friar as we learn the opera. There is also a Celestial Voice that is heard briefly during the auto-da-fé scene. Again, this voice (we never see the singer) is one of pure spirituality penetrating this corrupt atmosphere of a power struggle between Church and State.

Some people assert that Verdi was anti-Church. As you learn this opera, you can come to your own conclusions on this and other topics. You may want to look at the very blurred lines between Church and State in our own times and assess Verdi's view of organized religion as compared to a divine presence in the lives of his characters.

Start by reading the names of the roles and the artists in the cast (page 3). You will notice that each singer's voice category is mentioned. This is a good practice in that it helps us identify characters as we listen to the recording. Then read Andrew Porter's essay on pages 8–12. Porter, the former music critic for *The New Yorker,* is also a formidable scholar and translator of libretti. Porter was one of those who found much of the missing music from the Paris version of *Don Carlos,* and he has been instrumental in promoting the use of French in performances of the opera.

Now turn to the synopsis on page 13. Because this is a long and complicated opera with many plot twists, you should read the synopsis one scene at a time. I will mention in passing that this story was indeed drawn from history, although the characters were elaborated on by Schiller and Verdi in ways that had little to do with their real-life antecedents. But it is nonetheless important to view this drama in its setting, which was the time of the Spanish Inquisition and the slow unraveling of Spanish power. (Spain would be eclipsed by England in 1588 as the major European power.)

As you read the synopsis and the libretto, bear in mind that this opera exists in several versions, and you may at some point see a production in which the acts are divided differently than they are here. Our discussion of the breakdown of acts and scenes refers to the Modena version, used on this recording. What this recording's libretto sorely lacks is the indication of the track numbers next to the words in the text where a new track begins. The list of the tracks on pages 4 through 8 is a slight compensation, but I will give you specific indications when I make references to the text.

After reading Act I, start playing the recording and reading the text on pages 34–35. (When I make references in this opera to page numbers, it will be to the English-language translation unless I state otherwise.) Act I (Fontainebleau) opens with hunting horns and two groups of hunters. Here is a good example of how members of the same chorus can be divided to play different characters within a scene. Soon Carlo arrives and sings his aria "Io la vidi" (page 37, track 2, 2:00) in which he describes his first sighting of Elisabetta. (When *Don Carlo* is performed in its four-act version, this aria appears in what is here Act II, scene 1.) This is Carlo's only solo aria, which is remarkable when you think that he is the title character in a very long opera. When other characters sing, however, it often is in response to Carlo's actions or statements. You are familiar with other operas in which the title character has very little solo music. Tosca has only one real solo, while Cavaradossi has two. Don Giovanni basically has only two brief songs while other characters have long arias.

When Elisabetta arrives and meets Carlo, she does not yet know that this is the man to whom she is betrothed. When she discovers his identity—"Possente Iddio!" ("O great heavens!" page 44, track 4, 4:11), listen to the orchestra: it is telling us what is happening in her heart at the moment of recognition. Throughout this opera, and in much of Verdi's work, the essence of a character's feelings can be learned when you combine the words, the sound of the vocal line, and the sound of the orchestra. While this statement can apply to just about any composer, Verdi reaches an eloquence that is astonishing. What he tells us is accurate, succinct, and moving. As you listen to *Don Carlo,* you will find Verdi at his fullest powers of expression. You will discover that this opera is full of these great moments of dramatic insight.

This is quickly followed (at the start of track 5, page 45) with Elisabetta's singing "Di qual amor, di quanto ardor" ("With what love, with what passion"). This melody, the first of several that will appear as recurring themes, represents the love of Elisabetta and Carlo. Whenever you hear it, whether from them, or from the orchestra, Verdi wants to bring their love to your mind. If played or sung at a different tempo or in a different key, it will indicate a change in the nature or the fate of Elisabetta and Carlo's love. This use of a melody or musical passage is a *motive,* a fundamental dramatic device in many operas. Wagner is the most famous employer of this method—in his operas, these melodies are referred to as *leitmotivs,* although he did not coin this term. When a composer weaves various motives together, the result usually indicates an overlapping or conflict in the subjects that these motives represent. This is another musical function that you should listen for in *Don Carlo.* It is precisely this use of interwoven motives that gives this opera its great depth and texture.

You will notice that Elisabetta frequently refers to heaven ("ciel"). For her this is a place of refuge, salvation, and guidance. In an opera that closely examines the role of the Church (representing organized religion) as opposed to pure faith and sanctity, it soon becomes clear that Elisabetta's faith is indeed pure and unpolitical. This will mark our view of her throughout the opera. Notice the change in events in track 6 (page 51) as Elisabetta learns that she has been pledged to marry Philip, king of Spain, and not Carlo, his son. We learn (page 57) that King Henry leaves the decision up to Elisabetta. She must choose between love for Carlo and duty to her country. When she gives her answer (the top of page 58), her "Sì" is delivered "con voce morente." The English translation of this vocal marking is given as "faintly," but the more precise translation is "with a dying voice." Notice how carefully Montserrat Caballé has read this direction and how well she communicates it (track 9, 1:33). As Carlo and Elisabetta express their private anguish, the people express joy that Elisabetta will become the Queen of Spain and their miserable lot will be improved. Listen to how Verdi juxtaposes the public joy and the private anguish. The chorus is jubilant, the lovers despair, and the orchestra effectively communicates both emotions. As the scene closes, festive music plays as Elisabetta is escorted away. Carlo sings of how cruelly fate has treated him as the festivity fades into the distance.

Now read the synopsis for Act II, scene 1 (page 13). The setting is now the cloister of San Yuste. You will hear the voice of a friar in this scene. Depending upon the stage director of the production you attend, you may or may not see the friar inside the walls of the monastery. Sometimes there will be a hooded figure whose face cannot be identified. This may seem like a small point, but it is of great consequence. This is because Carlo thinks he has heard the voice of his grandfather, King Charles V, who abdicated the Spanish throne to Philip II in 1555 and entered the monastic life. Charles V was the grandson of Ferdinand and Isabella, known as the Catholic king and queen. They are most famous in America as the financiers of Columbus's journey to the New World. Yet in Spanish history, they are recalled as the ones who led the conquest of the entire territory of Spain and expelled the Moors and the Jews. They also established the Spanish Inquisition in 1478. The original intention of the Inquisition was to rid Spain of Moors, but it soon evolved into a form of secret police from which no Spaniard was safe. As you will discover in this opera, the power of the Inquisition (led by the Church) soon became greater than that of the monarchy.

In the cloister of San Yuste, the anguished Carlo (newly returned from France) encounters Rodrigo, who is a passionate advocate for the freedom of Flanders, which is under Spanish domain. It is important to note that Flanders was Protestant and Spain, of course, was Catholic. Track 10 opens with an orchestral theme representing Charles V. It will return in other forms when it accompanies music sung in later acts by Eboli and then Elisabetta. Note that at 5:35 of this track, the stage directions tell us that Carlo enters pale and agitated (page 67). Notice how Carlo's state is described by the orchestra at this moment.

At track 11, 0:49 (page 69), the friar tells Carlo that "earthly sorrow still pursues us in the cloister; war in the heart will abate only in heaven" ("Il duolo della terra . . ."). Here Verdi introduces another theme and motive. Register it in your head (replay it if necessary), because it returns at a key moment later in the opera. With the arrival of Rodrigo (track 12, page 69), the scene takes a new direction. Each expresses the subject that inflames his heart. For Rodrigo it is freedom for Flanders; for Carlo it is the love of Elisabetta. Both are forbidden topics in the Spain of King Philip II, so the confessions both young men make draw them close. They swear eternal friendship in the great duet "Dio, che nell'alma infondere amor" ("O God, who wished to instill love"; track 14, pages 74–75). This theme will return three times during the opera in different forms. The first is when the two men renew their friendship after Carlo is threatened by Eboli. Then, in the next scene (the auto-da-fé), as Rodrigo disarms Carlo, the theme is played by only two clarinets as a sad reminder that their friendship has taken a tragic turn. Toward the end of the opera, as Rodrigo is dying in Carlo's arms, the melody returns to reassert their devotion to one another. This theme, for many people, is the most beloved music in *Don Carlo*. Toward the end of the duet in the cloister, King Philip and Queen Elisabetta enter briefly to pray at the tomb of Charles V. The voices of monks return—we hear this music as a counterpoint to the renewed vows of friendship as Carlo quakes at the sight of his beloved Elisabetta on the arm of his father.

Now read the synopsis of the second scene of Act II. We are now in the gardens outside the cloister where we meet the flamboyant Princess Eboli, who sings the Veil Song that discreetly mocks Elisabetta and suggests that the King loves another woman. The song ends abruptly with the arrival of the Queen. Rodrigo enters with a letter for Elisabetta ostensibly from her mother in France, but really from Carlo, who then arrives and pleads with Elisabetta to help him obtain Philip's permission to go to Flanders. She rejects his plea and Carlo exits. The King arrives and finds the Queen unattended. He banishes her lady-in-waiting, the Countess of Aremberg, from court. This is actually a gesture to isolate Elisabetta: the Countess is the Queen's last remaining friend and confidante from France. The subtext of this is that Philip is angry that he is trapped in a loveless marriage that was arranged for reasons of state. In the last part of the scene, Rodrigo pleads the cause of Flanders with the King. Philip does not balk at Rodrigo's talk. Rather, he is impressed with the marquis's courage and idealism (here is a juxtaposition of youthful and aging political outlooks). The King warns Rodrigo to beware of the Grand Inquisitor—an important acknowledgment that no one in Spain, not even the king, is safe from the Spanish Inquisition.

The introductory music for this scene (track 15) speaks of light and of intrigue. This is the first bit of light we have been exposed to after two dark scenes. Notice, after the choral passage by the ladies, that the introductory music returns with more energy (track 15, 2:43). This is the dramatic entrance of Eboli. In many productions, this character wears an eyepatch, which makes her that much more compelling to watch.

The real-life Eboli also wore an eyepatch. Her Veil Song, "Nei giardin" ("In the gardens;" track 17, page 81), has a pronounced Arabic or Moorish sound to it, leading one to believe that perhaps Eboli has some North African blood in her that further fuels her fiery temperament. At the least, the metaphor of illicit romance in the song is not lost on the ladies listening to this story of a woman hidden by a veil who is wooed by a king.

Next is the sudden entry of the Queen (track 18, page 85), who is clearly sad. Then Rodrigo enters and slips Elisabetta a note from Carlo. After reading it, she talks to herself of Carlo. At the same time, Rodrigo mentions how sad Carlo is. Eboli assumes he is sad because he loves her (which is her way of saying that she actually is attracted to him). Elisabetta summons her "son" Carlo (page 93) and all the other characters leave the gardens.

The scene that follows with Elisabetta and Carlo is fascinating ("Io vengo a domandar grazia"—"I come to beg a favor"—track 21, page 93). For Carlo it represents a near nervous breakdown. We see for the first time the very unstable aspects of his character. You can hear his mental frenzy in both his vocal part and the orchestral music. Compare this music to that of Elisabetta as she answers his pleas. As we observe Carlo's capacity for mental delusions, we think of him differently. For example, was he hearing imaginary voices when he thought he recognized the voice of his grandfather within the cloister? What unsafe actions will Carlo take during the opera whenever his mental instability overtakes him? Can Elisabetta trust him to keep their secret?

Carlo tells Elisabetta that he wants to go to Flanders so that he does not have to see her each day with his despised father. Through all of this (pages 95–99), note how passionate and beautiful the music is in the dialogue between Carlo and Elisabetta. (The scene continues on disk 2, track 1, page 101.) Elisabetta, in a rare departure from her placid resignation, implores Carlo to "hurry to kill your father, and then, spattered with his blood, you can lead your mother to the altar. Go, go, go and kill your father!" This unusual outburst reminds one of the type of plot one sees in Greek tragedy. These potent lyrics, and the powerful music that goes with them, turn the heat up on the drama moments before the King will enter the scene. After the King has banished Elisabetta's lady-in-waiting, the Queen sings an exquisite, plaintive aria ("Non pianger"—"Do not weep"—track 3, pages 102–103) that is really an acknowledgment of the desperate situation she is in. The Queen and her attendants exit, including Eboli, who dishonestly pretends to show compassion.

Track 4 (page 105) is a detailed conversation between Philip and Rodrigo. This was the scene that Verdi enlarged and amplified for the 1872 production in Naples. Rodrigo screams at the King that the sort of peace that exists in Spain is "the peace of the tomb!" Philip remarks that Rodrigo is a strange dreamer who speaks as someone who does not understand "the anguish and grief" within a head "weighed down by the crown." He then confides to Rodrigo that he is an unfortunate father and a still more miserable husband. Rodrigo, of course, knows this already from Carlo. The King asks Rodrigo to spy on Carlo and Elisabetta, granting him free access to the Queen. Philip's last words are a repetition of an earlier admonition: "Beware of the Grand Inquisitor! Beware! Beware!" The actual words "Ti guarda" also mean "He's watching you!"

Read the synopsis for Act III, scene 1 (page 13–14). The plot in this scene is self-explanatory. Eboli sends a note of assignation to

Carlo, who thinks it is from the Queen. When Eboli discovers this, she swears revenge. The orchestral prelude to this scene (track 8) recalls Carlo's aria in Fontainebleau in which he recalls the first time he saw Elisabetta. When Eboli enters wearing a veil (track 9, page 117), it is an inversion of the story of the Veil Song: Carlo desires not the actual woman in the veil but the woman he assumes her to be—the Queen. Eboli refers to herself as a wounded tigress (a very apt phrase) and vows revenge against Carlo. This comes thrillingly forth in Eboli's dramatic declamation "Trema per te, falso figliuolo, la mia vendetta arriva già" ("Quake for yourself, false son, my vengeance is nigh"—track 10, 1:15, pages 126–127). After Eboli storms out in a rage, Rodrigo tells Carlo that for his own safety he should turn over any sensitive or incriminating papers he may be holding. This briefly arouses doubts in Carlo about Rodrigo's trustworthiness, but these are quickly dashed as the two men return briefly to their friendship theme, which is sung more slowly, more desperately than before.

Now read the synopsis for Act III, scene 2 (page 14). This is the famous auto-da-fé scene. An auto-da-fé was the ceremony that accompanied the pronouncement of judgment by the Spanish Inquisition, followed by the execution of the condemned. In most cases, the guilty party was declared a heretic who would then be burned at the stake as punishment. Interestingly, although the judgment came from the Church, the punishment came from the State. This scene was to be the great Meyerbeerian spectacle to please the Parisian audience. It includes several large choral sections: nuns, priests, monks, civilian onlookers, members of the court, Flemish deputies. In addition to the orchestra in the pit, there is a band onstage, all members in costume, led by an assistant conductor, also in costume. Philip and Elisabetta are present for what is actually the King's coronation. Carlo and Rodrigo also appear. And, of course, we witness the heretics being put to a gruesome death. Some productions I have seen include a rather graphic burning at the stake. This may or may not be faithful to the original Paris production, but it serves to show how grisly these events were. This scene includes grand processions and opulent clerical and secular costumes. Banners and flags blow in the wind. The bells of the church chime.

Track 11, page 133: Notice the text in the first two choruses we hear. The crowds sing that a day of rejoicing has dawned (in honor of the King's coronation), while the monks sing that a day of terror has dawned: Heretics will be forgiven in heaven if they repent. Compare the music of the monks with that of the festive crowd.

As you continue to read the text of this scene, with its many characters and conflicting priorities, make a special effort to create a mental picture of what is going on. Note each entrance and exit and imagine where each character is in relation to the others. When the Flemish deputies, led by Carlo, come to plead their cause to Philip, the King is infuriated not so much by their request as by his public humiliation by his son in the presence of the Church and the public. Carlo asks his father to let him rule Flanders, which Philip will not do. Track 16: The King orders that his son, the Prince, be disarmed. When no one will do this, Rodrigo, defender of Flanders and Carlo's friend, steps forward to take away Carlo's sword. For this act, Philip dubs him duke. The King has asserted his authority before his people.

As the auto-da-fé proceeds, a voice suddenly is heard. This Celestial Voice represents the spirit of forgiveness for the heretics. It is as if a higher power has overruled the judgment and actions of the Church on earth. This voice, like the voice of the friar in the cloister, is the sound of faith. It has frequently been remarked that Verdi was anticlerical, but he was a believer in a greater force and in the value and meaning of true faith. The Flemish deputies remark ironically that the pyres are being lit in the name of the Lord. King Philip and the monks sing "Glory to God." In response, the Celestial Voice simply says "Peace."

Now we go to the third compact disk. Although the auto-da-fé is visually and musically impressive, the great scene of the opera is coming up. Carefully read the synopsis of Act IV, scene 1. It begins and ends with two stupendous arias. At the start, in "Ella giammai m'amò" ("She never loved me"—track 1, pages 148–149), King Philip sings emotionally about his failed marriage to Elisabetta. This is one of the greatest arias for bass in all of opera. It lasts about ten minutes, and in its changing moods and introspection it is a set piece in the manner of Tatyana's letter scene in *Eugene Onegin*. Of course, the theme could not be more different, but there is a sense of tour de force about both when they are put in the hands of brilliant artists.

Next comes the powerful confrontation between the old, blind, and thoroughly unyielding Grand Inquisitor and the weak and vulnerable King. Read the text carefully. There is a slow transfer of authority in the scene. At first the King seems in charge, but he is steadily undercut by the Inquisitor. After Philip observes that Carlo must be punished, it is agreed that Carlo must be executed. As the Inquisitor explains, if the Son of God can die, so can the son of a king. Then the Inquisitor demands that Rodrigo, now a trusted friend of the King, also be executed. The King resists this, and the Inquisitor implies that even Philip might be subject to condemnation and execution at the hands of the Spanish Inquisition. The King's last words say it all: "So the throne must always bow to the altar!"

After the Inquisitor leaves, the Queen rushes in: someone has stolen her jewelry case. The King produces it, forces it open, and removes a picture of Carlo. He accuses her of various improprieties, which she denies. He raises his hand to slap her, but before he hits her, she faints. The King calls for help. Eboli and Rodrigo arrive and then Rodrigo and the King depart. The Queen and Eboli have their confrontation (track 6, pages 170–171) that leads to Eboli being offered the choice of exile or the convent for her sins. She chooses the veil. With her last day of freedom, she vows to save Carlo from execution.

The scene ends with "O don fatale" (track 7, pages 172–173), in which Eboli curses her beauty as the cause of her misery. She has made several confessions to Elisabetta: that she loves Carlo, that she has been the mistress of the king ("the sin which I accused you of I myself committed!"), and that it was she who made the king believe that Elisabetta and Carlo were being unfaithful. "O don fatale" is a thrilling end to the scene. When it is sung in a show-stopping manner by a talented, impassioned mezzo, it is often the moment that audiences most remember from the entire opera.

Have you noticed that in this, the most important scene in the opera, the title character is nowhere to be seen or heard? This is a rather remarkable occurrence: highly unusual but completely logical. Verdi understood that the behavior of all of these characters grew out of their relationship with, and feelings about, Carlo. In effect, he is the silent character who makes this scene so powerful and vivid.

Now read the synopsis for Act IV, scene 2 (page 14). Carlo is in prison, suddenly joined by Rodrigo. Carlo's documents, found on Rodrigo, have implicated Rodrigo in the Flanders rebellion. Carlo will be spared and Rodrigo will die. Suddenly a shot is fired and Rodrigo is hit. What follows is a rather slow death. Rodrigo tells Carlo that Elisabetta will be waiting for him the next day at the cloister of San Yuste. In Rodrigo's two final arias (tracks 9–10, pages 176–77 and 180–81), the dying man encourages Carlo to take up the cause of Flanders and envisions a happier Spain. One last time we hear the strains of the friendship duet. The King arrives to free Carlo, who rejects him. Suddenly, a surging crowd appears, demanding Carlo's release. In the confusion, Eboli slips in and helps Carlo escape. The Inquisitor appears in this chaotic scene and orders that everyone prostrate himself before the King. Again, in public the King is defended, but in private he will be beholden to the Inquisition.

Now read the synopsis for Act V (page 14). We are back in the cloister at the tomb of Charles V. After the commotion in the previous scene, the silence here is notable. Elisabetta, who has been victimized and forced to suffer throughout the opera, has come here to be alone and reflect while waiting for Carlo. She has decided that she will not go with him. In the magnificent aria "Tu che le vanità" (track 12, page 188), she claims to want only peace. After all the excitement of the previous three scenes (the auto-da-fé, the huge Act IV, scene 1, and the death of Rodrigo), it might seem unusual to assign an eleven-minute aria to the quietest of the major characters. This aria, musically and in terms of the text, is an extraordinary summation of everything that has occurred. The introductory music is initially that of Charles V, and then the churning violins suggest the anguish in the Queen's heart. Elisabetta recalls her years of happiness in France, her love of Carlo, the extinguishing of her hopes and illusions. (There is a typographical error in the seventh line of the English translation on page 191: it should say "the knot has been cut.") She wants to die: "Yielding to cruel pain, the heart has one sole desire: the peace of the grave!" Montserrat Caballé sings this aria with unsurpassed beauty (although you should also try to hear a recording of Mirella Freni, who is equally good).

Suddenly (track 13, page 191), Carlo enters the cloister. He tells Elisabetta, in a beautiful duet, that he will go fight for Flanders even if it means leaving her forever. As you will hear, although they have decided to part, this is a love duet of the highest order. They will meet in heaven. Elisabetta, who has spoken of heaven ("ciel" or "cielo") throughout the opera, knows she will be happy in death: "Ma lassù ci vedremo in un mondo migliore" ("But above we shall meet in a better world"—track 14, pages 196–97).

As Elisabetta encourages Carlo to flee to Flanders, Philip, the Inquisitor, and troops arrive to capture him. The King states "I shall do my duty," and seizes Elisabetta's arm as the Inquisitor chillingly adds that "the Holy Office will also do its duty." As the guards corner Carlo, he cries, "God will avenge me! His hand will shatter the tribunal of blood!" As he backs away from the guards, the gates of the cloister suddenly open. It is the friar from Act II, dressed in royal robes and wearing a crown. It is, in fact, Charles V, the father of Philip and the grandfather of Carlo. He intones words similar to what he said in Act II: "Earthly suffering still follows us into the cloister, the heart's strife will abate only in heaven." With that, he pulls Carlo into the cloister and the gates close. The Inquisitor recognizes the voice of the former king. Philip recoils in horror and Elisabetta cries, thrillingly and dramatically, to heaven. Remarkably, this rich and complex opera, which is four and a half hours long, is summed up in the heavenly cry of Elisabetta.

In the original libretto, there was no doubt that the friar was Charles V. In subsequent versions, Verdi was less explicit about who the friar might be. You can debate whether the friar was indeed the former king of Spain or was an apparition guided by the hand of God. One of the many themes in this opera is that corrupt power, whether in the hands of the State or of the Church, is impure and guided by immoral values. But divine grace, whether it comes from a superior being or resides in a human being (Elisabetta), is the greatest force of all. This is why Elisabetta is given the last great aria and the last note in *Don Carlo*. It is remarkable that now, as then, both atheists and deeply religious people can find meaning in this extraordinary opera.

Don Carlo is by far the longest opera you have yet learned. I saved long operas for later on in your training. By now you have developed not only the patience and the involvement but the concentration required for enjoying and getting the most out of an opera. You will find that when an opera is as thrilling and compelling as *Don Carlo,* you exit the theater feeling excited and enriched. There are many lesser operas that are much shorter than *Don Carlo* but seem much longer. Among the thrills that come with this opera and several long ones by Wagner is the sense of fulfillment derived from spending a long time focused only on it. The mind is cleared of other distractions and is filled with the music, the drama, the visual elements, and the ideas that these great works contain.

Our next opera, *Tannhäuser,* is our first venture into the art of Richard Wagner. This work actually shares many elements with *Don Carlo.* The leading character is passionate, principled, noble, flawed. The saintly woman who loves him (coincidentally named Elisabeth) is different from Verdi's queen but no less admirable. Religion is also a conditioning factor in the outlook of many characters. There is a spectacular ballet (as in some versions of *Don Carlo*) and a great series of choruses.

Yet in spite of these similarities, these operas are all unmistakably products of their respective creators. First of all, *Tannhäuser* is a German opera—your first—and the flavor and atmosphere are completely different. With it, we enter the realm of Wagner, a singular genius who was a complete man of the theater. He wrote his own libretti as well as the music. While Verdi used his ideals to explore drama and promote the cause of freedom, Wagner used his music and drama to expand his artistic and philosophical ideas and to challenge the status quo in his society and in all of art.

12.

TANNHÄUSER

OPERA AND IDEAS

Since its beginnings, opera has been a platform for the expression of the ideas of composers and librettists. Monteverdi sought a new form of expression. Mozart and da Ponte introduced the egalitarian ideas of Beaumarchais in *Le Nozze di Figaro* and all of the dangerous possibilities that lurk in *Don Giovanni*. Beethoven explored the best and the worst in human potential in *Fidelio*. Verdi pushed the political, social, and moral limits of his society in many of his works, including *Nabucco, Rigoletto, La Traviata, Un Ballo in Maschera,* and *Don Carlo.*

Richard Wagner, in almost all of his work, gave great emphasis to his ideas, which frequently were viewed as dangerous and revolutionary. It is unfortunate that as we look back in history at Wagner, we see him through the filter of Nazi Germany. The fact that the Nazis embraced Wagner fifty years after his death has tainted the way we see him now. Wagner was a rabid anti-Semite and had heinous ideas on many subjects, but he also wrote and spoke eloquently on the social conditions of his time, on men and women, on the place of the artist in society, on the redemptive power of love, on the Apollonian and Dionysian ideals of sex, on environmental devastation, ecological balance, and the overwhelming power of nature. Whether or not one agrees with his theories, one must read the writings and learn the operas of Wagner to understand the intellectual climate in Europe in the nineteenth century. Wagner's ideas are an important part of what thinkers of that time debated and took positions on.

Wagner was a good example of what E. T. A. Hoffmann considered a model of the creative artist in the Romantic era: highly sentimental yet caustic, rebellious, in conflict with the world, and deeply, obsessively involved in a rather tortured inner life that was fertile ground for his artistic output. In other words, not easy, but not easily ignored.

The title character in *Tannhäuser* is in many ways a surrogate for Wagner himself. Like Wagner, Tannhäuser is a stubborn, passionate man who struggles within himself and against others to define his beliefs about spiritual and erotic love and about the role of an outsider in society.

Wagner had many detractors, but he also had many powerful supporters, including Franz Liszt and King Ludwig II of Bavaria. Although Wagner seemed to be in perpetual financial distress, his career was highly successful, despite the controversy and acrimony he experienced (and provoked) with patrons, political figures, ideological opponents, artistic rivals, family members, and lovers. The only disaster in his career was, however, one of epic proportions: the Paris premiere of *Tannhäuser* in 1861. Although the opera was by then sixteen years old, Wagner made significant revisions in the work for its Paris production. It can be fairly said that *Tannhäuser* was not an artistic failure, but the Paris production was undone by political machinations and conflicting ideologies. More on this later.

Richard Wagner was born into a large family in Leipzig in 1813. His father was a lawyer who also loved the theater and counted among his acquaintances the ubiquitous E. T. A. Hoffmann. Wagner's father died when Richard was six months old, leaving his mother and nine children. Less than a year later, Wagner's mother married Ludwig Geyer, an actor, writer, and painter who was a family friend. Soon they all moved to Dresden, where he had his first contact with music. In 1817 Carl Maria von Weber became director of the local opera house. The composer of *Der Freischütz* was a frequent visitor in the Geyer home. In 1821, Geyer died, and again

Wagner's mother was left in charge of the family.

Left to his own devices, Wagner showed a strong interest in literature and read widely in history, art, and, when he was older, philosophy. This interest was abetted by his uncle Adolf Wagner, who gave the young man access to his vast library and engaged him in debate on the ideas he was studying. Wagner also became more interested in music and frequently attended concerts and opera. A performance of *Fidelio* he saw as a teenager profoundly influenced him. Here was the possibility to take ideas and set them in a theatrical context. Beethoven's opera must also have made it abundantly clear to Wagner that music can provide a strong texture for the theatrical exploration of ideas and feelings.

While he did have some formal training in harmony, Wagner was in many ways self-taught in music and composition. In 1830 he had the first public performance of one of his own compositions, an overture in B-flat. In July of that year he had his first contact with politics in action rather than in theory as he witnessed demonstrations by students and workers in Leipzig in support of unrest in France. For the rest of his life Wagner would be profoundly affected by the political events of his time. He frequented societies that advocated revolution against the existing political institutions.

A detailed description of German political affairs in Wagner's time would take more space than we have here, but it should suffice to say that Germany in the middle of the nineteenth century was a confederation of sovereign states and free cities. Some of these had strong foreign influence, especially from Austria, but also from Denmark and the Netherlands. In 1848–49 there was a failed attempt to get rid of the Austrians and unite these states to form a German nation. In his work Wagner glorified German-ness, which gives his art a very nationalist and sometimes disagreeable stripe. But, as I mentioned earlier, his promotion of German ideals came during the nineteenth-century movement to form a German nation, not the twentieth-century German attempt to rule the world.

Wagner was a strong advocate of socialism (Marx's *Communist Manifesto* was published in 1848) and joined an organization called the Fatherland Union, which was on the side of unification. In 1849, he met Mikhail Bakunin, the famous Russian anarchist who believed that anarchism, collectivism, and atheism would give man complete freedom. Bakunin also was a believer in violence as a means of revolution. After an uprising in Dresden in 1849, a warrant was issued for Wagner's arrest, and he fled, with the help of Liszt, to many years of exile in Switzerland. German unification finally occurred in the late 1860s, at the same time that Verdi's Italy was becoming a nation.

When he was in his twenties, Wagner became part of a philosophical movement called Young Germany, which emphasized free love and what was termed "the emancipation of the flesh." Wagner's views on love and sex, on human expression in an erotic context, and, especially, on spiritual uplift and redemption through love are central themes in his thought and writings. Great chunks of his music are so unabashedly sensual that they startle new listeners who think of Wagnerian music as pompous or militaristic. For example, more than a few critics have described the "Liebestod," the soprano's aria at the end of *Tristan und Isolde,* as the musical depiction of female orgasm.

As you develop your interest in Wagner and listen to his music on a regular basis, you will probably want to read about him. The card catalog in your library will reveal dozens of works of Wagnerian biography and criticism—adoring and scathing. However, you should start with many of Wagner's own essays, including "Art and Revolution," "The Artistic World of the Future," "The Art Work of the Future," "Opera and Drama," and "A Communication to My Friends." In the first of these, he introduced his idea of the *Gesamtkunstwerk,* or total work of art. He wrote: "As a Greek work of art encompassed the spirit of a fine nation, so the art work of the future must encompass the spirit of free humanity across the barriers of nationality; the national character within it must be a mere adornment, an enticing element of individual diversity, and not an obstructive barrier." Wagner believed this freedom to create universal art would come through revolution and the consequent social improvement.

It is difficult to understand how the same person who could entertain such noble views on art could also produce an essay such as "Jewry in Music" and be an unrepentant anti-Semite. This is but one of the many contradictions in Wagner that make him fascinating and controversial. Is it possible to despise the artist but love his art? That is something for you to decide.

For much of his life Wagner was a wanderer, moving from town to town in search of work or, occasionally, to escape from a contretemps in the place where he was living. He had a few long-term positions in his life that gave him the opportunity to conduct, to read, and to develop ideas for future works, but invariably Wagner left these posts, because he felt confined by the routine or because he had a falling out with his employer. His travels, of course, exposed him to more ideas and inspiration and enabled him to meet the leading artists of his day.

After holding a conducting post in Riga, he traveled to Paris in 1839. He would remain there until the spring of 1842. This was a period of hard work and poverty. He was appalled by what he considered the commercialization of art at the Paris Opéra, yet at the same time he was impressed with the scenic potential of that theater and, as you might expect, the prospect of earning the kind of fees that the Opéra could pay. Yet he would not have an opera of his produced there until the disastrous production of *Tannhäuser.*

By the time he reached Paris, Wagner had already composed two complete operas, *Die Feen* (The Fairies, 1834) and *Das Liebesverbot* (The Ban on Love, 1836). The latter is a comedy that drew freely from his involvement with the "emancipation of the flesh" crowd of the Young Germany movement. Neither of these works is seen much nowadays. He had also begun *Rienzi,* a massive five-act work, which he completed in Paris in 1840. He also wrote *Der Fliegende Holländer* (The Flying Dutchman, 1841) there, produced novellas, and did a lot of the initial reading and thinking that led to *Tannhäuser* and *Lohengrin.* In Paris Wagner came into contact with thinkers advocating anticapitalism and atheism. This period is also when he met Giacomo Meyerbeer, then at the zenith of his popularity as a composer of grand opera. Although Meyerbeer (who was Jewish) was friendly and encouraging, Wagner had ambivalent feelings about him; he admired and envied Meyerbeer's success and ridiculed his art. He enjoyed referring to Meyerbeer as a "musical banker." His experiences during this long sojourn in Paris left Wagner with a lasting insecurity about that city and its cultural values and institutions.

It is therefore worth noting that none other than Meyerbeer helped Wagner gain his first major success. The composer was instrumental in arranging for the opera house in Dresden to give the monumental *Rienzi* its premiere in 1842. The opera was a huge success. Its overture was soon heard in bands and orchestras throughout Germany, and Rienzi's prayer became a popular song for parlor tenors.

As Wagner traveled across the German lands in April 1842 en route from Paris to Dresden, he crossed the Rhine River for the first time. This waterway, of course, became central to Wagnerian mythology in *Der Ring des Nibelungen* (the "Ring Cycle," as it is often called). We will study *Die Walküre*, the second of the four *Ring* operas, in the next chapter. As he journeyed farther east, Wagner passed through Thuringia and saw Wartburg, the setting of *Tannhäuser*.

His next years in Dresden were important in his development in many areas. After the triumph of *Rienzi*, the premiere of *Der Fliegende Holländer* in January 1843 was a major disappointment, although this opera now enjoys great acclaim while *Rienzi* is produced infrequently. On February 3, 1843, Wagner was appointed Kapellmeister of the Royal Court of Saxony. This position represented money and security, but Wagner feared that it would be confining and would deny him the freedom of time and thought to produce his art. His wife, Minna (whom he had married in 1836), craved the stability and prestige that the position implied, and Wagner accepted the offer.

His marriage to Minna was never a good one. They were temperamentally incompatible; Wagner was so focused on his work and his ideas, while Minna was interested in domesticity. Wagner had numerous affairs through the years of their marriage as he roamed Europe in search of fulfillment of his goals and ambitions. Some of his affairs were with women who became his patrons. After many separations and stressful reconciliations, Richard and Minna Wagner separated in 1862 and never saw one another again. Minna died in 1866.

On a brief trip to Paris in 1853, Wagner met his future second wife, Cosima Liszt (1837–1930), the daughter of the great pianist and composer who was a steadfast ally of Wagner. In 1857 Cosima married Hans von Bülow (1830–1894), a conductor who would become one of Wagner's favorite interpreters of his work. Cosima divorced Bülow in 1869, when she and Wagner had already been involved romantically for several years. Their first daughter, Isolde, was born in 1865; a second girl, Eva, came in 1867; their son, Siegfried, was born in 1869. Cosima began keeping a diary on January 1, 1869, making daily entries until the day of Wagner's death in Venice on February 13, 1883. Cosima's diaries are among the greatest sources available on Wagner's last years.

The first opera Wagner completed in his Dresden years was *Tannhäuser*. Among the many ways in which Wagner is distinctive as an opera composer is that he also wrote his libretti. Critics have argued for years about the literary quality of Wagner's libretti. Some consider them great works in their own right; others find the language pedestrian or archaic. What is indisputable, however, is that Wagner had the unique opportunity to determine the shape, sound, and texture of his music dramas. When we think of famous teams of composers and librettists, such Mozart and da Ponte or Strauss and Hofmannsthal, we understand and admire the contributions of both partners, but assume that the composer probably had the upper hand and the final say. Wagner, as composer *and* librettist of his operas, could forge a creative vision free from collaboration and compromise. Given Wagner's intellect and temperament, one wonders how successful his collaborations would have been.

As the originator of his story ideas and the author of his libretti, Wagner the composer could envision his musical and scenic concepts as the stories and words evolved. This means that he spent years with operas growing inside of him, frequently with more than one work in his mind at a given time. His wide reading early in life and his continuous probing and intellectual inquiry throughout his life meant that he had a vast store of references and influences to call upon. As a result, his libretti often were derived from a principal source but also contained components from many other sources. In this regard *Tannhäuser* is no exception.

The story of Tannhäuser, who was born at the start of the thirteenth century in Salzburg, was recounted by the Brothers Grimm in the *Deutsche Sagen* (1816–18). Their source was an anonymous poem from three centuries earlier. Tannhäuser was a minnesinger, or knightly minstrel, who wandered about Central Europe seeking patrons to support him in exchange for his services as an artist. A book by E. T. A. Hoffmann, *Die Serapions-Brüder* (1819), was also probably on Wagner's reading list as a young man. This is the story of Heinrich von Ofterdingen, a minnesinger who participated in a song contest at the Wartburg (seat of the medieval landgraves of Thuringia) in 1207 and sang love songs that were more erotic than courtly. Wagner also knew the *Legend of Saint Elisabeth,* a poem in High German about a young woman who in many ways resembles the soprano role in the opera. There was also a sixteenth-century folk song called "Danhauser" and the writings of Heinrich Heine, Joseph Eichendorff, and Ludwig Tieck, all active when Wagner was at work on this opera. With all of these influences, Wagner could have created an artistic muddle. Instead, he used these elements to plumb many of the ideas he wrestled with for most of his life.

As you will discover when you learn the story, the title character resembles Wagner in several ways. He was an itinerant musician who, as an outsider, did not fit in because of his beliefs and behavior. Tannhäuser and Wagner were, to use a general term, womanizers, but not in the Don Giovanni sense. Rather, they viewed women as both a source of physical pleasure and a means of spiritual uplift. Their self-definition came in part from their views of the women in their lives. In this opera women represent the conflict between the sensual and the spiritual, the nurturing of the body and the soul. Wagner's lifelong obsession with the idea that a man can be redeemed by the love of a woman, with this redemption often coming only in death, is given extensive play in *Tannhäuser.*

Wagner began writing the libretto in June 1842 and completed it in April 1843. He began composing two months later and completed the score on April 13, 1845. The premiere of *Tannhäuser und der Sängerkrieg auf Wartburg* (Tannhäuser and the Song Contest at the Wartburg) was given in Dresden on October 19, 1845, with Wagner conducting. The title role was taken by Joseph Tichatschek, who had had a great success as the first Rienzi. The part of Elisabeth was sung by Wagner's nineteen-year-old niece, Johanna, at the beginning of a well-regarded career. Wagner revised the third act soon after the production was staged. *Tannhäuser* represented a large step forward in Wagner's development of his aesthetic ideal: the fusion of words, vocal music, dramatic action and the expressive capabilities of an orchestra. Although it was a moderate success in its Dresden premiere, *Tannhäuser* did not become popular until it received other productions. By the 1850s, however, it was the most frequently staged of Wagner's operas. It was the first Wagner opera to be staged in America when it appeared in New York in 1859. It was not heard in England until 1876, when it was staged in London (in Italian!).

Although he worked intensively in the 1850s—primarily on the libretti of the four *Ring* operas, on much of their music, and then, in the latter part of the decade, on the composition of *Tristan und Isolde* (completed 1859), he had to live on income from productions of his earlier operas and the support of his patrons. Since leaving Paris in 1842, his ambivalence regarding that city never diminished. He journeyed there in May 1849 in a fruitless attempt to find work. Another trip there, in 1850, was no more productive. In October of that year he wrote, "With all due consideration and all sincerity I assure you that the only revolution I still believe in is the one that starts by burning down Paris."

In the 1850s he continued to visit Paris, but nothing materialized. It was in Paris, however, that he met Cosima in 1853, so that the city he resented was also the place where he met the love of his life. He made another emotional trip there in 1858, to escape Minna and Mathilde Wesendonck, the Zurich patron with whom he probably was romantically involved despite the proximity of her husband, Otto. It was a measure of his involvement with Mathilde (or perhaps his sense of obligation) that Wagner agreed to set to music five poems written by Frau Wesendonck even though he otherwise was willing to set only his own words to music.

After completing *Tristan und Isolde,* Wagner again returned to Paris in September 1859, this time with the resolve of staging his popular *Tannhäuser,* which would surely bring him some income now that he was no longer welcome in the home of Herr Wesen-donck. Minna joined him in November.

In March 1860 Wagner gave three concerts of his music in Paris in the hopes of attracting ideological supporters and moneyed pa-trons. At these performances he came to know the poet Charles Baudelaire, who became his loyal champion. These concerts also left him further in debt. Although the score of *Tristan und Isolde* was published at this time, no opera company was willing to present it.

Wagner had attracted enough attention at his concerts that Em-peror Napoleon III ordered that *Tannhäuser* be given a production at the Opéra. This came about largely through the persistence of Princess Pauline Metternich, wife of the Austrian ambassador. Re-hearsals began on September 24, 1860. It should be noted that Giacomo Meyerbeer remained a faithful proponent of Wagner despite the contempt in which he was held by the composer from Dresden.

As you know, the Paris Opéra had a tradition of having elaborate ballets in all of its operatic productions. If a ballet was not part of the opera as it was written, it was not uncommon for a ballet having nothing to do with the opera to be inserted between two acts. It did not have to bear any dramatic or musical resemblance to the opera being presented; it would form a parenthetical divertissement before the thoughts of the audience returned to the opera of the evening.

Why did Paris have this curious tradition? Dance had been a cen-tral part of the city's social and cultural life for centuries, and the Opéra was proud of its excellent corps de ballet. And there was another reason: the Jockey Club. This group of gentlemen-about-town actively patronized the Opéra. Its members included promi-nent members of government, commerce, and high society who had great influence at the Opéra even if they were not the most enthusi-astic of opera fans. Traditionally, many of these men had mistresses in the corps de ballet. It was their custom to dine at their club while the first act of an opera was being performed, then go to the opera house, watch their girlfriends perform, and take them home for des-sert.

Wagner resisted the idea of composing a ballet for his opera. As you will discover, there is no logical place for a ballet in the second act of *Tannhäuser*. The opera management proposed that the act be divided into two scenes, which Wagner rejected. He also refused to permit someone else's unrelated ballet to be presented between two acts of his opera. So there was a great deal of similarity between the creator and his creation. The lead character in *Tannhäuser* is a stubborn, not always likable man who refuses to compromise his vision and his ideals in order to conform. After weeks of threats and counterthreats, Wagner agreed to write a ballet—to *open* the opera. He knew this would rankle the Jockey Club, but he also realized that a ballet at the start of the opera would give him expanded dramatic possibilities for that scene. At the beginning of *Tannhäuser,* the title character is in the arms of Venus, goddess of love, in a grotto of her domain, the Venusberg, which often has been slyly referred to as the "mountain of ill repute." The bacchanal that the audience observes when the curtain rises can be highly erotic, depending on where it is produced. Some modern productions have included nude dancers, which is not illogical—how many people at an orgy have their clothes on? If poorly staged, this ballet can be very campy and get a production off to a bad start. This scene is important because it must be the sensual counterpoint to the ascetic behavior that comes later in the opera. One of the themes throughout the work is the struggle within Tannhäuser between the Dionysian and the Apollonian, the pleasure of the flesh and the ennoblement of the spirit. It is a mistake, I believe, to put this struggle in terms of "sacred" and "profane," because profanity is always defined by those who align themselves with what they consider sacred. As you know, Wagner was not against sex.

Tannhäuser had a remarkable (and perhaps excessive) 163 rehearsals before opening in Paris on March 13, 1861. Whatever the Venusberg ballet was like that night is but a footnote to the real events of that evening. Wagner had antagonized many in Paris by thumbing his nose at their conventions. His political positions were well-known and did not sit well with German officials based in France. They helped foment opposition to him among an already hostile populace. Many ballerinas refused to appear in the Act I ballet because their sympathies lay with their gentlemen friends. When the men of the Jockey Club appeared for Act II and discovered that there was no ballet, they led a demonstration that surely was premeditated since word of Wagner's intentions had spread before the opening night. Fistfights broke out and arguments raged well into the night in the streets of Paris.

Albert Niemann, who sang the title role that evening, described the scene: "At yesterday's performance, *Tannhäuser* made a fiasco such as probably had never been known in Paris before. It was literally hissed off, hooted off, and finally laughed off. . . . The row was beyond belief: even the presence of the Emperor could not keep it within bounds. Princess Metternich was compelled to leave the theater after the second act, the audience continually turning around toward her box and jeering at her at the top of its voice."

The opera had two more equally disastrous performances before it was withdrawn. Many audience members produced whistles from their pockets to disrupt the later performances. Other audience members began to chant the word "ballet" during the second act.

Wagner carried the psychic wound of this failure for the rest of his days. His aspirations of financial reward and approval in Paris— the operatic heart of Europe—were destroyed. Yet out of this debacle came some good: the new Venusberg ballet sharpened and strengthened the first act and made the conflicts and dilemmas explored throughout the opera more tangible. Ironically, his failure in Paris in the era before the Franco-Prussian War (1870) made Wagner more popular in the German lands and led to more productions of his operas and, occasionally, to much-needed infusions of cash.

Tannhäuser has become one of Wagner's most popular operas, limited only by the paucity of tenors available to sing the highly demanding title role. It has a high tessitura (from the Italian for "texture," suggesting the part of a voice in which a role predominantly lies) that puts it out of reach for many singers. After two long acts, Tannhäuser's most taxing music comes in the Rome Narrative in Act III. A tenor who can sing this role must have stamina, ease in summoning high notes, and an almost trumpetlike quality to bring drama and meaning to the part. Heldentenors—the heroic tenors most often used in Wagner—are few and far between.

Modern audiences attend *Tannhäuser* because of its glorious music and seem not to be put off by the sexuality. This is in part because Tannhäuser ultimately dies beside Elisabeth, having rejected the carnality of Venus for the spiritual purity of Elisabeth. But audiences also respond to the Venusberg ballet and the opera's exploration of Eros. Wagner is more like Mozart and da Ponte than like Verdi in that he presents many sides to complex issues but does not necessarily take a firm stand on one side or another.

It is important to recognize that in the evaluation of Wagner's ideas—and perhaps all ideas—adopting a black/white, yes/no, either/or approach is not productive. In *Tannhäuser,* Wagner shows two polar opposites in the depiction of love and perhaps of womanhood. Yet the fact that Tannhäuser ultimately renounces one for the other does not mean that one is bad and the other is good. Righteous bigots often look to Wagner's work, as they do to the Bible, to find the aspects that support their own narrow contentions. When in a four- or five-hour Wagner opera we focus on ideas and issues as symbolized by different characters, the goal is not to pick the winner and the loser, the saint and the sinner, but rather to explore these concepts in a profound way. I often view attendance at a Wagner opera as the chance to go on a journey. On this trip, as I leave thoughts of my own life and my own world behind, I am afforded the luxury of dwelling in the deepest of ideas and emotions for a prolonged period. The way a Wagner opera works its magic is that the music, in beautiful abstraction, is one of the chief guides through these faraway worlds Wagner creates. His art is that of the nineteenth century, when works of art provided insight, reflection, refuge, and escape. Think about the total immersion that happens while reading Dickens, Hugo, or Dostoevsky and you will have an idea what I mean about going on a journey in a Wagner opera. Each time I make the journey again, it is at least as meaningful. In *Tannhäuser,* which I have seen more than twenty-five times, I observe new things on each journey and see the familiar things differently. One of the glories of a lifetime of operagoing is that as we grow and change, so does our perception of these great masterpieces. I hope these words alleviate any anxiety you might have about approaching Wagnerian opera, the prospect of which tends to provoke groans of disdain among people who have not yet learned to enjoy this composer's challenging works. I think that *Tannhäuser* is Wagner's most accessible work for the newcomer. Some people take to Wagner immediately; most of us require some time and exposure. If your first contact is less than optimal, don't give up on Wagner because of that.

Tannhäuser is your first opera in German, which is your fourth operatic language overall. Chances are that you will hear more operas in Italian than in any other language and that German will be second. You will soon discover that "guttural," the adjective most frequently used to describe the sound of German, does not really obtain as regards operatic German. Mozart, Beethoven, Weber, Wagner, Johann Strauss, Humperdinck, Richard Strauss, Berg, Schoenberg, and Korngold all found great means of expression in this language. German can sound harsh, but it is also lyrical and poetic. Despite the abundance of consonants, it too has vowels that are as musical as those in any other language.

Let us talk about what I call the "architecture" of a Wagner opera—the style and assumptions on which it is built. In Mozart and some Rossini, there are many scenes and much movement and spontaneous interaction among the characters. In bel canto, where many of the characters are introspective, the emphasis is on the beauty and dramatic expressiveness in sound. In Verdi there is an alternation in pacing: we have concise moments of great impact, longer choruses and orchestral sections, and then periods of introspection. All of these elements serve drama and the definition of the characters. In Offenbach (at least in *Les Contes d'Hoffmann*) and Tchaikovsky, there is also a great deal of character development, a desire to emphasize beauty and drama, and an interest in the sounds and the feelings communicated by the use of French or Russian.

Wagner's operas will sound different from anything you have yet heard, in part because of the German language and in part because of his own musical language. His operas are frequently lengthy because he gives the characters, the orchestra, and the audience more room to breathe, to reflect, and to interpret. Rather than feeling closed in by the heft of a Wagner opera, you should feel that he has given you a great deal of room. People often say, "Why does Wagner take twenty minutes to say what Mozart or Verdi can say in five?" The answer is that Wagner is not saying the same thing. A character by any of these composers may say "I love you," but the context, background, and impact is different in each case. In Wagner's operas, that declaration may be accompanied by an orchestral passage telling us why such a love would never work. This is another example of why I consider supertitles a scourge on opera. Many audience members might read the words "I love you" and then sit back without focusing on the message in the music, waiting instead for the next title to appear.

In Wagner the orchestra plays a much greater role in supporting, defining, and shaping the story and emotions in the libretto. If you do not listen closely to the orchestra in a Wagner opera, then you are not hearing one of the most important voices of all. You will realize that the orchestra picks up melodies from the singers and restates them. You heard some examples of this in *Don Carlo* (such as the friendship duet of Carlo and Rodrigo), but the practice is much more fully developed in Wagner. When the singer sings one melody (signifying erotic love, for example) while the orchestra plays two other melodies (signifying death and family), we hear all three and draw from this a more complicated dramatic moment than the singer could express alone. In some cases, these orchestral commentaries tell us what is going on in the character's head while he or she sings of something else. In other cases, the commentary makes allusions to things that the character either does not know or refuses to acknowledge. This may sound complicated to you, but it becomes very evident when you hear a performance.

The sound of Wagner's vocal music is also different from what you know. The composer created relatively few arias as we know them. This opera probably has only three—Elisabeth's "Dich, teure Halle" in Act II and her prayer and Wolfram's "O du mein holder Abendstern" in Act III. Even these flow directly into the action that follows and do not call for applause. (Never, in fact, should one applaud until after the very last note of an act in any Wagner opera.) On the other hand, Wagner did not employ recitatives as we know them; his style is more arioso. There is no real translation for this word; the literal translation would be "airy," but in fact it means "in the nature of an aria." The arioso style means that the action does not come to a halt as it might in some arias or recitatives.

Rather, there is ongoing verbal expression typically accompanied by a full orchestra. When two or more Wagner characters are onstage, theirs is an expansive conversation rather than the fast patter of Mozart or Rossini. In many ways this is more like human speech than the rhythmic cadences of typical recitative. You will quickly get used to this when you hear the first conversation between Tannhäuser and Venus following the bacchanal that opens the opera. Arioso singing requires a singer who is flexible and intelligent. The words must be remembered and given meaning in a musical structure that is much less formal than in Mozart and many other composers.

The recording we are using is the Paris version of *Tannhäuser,* generally accepted as the more cohesive and involving one musically and dramatically. The Dresden *Tannhäuser* has been recorded often and is staged periodically, but the Paris version represents Wagner's most advanced thinking about his opera. In this regard, *Tannhäuser* is distinct from *Les Contes d'Hoffmann* and *Don Carlo,* which have proponents for the several different versions of those operas. Sir Georg Solti has had a brilliant career as a conductor and is also distinguished by his great recorded legacy. He led the groundbreaking recording of the *Ring* cycle for London/Decca that set new artistic and technological standards and remains one of the high points in the history of recorded music. Solti, talented in the work of many composers, has garnered special acclaim for his Wagner.

The singers in this cast are a solid group of expert Wagnerians, most of them native German speakers. René Kollo's voice has beauty and the power necessary for the title role. That he was able to record the role over several days rather than singing it in one evening means that his voice sounds more rested in Act III than you are ever likely to hear from a Tannhäuser at a live performance. Helga Dernesch makes an impassioned Elisabeth. Later in her career, as her voice darkened, she began to sing roles in the mezzo repertory but at this stage she was still a soprano. (Probably the greatest interpreter of Elisabeth in our era was Leonie Rysanek, who brought beauty, pathos, and strength to this character who is too often portrayed as a virginal weakling. If you ever meet someone who saw Rysanek's Elisabeth onstage, ask him or her to describe the performance.) Venus is sung by the great Christa Ludwig, who ended her long and brilliant career in 1994. In addition to her work in opera, Ludwig was one of the greatest recitalists and lieder singers; her recordings of songs by Schubert, Wolf, Mahler, and Strauss are masterpieces. Victor Braun is a good Wolfram von Eschenbach, Tannhäuser's faithful friend and competitor in the singing competition in Act II.

The other musical forces on this recording are first-rate. The orchestra is the Vienna Philharmonic and the chorus is from the Vienna State Opera. The roles of pages and the shepherd boy are sung by members of the Vienna Boys' Choir. Notice the beauty of their unchanged voices—theirs is the sound of the purity and innocence that is often mistakenly ascribed to Elisabeth. She may be a virgin, but she is an adult woman with comprehension and sensitivity that extend far beyond her personal experience.

Let's begin. After familiarizing yourself with the characters and singers on the cast page (page 5), read the essay by Patrick Carnegy (pages 10–14) and the producer's note (pages 14–15). Then read the synopsis for Act I (page 16).

Track 1: The overture contains many of the musical motives of the opera. These are symbolic and serve as references in the manner I described above. Whether sung or played by the orchestra, they are intended to bring our mind back to a particular idea. After you hear this recording, replay the overture and you will discover how much music you recognize from the opera: the pilgrims' music, Tannhäuser's paean to the charms of Venus, and so on.

Wagner, in his Paris revision, had the curtain rise toward the end of the overture as the music moves directly into the bacchanal (around 10:00 on your recording). Notice in the music how there are scenes of tender love and unbridled lust. This is, in fact, not only an orgy; it is a celebration of sex as something liberating and enriching physically and spiritually. In reading the italicized description of the Venusberg, you see that Wagner is very specific about the setting: emerald-green waterfalls, the white foam of waves, rocks, a brook, bathing women, corallike tropical growths, roseate halflight. This must have been a beautiful setting at the Paris Opéra. The current production at the Metropolitan Opera, designed by Günther Schneider-Siemssen, is wonderfully evocative of this imaginary setting.

This opera, by the way, does call on your imagination more than many of the others we have studied. There is very little realism in this work, even if much of the scenery seems realistic. The characters live in a time and a place far removed from our own. They may have some basis in reality in that they existed, but Wagner knew of them through poems, fables, and songs and then reinterpreted them for us. In this regard they are more like the fantastical characters in *Les Contes d'Hoffmann* than the very human characters in *Rigoletto, Tosca,* and *Eugene Onegin.* Yet the characters in *Tannhäuser* have human responses, feelings, reactions, and frailties. It is on these levels that we respond to them and care about them so profoundly.

Track 2: We have had nearly twenty-two minutes of music before one of the principal characters begins to sing. This is certainly different from anything you are used to. Wagner has allowed us to become deeply immersed in the mood and setting before focusing on the characters. The music right before Venus sings speaks to us of postcoital rapture as she and Tannhäuser cuddle and nuzzle. In the first notes of track 2, Tannhäuser has a sudden disquieting thought and lifts his head with a start. You read this in the stage directions, but you can fully hear it in the orchestra. From this point forward, never neglect to listen carefully to the orchestra as you read the stage directions and the lyrics.

Track 3: This is Tannhäuser's ode to Venus, his paean to physical love. You heard it in the overture and it will return at a crucial moment in Act II. Although he enjoys the carnal delights of the Venusburg, he adds, "Not pleasure alone lies close to my heart—in the midst of joy I crave pain." One wonders if Wagner ever said this to a mistress before returning to Minna. Notice the curious and evocative way the argument between Venus and Tannhäuser subsides with the slow, descending sound of a clarinet.

Track 4: Listen to the dewy eroticism of this music as Venus works all of her considerable charms trying to prevent Tannhäuser from leaving.

Track 5: We begin to discover Tannhäuser's conflicted, unsettled nature, much like that of Wagner. He resists confinement (whether the post of Kapellmeister in Dresden or belonging to one woman). He needs to roam, to follow his creative and emotional impulses, even if these result in pain and suffering. It is freedom he wants—freedom, struggle, and strife.

Track 6: Make special note of the dialogue on page 62 of the libretto. Tannhäuser says he carries death in his heart—through repentance and atonement alone will he find rest. Venus insists that repose will never be his lot and that she offers salvation. Then, suddenly, Tannhäuser replies, "Goddess of pleasure and delight, no! Oh, not in you shall I find peace and repose! *My* salvation lies in Mary!" With that, Venus vanishes and the Venusberg gradually disappears. Notice that the music does not stop. Rather, it evolves from the mood of the first scene to that of the second.

You will notice that at a crucial moment in each act, the name of a different woman will be invoked and there will be the sound of an orchestral spell. In this act it is the Virgin Mary, a godly figure who represents different virtues than does Venus.

Track 7: We are now on earth. The elements Tannhäuser spoke of—birdsong, blue sky—are present. The voice of true purity, that of the shepherd boy, is the first that we hear. In some productions this is sung by a woman (Kathleen Battle made her Metropolitan Opera debut in this role), but it is often assumed by a young boy. At the end you hear the faint voices of a chorus of pilgrims.

Track 8: The pilgrims, who are headed to Rome, arrive in the valley. The shepherd boy asks them to pray for him. Tannhäuser is overcome by the weight of sin and sings the praises of God. As the shepherd boy sings before Tannhäuser's outburst, listen to the discordant strings in the orchestra that indicate his turmoil. Tannhäuser then sings the prayer sung by the pilgrims. This musical motive represents Christian faith. (At this point you may want to start thinking about whether Tannhäuser is a genuinely religious man or simply someone casting about for meaning. In other words, in the absence of Venus, is he looking for a substitute? This is, after all, the way many people find religion.)

Track 9: Notice in the music how we have three different motives. The song of the shepherd fades in one direction as the voices of the pilgrims recede in the other. Hunting horns herald the arrival of

Hermann, the uncle of Elisabeth and Landgrave of Thuringia (he is, in effect, the governor of this region). He is traveling with other knights, including Tannhäuser's old friend Wolfram. When Wolfram asks him to join them, Tannhäuser resists, insisting that the road calls. He is a wanderer and a seeker who cannot rest. He invokes a line from Orpheus (who carried a lyre just as Tannhäuser carries a harp): "Alas, never may I cast a backward glance" (page 74). But Wolfram knows the secret of Tannhäuser's heart: "Stay for Elisabeth" (page 74, 3:45).

Track 10: Wolfram explains to Tannhäuser that with his singing at the song contests he had captured Elisabeth's heart. She has not returned to any festival since he left. In a beautiful and rousing conclusion, Tannhäuser agrees to follow the other men "zu ihr!" ("to her!"). Listen, then, as the valley fills with huntsmen, the Landgrave sounds his horn, and the hunters answer with theirs. You will soon realize that Wagner had a special skill for creating thrilling, extraordinary conclusions to acts of his operas. Some cynics remark that these are there to wake up the audience members who fell asleep during the act, but I think you have recognized the beauty and excitement of Act I of *Tannhäuser*.

Now to Act II, on the second disk. Read the synopsis of Act II on pages 16–17 of your libretto. The setting for this act is the empty minstrels' hall in the Wartburg, site of the singing competitions. Such events were popular in Central Europe during the Middle Ages. The participants were judged not only on the beauty of their voices and the quality of their singing but on their ability to express themselves eloquently on a particular subject. The topic for the singing competition is "What is the true nature of love?"

On track 1, at the start of the act, Elisabeth enters the vast hall, which she salutes in her famous aria "Dich, teure Halle." One of the most difficult challenges a singer can face is to make one's first entrance onto an empty stage and then sing a difficult aria. Even if the singer has warmed up backstage, to come out onstage and immediately have to fill a hall with sound is difficult indeed. This aria is also, despite its exultant music, a good example of some of Wagner's clumsier libretto writing. While much of the rest of this opera is rather poetic, "Dich, teure Halle" sounds somewhat awkward in

German and in translation. The important subtext of this aria is that Elisabeth, who may in other (but not all) circumstances seem reticent, rejoices in the news that Tannhäuser is returning. For the first time since his departure she has agreed to be present at a singing competition.

You probably have noticed that the sound of Helga Dernesch's voice, which is very suitable for Elisabeth, has a different quality from that which we have heard in other female voices. Perhaps the only sound that is somewhat similar is Edda Moser's as Donna Anna. As I mentioned in the chapter on *Don Giovanni,* that role is occasionally sung by dramatic sopranos who specialize in Wagner. There is a certain steeliness in this type of voice that one does not find, for example, in Mirella Freni or Kiri Te Kanawa. The role of Elisabeth is actually among the more demure in the Wagner repertory, along with Senta in *Der Fliegende Holländer,* Elsa in *Lohengrin,* Eva in *Die Meistersinger.* The roles that call for the galvanic energy and penetrating sound we associate with heroic sopranos are Isolde and Brünnhilde (the heroine of three *Ring* operas), Strauss's Salome and Elektra, and Puccini's Turandot. We will be hearing a heroic soprano in the next chapter as Hildegard Behrens stars in *Die Walküre.*

Track 2: Listen to the orchestra as Tannhäuser first observes Elisabeth and then the clarinet accompaniment that introduces their tender reunion. He is evasive when she asks where he has been. After they praise the miracle that has brought Tannhäuser back to the Wartburg, Elisabeth gingerly tells him how she loves him. This is not a simple declaration in which "I love you" is repeated multiple times. Rather, it is a woman explaining what is in her heart. Wagner set these words to exquisite music.

For anyone who loves music it will one day happen that a particular melody will suddenly sound like the most beautiful thing he or she has ever heard. One of the joys of loving opera, and all music, is that each one of us has his or her own treasured melodies that go beyond the words and the drama to which they are set and reach us so deeply in a way that only an abstraction such as music can do. The principal melody in this passage ("Der Sänger klugen Weisen"—track 2, 3:55) is such music for me. I raise this example only to reinforce something I have said before: that with each listening of a familiar work we hear something new. The first few times I heard this opera, I was so focused on how "Dich, teure Halle" was performed that my concentration slipped afterward. Then, one day, this particular passage suddenly reached me and I felt a sense of sublime contentment. I am not suggesting that this passage will affect you that way, only that there will be special music somewhere in opera that you particularly will cherish.

The duet continues with further rapturous confession of mutual adoration. Such expression may seem trite, but not when it is accompanied by such uplifting music as when the two join voices ("Gepriesen sei die Stunde," 7:47). Later, Wolfram privately remarks that any hope he had of winning Elisabeth is gone. After Tannhäuser and Wolfram leave to prepare for the competition, the Landgrave enters. He quickly realizes that Elisabeth is in love with Tannhäuser and that she intends to preside at the singing competition.

Track 3: The next portion of the scene is the Entry of the Guests. This famous music has been used at events and convocations in government and academia because it so appropriately conveys the joy of a festive gathering. Even if you don't recognize this music, you certainly will be able to envision the scene in this great hall. Guests enter alone or in small groups and bow to Elisabeth and the Landgrave before taking seats. Each guest then joins in song with those who have already arrived. The result is a scene that slowly, inexorably builds with great majesty to a thrilling conclusion.

Track 4: The Landgrave announces the theme of this contest: "Can you fathom the true nature of love?" Elisabeth will present the prize to the winner. Wolfram is summoned to sing first.

Track 5: Wolfram's song bespeaks the chivalrous ideal of courtly love. He says he would gladly expend his heart's last drop of blood in devotion and sacrifice to his beloved. These sentiments are met with praise by the listeners and onlookers. Carefully read Wagner's description of the changes that overtake Tannhäuser during and after this song. He is gripped with an idea, with a strange music within him, and has become oblivious to all present, especially Elisabeth.

Track 6: Tannhäuser ridicules Wolfram's expression of love, telling him that these sentiments are cold and sexless. He extols instead the glories of physical love—that his desire may ever burn to refresh himself at the fount of delight. Wagner tells us that Elisabeth is prey to conflicting emotions: rapture and anxious astonishment. In other words, this woman so often thought of as chaste and passionless responds with empathy to Tannhäuser's words as others around him express horror.

Track 7: Biterolf, another knight, challenges Tannhäuser to a duel to defend the honor and virtue of all women. Other knights want a piece of the action as well.

Track 8: Tannhäuser further angers Biterolf by belittling his notions of love. The Landgrave attempts to keep the peace. Wolfram then rises to reassert his views of love, further inciting Tannhäuser.

Track 9: Here returns Tannhäuser's ode to Venus and the glories of carnal pleasure. It is also in this passage that Tannhäuser's speaking the name of a woman causes a crucial turn in the scene. In Act I, it was by naming the Virgin Mary that he escaped the Venusberg.

Track 10: Now, with the mention of Venus, he provokes a riot in the Hall of Song. The ladies flee in horror; the men draw their swords and are rushing to attack Tannhäuser when Elisabeth steps in front of him and orders the knights to halt. Her order to halt (track 10, 0:48) is an unbridled cry that blends passion, fear, and bravery. Such a cry from this previously temperate woman pierces the heart and conscience of every man present. They must kill her first, she says.

Track 11: In her impassioned appeal that Tannhäuser's life be spared, Elisabeth argues that no man should be denied the right to seek salvation through repentance and atonement. This music—the motive of redemption through atonement—will appear again in the third act. Then listen (4:25) as the orchestra describes the rising sense of misery in Tannhäuser before he sings "Woe is me" (page 106). He continues to express his shame at his betrayal of the goodness of Elisabeth (track 12). Within this passage, her grieving voice soars above all of the men's in a powerfully dramatic piece of musical scoring.

Track 13: The Landgrave banishes Tannhäuser from the Wartburg, but wisely gives him an option for redemption. He is to go to

Rome with a group of pilgrims, atone for his sins, and receive absolution from the Pope.

Track 14: As we near the conclusion of this act, remember what I mentioned in Act I about Wagner's skill in this area. All of the characters speak their feelings in overlapping voices that are occasionally in unison, often in harmony, and sometimes discordant. The Landgrave and the knights agree that Tannhäuser must go to Rome to repent. Elisabeth tells God that she will offer her life in sacrifice to save Tannhäuser. He is wracked with guilt and resolves to fall prostrate in the dust as an act of contrition. These characters are suddenly interrupted by the ethereal voices of young pilgrims. Suddenly (at 4:20) Tannhäuser falls to kiss the hem of Elisabeth's gown before crying "Nach Rom!" ("To Rome!") as others echo him. The curtain falls as Tannhäuser heads unsteadily to Rome, uncertain of his fate. Elisabeth kneels in prayer.

There are as many ways to interpret the character of Elisabeth as there are to interpret Tannhäuser. He can be brave and heroic, selfish and dissolute, a free thinker who wanders aimlessly, never fitting in and never content unless he challenges the standards of his society. Does he really believe he will be absolved, or, for that matter, that he needs to be absolved? What will happen if he is not pardoned? Was his outburst in praise of physical love an expression of his true feelings or was he under some spell cast by faraway Venus?

Elisabeth may be thought of as pious at all costs and a woman with a death wish. Or she can be seen as the essence of love—exactly what the Landgrave asked the singers to describe. It is often said that for Tannhäuser, for Wagner, and for many other men, the ideal woman combines the spiritual aspects of Elisabeth and the physical aspects of Venus. Such an ideal woman is commonly defined in modern times as a combination of madonna and whore, wife and mistress. I disavow those terms since they are examples of how men can simplify, compartmentalize, and degrade the image of women. I think it is fair to say that both Venus and Elisabeth are more complex women than they are given credit for. Both feel love and are aroused by this man. Both hurt when he impulsively disrupts the peace and contentment they crave.

In a few productions of *Tannhäuser,* the two roles have been sung by the same singer. This concept, resembling the operatic Hoffmann's ideal of three women in one, is successful only if you believe that Elisabeth would not be *capable* of physical pleasure. (That is, if our image of Elisabeth is purely spiritual and not sensual.) Think about this before going on to the final act of *Tannhäuser* on disk 3.

Read the synopsis for Act III on page 17 of the booklet. We are back in the valley where we first heard the shepherd boy in Act I. We hear a prelude depicting Tannhäuser's pilgrimage. The first notes played uncertainly by the orchestra are Elisabeth's motive of redemption through absolution. Soon the orchestra takes up the melody of the pilgrims. Then a disquieting new theme is played, followed by one of hope. These motives do not only depict Tannhäuser's journey; they can be considered conflicting thoughts swirling around in the head of Elisabeth, who is at prayer. Wolfram, who still loves her, watches. He remarks (track 2) that she has been praying day and night for Tannhäuser's absolution.

Track 3: Elisabeth is roused by the voices of pilgrims returning from Rome. This scene of the pilgrims' chorus is remarkably powerful in the hands of an Elisabeth who is a good actress. Leonie Rysanek would walk through the mass of pilgrims like a salmon going upstream. She would stare into each hooded face before moving to the next one. Although her back was to the audience, it gained tension and stiffness as her increasingly desperate search proved fruitless. Tannhäuser was not among the returning pilgrims who had received the papal blessing. Rather than overact, as many singers do in this scene, Rysanek used economy of gesture (in tandem with Wagner's evocative music) to make this moment unforgettable.

Track 4: This is the famous prayer to the Virgin Mary in which Elisabeth asks to die so that Tannhäuser may be pardoned. She then kindly refuses Wolfram's offer of assistance and slowly, very slowly (to the music of clarinet and flute), walks up the hill and disappears from our view. You might consider this last image of Elisabeth that of a woman at peace with her lot or, rather, that of a woman whose broken heart will cause her to die in great pain and sadness. This is open to your interpretation and that of the singer playing Elisabeth.

Tracks 5–6: Wolfram sings to the evening star of his beloved Elisabeth, asking it to greet her as she goes to become an angel in heaven. This song acquired immense popularity at the Dresden premiere in 1845 and has had a life of its own on concert programs ever since.

Track 7: At nightfall, a ragged Tannhäuser appears. He is trying to find the way to the Venusberg since he failed to gain a pardon from the Pope. He encounters Wolfram, who at first does not recognize this haggard, dejected wanderer. Tannhäuser recounts the story of his pilgrimage (track 8: the Rome Narrative). He describes his penitence as he sought the path to Rome, his joy at seeing so many of the pilgrims being absolved of their sins, and then the Pope's rejection of his entreaties. The Pope told him that he could no more be forgiven of his sins than the papal staff could suddenly sprout fresh leaves and flowers. In other words, it would take a miracle for Tannhäuser to be pardoned.

Track 9: With no hope of redemption, Tannhäuser summons Venus. As Wolfram attempts to restrain him, the perfumes and mists of the Venusberg suddenly materialize in the distance.

Track 10: Venus asks Tannhäuser if he seeks to return because he has been ostracized by the world. This scene is vaguely reminiscent of *Don Giovanni*: the Don did not fear hell and Tannhäuser seeks refuge there (both Wolfram and he refer to the Venusberg as hell). The tug of war between Venus and Wolfram concludes at his mention of Elisabeth (page 138, track 10, 1:50). This is the third time the mention of a woman's name (first Mary, then Venus, then Elisabeth) has suddenly turned the action in a new direction. Tannhäuser no longer seeks to join Venus. She cries "Lost to me, alas!" (page 140) and vanishes.

It is now dawn. As the last strains of Venus fade away, we hear the voices of a funeral procession. It is for Elisabeth. The mourners place Elisabeth's bier next to the cross at which she had earlier prayed. Tannhäuser kneels beside her and implores Elisabeth to pray for him in heaven (page 142). At that, he collapses and dies. Suddenly, the red glow of dawn floods the stage and young pilgrims enter carrying a staff that has sprouted fresh green leaves. Tannhäuser has gained redemption through the death of Elisabeth.

A beautiful chorus, led by the pure voices of young boys, concludes the opera.

One might come away from *Tannhäuser* with the impression that

Wagner was an intensely devout Christian who tried to create a moralizing story about the wages of sin. However, if you look at all of Wagner's oeuvre, you will find that he explored widely through all of the myths and symbols of world civilization. He was very interested in Buddhism and other Eastern philosophies and even considered moving to Asia to escape his difficult life in Europe. In his largest work, the *Ring* cycle, Wagner created a lengthy and detailed parable of pagan gods and mortals. The entire tetralogy is devoid of Christian myth. *Parsifal,* by contrast, has been seen by some as an allegory of the story of Jesus. It is probably fair to say that Wagner knew a good story when he saw one and was eager to inject his philosophical musings into these tales. One of the themes that he did return to throughout his career was that of redemption of a man through the love (and usually death) of a woman. This appears in *Der Fliegende Holländer, Tannhäuser, Götterdämmerung,* and *Tristan und Isolde.*

As you learn more about Wagner, you will probably want to read a lot of background material on the composer's ideas and artistic influences. The study of Wagner can become a lifelong fascination because it is, in effect, the study of Western culture, philosophy, politics, history, religion, and ethics.

I have selected Beethoven's *Fidelio* as the alternate work for the study of opera and ideas. This seminal opera, which influenced so many nineteenth-century works, has already been described in chapter 1. Beethoven's work is a cry for universal freedom for all humans but is also devoted to marital love and devotion. Leonore, the heroine, dresses as a young man (named Fidelio) and gets a job at the jail where Florestan, her husband and a political prisoner, is incarcerated. Through cunning and bravery, Leonore liberates Florestan, and a general amnesty is issued at the joyous conclusion of the opera. My recommended recording, conducted by Herbert von Karajan, stars Helga Dernesch as Leonore and Jon Vickers, one of the great heldentenors, in one of his best roles. (Vickers had the vocal resources to make a great Tannhäuser but never sang the role, which he considered immoral.)

We will now move on to *Die Walküre,* the most popular of the *Ring* operas, and a good introduction to the world of epic opera.

13.

DIE WALKÜRE

EPIC OPERA

*D**ie Walküre** is the second opera of Richard Wagner's famous cycle *Der Ring des Nibelungen*. This opera is preceded by *Das Rheingold* and followed by *Siegfried* and *Götterdämmerung*. To be perfectly accurate, let us use Wagner's terminology to describe the cycle: "a Stage Festival Play for Three Days and a Preceding Evening." By this definition, *Das Rheingold* is the prelude to a trilogy. However, it is generally accepted nowadays that *Das Rheingold* is an opera every bit as much as the other three, and therefore the *Ring* cycle is referred to as a tetralogy.

There can be little doubt that *Die Walküre* is the most popular of the four operas. There are two main reasons for this. The first is its sublime music, which has thrilled listeners since its premiere in Munich on June 26, 1870. The second is that *Die Walküre* forms something of a dramatic parenthesis in the *Ring* cycle. While two characters from *Das Rheingold* (Wotan, the chief god, and his wife, Fricka) return in *Die Walküre,* and some of the first opera's themes are addressed in the second one, Wagner used *Die Walküre* as a departure from the first work. *Das Rheingold* set up many of the

**If you have not read the previous chapter on* Tannhäuser, *you will not understand most of the references and allusions I make about the life and art of Richard Wagner in this chapter.*

364

characters, leitmotivs, and philosophical issues that would be explored throughout the cycle. *Die Walküre,* on the other hand, goes from symbols and action to the human and emotional side of Wotan, Fricka, and three characters we will meet in this opera: Siegmund, Sieglinde, and the heroine of the *Ring* cycle, Brünnhilde. I use the word "human" advisedly. Many of the characters in this epic saga are gods. They are certainly not godly, but neither are they subject to the laws of man.

There are many literary sources for the cycle. As early as 1846 Wagner wrote in letters that he was reading the *Nibelungenlied,* a collection of Germanic myths about a corrupt family that possesses an accursed hoard of gold. The myths were collected in a long Middle High German epic written around the year 1200. Wagner also was deeply influenced by the *Völsunga Saga,* an Icelandic prose saga that was assembled around 1200 using various older myths and legends. To these characters he brought his own philosophical musings and concerns and created a monumental story that is much greater in scope and ambition than the myths of old.

In other words, Wagner attempted to create myth and legend for our times. The *Ring* cycle has been exhaustively studied as an allegory on all of the ills that afflict modern society. George Bernard Shaw, a socialist, thought the cycle was an eloquent diatribe against capitalism. Certainly, the corrosive effect of greed and materialism is a central theme in the cycle. There is also Wagner's ongoing interest in the relations of men and women and the search for redemption. However, in the *Ring* this redemption does not come about thanks to God, Jesus, or the Virgin Mary; rather, it is won through love and death. With this redemption comes the possibility of renewal, if not for the characters, then for the world they left behind. I have long held that the *Ring* cycle is a treatise about how man's tampering with nature will lead to his own destruction. There are examples of this throughout the cycle as the natural forces of earth, air, fire, and water caution against environmental desecration and ultimately, when the gods and mortals who populate these operas have wreaked too much destruction, the forces of nature rise up and reclaim the planet, restoring the ecological balance.

One of the glories of the *Ring* cycle is that it enables us to search for its meaning, and meaning in our own lives, on so many levels. This cycle is what Wagner envisioned as his theater of the future.

Wagner began work on this story in the late 1840s in Dresden. His original intention was to create one opera, *Siegfrieds Tod* (Siegfried's Death). This conception later evolved to become *Götterdämmerung* (The Twilight of the Gods). He wrote this libretto first (1848, revised 1852). As he dug deeper into the story and its implications, Wagner then found it necessary to create an opera about the earlier life of Siegfried to set up events that would lead to the hero's tragic end in the later opera. This work is called *Siegfried,* and it was the second libretto he completed (1851, revised 1852). Next Wagner focused on four other characters who are important to Siegfried: his parents, Siegmund and Sieglinde, his grandfather Wotan (who appears as the unnamed Wanderer in *Siegfried*), and Brünnhilde, a daughter of Wotan, and Siegfried's future wife (which means he marries his aunt, but we won't worry about that!). These characters appear in *Die Walküre,* whose libretto Wagner completed in the spring of 1852. The composer then felt it was necessary to have an introductory work that would explain the structure of this society of gods and mortals and to present much of the thematic material that would be employed throughout the cycle. Thus was born the libretto for *Das Rheingold* (November 1852).

It is not enough to say that Wagner had his first idea with the death of Siegfried and then worked backward. He had a sketch of the entire story and all of its characters, but only gradually found it necessary to introduce the many characters and subplots we know today. Although the libretti were written in reverse order, the music was composed in the right direction. *Das Rheingold* was completed in 1854, then *Die Walküre* (1856), then *Siegfried* (begun in 1856, laid aside, then resumed in 1864 after the composition of *Tristan und Isolde,* the Paris *Tannhäuser,* and *Die Meistersinger von Nürnberg,* and finally completed in 1871). *Götterdämmerung* was begun in 1869 and completed in 1872.

Although *Das Rheingold* was first staged in 1869 and *Die Walküre* the following year, it was Wagner's vision that these operas be presented in true epic fashion—in a cycle of performances over five or six days. Although each opera is wonderful on its own, attendance at a complete cycle is an entirely different experience. You can focus more fully on the music and the story. By seeing and hearing these operas so close together, you live with their concerns as you would those of a great novel.

A man with vision and dreams as lofty as Wagner's would undoubtedly want his own theater in which his epic music drama could be staged. Although the wonderful stage facilities of Paris could have done justice to the many scenic effects in the *Ring* cycle, that theater was obviously not a possibility for Wagner after *Tannhäuser*. By the time the cycle was complete, following the Franco-Prussian War, German nationalism was cresting, and these operas based in Germanic myth perfectly fit the mood of the rising nation. Wagner thought that the town of Bayreuth in upper Bavaria would be a suitable site for his first stage festival play. He was not pleased with Bayreuth's theater and decided that a new one had to be built to house *Der Ring des Nibelungen*.

Wagner, who was always in personal financial straits, embarked on the huge mission of trying to raise enough money not only to build a theater but to produce the four operas. As his work and his legend became more popular in the new Germany, Wagner societies sprang up that devoted themselves to the study and appreciation of his work. These became great sources of income for the construction of the Festspielhaus (Festival House), with the largest contributions coming from Munich. King Ludwig II of Bavaria provided a guarantee of 216,152.42 marks, which the Wagner heirs repaid over many years. Wagner raised additional money from a series of concert tours.

The theater was built and the first complete *Ring* cycle was given on August 13, 14, 16, and 17, 1876. The performances were attended by monarchs, intellectuals, artists, and friends of Wagner and Cosima from across Europe. Two more cycles were given in August, and the festival was a resounding success. Wagner and his art were heaped with encomia. All of this must have been very gratifying for the composer—until he received word that the festival had ended its first season with a deficit of 148,000 marks.

Wagner spent much of 1877 on a strenuous concert tour to raise some of the money to meet his debts. He also was at work on his last opera, *Parsifal,* and despite all of his exertions (or perhaps because of them) he developed a new love interest in a young woman named Judith Gautier-Mendès. While apparently it was not of consequence in physical terms, this relationship did provide him with renewed inspiration to work on *Parsifal.*

The doors at Bayreuth did not open again until the 1882 premiere of *Parsifal.* On the final night, Wagner, unseen by the public, took the baton away from the conductor and led the performance from the second scene change until the end of the opera. Did he know this would be his last performance? Wagner, by then frail and suffering from a severe heart condition, died in Venice in February of 1883. Although his son, Siegfried, had been groomed to run the theater in Bayreuth, he was still a teenager when Wagner died. Besides, Cosima had other ideas. She became a highly capable administrator and very carefully burnished the Wagner myth. A new *Ring* cycle was produced in 1896, twenty years after the first one. Bayreuth became a cultural mecca in Europe as well as a destination for members of high society. It was a place where all of Wagner's work could be produced and glorified.

Cosima lived until 1930 and was actively involved in the theater for most of her life. Siegfried also was actively involved but died only a few months after his mother, never able to realize his own dreams. The festival remained in the hands of Siegfried's English-born wife, Winifred, and later their children. But the connection to the original visionary, Richard Wagner, had ended.

During the rise of Nazism, Bayreuth was a showplace for the glorification of what was considered the superiority of the German people. The character of Siegfried was considered the prototype of the model German: fearless and strong. Hitler visited the festival every year until 1940, so that Bayreuth and Wagner acquired an indelible Nazi taint. Winifred was, by all appearances, highly sympathetic to the Nazi cause, although some observers claimed that she had to make the best of a horrible situation and should be commended for helping the festival maintain a certain degree of artistic independence throughout the Nazi era. Winifred wanted to shut the theater in 1941, but the Nazi regime ordered "war festivals" in which wounded soldiers and other heroes would be able to gain inspiration and hope from Wagner's work. Winifred reasoned that the government payments for these festivals would help maintain the architectural and physical integrity of the theater. When Bayreuth was bombed, the theater was spared, although much of Wahnfried, the Wagner family home, where the composer is buried, was destroyed.

After the war the administration of the theater was entrusted to the town of Bayreuth. Artistic matters, however, would remain in Winifred's hands. In 1949, she gave authority to her two sons, Wieland and Wolfgang. In 1951, the festival presented Wieland's first new production, *Parsifal,* which revealed that he had a special genius and vision of his own. Many of his productions departed from traditional stagings but were nonetheless faithful to the composer's ideas. These productions, often quite abstract and rich in symbolism, galvanized the Festspielhaus, attracted the world's attention, and had a great influence on other stage directors and producers. With the availability of singers such as Birgit Nilsson, Leonie Rysanek, Astrid Varnay, Martha Mödl, Elisabeth Schwarzkopf, Wolfgang Windgassen, Ramon Vinay, Hans Hotter, George London, and others, there was a group of artists up to the musical and intellectual challenges that Bayreuth productions of the 1950s and 1960s entailed. Wieland died relatively young in 1966. Since that time, his brother, Wolfgang, has been the sole director of the Bayreuth Festival.

In this era of advanced technology, the art of Bayreuth has spread elsewhere thanks to the many audio and video recordings of its productions. Every production since 1978 has been preserved on video.

I often wonder what Wagner, a man who spoke often about the art of the future, would have said about the technology that preserves his art. Audio recording in Bayreuth began in 1927, so that scratchy performances exist from a time when Cosima and Siegfried were still present and there was a direct link to the creator. Nowadays, as in all opera, the works of Wagner have evolved to reflect the styles and tastes of the many stage directors and conductors who approach them.

With this is mind, let us begin our exploration of *Die Walküre.* This is only your first foray into the world of the four epic operas that form the *Ring* cycle. If you find that at first you cannot understand or appreciate them, do not give up. Return to them periodically as your love for and knowledge of opera grows and you will make many gratifying discoveries.

What do I mean by "epic" opera? These operas rely on myth and legend for their subject matter. This is notable because they compel audience members to depart from any familiar setting in reality and to immerse themselves entirely in the mythic worlds of the opera. In this regard, *Tannhäuser* is to some degree an epic opera, yet it has certain touchstones of realism. Elisabeth is a pious woman of the Middle Ages, and there were probably many others like her. The singing competitions and the pilgrimages to Rome were all part of medieval life in central Europe. On the other hand, Venus and her love grotto are more mythical concepts which conceivably could find a place in the *Ring*.

Another important aspect of epic opera is the presence of a heroic central figure, usually a man. We are asked to focus on the exploits of this hero in war and in love. We admire his courage and feel his suffering, usually depicted with music of great grandeur and sweep. But an important difference between an epic hero and one such as Don Carlo or Cavaradossi is that the epic opera is usually set against a cultural or historic abstraction. Therefore, the behaviors and attitudes of this character are not tied to a time and place for which we have preconceived ideas. That is why an opera set in antiquity can be heroic—most audience members do not have a strong sense of the cultural mores of ancient times, so they can accept on the part of the principal character a heroic comportment that would seem ludicrous in an opera set in the nineteenth century. While many epic sources are drawn from the ancient Mediterranean, the mythology of Central and Northern Europe has also provided material for operas, particularly those of Wagner.

Epic opera differs from grand opera in that the latter had as one of its ideals the creation of massive physical productions with crowds, choruses, and obvious financial outlay. In other words, grand opera features the glorification of spectacle, often at the expense of cohesive storytelling. Epic opera puts the occasional spectacular effect at the service of the story. This certainly is not a style that is exclusively Wagner's. A strong argument could be made that Monteverdi's *Il Ritorno di Ulisse in Patria* (1640), a retelling of the last pages of the *Odyssey,* was among the first epic operas. Although the orchestral scoring is hardly of epic proportions, *Ulisse* is an epic opera because of its subject and because of the way its librettist and composer explored the theme of heroism cast against a broad range of challenges and dilemmas.

Another epic opera, and the one I recommend as the alternate to our study of *Die Walküre,* is Hector Berlioz's *Les Troyens.* This massive work, drawn from the story of Dido and Aeneas in Vergil's *Aeneid,* was called a "lyric poem in two parts." The first part is *La Prise de Troie* (The Capture of Troy) and the second is *Les Troyens à Carthage* (The Trojans at Carthage). This two-part opera is often referred to as the French *Ring.* Its music and sweep is every bit as rich as Wagner's, although this is more a splendid retelling of a heroic epic than a context in which the composer explores his philosophical ideas. The recommended recording is on Philips, conducted by Sir Colin Davis and starring Josephine Veasey, Berit Lindholm, and Jon Vickers. There is also an excellent video from the Metropolitan Opera, conducted by James Levine and starring Tatiana Troyanos, Jessye Norman, and Plácido Domingo.

Die Walküre is the first opera you will learn that has no chorus. The Valkyries in Act III are eight women with names and personal characteristics who sing both together and alone. *Die Walküre,* by the way, is the way to say "The Valkyrie" in German.

The essays in the libretto booklet give you a good deal of background about the *Ring* cycle and, especially, the development and special characteristics of *Die Walküre.* But it probably would be useful for me to give you a little background about the story of *Das Rheingold* so that you know where we are when the curtain rises on *Die Walküre.*

The first opera of the cycle begins in the Rhine River—that is, underwater. The three Rhine maidens who protect the magic gold frolic and swim about until Alberich, the evil dwarf, arrives. He make a clumsy pass at the maidens, who laugh off his advances. They tell him that whoever possesses the gold will have power over the world but must renounce love forever. Since Alberich's flirtation is not getting anywhere, he decides to steal the gold. Darkness suddenly fills the river as the gold disappears.

Meanwhile, high in the mountaintops, Fricka, the goddess of marriage, awakens her husband, Wotan, the most powerful of all the gods. Wotan had contracted with two giants, Fafner and Fasolt, to build the gods a magnificent new castle called Valhalla, which looms above. Wotan had promised the giants an unusual form of compensation: Freia, the goddess of youth and Fricka's sister. When the giants arrive, Wotan hedges, saying he never really intended to offer Freia as payment. Three other gods, Donner (thunder), Froh (spring), and Loge (fire) help him stall the giants until another form of payment can be determined. Loge recommends that he and Wotan steal the Rhinegold from Alberich to give to the giants. Fafner and Fasolt agree to accept the gold, but they abduct Freia as collateral. With the goddess of youth gone, the gods begin to wither and weaken. Wotan and Loge make haste as they head down into the earth to find Alberich.

Alberich lives in the Nibelheim, an ugly hollow in the earth where he has enslaved the Nibelungs, a race of dwarfs who live like worms in the ground. They have been forced to turn all of the gold into ingots. Also there is Alberich's churlish brother, Mime. Some of the gold has been used to make two important objects. The Tarnhelm is a magic helmet that enables the wearer to disappear or to transform himself into any shape. The other object is a ring—*the* ring for which the entire cycle is named. The wearer of this ring will have absolute power.

Wotan and Loge arrive and claim they have heard rumors of Alberich's magic powers. When they challenge Alberich to show them how the Tarnhelm works, he turns himself into a large dragon. Loge pretends to be frightened and asks Alberich if he can transform himself into something small. At that, Alberich turns himself into a toad, which Wotan captures and Loge then strips of the Tarnhelm. They bind Alberich and return with him to the mountaintops.

Wotan makes Alberich command the Nibelungs to bring up all of the gold. Wotan also craves the ring and its power; he demands that Alberich turn it over to him. When the dwarf resists, Wotan pulls it off his finger and places it on his own. Alberich places a curse on the ring that will remain throughout the cycle: until the ring is returned to Alberich, anyone who wears it is doomed to ceaseless worry and death.

The giants arrive with Freia. Fasolt, who has fallen in love with Freia, agrees to accept the gold only if it can be piled high enough to hide Freia completely from view. After the gold is stacked up, the Tarnhelm must be added to bring the heap higher than Freia's head. But one of her eyes can still be seen through a hole in the pile. Fafner insists that the ring be added to close the hole. Wotan resists until, suddenly, Erda, goddess of the earth, rises from the ground and cautions Wotan to give up the ring, which would only bring the downfall of the gods if they were to keep it. Wotan reluctantly adds the ring to the pile.

Fasolt places the ring on his finger and is quickly clubbed to death by Fafner. So the curse claims its first victim. Fafner lumbers off with all of the gold and the gods file into their new castle. From below come the cries of the Rhinemaidens, pleading for the return of their gold.

It is at this point that *Das Rheingold* ends. You might expect *Die Walküre* to be a direct continuation of the story of the Ring and its curse. But *Die Walküre* is distinct among the four operas in the cycle because it is the only one in which no character has the ring. It remains with Fafner until *Siegfried,* the third opera of the cycle.

As you might imagine, staging the *Ring* cycle is a massive undertaking requiring inventive scenic and special effects as well as singers with acting skills, physical endurance, and dexterity. And, of course, these singers must possess formidable voices and intelligence to handle this very difficult music. In scenic terms, *Die Walküre* is the least challenging of the four operas. There is only one special effect—the magic fire that encircles Brünnhilde at the end of the opera. *Die Walküre* also is distinguished by one of the most erotic scenes ever written. If this doesn't heat you up, nothing will.

Perhaps the greatest "special effect" in *Die Walküre* is the music itself. When he began composing this opera, Wagner had recently undergone a change in philosophy about music in his operas. Previously, he wrote music that sometimes was more restrained in its beauty and power. Music, he felt, was meant to be but one component, and not the dominant feature, in the music dramas he created. Perhaps because he was his own librettist, Wagner gave more importance to the words than other composers do. But by the time he set about to write the music for *Die Walküre*, he was interested in how far the musical element of an opera could be taken and still bring meaning to the story. With this opera he pushed his boundaries, and he had the talent to fulfill these greater demands. *Die Walküre* is filled with thrilling music that sets audiences cheering. The drama, in fact, is heightened by the raw power of the music, as you will discover. This marked the beginning of the mature Wagner style that he developed for the rest of his life.

Let's begin. Familiarize yourself with the names of the characters and the singers (page 3 in your libretto book). Then read the two essays by John Deathridge (pages 41–58). These may be a bit too full of unfamiliar names and terms (although I gave you some grounding in these pages), but the chronology about the composition of the *Ring* cycle (pages 48–51) is very valuable for understanding how this magnum opus evolved. Then read the synopsis of Act I, scene 1 (pages 60–61). Please carefully read the italicized indications and stage directions and try to have a good mental image of what the set looks like. For example, you have probably never seen a house with an indoor ash tree as its most prominent feature.

Disk 1, track 1 (page 123): *Die Walküre* begins with a raging storm depicted in the prelude. The pounding cellos carrying the original theme, followed by the riotous orchestral voices of horns, cellos, drums, and other instruments, make this a storm distinct from others you have heard. The music begins with the curtain down. It opens only toward the end of the storm, to reveal the home of Hunding and Sieglinde.

Track 2: Siegmund bursts into the house to take refuge from the storm and collapses. He is discovered by a startled Sieglinde. From this point forward, carefully read the text as you listen. I will make periodic comments along the way. This scene depicts the slow, tentative reaching out of Sieglinde to Siegmund, and vice versa. They begin to sense a special feeling about each other, but they do not understand it. Note that all of this singing is in arioso style. Only two passages in this opera resemble arias: Siegmund's "Winterstürme" (track 10) and Sieglinde's "Du bist der Lenz" (track 11), both in this act.

Track 4 (page 127): Press the pause button on your CD player and go back to read the synopsis (pages 61–62) for the second scene. This is important because all of Wagner's notes for the scene are italicized in the synopsis. You must create a strong, clear mental picture of this scene. With the arrival of Hunding, Sieglinde's brutish husband, the dynamic changes. An intruder has broken the strange intimacy that suddenly developed between Siegmund and Sieglinde. Hunding's arrival is signaled by the sound of the Wagner tuba (track 4; 0:28). These are actually horns, not tubas, that were designed for Wagner to meet specific sonic needs he desired. Hunding privately remarks how like his wife Siegmund is ("That snaky shiftiness gleams out of his eyes as well").

Track 5 (page 131): Siegmund is reluctant to reveal his name to the prying Hunding. He says his name is Wehwalt (Woeful) and that his father's name was Wolf. He then tells the story of being separated from his twin sister and of the wars and misery he endured. He speaks of the slaughter of his mother and the simultaneous disappearance of his sister. It may not yet be clear to you that Siegmund's father was none other than Wotan. This master of the gods wandered the earth, having many affairs (not unlike Wagner). In one of them, as "Wolf," he impregnated a mortal woman, who gave birth to twins: Siegmund and Sieglinde. In this scene, Siegmund has not yet figured out that he has entered his sister's home.

Note, at 3:55 of track 5, after Siegmund says "den Vater fand ich nicht" ("I did not find my father"), that the horns in the orchestra break in with a particular melody. This is the Valhalla motive, referring to the castle and the chief of the gods. Whenever you hear this music in the *Ring* cycle, Valhalla should come to mind.

Tracks 6 and 7: As you read the scene, you will learn that Siegmund's knack for running into people who don't like him has continued. Hunding is from the family that Siegmund recently battled with. Hunding says that the laws of hospitality require him to let Siegmund stay the night, but in the morning they will duel over the honor of Hunding's clan. He directs Sieglinde to prepare his bedtime drink. As she leaves she attempts, without success, to direct

Siegmund's gaze to something strange stuck in the ash tree in the middle of the house. Notice how the music evolves to what we hear at track 7, 4:40: a beam of light shines into the room, illuminating a sword that has been plunged into the tree. This music is the sword motive, another of the many important leitmotivs in the *Ring* cycle.

Track 8: Now go back to read the synopsis for scene 3 (page 62). Wagner divided this act into scenes for purposes of defining the presence and absence of Hunding, but the action is continuous. What follows is one of the most exciting, erotically charged scenes in all of opera. As soon as Hunding has gone to bed, followed for now by his wife, Siegmund muses aloud about a sword his father promised him. When he thrillingly sings "Volsa, Volsa, where is your sword?" (2:25, page 139), he is talking about himself. He and his sister are the Volsung twins. Wagner drew this story line from the Icelandic *Völsunga Saga* I referred to above. At 3:02, light again illuminates the sword as we hear the orchestra play that motive. This time Siegmund sees it. Through all of this, he also sings of the mysterious attraction he feels for the lady of the house.

Track 9: Sieglinde returns and tells Siegmund that she has drugged Hunding. She recounts the story of her wedding. She was captured and brought to Hunding as an unwilling bride. During this evening, a mysterious old man (Wotan) entered the house and plunged into the tree the sword, which only the bravest hero will be able to extract. Many have tried without success. Could Siegmund be the one to pull the sword out of the tree? Siegmund, who still does not suspect the identity of this woman, tells her (page 143) that "both sword and woman will be his. Fiercely in my heart burns the oath that makes you my noble wife."

Track 10 (page 145): Siegmund tells Sieglinde that, for them, spring has just replaced winter. He, in fact, is the spring, and she is love. He refers to her in a general way as his sister, but this will not be formally declared until the last words of this act. You will notice, in the rapturous music that follows, as they declare love and prepare to engage in ecstatic lovemaking, that neither seems to realize that they are brother and sister. If you doubted my assertion that Judeo-Christian teachings did not influence the values of the characters in the *Ring*, this is Exhibit A. We audience members do not judge them harshly. Rather, we are swept along in the musical delirium that Wagner has created (tracks 12 and 13).

At the moment that Siegmund pulls the sword (which he names Nothung) from the tree (track 13, 1:28), a magic spell is heard in the orchestra. Listen to the shimmering sounds at this moment, which represents not only Sieglinde's joy that someone finally has rescued her, but the erotic quiver that Siegmund's wielding of the sword— undoubtedly a phallic symbol—sends up Sieglinde's spine. In a production in the 1960s, Leonie Rysanek spontaneously emitted an orgasmic yell that was so astonishing that it subsequently became part of her performance. Since then, other singers have imitated, but never equaled, that rapturous sound. Wagner did not write it (and Jessye Norman does not scream in this performance), but here is an example of a small piece of performance practice that has crept into the sacrosanct world of Wagner.

In the final moments of this act, brother and sister give themselves to one another, vowing to increase the bloodline, and as the music whips up to a wild frenzy, they waste no time in acting on their passions. In some productions this is rather graphically suggested—no nudity, mind you, but very aggressive kissing, hugging, and rolling around on top of one another. In others, especially those with larger singers, they might exult and then move out of the house to a setting that was at first wintry but is now in the full bloom of spring. When well performed, this act is usually greeted with delirious ovations during the curtain call.

Now comes the second act (disks 2 and 3). This is a rather long act, darker and slower than the others. Here we see Wotan and his favorite daughter, Brünnhilde, the chief warrior goddess of the Valkyries, and hear the famous Valkyrie motive for the first time. Wotan has summoned Brünnhilde to lead the defense of Siegmund. Wotan sees in his son the possibility of a hero who can wrest the ring from Fafner. Throughout this opera you should bear in mind that Brünnhilde is Wotan's most beloved child. He thrills to hear her as she cries her celebrated warrior yell ("Hoyotoho!"). She warns him of Fricka's arrival in a chariot drawn by bleating rams (a funny and very accurate image of the character of Fricka).

Viewers of the whole cycle already have met Wotan's nagging

wife in *Das Rheingold*. With her husband siring children right and left (we know of nine Valkyries and two Volsungs, and there are probably many more), Fricka, the goddess of marriage, decides to give her husband a lecture on fidelity. She is also appalled that Siegmund and Sieglinde have had sex (word gets around). Christa Ludwig does a superb job with this scene. Incidentally, the mother of the Valkyries is Erda, the goddess of the earth who rose from the ground to insist that Wotan turn over the ring to the giants.

Fricka does not care that Siegmund might be able to save the gods by capturing the ring. For her, the sanctity of marriage is the most important issue. To atone for his infidelities, Wotan must allow Hunding to slay Siegmund. He must instruct Brünnhilde to stay out of the fray as well. The return of Brünnhilde (track 5) only further annoys the irate Fricka. She departs.

It is generally accepted that Wagner drew inspiration for the Wotan/Fricka relationship from his own marriage to Minna. On the other hand, he also thought of himself as Siegmund to Mathilde Wesendonck's Sieglinde, even though that liaison did not produce children. In the dramatic scheme of things, Fricka and Hunding represent the dreary confines of conventional marriage, which were a constant irritant to Wagner.

The second scene of this act is a long, personal conversation between Wotan and Brünnhilde (disk 2, tracks 6–10; disk 3, track 1). Stop your CD player and read the synopsis (page 63). This scene is almost thirty-five minutes in length and can be rough going for people not used to this kind of prolonged operatic conversation. However, it can also be very rewarding in terms of our learning about the relationship between these two crucial characters. Both James Morris and Hildegard Behrens bring great drama and insight to the scene. Throughout, by the way, you should note Behrens's passionate and expressive use of German. Hers is not a matter of consonant-popping enunciation for effect; rather, she brings a clarity to the words that indicates her character's feelings at every moment. Even if you do not speak German, listen to the sounds as you read the English and you will understand the subtle shadings and mood changes that come with each sentence.

Read the libretto carefully as this scene progresses. In this scene,

Wotan undoes his edict to protect Siegmund. Brünnhilde objects to this, seeing in her half-brother the ideal hero to retrieve the ring. Wotan says he must accede to Fricka's will, suggesting that this is the lingering curse he must endure for having held the ring. You will hear wonderfully varied orchestral commentary, which gives the drama great texture. Many leitmotivs come to the fore as Wotan tells Brünnhilde the whole story of the sorry state of the gods. You will also hear Alberich's curse on the ring (track 9, 1:00). Whenever you hear the sound of cascading trombones, they signify Wotan's railing against whatever has angered him. This may be Fricka or, later on, Brünnhilde's disobedience.

Brünnhilde's inability to comprehend her father's sudden weakness of resolve is described not only in her words but in the orchestra. Finally, filled with sadness at having to defend Hunding rather than Siegmund, she gathers up her weapons and leaves.

Scene 3 (disk 3, tracks 1–2): After reading the synopsis (pages 63–64), keep following the libretto. Sieglinde and Siegmund arrive. She feels guilty for having subjected her brother to danger. Although she is exhausted, she wants to push on. Siegmund insists that she rest. He tries to tell her that Nothung will protect them from any attack. With the sound of Hunding's horns, she faints. She will remain unconscious throughout the fourth scene.

Act II, scene 4 (synopsis, page 64; tracks 3–6): Brünnhilde is filled with compassion for Siegmund's resolve to forgo the company of heroes in Valhalla if it means leaving behind Sieglinde. This is Brünnhilde's first glimpse of romantic love between a man and a woman; the only other love she has known is that between devoted daughter and a loving father. She decides to defend Siegmund after all, despite Wotan's orders. Notice how the clarion sound of Behrens's voice brings extra dramatic imperative to everything that Brünnhilde resolves to do. This is a virginal warrior goddess who, though trained to fight, also has developed impulses and feelings about what is just. Too often the role of Brünnhilde is played as an aggressor without the compassion that Behrens so effectively communicates.

Scene 5 (tracks 7–8) is a gripping conclusion to this intricate act. Read the synopsis carefully (page 64). Sieglinde awakens to see

Hunding dueling Siegmund. Just as it seems that Siegmund, with Brünnhilde at his side, will win, Wotan reluctantly waves Brünnhilde aside and shatters Nothung, Siegmund's sword, with his spear. Hunding kills Siegmund. Sieglinde collapses, but Brünnhilde gathers her up, along with the broken sword, and they ride off atop Grane, Brünnhilde's horse. Wotan avenges his son's death by killing Hunding with a single wave of the hand (track 8, 4:21) and then vows to punish Brünnhilde as the trombones lead the charge in one of those great "wake-up call" endings in which Wagner specialized.

Was this act too long and difficult? It is not much shorter than all of *Elektra*, our next and last opera in this book. There was a lot of talk and relatively little action. It is surely the hardest act of any we will study in this book. The lesson here is that great preparation, stamina, and concentration are required to give Wagner his due. There are other acts in Wagner that are even longer—in *Die Meistersinger* and *Parsifal*, for example. But one day you will attend a performance of *Das Rheingold*, a one-act opera that is two and a half hours long, and if it is a good performance, you won't notice how long you are in your seat.

There is no easy answer to this problem. If you cross that threshold in Wagner in which you revel in his music and drama, the length of an act or of an entire opera will not seem onerous. Otherwise, you may have to approach the *Ring* cycle gradually by listening to recordings and watching videos so that you can take breaks as you feel the need. I remind you of my view of a night at a Wagner opera as a long journey. Approach these works with an open mind and don't feel pressured to love them at first listen or sight.

Now on to disk 4 and the exciting third act of *Die Walküre*. Read the synopsis on page 65 for Act III, scenes 1 and 2.

Track 1: No matter how many times I hear the famous Ride of the Valkyries, which opens the act, the music never fails to thrill me. You may have heard this music only in its orchestral version—that is, without the voices of eight healthy Valkyries. There is excitement in the sheer power of their sound. This is *singing*, by the way, and not yelling, as bad imitators would have us believe. With the arrival of each sister, the salutations are renewed, which is why the music goes on longer than you'd have imagined. In productions of old, these were the women wearing helmets with horns. In recent years the clothing of warrior goddesses has evolved to be considerably more formfitting.

The Valkyries each have a horse that they use to carry the bodies of dead heroes back to Valhalla. The Ride of the Valkyries is actually a musical depiction of this activity. In most productions, the horses are implied. In an imaginative production done some years ago at the Seattle Opera, which specializes in productions of the *Ring* cycle, the Ride of the Valkyries was done on a merry-go-round. It might sound gimmicky, but it was really very effective. The dizzying motion and the ascending and descending motion of each horse was very persuasive with this music. Brünnhilde's horse, Grane, figures not only in *Die Walküre* but in the next two operas as well. In *Götterdämmerung,* a literal staging of the immolation scene—in which the world begins tumbling down when Brünnhilde mounts Grane and rides into the flames—would require a horse with a wonderful temperament and a singer who is a great horsewoman, both with nerves of steel. As you might expect, the appearance of Grane is more often than not left to the imagination.

Track 2: The tension in the scene escalates as Brünnhilde arrives with the exhausted and shell-shocked Sieglinde. The Valkyries, upon hearing of Wotan's wrath, fear offering protection to Brünnhilde and Sieglinde.

Track 3: Sieglinde says she has nothing to live for and hopes only for a speedy death. Brünnhilde informs her that she must live for love: she is carrying Siegmund's child. This is important for two reasons. The obvious one is Sieglinde's pregnancy: this child will be Siegfried, the great male hero of the *Ring* cycle. (It is Brünnhilde who selects the name of the unborn child, which means "peace in victory.") The less obvious point is that Brünnhilde again is extolling conjugal love; these remarks represent notable growth and evolution for the once coltish young warrior goddess. The theme of love is picked up in Sieglinde's last music: "O hehrstes Wunder!" ("Oh mightiest of miracles!"—track 3, 5:23). This is the first time we hear one of the most important motives in the *Ring* cycle: the love motive. It will return at the very end of *Götterdämmerung* as Brünnhilde has begun the process of redemption for Siegfried (and the world) by immolating herself on his funeral pyre.

Track 4: Wotan and his angry cascading trombones in the orchestra have arrived looking for Brünnhilde, whom the Valkyries are shielding from his wrath.

Track 5: Brünnhilde bravely steps forward to accept her punishment. Wotan tells her that she will no longer enjoy his love and protection or have the honor of carrying out his will. The Valkyries bemoan the fate of their sister, but they are too intimidated by Wotan to oppose him.

Stop your CD player and return to pages 65–66 to read the synopsis for Act III, scene 3, the moving conclusion to the opera. This scene is filled with emotion and tenderness. Duty forces Wotan to punish his beloved daughter. Although he is the chief god, even he has restraints on his power (think of King Philip II in *Don Carlo*). Brünnhilde has sacrificed her divine powers in the defense of her principles. You might think that she was defending the wrong party: an incestuous brother and sister whose affair broke up the sister's marriage. On the other hand, if you believe in true love triumphing over the legal constraints applied by traditional marriage, then you are on the side of Siegmund and Sieglinde. Did Brünnhilde behave correctly? Should she have disobeyed her father?

Tracks 6–8: Brünnhilde explains that she did not do what Wotan ordered but, rather, what he wanted in his heart. She prophesies that her action will produce a hero to save the Volsung line. Wotan rejects this, saying that it is her duty to carry out his commands, not to interpret them. Yet he is moved and admiring of her courage and her faith in steadfast love.

Tracks 9–10: Wotan decides to honor Brünnhilde's request to be put asleep encircled by magic fire. Only a true hero can penetrate this fire. Both sense that this man will be the future son of Sieglinde. Wotan passionately bids her farewell ("Leb' wohl"), kissing Brünnhilde's eyes shut, in the process removing her divine powers. He then gently lays her down, summons Loge, the god of fire (track 11), and as fire encircles the Valkyries' rock (track 12), without looking back, he leaves his best-loved child forever.

The Magic Fire music is justifiably famous. Sit back and listen to it. Imagine a fire igniting in flames that flicker and then spread until a circle of fire is formed in the middle of the stage. Smoke rises, the sky turns red, and gradually this opera, filled with so much epic conflict, comes to a quiet close.

Throughout our discussions of the first ten operas we have studied, I have alluded to psychological attitudes and insights of characters as described by the librettist and composer of an opera. Whether it is the death wish of Gilda, the conflicted sexual motivations of Donna Anna, or the inability of Eugene Onegin to maintain a meaningful relationship, we have asked ourselves why characters behave as they do. Yet there is a special category of opera that must be referred to as "psychological opera" in which the riddles and mysteries of the human mind become the central theme. We will learn Richard Strauss and Hugo von Hofmannsthal's *Elektra,* which was written in the intellectually charged atmosphere of Freud's Vienna. This opera also presents our first contact with dissonant music in an outstanding score that points toward modern music.

14.

ELEKTRA

PSYCHOLOGICAL OPERA

In our times, which is to say the era since Sigmund Freud (1856–1939) gave a vocabulary to the passions of the mind, all of us claim to have some sense of what the term "psychology" means. Although the word simply suggests "the study of the mind," it has acquired carloads of baggage in the post-Freudian era. Yet opera, the focus of this book, had existed for almost three hundred years when Freud's discoveries of human behavior started to appear.

Psychological opera is not an actual genre, such as opera seria or opera buffa, yet I believe that you are at the point in which you should consider the art form in a new way. What I propose in this chapter is that we think of psychological opera not so much as Freudian opera but, rather, as opera that explores or depicts the vagaries of human behavior. This does not necessarily imply insanity. If we were to use Freud's method of studying behavior and motivations, we could have a field day with the psyches of such pre-Freudian women as Gilda (did she have a death wish?), Lucia (was this a case of temporary insanity or a progressively deteriorating mind?), Donna Elvira (why does she forgive the man who abuses her?), Donna Anna (why is she sexually attracted to her father's murderer?), Tatyana (was her letter a healthy expression of her feelings or a deliberate act to bring misery upon herself?), Elisabetta (did she marry her fiancé's father so that she could become both mother and lover to him?), Elisabeth (was she afraid of sex?), Sieglinde (why did she knowingly commit incest?), and Fricka (does she have an unrealistic view of fidelity and the male sex drive?).

Yet the study of psychology in opera does not require us to look at characters through a Freudian prism. Rather, it should be an examination of the motivations of characters in the settings in which we find them. In *Don Carlo* there are characters whose psychological profiles are several layers deep. King Philip is a fatalist who exercises empty power. He has the love of neither his wife and his son nor of much of his nation. Elisabetta denies herself gratification, provoking her own misery. Carlo has periods of mental and emotional collapse. Verdi lets us see the psychic wounds of these characters, but he had no Freudian terminology to define them. These are psychological characters before the language of psychology was invented.

While there are many operas in which we accept the actions of characters without exploring their psychological motivations and impulses (*Il Barbiere di Siviglia* is a good example of this), there are many more that we can explore in pre- and post-Freudian psychological terms. Certainly *Boris Godunov* is as much a psychological opera as it is a grand opera.

Yet our choice for study of psychological opera is *Elektra*, a work deeply tied to the intellectual and psychoanalytical currents of Vienna at the beginning of the twentieth century. Hugo von Hofmannsthal wrote his play *Elektra* in the summer of 1903. It was an adaptation of the play by Sophocles but undoubtedly showed the influence of modern Vienna. Sigmund Freud and Josef Breuer published their landmark work, *Studies in Hysteria,* in 1895. In 1900, Freud produced his equally famous and controversial *Interpretation of Dreams.* In *Studies in Hysteria,* the most famous case study was probably the woman called Anna O., who became hysterical and deranged following the death of her father. This model influenced the creation of the title character in Hofmannsthal's *Elektra.* Although this heroine is definitely the woman Sophocles wrote of, she has taken on the modern psychological profile of a woman who was famous in Viennese intellectual circles through the writings of Freud. Therefore, Hofmannsthal's characters work on two levels: as their ancient selves and with the mantle of Freudian theory wrapped around them.

Elektra is distinctly un-Freudian in one important respect. Freud's subjects typically suppressed their visions, memories, and fears. It was only through extensive psychoanalysis that these issues would come forth. Elektra, on the other hand, does not suppress her memories and feelings; in fact, she relives them every night. The more Freudian character may be Klytämnestra, Elektra's mother, who murdered her husband Agamemnon seven years before we meet these characters. Klytämnestra is in a great deal of denial about her act, yet has nightmares that make her sleepless and wrack her with guilt and foreboding.

Hofmannsthal was not alone in bringing Freudian theory to art. It influenced the plays of August Strindberg, the paintings of Edvard Munch, and, as we will see, the music of Richard Strauss. The composer, in this opera, responded viscerally to Hofmannsthal's play, which was pared further to produce the libretto for the opera. In effect, Strauss's stupendous music makes the play speak in nonverbal ways. It takes the story and the psyches several steps beyond what the play describes.

It has been argued for years whether what Strauss wrote is cacophony or music. It is alternately tonal and dissonant. Yet it works perfectly in this story of primal emotions in which there is family betrayal, mother-daughter conflict (to put it mildly), an absent father, sisterly love and rivalry, a strong whiff of brother-sister incest, and smoldering, unresolved feelings of all types.

Bear in mind that this is a pre-Christian story even though it was written in this form in 1903. Our values based on the Judeo-Christian tradition, which we normally use to explain human behavior and failings, simply do not apply here. The whole notion of manners and proper comportment also do not apply. We have instead the rawest, most primal emotions and music that matches them: fiercely scraping violins, growling cellos, blasting brass, screaming woodwinds, and strange percussion: cracking whips and sounds of beating. To these add the growls, groans, cackles, and screaming by the singers, and it might seem hard to believe that the same composer produced the luscious waltzes in *Der Rosenkavalier* a couple of years later. Yet for all of its crashing and screaming, the score of *Elektra* is also filled with gorgeous melody. By now your skills at opera appreciation are advanced enough that you will be able to hear the beauty amid the chaos.

This opera uses more orchestral instruments (111) than almost any other. The sheer volume of *Elektra* is one of its arresting features. The singers must work to be heard over this thunderous orchestra. The recording we will use to learn *Elektra* is a landmark. Its vivid realism is still rather shocking more than twenty-five years after it was recorded. One of its stars is the Vienna Philharmonic, which first played this score under Strauss's baton and has total mastery of this fiendishly hard music. The conductor is Sir Georg Solti, one of the legendary maestros of the twentieth century. Birgit Nilsson, one of the greatest dramatic sopranos ever, plays the title character. Few artists have had the supreme command of vocal resources to handle the punishing role of Elektra. Although this one-act opera is only about 110 minutes long, Elektra is onstage for almost the entire time. Matching Nilsson at every step is Regina Resnik as Klytämnestra, Elektra's mother. Resnik's is a harrowing psychological portrait of a woman alternately evil, vain, demented, controlling, and shallow.

Throughout the opera, Strauss has created moments of unmistakable psychic horror. The first three notes of the opera (the motive of Agamemnon, Elektra's murdered father) jolt you from your seat. These are the same notes we will hear at the end of the opera after Elektra does the manic, frenzied dance that results in her own sudden death. The music of this death evokes the sound of a heart that has exploded. Or listen to the restless growl of the orchestra as Klytämnestra makes her entrance (track 6 on the first disk). Later on, note how the orchestra suggests the sound of yelping, starving dogs. Throughout, the blood-curdling laughs and screams are not the stuff of horror films. These are primal screams of pain and joy. It is interesting to note that although Strauss did not acknowledge or speak much about his mother, she was mentally deranged. This must have contributed to his musical portrayal of Klytämnestra and his attraction to this story with its turbulent emotional extremes.

Elektra had its premiere in Dresden on January 25, 1909. It enjoyed some success, but it was not until a 1910 production at Covent Garden led by Thomas Beecham that it was considered a masterpiece. No less an observer than Shaw remarked that Strauss and Hofmannsthal made tragedy accessible again, stating "with an utterly satisfying force, what all the noblest powers of life within us are clamoring to have said, in protest and in defiance of the omnipresent villainies of our civilization; and this is the highest achievement of our highest art."

Let us begin. First read the two essays in the libretto booklet. One, by Michael Kennedy (page 12), explores this opera as a product of the Expressionist movement in art. Gerd Uekermann's is an excellent study of myth and psychoanalysis in Hofmannsthal's play. Then read the synopsis on page 20.

One of the first things you will realize about this opera is its remarkable compactness and concision. It is by far the shortest opera we have studied, yet its impact is as strong as anything else you have learned. You should play this recording loud. Years ago I purchased the Rolling Stones' album *Let It Bleed*. On the album cover was the recommendation that the music be played at high volume to be fully appreciated. That applies to this recording as well. With 111 instruments in the orchestra and a powerful dramatic soprano like Birgit Nilsson in the title role, this music should be heard in all of its sonic splendor.

Bear in mind too that this is a one-act opera that takes place in one location: the courtyard of the house of Agamemnon in ancient Mycenae. The scenic aspect of the opera is actually rather static. The murders that occur take place within the palace, so our imaginations—fueled by the orchestral music and the singers—are called upon to envision their full horror. This convention of Greek tragedy is a brilliant dramatic move in this opera too, since what we imagine can be much more horrible than anything that could be represented onstage.

Disk 1, track 1 (page 54): The first notes we hear are the motive of Agamemnon. In fact, they almost speak his name. If you say the name as you hear the chords, you will understand what I mean. The servant girls talk about Elektra, who suddenly darts onto the scene. She is mad, the women remark. Their descriptions and imitations of her give us a good idea of who she is before we meet her. In track 2 (page 60), we see Elektra in all her fury. The orchestral lead-in to her first words tell us of her miserable torment. Her long monologue ("Allein!") is her nightly retelling of the murder of her father, Agamemnon, at the hands of her mother, Klytämnestra, and her mother's lover, Aegisth. Elektra, in addressing her dead father, calls the murderous couple "your wife and the man who sleeps with her." Throughout this monologue, with increasing power, Elektra calls the name of Agamemnon. These repeated cries have the effect of rattling the listener and drawing us into the tension of the opera. The graphic lyrics of slit throats, splattered blood, and slaughtered animals in Elektra's monologue bespeak her desire for revenge. For the next hundred minutes, Strauss creates a slowly calibrated buildup of seething tension. We are sucked into the sickness and depravity of these characters and live with them until Klytämnestra and Aegisth are killed and Elektra drops dead. Even then, as you will hear, Strauss's music keeps pulling us in until two heart-stopping drumbeats jolt us to our senses in one of the greatest closing moments in all of opera.

Track 3 (page 62): We now meet Chrysothemis, Elektra's sister and, to apply some modern terminology, a codependent if ever there was one. She is also a very sympathetic character who symbolizes love amid all of this depravity and hatred. If Elektra has the musical sound and personality of a Valkyrie, then Chrysothemis has the musical temperament of Sieglinde. This parallel cannot be stretched too far, because Brünnhilde, the chief Valkyrie, is a far more appealing personality than Elektra. Nonetheless, the *vocal* personalities are similar. Chrysothemis tells Elektra of Klytämnestra's plan to lock her in a tower. The sister then begs Elektra to get over her obsession with revenge (which has gone on now for seven years) and attempt to live a normal life (track 4, page 64). If Elektra relents, Chrysothemis will also be freed. Her hope is to leave this place and have children. Notice, in the conversation between the two sisters, how hysterical the orchestral accompaniment is for Elektra while the one for Chrysothemis is lyrical.

Suddenly (tracks 5 and 6, pages 66–68) there is a sort of unrest in the orchestra that suggests the beating of animals, especially dogs.

This tells us that Klytämnestra is approaching. This music builds for more than four minutes as Chrysothemis tells her sister that their mother has had a nightmare about their exiled brother, Orest, and cautions Elektra to avoid her. Chrysothemis flees while Elektra stays to relish the encounter with Klytämnestra.

Track 7, page 69: The queen is clearly in an angry and vindictive mood. Notice again the wild mood swings in mother and daughter as depicted in the orchestra. The queen's imperious mood changes, by tracks 8 and 9 (pages 71–74), to a recitation of her nightmares and a complaint about how poorly she has been sleeping. This is the most Freudian passage in the text, surely influenced by Freud's *Interpretation of Dreams,* published two years before Hofmannsthal set to work on his play. Pay close attention to the sound of the German words in the queen's recitation of how she is tormented. The richest part of this linguistic sound of torment starts in track 8, 0:31, page 71 ("Schreist nicht du . . .") and continues to become more pungent and strangely decadent at 1:21 ("schlachte, schlachte, schlachte") as the sound of words and music become one in the description of grisly slaughter.

The descriptions become even more vivid on page 73 ("a something crawls over me . . . Can one then perish while still alive, like a rotting carcass? . . . And then I sleep and dream, dream that the marrow is melting in my bones" . . . "Every demon leaves us alone, as soon as the correct blood has flowed") as the orchestral music becomes ever more lurid and psychotic. What is remarkable about this music is that although it depicts horrific ideas, it has a beauty all its own. The words Klytämnestra speaks are those of a tormented woman of ancient Greece, not a prototype of an hysteric in 1903 Vienna. Yet they certainly had double resonance for anyone in Strauss's audience familiar with Freud's theories.

After mother and daughter carefully take verbal swipes at one another, Elektra explodes (track 11, page 80) as she tells her mother that the only way Klytämnestra can sleep again is for her own blood to be spilled. After this powerful tirade, the queen's confidante suddenly rushes in and whispers something in her mistress's ear. Carefully read the stage directions on page 82 as you listen to what the music tells you about Klytämnestra's reactions to what she is hearing. You can hear sick, cynical laughter as news has come that will surely devastate Elektra. We will find out what it is in the very first words on the second CD.

Track 1: Orest, beloved brother of Elektra and her last hope to murder her mother, is dead. Chrysothemis brings Elektra the news, although surely the orchestral music gave you a clue. At first Elektra cannot believe this, but as two servants talk of sending word to Aegisth (track 2), Elektra accepts the possibility of her brother's death and tells Chrysothemis (track 3, page 86) that the task of vengeance has fallen to them. In track 4 (pages 88–91), as Elektra attempts to convince Chrysothemis to help her do the killing, her words become frankly erotic and sexual. One wonders if Viennese audiences took this as a moment of Eros inspired by thoughts of murder, or viewed it merely as rather pearly dialogue between two women in ancient Greece. Or, with such beautiful music, did they not notice the words?

When Elektra fails to enlist her sister's aid, she curses her and starts digging with her hands to find the axe that was used to kill her father (track 5, page 93). Strauss's music here is very pictorial: both of the digging and of Elektra's frenzy and dementia. Read the stage directions on page 94 as you listen to this music.

Orest, who was supposed to be dead, appears.

Track 6 (pages 94–97): The crazed Elektra does not recognize her own brother. He has come, he tells her, to bring the queen the news of her son's death. Eventually, the stranger convinces Elektra to reveal her name.

Track 7 (pages 97–99): Elektra still does not realize this is her brother, even though the servants of the house and even the dogs recognize him.

Track 8 (page 100): In one of the opera's most magnificent moments ("Orest!"), Elektra realizes that the man she is looking at is her brother. The orchestra speaks of her joy and also of the rising sense of possibility in her mind that the vengeful murders can take place after all. With this renewed hope comes introspection and self-awareness. Elektra knows that she has gone from being a healthy, beautiful young princess to a haggard woman living like an animal among animals outside her mother's palace. In these words, too, come lines that bespeak the famous "Electra complex" that Freud spoke of: "These precious feelings I have had to sacrifice to our father. Do you think, when I rejoiced in my body, that his sighs and groans did not penetrate to my bedside?" ("Diese süssen Schauder . . ."—track 8, 8:42). These words are just ambiguous enough to be open to interpretation. In this scene, Elektra also shows more than a slight sexual attraction to her brother. What does all this incestuous sexuality represent in Elektra? Think about it.

Track 9 (page 101): Orest agrees to commit the murders.

Track 10 (page 103): Orest's tutor tells the rejoicing siblings to be silent lest they be heard in the palace (a nice touch of realism that also serves to lower the volume of the music before the big events to come). In the orchestral music that follows you can hear the flickering light at the door to the palace. Orest enters the palace.

Track 11 (page 103): Listen to how the music describes what is going on in Elektra's head. Elektra suddenly realizes that she forgot to give Orest the axe (a Freudian slip?). Keep listening to the mounting tension in the orchestra. A scream is heard. Orest is killing Klytämnestra.

Track 12 (page 104): We cannot see the murder, but the sounds of the orchestral music, the scurrying of the maids, and the frightened arrival of Chrysothemis all create terrible thoughts and images in our head. Everyone except Elektra runs offstage.

Track 13 (page 106): Instead of focusing our thoughts on the death of the queen, the orchestra breaks in with a lilting melody on the clarinet. Here is the ridiculous Aegisth. Elektra lights his path as she guides him up the palace steps. He silently goes into the house. Now listen to the orchestra. In a spine-tingling musical passage, Aegisth is killed as well. "Can no one hear me?" the doomed man screams. "Agamemnon can hear you!" cries Elektra. The deed has been done.

Tracks 14–16: Chrysothemis leads the rejoicing. The explosion of joy in the orchestra tells us that things should end happily. Elektra says that from the seeds of adversity she has reaped joy. Then she says, "Love kills! But no one dies without having known love!"

Suddenly, at track 17 (page 113), Elektra breaks into a wild, disjointed dance of joy. Listen as the orchestra tells you how she dances. Do you hear the chaos and confusion creep into her brain? This dance of joy accelerates and, suddenly, alarmingly, becomes a frenzied dance of death. Her movements become more labored, but she cannot stop. In an instant, as the orchestra clearly tells you, her heart explodes (track 17, 2:41–45). The Agamemnon motive, now more appropriately that of the curse on the house of Agamemnon, tells us that another victim has been claimed. Now that the deed Elektra lived for—the murder of her mother and Aegisth—has been done, her reason for living has gone. Chrysothemis forlornly calls out for her brother.

A magnificent orchestral sweep gathers us up, and then, unexpectedly, two final beats of a drum—like two final beats of a heart—shatter the music's grandeur and give the audience one last shock. The final psychological jolt is ours.

As you probably have realized, this opera is not an academic Freudian exercise. It is living, fire-breathing theater. I believe it is worth noting that if one were to be watching supertitles of this very literal play, one would miss a great deal of the drama where it counts—onstage.

Since the beginning of the twentieth century, many operas with powerful psychological components have come forth, more often than not in the form of a character with a great tragic flaw. Look at Janáček's *Jenůfa* (the character of Kostelnička in particular), Berg's *Lulu,* and Benjamin Britten's *Peter Grimes.* Also, when you study Mussorgsky's very grand *Boris Godunov* (1874), note its strong psychological elements.

However, for an alternate psychological opera I have selected a work from the pre-Freudian era: Mozart's *Così fan tutte.* For too long this work was thought of as a silly sex farce about partner swapping. In fact, it is a very sophisticated exploration of the male and female psyches. Why do men and women behave as they do? While da Ponte's libretto is a series of clever scenes, if you look closely at the lyrics in several arias, you will see that he created four distinct personalities in these two pairs of young lovers. We wonder whether women behave as they do by choice or whether they behave in a manner intended either to gratify or repel men. In other words, do these women exist to react to men, or do they understand and follow their own feelings and instincts? The internal monologues of the pensive character of Fiordiligi are fascinating forays into a complicated and conflicted psyche. To da Ponte's libretto Mozart brought music of sublime beauty and great mystery. Its sounds are so beguiling that you must listen carefully to realize how sensitive and specific it is to the story. As was their wont, da Ponte and Mozart present the circumstances and then leave it up to us to decide and analyze what we perceive.

Our course has ended, and you now have the skills to learn and appreciate any opera that you may come in contact with. You are now ready to begin a lifelong love affair with opera, that most intoxicating and beguiling of art forms.

Bravo! Brava! Bravi! Brave!

15.

OPERA AND YOU

A LIFELONG LOVE AFFAIR

Operagoing is all about passion. We operagoers are dedicated people: we collect recordings, hear and rehear favorite singers in roles we love, read everything we can about opera, and plan our vacations based on which opera or operas are playing in a particular place. We relate events and emotions in our lives to memorable moments in opera. When we feel love, we think of operatic lovers. When we are sad, the music and stories from opera often give us insight or solace.

Perhaps the greatest thing about being a devoted operagoer is that there is so much room for growth. Just because you have heard an opera once does not mean that you can't hear it one, five, or twenty times more. I have heard at least twenty performances of each of the operas you learned in this book, and I would happily hear them twenty more times. With each rehearing, you refine what you know. The better you know an opera, the more you will be challenged by the ideas of new singers, conductors, directors, and designers.

Your first experience with *Rigoletto* or *Tosca* is only your introduction to those masterpieces. Each time you hear a different singer in any of the key roles, you are hearing a new interpretation. Even the same singer will vary on two different occasions. Artists grow and change in their approach to a character based on their own life experiences and their moods. For example, I saw a famous soprano from Eastern Europe sing Tosca twice within ten months. The first time was a good, honest performance that pleased the audience. The second, however, was stunning. In the intervening months, the singer's husband had suddenly died. The love scenes in the second performance seemed much more deeply felt, and her response to the torture and death of her lover was riveting. While I attended the second performance with the knowledge that the artist's husband had died not long before, that information was not necessary to appreciate the powerful performance that was being given.

When a different conductor approaches a score you are familiar with, you will hear something new. For example, you will notice that recordings of the same opera are often faster when conducted by Georg Solti and slower when conducted by Herbert von Karajan. (Each led recordings of *Don Carlo* and *Lohengrin* which make for good comparisons.) There is no right and wrong in this: each conductor has his valid point of view, and you will come to your own conclusions as you listen. Every director or designer who tackles the ideas and the drama of an opera will give you something new to think about. I have seen two productions of *La Traviata* by Franco Zeffirelli. His ideas and his approach to the main character changed as he grew older, and I had the chance to explore his views by comparing my memory of the first production with the performance of the second one.

It is usually the performances of favorite singers, and the discovery of new ones, that keep us coming to the opera house. I feel fortunate that since the 1960s I have heard and seen most of the great singers in live performances. Some, such as Maria Callas and Renata Tebaldi, I heard toward the end of their careers, and I cherish those few performances that inspired me so. Other artists, including Leontyne Price, Joan Sutherland, Montserrat Caballé, Marilyn Horne, Jon Vickers, Luciano Pavarotti, and Plácido Domingo, I heard in all their glory. These artists are part of my operatic golden age. But I approach the future with enthusiasm. Every time I hear a wonderful new singer my hopes for the future are renewed. I attend every performance with the happy anticipation that I may be in the presence of the next Sutherland or Rysanek.

While this does not always happen, hope is central to the emotional makeup of many opera lovers.

You will soon discover that one of the special things about operagoing is that you, the audience member, are not a passive participant in the performance. The audience member is not merely a witness to the arrival of new artists. You are also someone whose life and growth can be charted by your responses to various operas. A work that had little significance to you when you were younger may, as you mature, take on profound meaning. In my case, *Eugene Onegin, Andrea Chénier, Così fan tutte,* and *Elektra* now speak to me in ways that eluded me when I was a teenager. Each is a meditation on the beauties and burdens of love, and with greater maturity, I see and feel subtleties of meaning that did not reveal themselves to me before.

Because we know opera characters over the arc of years, they live and breathe within us in ways that characters from books, theater, or film usually do not. In those art forms, we usually encounter characters once and then they become a memory. In opera, we revisit characters periodically and see them differently based on the singers and the production they are in, and on who we are when we see them again. Each time we hear music related to those characters, we make associations that may be by turns comforting or disturbing, but always vivid.

And with so many operas being performed, there is always something new to hear. When a company stages a lesser-known work by Handel, Mozart, Rossini, Donizetti, Verdi, Wagner, Puccini, or Strauss, we not only learn something new but come to appreciate again the works we already know by those composers. For example, nearly all operagoers know Mozart's *Le Nozze di Figaro, Don Giovanni, Così fan tutte,* and *Die Zauberflöte.* But if you hear an earlier work such as *Il Rè Pastore* or a later one such as the magnificent *La Clemenza di Tito,* you will better understand the range of Mozart's talent as well as the greatness of his four most famous operas.

For the devoted operagoer, there is also the sense of community and belonging that the art form provides. In general, people are seated in an opera house because they want to be there. Since being an opera audience member is an active rather than a passive experience, there is a thrilling, communal charge that happens during a great performance that you seldom see elsewhere. Opera audiences know what they are seeing; they arrive with expectation and anticipation; and they respond with ardent passion.

In the introduction to this book, I opened the curtain with the first lines from *Pagliacci:* "Si può?" *Pagliacci* rings down the curtain with four of the most famous words in all of opera: "La commedia è finita!"—loosely, "The show is over!" But for you this is only the beginning.

Following this chapter are three appendices that will help you get further involved in opera. The first is a list of magazines and books that merit your attention. The second is an extensive list of recommended recordings and videos of many operas you may want to learn. These are only suggestions. If you have a favorite singer or conductor who does not appear on the recording I suggest, go for the one with your preferred artists. This list was compiled to give you the broadest view of talent available in recordings, although it certainly reflects some of my preferences. But one of the glories of collecting recordings is to compare several performances of the same opera. There are at least five good recordings each of *Don Giovanni* and *Don Carlo,* and if these become favorite operas of yours, you will likely wind up buying several different versions. The third appendix is probably the most complete listing you will ever see of addresses and phone numbers of opera houses around the world. As you become a more devoted opera fan, consult this list when you make your travel plans. Every night, somewhere in the world, there is a great performance of opera being given.

And when you take your seat, look down your row and you'll see me there.

APPENDIX A

SUGGESTED READING

ABOUT OPERA

As you might expect, a person can devote a lifetime to reading about opera. Most major opera-loving nations have at least one magazine that covers the art form. Libraries and good bookstores have shelves overflowing with volumes about every aspect of opera. In addition to books containing the stories of popular operas, there are biographies of composers, librettists, singers, designers, and conductors. I enjoy reading the letters of composers such as Mozart, Wagner, and Verdi, in which they explore the pain and pleasure involved in the creation of their masterpieces. Libraries are also full of critical analyses of all of the major operas. Some, such as Shaw's *The Perfect Wagnerite,* are as entertaining as they are enlightening. Unfortunately, others are quite dry or represent some of the narrow and outdated values of bygone days. This is particularly true in men's descriptions of the nature of women. I believe that composers had a much fuller understanding of complex human emotions than did the critics who sought to explain the composers' works.

This suggested reading list contains books and publications that will give you, the blossoming opera lover, more insight into various aspects of the art form. I have included only two singers' autobiographies, even though there are many more; but the books by Tito Gobbi and Marilyn Horne give you a good idea about how the lives and careers of two great artists developed in the years before and after the Second World War. Of course, you should read the biography of any other singer who interests you. The other books on this very selective list are intended to give you a sense of different aspects of the art form: the voice, the personal and creative lives of composers, the backstage life of an opera house, opera in other media.

In a class by itself is *The Grove Dictionary of Opera,* edited by Stanley Sadie. This is probably the most comprehensive compendium of opera ever created. Anything you would ever want to know about opera can be found in its four volumes. One of the great pursuits of true opera lovers is to spend endless hours reading the esoteric entries about forgotten composers and operas and the illuminating essays on familiar topics. With a price tag of more than $800, the Grove is only for the most ardent or well-heeled opera fan. If you can afford it and you have fallen in love with opera, this unparalleled collection will provide boundless pleasure and enlightenment.

BOOKS

Ardoin, John, *The Callas Legacy* (Charles Scribner's Sons, 1991). Ardoin is probably the leading chronicler of the life and career of Maria Callas, the most influential opera singer in the second half of the twentieth century. You should read other of Ardoin's books and articles to learn about Callas onstage and at home, but read this one for his expert analysis of how Callas's artistry is preserved on disk. This detailed yet accessible volume will give you valuable insight about how to listen to an opera recording.

Bing, Sir Rudolf, *5,000 Nights at the Opera* (Doubleday, 1972). Bing was one of the last great opera impresarios; in his time, decisions were made by one person rather than by committee. So his very entertaining memoirs are an artifact from another era in opera. They also will give you a great perspective into backstage life at the Metropolitan Opera during an era when most of the world's great stars appeared on its stage.

Culshaw, John, *Ring Resounding* (Secker and Warburg, 1967). There is probably no better book on the agonies and ecstasies of making an opera recording. Culshaw makes the reader feel as if this first stereo recording of Wagner's *Ring* cycle was akin to the exploration of uncharted terrain. We follow the story with all the excitement of reading a great adventure story.

Gobbi, Tito, *My Life* (Doubleday, 1980). A good, old-fashioned opera autobiography that combines humility, ego, wonderful anecdotes about colleagues, and insights into the craft of singing and acting. This book, without trying, is very moving, because it makes the reader realize that the precious generation of artists of which Gobbi was a part has largely disappeared, and that with them has gone a whole style of performance and dedication to the art form.

Grout, Donald Jay, *A Short History of Opera* (Columbia University Press, 3rd edition, 1988). Probably the standard text for learning all about opera. It can be a bit technical for the beginner, but it is valuable for reference even if you don't read it cover to cover.

Hamilton, David (editor), *The Metropolitan Opera Encyclopedia* (Simon & Schuster, 1987). A valuable basic book to keep on your shelf for frequent reference for names of singers, operas, theaters, composers, conductors, and designers. Particularly enjoyable are twenty-four essays by singers, conductors, and critics about specific roles or operas. Even if you are unfamiliar with the topics, they make good, instructive reading. This volume is also valuable for its definitions of technical terms that you may come across in your reading about opera.

Higgins, John, *The Making of an Opera* (Atheneum, 1978). A detailed description of the creation of one opera production, in this case a staging of *Don Giovanni* at the Glyndebourne Festival in England. You will learn about all the work that occurs before the first day of rehearsals and then about the exhilaration and tribulations of the days leading up to opening night.

Horne, Marilyn, with Jane Scovell, *My Life* (Atheneum, 1983). Blunt, forthright, intelligent, funny, dedicated, trailblazing—all of the attributes for which this artist is renowned come forth in this volume. This is the story of a modern opera star who was trained by great old masters but had to face an art form that was changing radically. It will let you know how opera stars of today live and work.

Lebrecht, Norman, *The Maestro Myth* (Birch Lane, 1991). An interesting and challenging book about the changing role of conductors in the music world. Some of your notions about the almighty maestro may be shattered as your knowledge of conductors grows.

Mordden, Ethan, *Demented: The World of the Opera Diva* (Watts, 1984). Perhaps too catty and bitchy for some tastes, but also filled with insights and humor. This book is a report from the front lines of opera fandom by a writer who understands why we cherish divas and overlook their foibles.

Mordden, Ethan, *Opera Anecdotes* (Oxford University Press, 1985). It behooves you as a budding opera fan to be conversant in these (usually) true and accurate stories from the annals of opera, many of which are riotously funny.

Mozart, Wolfgang Amadeus, *Letters* (Little, Brown, 1990). First published in 1938 in the translation by Emily Anderson. The brilliant and often sad life of this peripatetic genius is revealed in his letters. While his operas are not dwelt upon too much, reading his comments about the singers, musicians, and patrons of the late eighteenth century will give you a vivid sense of the Classical era in European music.

Newman, Ernest, *Wagner as Man and Artist* (Limelight Editions, 1985). First published by Knopf in 1924, this is still the starting point for reading about Wagner. Newman attempted to sift through the myths and legends about Wagner, many created by the composer himself. This book is also interesting because it is an attempt at psychobiography written decades before that became a dominant style in exploring famous lives in print.

Osborne, Charles, *Verdi: A Life in the Theatre* (Knopf, 1987). Verdi led such a long, rich, and complex life that it is hard to gather all of it in one volume. This book is an excellent introduction to the composer, but you should continue to explore his life and work in more detail by reading others of the dozens of books about the colossus of Italian opera.

Robinson, Paul, *Opera & Ideas* (Harper & Row, 1987). Though not for beginners, this book is a full, rich, engaging essay about how various operas relate to the political, social, and sexual realities of the times in which they were created and, for that matter, how these themes speak to us today.

Rosenthal, Harold, and John Warrack, *The Concise Oxford History of Opera* (Oxford University Press, 1992). Although the Grout *Short History of Opera* is more comprehensive, this good volume is more portable if you plan to read about opera while you travel.

Schmidgall, Gary, *Literature as Opera* (Oxford University Press, 1977). A very important and enlightening book that will help you understand how composers from Handel through Britten drew inspiration from literary sources to create operatic masterpieces. It may be tough going when you are new to opera, but bear it in mind once your knowledge of opera grows.

Schonberg, Harold, *Lives of the Great Composers* (W.W. Norton, 1981). A fine collection of profiles by the former chief music critic of *The New York Times*. This is the perfect book to inspire you to read more about the composers who interest you most.

Simon, Henry, *100 Great Operas and Their Stories* (Doubleday, 1989). A collection of synopses of the operas you are most likely to attend. This is a good starting place when you want to prepare to see an opera, but you should also be sure to listen to the music and have a look at the libretto.

Steane, J. B., *Voices: Singers and Critics* (Amadeus Press, 1992). A wonderful, detailed explanation of every type of operatic voice, along with in-depth views of the special artistry of ten legendary singers. The book also contains excerpts from the writings of leading British critics of the beginning of the century, all of them provocative. Once you have become a connoisseur of voices, this book will give you great pleasure.

Story, Rosalyn M., *And So I Sing* (Warner Books, 1990). The important contributions of African-American singers to opera is explored in this valuable book. All of the singers profiled are women, a telling fact about the disparity between the gains achieved by African-American men and women in opera. You will also learn that Marian Anderson was not the first great African-American singer.

Wagner, Richard, and Franz Liszt, *Correspondence* (Vienna House, 1973). Two volumes of lively letters exchanged by the self-absorbed and ever-indebted Wagner and his patient, magnanimous father-in-law. These letters will give you insights into the musical and political life of Central Europe at the height of the Romantic era.

Weinstock, Herbert, *Rossini* (Limelight Editions, 1987). While Stendhal's biography of Rossini is vastly more entertaining, it is not terribly accurate. This book clears up many of the misconceptions and apocrypha that have attached themselves to Rossini but still is enjoyable to read.

PERIODICALS

Opera News, published by the Metropolitan Opera Guild, is the leading American magazine about opera. Although it gives more coverage to the Met than to other companies, it is a national publication that covers activities in opera companies around the world as well. *Opera News* is also useful for finding out when major companies are performing particular operas. In recent years the magazine has engaged leading writers from other fields to write about specific themes and topics addressed in individual operas. This has lifted the quality of writing and debate in the magazine's pages.

The *Opera Monthly* is a newer magazine devoted to the art form. It tends to have more profiles than *Opera News* but has not yet become as authoritative as the older publication.

The *Opera Quarterly* is a scholarly journal published in North Carolina. Valuable for the opera lover, it is probably daunting for the beginner.

Opera is an august British publication that has a decidedly Anglophilic point of view, which is part of its charm. It also has superb listings of performances around the world, lively writing, and a devoted following of opinionated readers.

Opera Now is a relatively new publication that could best be described as the British equivalent of *Opera News* in terms of style and content. It gives good coverage to performances throughout Europe and features good travel articles.

Opéra International is a very opinionated French magazine that makes for great reading if the cover story is about a singer you favor. But if one of your favorites is not admired by the editors, be prepared for severe commentary. Still, its profiles of opera stars are some of the best around.

Opernglas is the top German-language opera magazine. It is serious in purpose and thorough, though it lacks the flair of its French and British counterparts.

Corriere del Teatro is Italy's leading publication about theater and opera, with comprehensive reporting and coverage of the volatile Italian opera scene.

APPENDIX B

DISCOGRAPHY AND
VIDEOGRAPHY:
RECOMMENDED PERFORMANCES

What follows is a list of recordings and videos of many operas you will want to learn. This is by no means exhaustive and should be considered one man's view. Of course, collectors of opera recordings are as ardent as operagoers. Each has a different opinion about the best performance of, say, Mozart's *Don Giovanni*. In fact, there are many wonderful performances of that opera on disk, and I would never say that you should listen to one and exclude all of the others. Yet several factors informed my choices on the list below. The first is that whenever I had to choose between two equally good performances, I usually picked the newer one. There are two reasons for this: the recording quality is probably superior, and you are more likely to have the opportunity to hear some of these singers live. In a few cases, though, there are voices from the past that I wanted you to hear. For that reason, I have made an effort to include as many different voices and styles as possible. So, while singers such as Montserrat Caballé, Joan Sutherland, Luciano Pavarotti, and Plácido Domingo figure prominently, I have made certain that you also hear many other sopranos and tenors in roles that these four have recorded as well. Similarly, I have included performances by artists in roles where you would not normally find them, such as Sutherland as Turandot and Domingo as Lohengrin, to give you a sense of their artistic range.

A few recordings have music cut from the score but are recommended because of the quality of individual performances. A few others are live recordings—the sound of prolonged applause may be bothersome, so imagine you are in an opera house and envision the curtain calls, and the applause will make sense.

In terms of the videos represented here, I have selected memorable performances where possible, and interesting productions where available. Since I live in New York City, which is paradise for recordings in terms of price and selection, I am able to find almost anything I want to hear. Yet it is more difficult outside of large cities to find as big a selection. Therefore, in choosing between recordings on major labels or those that are less widely distributed, I usually opted for the majors. Note that some labels go by different names in different places. For example, what is London in North America is called Decca in Europe.

This list is alphabetized by opera. In most cases, the name will be in the original language, though Eastern European operas are cited by their usual English titles. Each opera's name is followed in parentheses by its composer. The next name you see is that of the conductor. Following a semicolon will be the names of one or two of the major singers. The second set of parentheses includes the name of the recording company or distributor. In every case, the recording (on CD) is listed first, followed by the video (V). In the rare cases in which there is a good video but no audio recording worth hearing, that will be indicated. After some of the videos you will find the name of the opera house or festival where the video was made. Some videos were made as motion pictures—this, too, will be indicated.

The Abduction from the Seraglio (Mozart). See *Die Entführung aus dem Serail*
Acis and Galatea (Handel). Hogwood; Dawson, Ainsley (Oiseau-Lyre)
Adriana Lecouvreur (Cilea). Capuana; Tebaldi (London)
    V: Gavazzeni; Freni; La Scala (Home Vision)
L'Africaine (Meyerbeer). V: Arena; Verrett, Domingo; San Francisco Opera (Home Vision)
Agnese von Hohenstaufen (Spontini). Muti; Caballé (Rodolphe)
Agrippina (Handel). McGegan; Bradshaw (Harmonia Mundi)
Die Ägyptische Helena (R. Strauss). Dorati; G. Jones (London)
Aïda (Verdi). Muti; Caballé, Domingo (EMI)
    V: Levine; Millo, Domingo; Metropolitan Opera (DG)
Akhnaten (Glass). Davies (CBS)
Albert Herring (Britten). Britten; Pears (London)
Alceste (Gluck). Baudo; Norman (Orfeo)
Alcina (Handel). Hickox; Augér (EMI)
Alzira (Verdi). Capuana; Zeani (Verona)
Amadigi (Handel). Minkowski; Stutzmann (Erato)
Amahl and the Night Visitors (Menotti). V: López-Cobos; Stratas, Sapolsky (World Vision). A popular film made for television of a favorite children's opera.
L'Amico Fritz (Mascagni). Gavazzeni; Freni, Pavarotti (EMI)
Andrea Chénier (Giordano). Santini; Corelli (EMI)
Anna Bolena (Donizetti). Bonynge; Sutherland, Ramey (London)
Apollo et Hyacinthus (Mozart). Hager (Philips)
Arabella (R. Strauss). Tate; Te Kanawa (London)
    V: Solti; Janowitz (London): Vienna State Opera
Ariadne auf Naxos (R. Strauss). Karajan; Schwarzkopf (EMI)
    V: Levine; Norman (DG) Metropolitan Opera
Ariane et Barbe-Bleue (Dukas). Jordan; Ciesinski (Erato)
Aroldo (Verdi). Queler; Caballé (CBS)
Armida (Dvořák). Albrecht; Caballé (Foyer)
Armida (Rossini). Franci; Deutekom (Memories)
Ascanio in Alba (Mozart). Hager; Baltsa (Philips)
Athalia (Handel). Hogwood (Oiseau-Lyre)
Attila (Verdi). Muti; Ramey, Studer (EMI)
Atys (Lully). Christie (Harmonia Mundi France)

Un Ballo in Maschera (Verdi). Leinsdorf; L. Price, Bergonzi (RCA)
  V: Patané; Ricciarelli, Pavarotti; Metropolitan Opera (Bel Canto)
Il Barbiere di Siviglia (Rossini). Chailly; Horne, Nucci, Ramey (Sony)
  V: Abbado; Berganza, Prey (Unitel)
The Bartered Bride (Smetana). Kosler; Beňačková (Supraphon)
La Battaglia di Legnano (Verdi). Gardelli; Ricciarelli, Carreras (Philips)
Bastien und Bastienne (Mozart). Leppard (Sony)
Beatrice di Tenda (Bellini). Bonynge; Sutherland, Pavarotti (London)
Béatrice et Bénédict (Berlioz). Nelson; Graham, Viala (Erato-Musifrance)
The Beggar's Opera (Gay). Barlow; Walker, Hoskins (Hyperion)
Benvenuto Cellini (Berlioz). C. Davis; Gedda (Philips)
Billy Budd (Britten). Britten; Pears, Glossop (London)
  V: Atherton; English National Opera (Home Vision)
Bluebeard's Castle (Bartók). Fischer; Ramey, Marton (CBS)
  V: Solti (London)
La Bohème (Puccini). Karajan; Freni, Pavarotti (London)
  V: Karajan; Freni; La Scala (DG) or Levine; Stratas; Metropolitan Opera (Bel
  Canto)
Boris Godunov (Mussorgsky). Fedoseyev; Vedernikov (Philips)
La Cambiale di Matrimonio (Rossini). V: Gelmetti; Schwetzingen Festival (Teldec)
Candide (Bernstein). Bernstein (DG)
Capriccio (R. Strauss). Sawallisch; Schwarzkopf (EMI)
I Capuleti e i Montecchi (Bellini). Abbado; Scotto, Pavarotti (Butterfly)
Carmen (Bizet). Abbado; Berganza, Domingo (DG)
  V: Levine; Baltsa, Carreras; Metropolitan Opera (DG) or the Francesco Rosi film
  (not on video) with Migenes-Johnson, Domingo
Cavalleria Rusticana (Mascagni). Cellini; Milanov, Bjoerling (RCA)
  V: Pretre; Obraztsova, Domingo (Philips); filmed in Sicily
La Cenerentola (Rossini). Abbado; Berganza (DG)
  V: Abbado; von Stade; La Scala (DG)
Chérubin (Massenet). Steinberg; von Stade (RCA)
Christopher Columbus (Offenbach). Francis; Arthur (Opera Rara)
Le Cid (Massenet). Queler; Domingo, Bumbry (CBS)
La Clemenza di Tito (Mozart. C. Davis; J. Baker (Philips)
  V: Levine; Troyanos; Metropolitan Opera (DG)
Cléopatre (Massenet). Fournillier; Harries (Koch-Schwann)
Le Comte Ory (Rossini). Gui (EMI)
Les Contes d'Hoffmann (Offenbach). Cluytens; Gedda (EMI)
Le Coq d'Or (*The Golden Cockerel*; Rimsky-Korsakov). Svetlanov (MCA Classics)
Il Corsaro (Verdi). Gardelli; Caballé, Carreras (Philips)
Così fan tutte (Mozart). Levine; Te Kanawa (DG)
  V: Pritchard (VAI)
The Cunning Little Vixen (Janáček). Mackerras; Popp (London)
La Damnation de Faust (Berlioz). Solti; Riegel, von Stade (London)
Daphne (R. Strauss). Böhm; Gueden (DG)
Daughter of the Regiment (Donizetti). See *La Fille du Régiment*
Death in Venice (Britten). Bedford; Pears (London)
The Death of Klinghoffer (Adams). Nagano (Elektra)

Dialogues of the Carmelites (Poulenc). Dervaux; Duval, Crespin (EMI)
Dido and Aeneas (Purcell). Leppard; Norman (Philips)
Don Carlo (Verdi). Giulini; Domingo, Caballé (EMI)
  V: Levine; Domingo, Freni; Metropolitan Opera (Bel Canto)
Don Giovanni (Mozart). Maazel; Raimondi, Te Kanawa (CBS)
  V: Joseph Losey film with same cast (Kultur)
La Donna del Lago (Rossini). Pollini; Ricciarelli (CBS)
Don Pasquale (Donizetti). Kertesz; Sciutti (London)
Don Quichotte (Massenet). Simonetto; Christoff, Berganza (Melodram)
Die Dreigroschenoper (The Threepenny Opera; Weill). Brückner-Rüggeberg; Lenya
  (CBS)
I Due Foscari (Verdi). Gardelli; Ricciarelli, Carreras (Philips)
Edgar (Puccini). Queler; Bergonzi, Scotto (CBS)
Elektra (R. Strauss). Solti; Nilsson, Resnik (London)
  V: Böhm; Rysanek (London); a riveting film
    Levine; Nilsson; Metropolitan Opera (Bel Canto)
    Abbado; Marton; Vienna State Opera (Home Vision)
Elisabetta, Regina d'Inghilterra (Rossini). Masini; Caballé, Carreras (Philips)
L'Elisir d'Amore (Donizetti). Molinari-Pradelli; Freni, Gedda (EMI)
  V: Rescigno; Blegen, Pavarotti (Bel Canto) 1981
L'Enfant et les Sortilèges (Ravel). Maazel (DG)
Die Entführung aus dem Serail (Mozart). Solti; Gruberova (London)
  V: Böhm; Gruberovà; Bavarian State Opera (DG)
Ermione (Rossini). Scimone; Gasdia (Erato)
Ernani (Verdi). Schippers; Bergonzi, L. Price (RCA)
Esclarmonde (Massenet). Bonynge; Sutherland (London)
Eugene Onegin (Tchaikovsky). Levine; Freni, Allen (DG)
  V: Kirov Opera 1950 film (Kultur)
The Fairy Queen (Purcell). Britten (London)
Falstaff (Verdi). Solti; Evans, (London) or Toscanini; Valdengo (RCA)
  V: Pritchard; Gramm; Glyndebourne Festival (VAI) or a very worthy production
    was taped at the Metropolitan Opera with Levine leading Freni, Horne, Plishka,
    in 1992. Watch for video release.
La Fanciulla del West (Puccini). Capuana; Tebaldi (London)
  V: Maazel; Zampieri, Domingo; La Scala (Home Vision)
Faust (Gounod). Cluytens; de los Angeles, Gedda (EMI)
La Favorita (Donizetti). Bonynge; Cossotto, Pavarotti (London)
  V: Rucci; Tamantini (View). Although it is the voice of Franca Tamantini, it is the
    figure of Sophia Loren that you will see in this Italian film.
Fedora (Giordano). Gardelli; Olivero (London)
Die Ferne Klang (Schreker). Albrecht (Capriccio)
Fidelio (Beethoven). Karajan; Dernesch, Vickers (EMI)
  V: Haitink; Söderström; Glyndebourne (VAI)
Fierrabras (Schubert). Abbado; Studer (DG)
The Fiery Angel (Prokofiev). Jarvi; Secunde (DG)
La Fille du Régiment (Donizetti). Bonynge; Sutherland, Pavarotti (London)
  V: Wendelken-Wilson; Sills (VAI)
La Finta Giardiniera (Mozart). Hager (Philips)
La Finta Semplice (Mozart). Hager; Donath (Orfeo)

Flavio (Handel). Jacobs; Gall (Harmonia Mundi)
Die Fledermaus (J. Strauss). Karajan (London)
  V: C. Kleiber; Bavarian State Opera (Unitel) or Bonynge; Covent Garden (Home Vision). The Act II party scene, featuring Horne and Pavarotti, was Joan Sutherland's farewell to opera.
Der Fliegende Holländer (Wagner). Dorati; Rysanek, London (London)
  V: Segersram; Behrens, Grundheber; Savonlinna Festival (Teldec)
Floridante (Handel). McGegan (Hungaraton)
La Forza del Destino (Verdi). Schippers; L. Price, Tucker (RCA)
Lo Frate 'nnamorato (Pergolesi). V: Muti; La Scala (Home Vision)
Die Frau ohne Schatten (R. Strauss). Böhm; Nilsson (DG)
Friedenstag (R. Strauss). Bass; Marc (Koch Classics)
Der Freischütz (Weber). Kleiber; Janowitz, Schreier (DG)
From the House of the Dead (Janáček). Mackerras (London)
La Gazza Ladra (Rossini). Gelmetti, Ricciarelli; Ramey (Sony)
  V: Bartoletti; Cologne Opera (Home Vision)
El Gato Montes (Penella). Roa; Berganza, Domingo (DG)
Gianni Schicchi (Puccini). See *Il Trittico*
Giasone (Cavalli). Jacobs (Harmonia Mundi France)
La Gioconda (Ponchielli). Gardelli; Tebaldi (London)
  V: A. Fischer; Marton, Domingo; Vienna State Opera (Home Vision)
Un Giorno di Regno (Verdi). Gardelli; Norman, Carreras (Philips)
Giovanna d'Arco (Verdi). Levine; Caballé (EMI)
  V: Chailly; Bologna Opera (Teldec)
Giulio Cesare (Handel). Jacobs; Larmore, Schlick (Harmonia Mundi)
  V: C. Smith (London), a famous production by the innovative Peter Sellars
Götterdämmerung (Wagner). Levine; Behrens (DG) or Solti; Nilsson (London)
Guglielmo Tell (Rossini). Chailly; Freni, Pavarotti, Milnes (London)
Guntram (R. Strauss). Queler; Goldberg (CBS)
Hänsel und Gretel (Humperdinck). Pritchard; Cotrubas, von Stade, Te Kanawa (CBS)
  V: Solti; Fassbänder, Gruberova; Vienna State Opera (London)
L'Heure Espagnole (Ravel). Maazel (DG)
Les Huguenots (Meyerbeer). Bonynge; Sutherland (London)
  V: Bonynge; Sutherland (Home Vision)
The Ice Break (Tippett). Atherton (Virgin Classics)
Idomeneo (Mozart). Pritchard; Pavarotti (London)
  V: Pritchard; Glyndebourne Festival (VAI)
Imeneo (Handel). Palmer (Vox Unique)
L'Incoronazione di Poppea (Monteverdi). Harnoncourt; Donath (Teldec)
Iphigénie en Aulide (Gluck). Gardiner (Erato)
Iphigénie en Tauride (Gluck). Gardiner (Philips)
Iris (Mascagni). Patanè; Tokódy, Domingo (CBS)
L'Italiana in Algeri (Rossini). Scimone; Horne, Ramey (Erato)
  V: If a Metropolitan Opera performance with Levine and Horne is released, grab it.
Jenůfa (Janáček). Queler; Beňačková, Rysanek (Bis), a live performance, or MacKerras; Söderström (London/Decca)
Le Jongleur de Notre Dame (Massenet). (Chant du Monde)

La Juive (Halévy). de Almeida; Carreras (Philips)
Kat'a Kabanová (Janáček). Mackerras; Söderström (London)
  V: A. Davis; Glyndebourne Festival (Home Vision)
Khovanschina (Mussorgsky). Abbado; (DG)
  V: Simonov; Nesterenko; Bolshoi Opera (Kultur)
Lady Macbeth of Mtsensk (Shostakovich). Rostropovich; Vishnevskaya (EMI)
Lakmé (Delibes). Bonynge; Sutherland (London)
The Last Temptations (Sallinen). (Finlandia)
A Life for the Tsar (Glinka). Tchakarov (Sony)
Lodoïska (Cherubini). Muti (Sony)
Lohengrin (Wagner). Solti; Domingo (DG)
  V: Nelsson; Bayreuth Festival (Philips) or Levine; Metropolitan (Bel Canto)
I Lombardi alla Prima Crociata (Verdi). Gardelli; Deutekom, Domingo (Philips)
Louise (Charpentier). Prêtre; Cotrubas (Sony)
The Love for Three Oranges (*L'Amour des Trois Oranges*; Prokofiev). Nagano (Virgin)
Lucia di Lammermoor (Donizetti). Bonynge; Sutherland, Pavarotti (London)
  V: Cillario; Moffo (VAI) a film made on location, or Bonynge; Sutherland, Kraus; Metropolitan Opera (Bel Canto)
Lucio Silla (Mozart). Harnancourt (Teldec)
Lucrezia Borgia (Donizetti). Bonynge; Sutherland (London)
Luisa Miller (Verdi). Maag; Caballé, Pavarotti (London)
Lulu (Berg). Boulez; Stratas (DG) (the three-act, completed version) or Böhm; Lear (DG) (the two-act version)
Die Lustige Witwe (Lehár). Matačić; Schwarzkopf (EMI)
Macbeth (Verdi). Leinsdorf; Rysanek, Warren (RCA)
  V: Chailly; Verrett, Nucci; a 1987 film.
Madama Butterfly (Puccini). Leinsdorf; L. Price (RCA)
  V: Karajan; Freni (London); a 1974 film
The Magic Flute (Mozart). See *Die Zauberflöte*
Makropoulos Affair (Janáček). Mackerras; Söderström (London)
  V: Klobučar; Sundine; Canadian Opera (VAI)
Manon (Massenet). Rudel; Sills, Gedda (EMI)
Manon Lescaut (Puccini). Sinopoli; Freni, Domingo (DG)
  V: Levine; Scotto, Domingo; the Metropolitan Opera (Bel Canto)
Maometto Secondo (Rossini). Scimone; Ramey (Philips)
Maria Stuarda (Donizetti). Bonynge; Sutherland (London)
The Marriage of Figaro (Mozart). See *Le Nozze di Figaro*
Martha (Flotow). Heger; Rothenberger, Gedda (EMI)
Maskarade (C. Nielsen). Fransden (Dansk Musik Antologi)
I Masnadieri (Verdi). Muti (Qualiton)
Mathis der Maler (Hindemith). Ludwig; Fischer-Dieskau (DG)
Il Matrimonio Segreto (Cimarosa). V: Griffiths; Cologne Opera (Home Vision)
Medea (Cherubini). Serafin; Callas (EMI)
Médée (Charpentier). Christie (Harmonia Mundi France)
The Medium (Menotti). V: Schippers (VAI); a memorable 1950 film
Mefistofele (Boito). Patanè; Ramey (Sony)
  V: Arena; Ramey; San Francisco Opera (Home Vision)

Die Meistersinger von Nürnberg (Wagner). Jochum (DG)
The Merry Widow (Lehár). See *Die Lustige Witwe.*
A Midsummer Night's Dream (Britten). Britten (London)
Mitridate, Rè di Ponto (Mozart). Hager (Philips)
    V: Harnoncourt. Filmed at the splendid Teatro Olimpico in Vicenza.
Mosè in Egitto (Rossini). Bartoletti; Christoff (GDS)
Moses und Aron (Schoenberg). Solti (London)
The Mother of Us All (Thompson/Stein). Leppard; Dunn (New World)
Muzio (Handel). R. Palmer (Newport Classics)
Nabucco (Verdi). Gardelli; Gobbi, Suliotis (London)
La Navarraise (Massenet). (Chant du Monde)
Nerone (Boito). Queler; Nagy (Hungaraton)
Nina, o sia La Pazza per Amore (Paisiello). Panni (Bongiovanni)
Nixon in China (Adams). de Waart (Elektra/Nonesuch)
Norma (Bellini). Bonynge; Sutherland, Horne, Alexander (London)
Le Nozze di Figaro (Mozart). Levine; Furlanetto, Te Kanawa, Upshaw (DG)
    V: Pritchard; Te Kanawa; Glyndebourne Festival 1973 (VAI)
Oberon (Weber). Kubelik; Nilsson, Domingo (DG)
L'Oca del Cairo (Mozart). Schreier (Philips)
Oedipe (Enesco). Foster; van Dam (EMI)
Oedipus Rex (Stravinsky). Salonen; Cole (Sony)
Orfeo (Monteverdi). Harnoncourt (Teldec)
    V: Harnoncourt; Zurich Opera (London)
Orfeo (Rossi). Christie (Harmonia Mundi France)
Orfeo ed Euridice (Gluck). Solti; Horne, Lorengar (London)
    V: Haenchen; Covent Garden (Home Vision)
Orfeo ed Euridice (Haydn). Bonynge; Sutherland, Gedda (Verona)
Orlando (Handel). Hogwood; Augér, Bowman (Oiseau-Lyre)
Orlando Furioso (Vivaldi). Scimone; Horne (Erato)
    V: Behr; Horne; San Francisco Opera (Home Vision)
L'Osteria di Marchiaro (Paisiello). Sanfilippo (Bongiovanni)
Otello (Verdi). Levine; Domingo, Scotto (RCA)
    V: Karajan; Vickers, Freni (DG)
Ottone (Handel). McGegan; Minter (Harmonia Mundi)
Padmâvatî (Roussel). Plasson; Horne (EMI)
Pagliacci (Leoncavallo). Cellini; de los Angeles, Bjoerling (EMI)
    V: Prêtre; Stratas, Domingo; La Scala (Philips)
Paride ed Elena (Gluck). Schneider; Alexander, McFadden (Capriccio)
Parsifal (Wagner). Barenboim; Meier, Jerusalem (Teldec)
    V: H. Stein; Bayreuth (Philips)
Partenope (Handel). Kuijken (Deutsche Harmonia Mundi)
Il Pastor Fido (Handel). McGegan (Hungaraton)
Paul Bunyan (Britten). Brunelle (Virgin Classics)
Les Pêcheurs de Perles (Bizet). Dervaux; Gedda, Micheau (EMI)
Peer Gynt (Egk). Wallberg; R. Hermann (Orfeo)
Les Pélérins de la Mecque (Gluck). Gardiner (Erato)
Pelléas et Mélisande (Debussy). Boulez; Shirley, Söderström (Sony)
Pénélope (Fauré). Dutoit; Norman (Erato)

La Périchole (Offenbach). Lombard; Crespin (Erato)
Peter Grimes (Britten). C. Davis; Vickers (Philips)
The Pilgrim's Progress (Vaughan Williams). Boult (EMI)
Il Pirata (Bellini). Gavazzeni; Caballé, Martí (EMI)
Platée (Rameau). Minkowski; Ragon (Erato)
Poliuto (Donizetti). Caetani; Carreras, Ricciarelli (CBS)
Porgy and Bess (Gershwin). de Main; Dale, Albert (RCA)
Prince Igor (Borodin). Tchakarov (Sony)
    V: 1969 Russian film (Kultur)
Le Prophète (Meyerbeer). H. Lewis; Horne, McCracken (CBS)
I Puritani (Bellini). Muti; Caballé, Kraus (EMI)
The Queen of Spades (Tchaikovsky). Ozawa; Freni (BMG)
    V: 1960 Russian film (Kultur)
A Quiet Place (Bernstein). Bernstein (DG)
The Rake's Progress (Stravinsky).
    V: Haitink; Glyndebourne Festival (VAI)
The Rape of Lucretia (Britten). Britten; J. Baker (London)
Regina (Blitzstein). Mauceri (London)
Il Rè Pastore (Mozart). Marriner (Philips)
Das Rheingold (Wagner). Levine; Ludwig, Morris (DG)
Rienzi (Wagner). Hollreiser; Kollo (EMI)
Rigoletto (Verdi). Bonynge; Sutherland, Pavarotti, Milnes (London)
    V: deFabritiis; Gobbi, del Monaco, Arnaldi; Rome Opera (View)—essential for
    Gobbi's great performance, or Chailly; Wixell, Pavarotti, Gruberova; filmed on
    location in Mantua (London)
Rinaldo (Handel). Fisher; Horne (Nuova Era)
Der Ring des Nibelungen (Wagner). Levine (DG) or Solti (London); also see individ-
    ual operas: *Das Rheingold, Die Walküre, Siegfried, Götterdämmerung*
    V: You should first see the excellent Metropolitan Opera production (DG)
    led by Levine to learn the cycle. Then see the provocative 1976 centennial
    production from (Philips) Bayreuth led by Pierre Boulez.
Il Ritorno d'Ulisse in Patria (Monteverdi). Harnoncourt (Teldec)
    V: Tate; Salzburg Festival (Home Vision)
Roberto Devereux (Donizetti). V: Rudel; Sills (VAI); one of Sills's great roles
Le Roi Arthus (Chausson). Jordan (Erato)
Le Roi de Lahore (Massenet). Bonynge; Sutherland (London)
Le Roi d'Ys (Lalo). Jordan; Ziegler, Hendricks (Erato)
Roméo et Juliette (Gounod). Plasson; Malfitano, Kraus (EMI)
La Rondine (Puccini). Maazel; Te Kanawa, Domingo (CBS)
Der Rosenkavalier (R. Strauss). Haitink; Te Kanawa, von Otter (EMI)
    V: Karajan; Schwarzkopf, Jurinac (Kultur)
Rusalka (Dvořák). Neumann; Beňačková, Ochman (Supraphon)
Saffo (Pacini). Capuana; Gencer (Hungaraton)
Salome (R. Strauss). Solti; Nilsson (London)
    V: Böhm; Stratas (DG) or Sinopoli; Malfitano (Teldec); the latter is a rather vivid
    Berlin Opera production that includes nudity.
Samson et Dalila (Saint-Saëns). Prêtre; Gorr, Vickers (EMI)
    V: Rudel; Verrett, Domingo (Home Vision)

Satyagraha (Glass). Keene (CBS)
Saul and David (C. Nielsen). Järvi (Chandos)
La Scala di Seta (Rossini). V: Gelmetti; Schwetzingen Festival (Teldec)
Der Schauspieldirektor (Mozart). C. Davis (Philips)
Schwanda (Weinberger). Wallberg; Popp, Jerusalem, Prey (CBS)
Il Segreto di Susanna (Wolf-Ferrari). Pritchard; Scotto (CBS)
Semiramide (Rossini). Bonynge; Sutherland, Horne (London)
La Serva Padrona (Paisiello). Vaglieri (Nuova Era)
La Serva Padrona (Pergolesi). Nemeth (Hungaraton)
    V: Ferrara; Moffo (View)
Si (Mascagni). Sanna (Bongiovanni)
La Siège de Corinthe (Rossini). Olmi (Nuova Era)
Il Signor Bruschino (Rossini).
    V: Gelmetti; Schwetzingen Festival (Teldec)
Siegfried (Wagner). Levine; Goldberg, Behrens (DG)
Silbersee (Weill). Latham-König (Capriccio)
Simon Boccanegra (Verdi). Abbado; Freni, Cappuccilli (DG)
    V: Solti; Te Kanawa, Agache; Covent Garden (London)
Siroe (Handel). Palmer (Newport Classics)
The Snow Maiden (Rimsky-Korsakov). Angelov; Zemenkova (Fidelio)
Il Sogno di Scipione (Mozart). Hager (Philips)
Die Soldaten (Zimmerman). Kontarsky (Teldec)
La Sonnambula (Bellini). Bonynge; Sutherland, Pavarotti (London)
Lo Sposo Deluso (Mozart). C. Davis (Philips)
Stiffelio (Verdi). Gardelli; Carreras (Philips)
La Straniera (Bellini). Guadagno; Caballé (Legato)
Street Scene (Weill). Mauceri (London)
Suor Angelica (Puccini). See *Il Trittico*
Il Tabarro (Puccini). See *Il Trittico*
Tamerlano (Handel). Gardiner (Erato)
Tancrède (Campra). Malgoire (Erato)
Tannhäuser (Wagner). Solti; Kollo (London)
    V: Levine; Metropolitan Opera (Bel Canto), or C. Davis; Bayreuth Festival (Philips)
The Telephone (Menotti). V: Serebrier; Farley (London)
The Tender Land (Copland). Brunelle (Virgin Classics)
Teseo (Handel). Minkowski; James (Erato)
Threepenny Opera (Weill). See *Die Dreigroschenoper*
Tiefland (d'Albert). Zanotelli (Eurodisc)
Timon of Athens (Purcell). Gardiner (Erato)
Tosca (Puccini). De Sabata; Callas, Di Stefano, Gobbi (EMI)
    V: Bartoletti; Kabaivanska, Domingo (London); or Mehta; Malfitano, Domingo, Raimondi. Both were filmed on location in Rome.
Die Tote Stadt (Korngold). Leinsdorf; Neblett, Kollo (RCA)
La Traviata (Verdi). Bonynge; Sutherland, Pavarotti (London); or Ghione; Callas, Kraus (EMI)
    V: Levine; Stratas, Domingo (MCA)—a film by Franco Zeffirelli with a superb performance by Stratas—or Patanè; Moffo (VAI)

Treemonisha (Joplin). Schuller; Balthrop, Allen, Hicks (DG)
   V: same company as recording (Kultur)
Tristan und Isolde (Wagner). Böhm; Nilsson, Windgassen (Philips)
   V: Barenboim; W. Meier, Kollo; Bayreuth Festival (Philips)
Il Trittico (Puccini). Gardelli; Tebaldi (London)
Trouble in Tahiti (Bernstein). V: Bernstein (Kultur)
Il Trovatore (Verdi). Cellini; Milanov, Bjoerling (RCA)
Les Troyens (Berlioz). C. Davis (Philips)
   V: Levine; Troyanos, Norman, Domingo; Metropolitan Opera (Bel Canto)
The Tsar's Bride (Rimsky-Korsakov). V: 1966 Bolshoi Performance (Kultur)
Turandot (Puccini). Mehta; Sutherland, Caballé, Pavarotti (London)
   V: Levine; Marton, Domingo (DG). A fabulous Zeffirelli production at the Metro-
     politan Opera.
Il Turco in Italia (Rossini). Chailly; Ramey, Caballé (CBS)
The Turn of the Screw (Britten). Britten (London)
   V: C. Davis (Philips)
Ugo, Conte di Parigi (Donizetti). Francis (Opera Rara)
Undine (Lortzing). Eichhorn (Capriccio)
Vanessa (Barber). Mitropoulos; Steber (RCA)
I Vespri Siciliani (Verdi). Queler; Caballé, Domingo (SRO)
   V: Muti; La Scala (Home Vision)
La Vestale (Spontini). Votto; Callas (Melodram)
Il Viaggio a Reims (Rossini). Abbado; Ricciarelli, Cuberli, Ramey (DG)
La Vie Parisienne (Offenbach). Plasson; Crespin, Mesplé (EMI)
A Village Romeo and Juliet (Delius). Mackerras; Field, Davies (Argo)
   V: Mackerras (London); a film
Le Villi (Puccini). Maazel; Scotto, Domingo (CBS)
Vincent (Rautavaara). Manchurov; Hynninen (Ondine)
Violanta (Korngold). Janowski; Marton (CBS)
La Voix Humaine (Poulenc). Prêtre; Migenes-Johnson (Erato)
   V: Serebrier; Farley (London)
Die Walküre (Wagner). Levine; Behrens, Norman, Morris (DG)
La Wally (Catalani). Cleva; Tebaldi (London)
War and Peace (Prokofiev). Rostropovich; Vishnevskaya (Erato)
Werther (Massenet). Prêtre; de los Angeles, Gedda (EMI)
Wozzeck (Berg). Abbado; Behrens (DG); or Böhm; Fischer-Dieskau, Lear (DG)
X (Davis). Curry (Gramavision)
Die Zauberflöte (Mozart). Marriner; Te Kanawa, Studer (Philips)
   V: Levine; Battle; Metropolitan Opera (DG)
Zaïde (Mozart). Klee (Philips)
Zelmira (Rossini). Scimone; Gasdia (Erato)
Zoroastre (Rameau). Kuijken (Deutsche Harmonia Mundi)

APPENDIX C

OPERA HOUSES AROUND
THE WORLD:
A COMPLETE LIST FOR
THE TRAVELER

Anyone who believes that opera can be found only in the world's largest cities at exorbitant prices need merely look at the list below. There you will find names of opera houses in forty-six countries on six continents. Opera is everywhere, and you, as an opera lover, can plan vacations in which opera plays a significant part. Whenever I travel to a foreign land, I always check with the national tourist office of the nation I will visit to find out which opera is playing where, and I schedule my itinerary accordingly.

The countries that gave birth to opera—Italy, Germany, Austria, France—have opera houses in most cities of any consequence. Many of these theaters receive generous government funding. For example, the arts budget for the city of Berlin in 1992 was approximately $600 million. Compare this with the $174 million spent by the National Endowment for the Arts for the *entire United States* in the same year and you will realize how important the arts are to many European nations.

Nonetheless, opera is alive and well in the United States, and I am proud, as an opera-loving American, to include the names of companies from forty-two states, Puerto Rico, and the District of Columbia. You should also check with the music department of your local college or university about attending campus productions. For example, the singer you hear at the University of Michigan may be the next Jessye Norman, who studied there in the 1960s. Cities such as New York, Philadelphia, Baltimore, and Cincinnati have excellent music conservatories that produce several operas each year with the potential stars of tomorrow.

In each state and country you find below, the listings are arranged alphabetically by city. Therefore, even though the San Francisco Opera is probably the finest company in California, you will have to look far down the list to find it. I have included telephone and fax numbers where possible, but if you intend to go to far-flung theaters such as the opera house in Quito, Ecuador, the phone number will not do you much good, and you will be better served by contacting the national tourist office.

For calling from outside the country you are interested in, dial the country and city code to the left of the slash. If you are in the country, use only the city code, preceded by a zero. If you are in the city where the opera house is, simply dial the numbers to the right of the slash. For example, to call La Scala, the country code for Italy is 39, the city code for Milano is 2, and the phone number is 887-9211. If you were to call from Rome, let's say, you would dial 02/887-9211. Note that to call all numbers in the United States and Canada from abroad, the country code is 01, which should be followed by all the numbers indicated.

In many cases it's as effective to call opera houses in North America as it is to write to them. In the rest of the world, it is better to write to a theater than to call, especially if you do not speak the language of the country. This book includes phone numbers and addresses as they were available to enable you to travel to see opera around the world.

ARGENTINA

Teatro Colón
Cerrito 618
1010 Buenos Aires, Argentina
tel. 54-1/358-924
fax 54-1/111-232

One of the world's most beautiful opera houses, with an educated, passionate audience. On the lower levels on the sides of the auditorium is a semienclosed section that for many years was reserved for widows who otherwise could not go out as single women in Argentine society.

AUSTRALIA

State Opera of South Australia
G.P.O. Box 1515
Adelaide, S.A. 5001
Adelaide, Australia
tel. 61-8/233-4811
fax 61-8/231-7646

Victoria State Opera
370 Nicholson Street
Fitzroy, Victoria 3065
Melbourne, Australia
tel. 61-3/417-5061
fax 61-3/419-5071

Australian Opera
P.O. Box 291
Strawberry Hills, N.S.W. 2033
Sydney, Australia
tel. 61-2/699-1099
fax 61-2/699-3184

The Sydney opera house is probably the most famous building in Australia. It has not always been successful as a home to opera because of problems with acoustics and stage equipment. Yet these problems have largely been overcome, and the company attracts international stars who are drawn to the friendliness of the Australians and the fact that, with reversed seasons from the northern hemisphere, Sydney becomes a great refuge from colder climates in Europe and North America.

AUSTRIA

Operetten Festspiele Bad Hall (late June–early August)
Hauptplatz 5
4540 Bad Hall, Austria
tel. 43-7258/2255
Operettas are given each weekend.

Bregenz Summer Festival (late July–late August)
P.O. Box 311
6901 Bregenz, Austria
tel. 43-5574/492-0224
fax 43-5574/492-0242

Mörbisch Seefestspiele (mid-July–August)
Schloss Esterhazy
7000 Eisenstadt, Austria
tel. 43-2682/66210
fax 43-2682/66211
Operettas are staged on a raft that floats on Lake Neusiedl, thirty miles from Vienna. During the performance season, you may contact the box office at:

Seestrasse 4
7072 Mörbisch, Austria
tel. 43-2682/8232
fax 43-2685/8855

Graz Festival (October)
Steirischer Herbst
Palais Attems
Sackstrasse 17
8010 Graz, Austria
tel. 43-316/823-0070 or 824-2170
fax 43-316/835788

Grazer Oper
Kaiser-Josef Platz
8010 Graz, Austria
tel. 43-316/827422
fax 43-316/826451

Hohenems Schubertiade (June)
Postfach 100
Schweizerstrasse 1
6845 Hohenems, Austria
tel. 43-5576/2091
fax 43-5576/5450

Brucknerhaus
Untere Donaulände 7

4020 Linz, Austria
tel. 43-732/275225
fax 43-732/283745

Named for Anton Bruckner (1824–96), a native of Linz best known for his symphonies.

Carinthian Summer (July–August)
9570 Ossiach, Austria
tel. 43-4243/2510
fax 43-4243/2353

Hellbrun Festival (August)
Postfach 47
5027 Salzburg, Austria
tel. 43-662/78784
fax 43-662/883220

The first opera ever staged in Austria, Monteverdi's Orfeo, *was given in the open-air Stone Theater in 1617.*

Mozartwoche (late January–early February)
International Stiftung Mozarteum
Postfach 34
Schwarzstrasse 26
5024 Salzburg, Austria
tel. 43-662/73154
fax 43-662/882419

An all-Mozart festival, centered around his birthday on January 27.

Salzburger Festspiele (late July–August)
Hofstallgasse 1
5020 Salzburg, Austria
tel. 43-662/42541
ticket office:
Box 140
5010 Salzburg, Austria

The Salzburg Festival is probably the world's leading summer opera festival—a megastar, high-profile event where all of the world's artistic managers, record-company executives, powerful conductors, singers, designers, and directors, and music-loving heads of state gather to conduct business, to see and be seen. In the midst of all this pushing and pulling, a great deal of fine music-making takes place before audiences clad in gowns and tuxedos who have spent a lot of money on tickets. The atmosphere is not unlike Christmas in an Aspen filled with movie stars or Cannes during the film festival. The Salzburg Festival saw its great ascent in the 1950s and 1960s, when the imperious Austrian conductor Herbert von Karajan made it a showcase for the opera productions that he conducted and occasionally staged as well. While there is always a strong presence of the music of Mozart, Salzburg's native son, the festival presents opera, chamber music, and symphonic music from all eras and composers. Any serious operagoer who visits Austria in the summer should try to go to a performance at the Salzburg Festival.

Oster Festspiele Salzburg (Palm Sunday–Easter Monday)
Festspielhaus

5010 Salzburg, Austria
tel. 43-662/842541361
An Easter festival in Salzburg, featuring one excellently prepared, starrily cast opera with a major conductor such as Georg Solti.

Salzburg Kulturtage (October)
Salzburg Kulturvereinigung
Waagplatz 1a
Trakl Haus
Postfach 42
5010 Salzburg, Austria
tel. 43-662/845346

Salzburger Marionettentheater
Schwarzstrasse 24
5024 Salzburg, Austria
tel. 43-662/72406
You might think that a production of a Mozart opera with marionettes moving about to recorded music is kitschy, but when done with the great skill and charm of this company, it becomes a delightful way to see opera, especially (though not exclusively) for children. This 335-seat theater is almost always sold out.

Jugendstil Theater
Baumgartner Hohe 1
1145 Vienna, Austria
tel. 43-1/922-2492
fax 43-1/911-2493

Theater an der Wien
Linke Wienzeile 6
1060 Vienna, Austria
tel. 43-1/58830
fax 43-1/587-9844
This theater, which saw the premieres of Die Zauberflöte, Fidelio, *and* Die Fledermaus, *also presents dance, plays, and Broadway musicals.*

Wiener Kammeroper (Vienna Chamber Opera)
Fleischmarkt 24
1010 Vienna, Austria
tel. 43-1/512-0100
fax 43-1/512-444826

Wiener Staatsoper (Vienna State Opera)
Opernring 2
1010 Vienna, Austria
tel. 43-1/514440
tel. 43-1/513-1513 *(phone orders for tickets, credit cards only)*
fax 43-1/51444-2330
The Vienna State Opera surely appears on anyone's short list of the great opera houses of the world, along with the Metropolitan and La Scala, and perhaps the houses of London, Paris, Munich, Hamburg, and Barcelona. For most of the year, one can see leading stars in great operas with a wonderful orchestra and chorus. There are only about sixteen hundred seats, so you must plan ahead, but there is

ample standing room for sale if you wind up without a seat. Viennese standees are very opinionated and knowledgeable, so you might learn a lot from them, but take their opinions with a grain of salt. They will often tell you that the singer onstage is the greatest of all or, more likely, does not compare with so-and-so, who sang the role in 1957. But the gossipy, naughty Viennese often make wonderful company for sharing an operagoing experience. A good way to find tickets for seats is through ticket agencies that can be recommended by the tourist office. There is a service charge on these tickets, but it is worth it if it means the difference between seeing a performance or not.

It is possible to purchase tickets for the Staatsoper and the Volksoper through the Austrian State Booking Office, Hanuschgasse 3, 1010 Vienna, Austria; tel. 43-1/514440, fax 43-1/51444-2969. Written ticket orders must arrive fourteen days before a performance, and phone sales begin six days before (tel. 43-1/513-1513).

Vienna Festival (May–June)
Box Office: Lehargasse 11
1060 Vienna, Austria
tel. 43-1/586-1676
fax 43-1/586-167649

Volksoper
Währingerstrasse 78
1090 Vienna, Austria
tel. 43-1/343627
Operetta is the chief draw here, though some operas and Broadway musicals are also staged.

Wien Modern
Kulturabteilung der Stadt Wien
Friedrich Schmidt Platz
1082 Vienna, Austria
tel. 43-1/42800-2741
Twentieth-century works, including opera.

BELGIUM

An organization called Balconop organizes arts tours in Belgium, including those of particular interest to opera lovers. Packages are created to include hotel and opera tickets. Address: Service Artistique de l'O.P.T., rue Marché aux Herbes 61, 1000 Brussels, Belgium.

De Vlaamse Opera/The Flemish Opera
Van Ertbornstraat 8
2018 Antwerp 1, Belgium
tel. 32-3/233-6808 or 233-6685
fax 32-3/232-2661
This company is recognized for its wide, innovative repertory, but its productions of Wagner operas have earned it the nickname of "the Flemish Bayreuth."

Flanders Festival—Antwerp (September–early October)
Theaterwinkel
Sint-Jacobsmarkt 74

2000 Antwerp, Belgium
tel. 32-3/233-7160
fax 32-3/232-2885

Cirque Royal
81 Rue de l'Enseignement
Brussels, Belgium
This theater hosts international opera companies bringing top casts and productions.

Théâtre Royal de la Monnaie
Place de la Monnaie at Rue Neuve
Box Office: Rue de la Reine
1000 Brussels, Belgium
tel. 32-2/218-1266
The leading opera house in Belgium.

Flanders Festival (April–October)
Eugene Flageyplein 18
1050 Brussels, Belgium
tel. 32-2/648-1484
fax 32-2/649-7597

De Vlaamse Opera
3 Schouwburgstraat
9000 Ghent, Belgium
tel. 32-91/252425
Shares productions with the Flemish Opera of Antwerp.

Festival de Wallonie
29, rue du Jardin Botanique
4000 Liège, Belgium
tel. 32-41/223248 or 223367

Opera Royal de Wallonie
1, rue des Dominicains
4000 Liège, Belgium
tel. 32-41/235910 or 237713
fax 32-41/210201

BRAZIL

Brazil is the homeland of the lovely Bidù Sayão, who sang many lyric soprano roles at the Metropolitan Opera in the 1940s and 1950s. Although the traveler to Brazil does not immediately associate opera with that country, it is possible to attend performances in Rio de Janeiro and São Paulo from May to October. It is often difficult to get accurate information about where and when performances will take place. Box office staff at the theaters seldom speak English, so that you would be better served by checking at your hotel, in local newspapers, or with the tourist office. A call to the Brazilian Tourism Board in Rio (55-21/273-2212) will put you in touch with an English speaker who can probably give you the most up-to-date information about opera at Brazil's three major theaters.

Teatro Amazonas
Praça São Sebastião
Manaus, Brazil
tel. 55-92/234-2776

If you have seen Werner Herzog's film Fitzcarraldo, *then you know about the world's most remote opera house, 1,000 miles (1,600 km) from the ocean, deep in the Amazon rain forest. About 100 years ago Manaus was the center of the world rubber market. People went there to make their fortunes and wanted to establish European culture in the jungle. After great effort to get the necessary supplies to build an opera house, the theater opened in 1910. Soon thereafter, rubber prices collapsed and the theater went unused for years. Manaus has risen again in recent years to become an urban center with more than one million people. Opera is again produced at the Teatro Amazonas, which surely is the most exotic destination for any opera lover.*

Teatro Municipal
Praça Floriano
Rio de Janeiro, Brazil
tel. 55-21/210-2463

This beautiful theater in downtown Rio is architecturally reminiscent of the Paris Opéra's Palais Garnier. A special treat is to dine at the Cafe do Teatro, a nice restaurant that is open to the public for lunch. The decor in the restaurant will make you think you are in a stage set for the second act of Aïda. This is recommended even if there are no performances going on at the theater.

Teatro Municipal
Praça Ramos de Azevado
São Paulo, Brazil

For information about opera in São Paulo, check with the tourist authority or the concierge of your hotel.

BULGARIA

National Theater-Opera National de Sofia
Bd. Dondukov 58
1000 Sofia, Bulgaria
tel. 359-2/877-011
ticket sources: tel. 359-2/881-658 *(tourist office) or:* 359-2/871-366

Sofia Music Weeks (late May–mid-June)
1 Bulgaria Square
1414 Sofia, Bulgaria
tel. 359-92/543041
fax 359-92/802042

Varna Summer International Festival (June–August)
Municipality People's Council
9000 Varna, Bulgaria
tel. 359-52/220101
fax 359-52/253011

CANADA

Banff Festival
Eric Harvie Theater
Banff, Alberta, Canada
tel. 403/762-6300

Edmonton Opera
10102 101st Street
Edmonton, Alberta T5J OS5
Canada
tel. 403/422-4919
(Jubilee Auditorium: 403/429-1000)

Opera Hamilton
Hamilton Place
Great Hall
Hamilton, Ontario, Canada
tel. 416/527-0089

Opéra de Montréal
Salle Wilfrid Pelletier
Place des Arts
1501 Jeanne-Mance Street
Montréal, Québec, H2X 1Z9 Canada
tel. 514/985-2258

Opera Lyra Ottawa
Theater of the National Arts Center, Ontario
Ottawa, Ontario, Canada
tel. 613/233-9200

Ottawa Festival Opera
Confederation Square
Ottawa, Ontario K1P 5W1
Canada
tel. 613/996-5051

Opéra de Québec
1220 Tache Street
Québec City, Québec G1R 3B4
tel. 418/529-4142
Performances are usually held at:
Grand Théâtre de Québec
269 Boulevard St. Cyrille East
Québec City, Québec G1R 2B3
Canada

Canadian Opera Company
O'Keefe Centre
1 Front Street East
Toronto, Ontario, Canada

or:

Elgin Theatre
189 Yonge Street
Toronto, Ontario, Canada
tel. 416/872-2262
fax 416/363-2895
Reportedly the first company to use surtitles (also called supertitles), the controversial innovation that has drawn new audiences to opera while alienating others.

Vancouver Opera (November–May)
1132 Hamilton Street
Vancouver, B.C. V6B 2S2 Canada
tel. 604/682-2871
Performances are held at:
Queen Elizabeth Theatre
630 Hamilton Street

Pacific Opera
McPherson Playhouse
Victoria, B.C. Canada
tel. 604/385-0222

Manitoba Opera
Centennial Hall
Winnipeg, Manitoba, Canada
tel. 204/957-7842

CHILE

Teatro Municipal
P.O. Box 18, Agustinas 794
Santiago, Chile
tel. 56-2/712900
fax 56-2/337214

COLOMBIA

Teatro Colón
Calle 10, Carrera 6
Bogotà, Colombia
This theater has a glass curtain!

CROATIA

Dubrovnik Festival (July–August)
Od Sigurate 1
5000 Dubrovnik, Croatia
tel. 38-50/27995
fax 38-50/27944

CZECH REPUBLIC

A good ticket source for performances in Prague is the Bohemia Ticket International Agency, P.O. Box 534, 1-11121 Prague, Czech Republic, tel. 42-2/261-889, fax 42-2/734632.

Dvořák Hall
Prague, Czech Republic
tel. 42-2/286-0111
A symphonic hall that may also include vocal performances.

Estates Theater
Prague, Czech Republic
tel. 42-2/228658

Narodni Divadlo (National Theater)
Narodni 2
P.O. Box 865
11230 Prague 1, Czech Republic
tel. 42-2/205364
Prague's leading opera house.

Prague Spring Festival (May–early June)
Hellichova 18
11800 Prague 1, Czech Republic
tel. 42-2/530293 or 533474
fax 42-2/536040
The Bohemian ticket agency listed above is a good source of tickets for this popular festival, which usually stages five operas.

Prague State Opera
Prague, Czech Republic
tel. 42-2/265353

Smetanovo Divadlo (Smetana Theater)
Wilsonova
Prague, Czech Republic
tel. 42-2/232-2501 or 269-746
A symphonic hall that may also include vocal performances.

DENMARK

Århus Festival (September)
Musikhuset
Thomas Jensen Alle
8000 Århus C, Denmark
tel. 45-86/121233
fax 45-86/194386

Royal Danish Opera
Det Kongelinge Theater
Holmens Kanal 3

1060 Copenhagen K, Denmark
tel. 45-33/141765 or 141002
fax 45-33/144606

Tivoli
3 Vesterbrogade
1620 Copenhagen V, Denmark
tel. 45-33/151001

People who don't know Tivoli tend to think of it as a theme park. Actually, it is a wonderful nineteenth-century park with lovely pavilions, restaurants, and theaters that have drawn crowds since 1843. Tivoli is also one of the leading presenters of musical performances in the world. Among the many events that occur there from May to October are several operas-in-concert featuring some of the world's top singers.

ECUADOR

Teatro Sucre
Plaza del Teatro
Avenida Guayaquil
Quito, Ecuador

ENGLAND

Aldeburgh Festival (June)
High Street
Aldeburgh, Suffolk 1P 15 5AX
England
tel. 44-728/453 543
fax 44-728/452 715

This festival was founded by Benjamin Britten, England's great twentieth-century opera composer. You can feel this place in his music, which is often featured at the festival.

Arundel Festival (late August–early September)
Arundel Festival Society
The Mary Gate
Arundel, West Sussex, England
tel. 44-903/883-690
fax 44-903/882-188

Bath International Festival (late May–mid-June)
Bath Festival Office
Linley House
1 Pierrepoint Place
Bath, Avon, BA1 1JY England
tel. 44-225/462231
fax 44-225/445551

Performs at various locations in and around Bath.

Brighton Festival (May)
54 Old Steine
Brighton BN1 1EQ England

tel. 44-273/676296
fax 44-273/822095

Buxton Festival (mid-July–mid-August)
1 Crescent View
Hall Bank, Buxton
Derbyshire SK17 6EN England
tel. 44-298/70395 or 78939
fax 44-298/72289

Cambridge Festival (July)
Mandela House
4 Regent Street
Cambridge CB2 1BY England
tel. 44-223/357851

Canterbury Festival (October)
59 Ivy Lane
Canterbury, Kent CT1 1TU England
tel. 44-227/488800

Cheltenham Festival (July)
Town Hall, Imperial Square
Cheltenham, Gloucestershire GL50 1QA England
tel. 44-242/521621 or 523690
fax 44-242/573902

Chichester Festivities (July)
Box Office: Hammick's Bookshop
65 East Street
Chichester, West Sussex PO19 1HL England
tel. 44-243/780192

Cricklade Music Festival (late September–early October)
The Coach House
Lotton, Swindon SNG GDF England
tel. 44-793/750338

Glyndebourne Festival Opera (May–August)
Glyndebourne, Lewes
East Sussex BN8 5UU England
tel. 44-273/812 321
fax 44-273/812 783
One of the most sophisticated summer opera festivals. Since 1934, audience members have brought baskets of caviar, pâté, and fine breads to enjoy with champagne as they relax in elegant clothes on the green lawn of Glyndebourne during intermissions. Oh yes, and the opera is usually superb too.

Opera North
The Grand Theatre
46 New Briggate
Leeds, Yorkshire LS1 6NU England
tel. 44-532/439999 or 459351
fax 44-532/440418 or 435745

Opera 80
Theater Royal Lincoln
Clasketgate, Lincoln LN2 1JJ England
tel. 44-522/25555
fax 44-522/545867

A touring company, based in Lincoln, that journeys around England.

Pavilion Opera (April–December)
Thorpe Tilney Hall
Lincoln LN4 3SL England
tel. 44-5267/231
fax 44-5267/315

Performances are staged in country homes and estates, with audience members close to the singers. For information in the United States, contact Lucy Tittmann, tel. 508/ 369-1152; fax 508/369-7919.

Empire Theater
Lime Street
Liverpool L1 1JE England
tel. 44-51/709-1555 or 709-8070

Early Music Centre Festival (October)
The Early Music Centre
Charles Clore House
17 Russell Square
London WC1B 5DR England
tel. 44-71/580-8401
fax 44-71/323-2133

English Bach Festival
15 South Eaton Place
London SW1 9ER England
tel. 44-71/730-5925
fax 44-71/730-1456

Despite the name, this festival also specializes in presenting operas by early music composers such as Rameau and Handel.

English National Opera
London Coliseum
St. Martin's Lane
London WC2N 4ES England
tel. 44-71/836-3161 or 836-0111
fax 44-71/379-1264 or 836-8379

Located between Covent Garden and the theater district of London's West End, the English National Opera (ENO) is notable for two things: its operas are all presented in English and generally receive high-quality productions drawing upon the sterling talent of London's theater community. It is sometimes jarring to hear beloved arias sung in English, but that is ENO's particular preference. And a night at ENO is highly commended for any visitor to London for its good voices and, especially, the great theatrical insights it brings to familiar operas. There are 100 low-priced balcony tickets sold at the box office on the day of the performance—first come, first served.

Opera Factory
8a The Leathermarket, Weston St.
London SE1 3ER
England
tel. 44-81/378-1029
fax 44-81/378-0185
Opera on the fringe, but you may get to see the stars of tomorrow in works the big houses won't produce, such as Monteverdi's L'Incoronazione di Poppea.

Monteverdi Choir and Orchestra Ltd.
Bowring Building
P.O. Box 165
Tower Place
London EC3P 3BE England
tel. 44-71/480-5183
fax 44-71/480-5185
Not only Monteverdi but Mozart and others.

The Royal Opera House at Covent Garden
London WC2E 9DD
England
tel. 44-71/240-1066 *(You may call this number from overseas and use a credit card to book tickets.)*
One of the world's leading companies has performed in theaters on this site for more than 250 years (fires destroyed earlier buildings here). You may remember that Henry Higgins (from Pygmalion *and* My Fair Lady*) first encounters Eliza Doolittle as he leaves a performance at Covent Garden. The building is the home of the Royal Opera and the Royal Ballet. Although the opera company has had rough times artistically and administratively in recent years, it remains an important destination for any operagoer and for many singers. Certainly worth attending a performance. Sixty-five tickets for the rear amphitheater (also called "the gods" because you feel closer to heaven than to the earth) go on sale at 10 A.M. on the day of the performance—first come, first served, one ticket per customer.*

Sadler's Wells Theatre
Rosebery Avenue
London EC1R 4TN England
tel. 44-71/278-8916
fax 44-71/837-0965

St. John's Smith Square
London SW1P 3HA England
tel. 44-71/222-1061
fax 44-71/233-1618
A baroque church with excellent acoustics.

Ludlow Festival (late June–early July)
Castle Square
Ludlow Shropshire SY8 1AY England
tel. 44-584/2150

Newbury Spring Festival (May)
Suite 3, Town Hall

Newbury, Berkshire RG14 5AA England
tel. 44-635/49919
fax 44-635/528690

Nottingham Festival (late May–early June)
Arts Department
51 Castle Gate
Nottingham NG1 6AF England
tel. 44-602/483504

Sevenoaks Summer Festival (June)
Sevenoaks School
Sevenoaks, Kent TN13 1HU England
tel. 44-732/455133
fax 44-732/456143

Winter Visitors' Season
Royal Shakespeare Theatre, Box Office
Stratford-upon-Avon CV37 6BB England
tel. 44-789/295623
More than just the Bard is staged at Stratford-upon-Avon.

FINLAND

When telephoning within Finland, dial 9 before the city code (for example, Helsinki becomes 90).

Finnish National Opera
Bulevardi 23-27
P.O. 188
00181 Helsinki, Finland
tel. 358-0/129255
tel. 358-0/129216 (advance reservations)
fax 358-0/1292301
Finland has perhaps the greatest contemporary opera scene in the world. Works by Finnish composers such as Leevi Madetoja, Einojuhani Rautavaara, Aulis Sallinen, and Joonas Kokkonen are produced as often as those by Mozart, Verdi, Wagner, Puccini, and Tchaikovsky. The Finnish National Opera commissions new operas by Finns and helps train many of the great singers—especially basses—that seem to come from this nation of five million music lovers. The company's new opera house opened in August 1993.

Helsinki Festival (late August–mid-September)
Unioninkatu 28
00100 Helsinki, Finland
tel. 358-0/659688
fax 358-0/656715

Ilmajoki Music Festival
Kahmankuja 6
60800 Ilmajoki, Finland

tel. 358-64/547049
fax 358-64/547171

Savonlinna Opera Festival (July)
Savonlinna Tourist Service (arranges tickets and hotels)
Puistokatu 1
57100 Savonlinna, Finland
tel. 358-57/273-492 or 273-493
fax 358-57/514-449

This festival is one of the most enjoyable in Europe. It takes place in the courtyard of Olavinlinna Castle (1475), which sits on a little spit of land jutting out onto a body of water. The courtyard has 2,200 seats. Performances of up to six operas are done in repertory every July.

FRANCE

Aix-en-Provence Festival (July)
Palais de l'Ancien Archevêché
13100 Aix-en-Provence, France
tel. 33-42/173400 or 233781
fax 33-42/961261

Tickets may also be booked through the tourist office:
Office de Tourisme
2 Place du Général de Gaulle
13100 Aix-en-Provence, France
tel. 33-42/161161
fax 33-42/161162

Albi Festival de Musique (mid-July–early August)
Office de Tourisme
Palais de la Berbie
81000 Albi, France
tel. 33-63/542888

Théâtre Musical d'Angers
7, rue Duboys
49100 Angers, France
tel. 33-41/604040
fax 33-41/603224

Opéra d'Avignon et des Pays de Vaucluse (July)
BP111-84007 Avignon, France
tel. 33-90/822344
fax 33-90/850423

Rencontres Internationales de Musique Baroque et Classique de Beaune (July)
2, square St. Irénée
75011 Paris, France
tel. 33-1/43574697

Held at the Notre Dame Basilica of Beaune, in wine country.

Grand Théâtre de Bordeaux
Place de la Comédie
BP 95 Bordeaux, France
tel. 33-56/447071
fax 33-56/819366

Grand Théâtre de Dijon
2, rue Longepierre
21000 Dijon, France
tel. 33-80/672323

Rencontres Musicales d'Evian (May)
contact: 47, rue de Ponthieu
75008 Paris, France
fax 33-1/42256066
Held at the spa of Evian-les-Bains.

Centre Culturel de l'Ouest
Abbaye Royale de Fontevraud
49590 Fontevraud l'Abbaye
tel. 33-41/537352

Opéra de Lille
2, rue des Bons Enfants
59800 Lille, France
tel. 33-20/554861
fax 33-20/511790

Opéra de Lyon
Opéra Nouvel
Place de la Comédie
69001 Lyons, France
tel. 33-78/280960
fax 33-78/278805
The new opera house in Lyons opened on May 14, 1993, with a performance, dubbed the world premiere, of Debussy's Rodrigue et Chimène (1890–92), a work that was seemingly never produced until then. The Lyon Opera also does very well by the works of Hector Berlioz, presenting a festival in late September in odd-numbered years.

Opéra de Marseille
2, rue Beauvau
13001 Marseilles, France
tel. 33-91/550070
fax 33-91/549415

Festival de Musique de Menton (August)
Palais de L'Europe
Avenue Boyer BP 111
06503 Menton Cedex, France
tel. 33-93/358222 or 575700
fax 33-93/575100
Held in a beautiful square in this beautiful town on the Riviera.

Metz Opéra-Théâtre
4–5, place de la Comédie
57000 Metz, France
tel. 33-87/754050
fax 33-87/753993

Opéra de Montpellier
11, boulevard Victor Hugo
34000 Montpellier, France
tel. 33-67/660092
fax 33-67/663819

Opéra de Nancy et de Lorraine
1, rue Sainte-Catherine
54000 Nancy, France
tel. 33-83/853060
fax 33-83/853066

Opéra de Nantes
1, rue Molière
44000 Nantes, France
tel. 33-40/697718
fax 33-40/419077

Opéra de Nice
9, rue de la Terrasse
06300 Nice, France
tel. 33-93/856731
fax 33-93/803483
performances at:
Théâtre de l'Opéra de Nice
4, rue St. François de Paule
06300 Nice, France
tel. 33-93/805983
fax 33-93/803483

Chorégies d'Orange (late July–early August)
18, place Silvain
B.P. 205
84107 Cedex Orange, France
tel. 33-90/342424
fax 33-90/348767
Opera is staged outdoors in a beautifully preserved Roman amphitheater which attracts eager audiences and excellent singers.

Châtelet, Théâtre Musical de Paris
2, rue Edouard Colonne
75001 Paris, France
tel. 33-1/4028-2828
fax 33-1/4236-8975
When in Paris, always check what is playing at the Châtelet. Many of the city's more daring productions take place in this historic theater near the banks of the Seine.

Festival d'Automne à Paris (September–December)
156, rue de Rivoli
75001 Paris, France
tel. 33-1/4296-1227
fax 33-1/4015-9288
Specializes in contemporary arts, including opera.

Opéra-Comique
5, rue Favart
75002 Paris, France
tel. 33-1/4286-8883 or 4297-5864
fax 33-1/4286-8578
At this old theater that produced opéra comique in the nineteenth century, you can still see many French classics and the occasional non-French work.

Opéra Garnier (The old Paris Opéra)
Théâtre National de l'Opéra
8, rue Scribe
75009 Paris, France
tel. 33-1/4001-1789
fax 33-1/4001-2560
One of the most important buildings in opera history sits in the middle of Paris, providing a social and psychological focus similar to those of La Scala in Milan and the Staatsoper in Vienna. This is the setting of The Phantom of the Opera. *The Palais Garnier has been, since the opening of the new opera house at the Bastille, the home of the Paris Opera Ballet. The theater should certainly be visited, and if there is a performance there, see it if only for the experience of being with the echoes and ghosts that are part of the history of this great theater.*

Opéra de Paris–Bastille
120, rue de Lyon
75012 Paris, France
tel. 33-1/4001-1789
fax 33-1/4001-1616 or 4344-9401
This new home of the Paris Opéra opened in the late 1980s and, like most new Paris landmarks, was met by a storm of controversy between those who loved it and those who hated it. Don't forget that the same thing happened with the Eiffel Tower and the Pompidou Center, so approach the Bastille Opera with an open mind. It has excellent stage facilities and better sightlines than the old Paris Opéra, though it will never have the special flavor of the old theater.

Péniche Opéra
Amarée face au 200, quai de Jemmapes
75010 Paris, France
tel. 33-1/42451820
Does smaller, more experimental operas.

Théâtre des Champs-Elysées
15, avenue Montaigne
75008 Paris, France

tel. 33-1/4952-5050
fax 33-1/4952-0741
Yet another place to see good opera in Paris.

Opéra de Normandie
Théâtre des Arts de Rouen
22, place des Arts (quai de la Bourse)
BP 1253
76177 Cedex Rouen
tel. 33-35/714136
fax 33-35/153349

Maison de la Culture et de la Communication
BP 237
42013 Cedex 02 Saint-Etienne
tel. 33-77/253518
fax 33-77/375656

Opéra du Rhin
19, place Broglie
67008 Strasbourg, France
tel. 33-88/754800
fax 33-88/240934
foreign sales: tel. 33-88/754843
Though based in Strasbourg, the Opéra du Rhin also performs in the Alsatian cities of Colmar and Mulhouse.

Festival de Sully, Orléans et Lorient B.P. 58 (mid-June–mid-July)
45600 Sully-sur-Loire, France
tel. 33-38/362346
fax 33-38/365332

Toulon Opéra
Boulevard de Strasbourg
8300 Toulon, France
tel. 33-94/927078

Théâtre du Capitole
Place du Capitole
31000 Toulouse, France
tel. 33-61/228022
fax 33-61/222434

Grand Théâtre de Tours
34, rue de la Scellerie
37000 Tours, France
tel. 33-47/053787
fax 33-47/661192

GERMANY

Stadttheater
Kennedyplatz 4
8900 Augsburg, Germany
tel. 49-821/513635

Freilichtbühne am Roten Tor (June–July)
Kasernstrasse 4
8900 Augsburg, Germany
tel. 49-821/36604
Outdoor opera and operetta.

Oper in der Stiftsruin (August)
Pavillion am Marktplatz
Postfach 91
6430 Bad Hersfeld, Germany
tel. 49-6621/72066
Performances, especially of early operas, are staged at the ruins of the local abbey.

Kissingen Summer Festival (June–July)
Postfach 2260
8730 Bad Kissingen, Germany
tel. 49-973/807110
fax 49-973/807200

Festspielleitung Bayreuth (August)
Festspielhaus
Postfach 100262
8580 Bayreuth, Germany
tel. 49-921/20221
Wagner's temple to his own art opened in 1876 with the first complete performance of Der Ring des Nibelungen. *Bayreuth remains the unrivaled destination for Wagnerites of every stripe. It gets hot there, and the seats are uncomfortable, but it is one of the operagoer's most memorable experiences. Tickets go on sale in November of the year before the performances, and demand far exceeds supply. One of Wagner's innovations was a covered orchestra pit, which enables you to focus more completely on the drama. The greatest Wagnerian conductors, including James Levine, Georg Solti, and Pierre Boulez, all work steadily in Bayreuth and seem to draw inspiration from the artistic legacy of this place. Wagner's wife Cosima, son, Siegfried, and grandchildren were all active keepers of the flame, and Bayreuth, more than any other city associated with a composer, has the atmosphere of a shrine.*

Margräfliches Opernhaus
Opernstrasse
8580 Bayreuth, Germany
tel. 49-921/25416
Where Bayreuth goes to the opera once the Wagnerites have gone home. Even Bayreuth cannot live by Wagner alone.

Berlin Festival (September)
Berliner Festspiele GmbH
Postfach 301648

1000 Berlin 30, Germany
tel. 49-30/254890
fax 49-30/254-89111

Deutsche Oper Berlin
Bismarckstrasse 35
1000 Berlin 10, Germany
tel. 49-30/34381
fax 49-30/3438232
for tickets, write to:
Deutsche Oper Berlin
Richard Wagner Strasse 10
1000 Berlin 10, Germany
tel. 49-30/341-0249
When Berlin was divided, this became the new opera house in West Berlin.

Deutsche Staatsoper Berlin
Unter den Linden 7
1086 Berlin, Germany
tel. 49-30/200-4762 or 203-540
The old Berlin opera house, on the street Marlene Dietrich made famous, became the home after World War II of the national company of East Berlin.

Komische Oper (Comic Opera)
Behrenstrasse 55/57
Postfache 1311
1086 Berlin, Germany
tel. 49-30/220-2761 or 292555

Theater des Westens
Kantstrasse 12
1000 Berlin 12, Germany
tel. 49-30/31903-193
Operetta.

Oper Bonn
Am Boeselagerhof 1
5300 Bonn, Germany
tel. 49-228/7281 or 773-6667

Cologne: *See Köln.*

Lake Constance Opera Festival (July)
Constanzsee, Germany
tel. 49-7531/52016

Staatstheater Darmstadt
Postfach 111 432
6100 Darmstadt, Germany
tel. 49-6151/281-1213

Sachsische Staatsoper Dresden (Saxon State Opera)
Theaterplatz in der Schinkelwache
8010 Dresden, Germany
tel. 49-351/48420

Semper Opera Dresden
2 Theaterplatz
801 Dresden, Germany
tel. 49-351/484-2731 or 48420
Dresden's major opera house, site of the premieres of Strauss's Salome, Elektra, *and* Der Rosenkavalier.

Dresden Music Festival (May–June)
Besucherdienst der Dresdener Musikfestspiele
Günzstrasse 31
Postfach 110
8012 Dresden, Germany
tel. 49-351/459-4040 or 495-5025
fax 49-351/459-3738

Deutsche Oper am Rhein
Neckarstrasse
4100 Duisburg 1, Germany
tel. 49-203/300-9100
fax 49-203/300-9200
Shares productions with the opera house in Düsseldorf.

Deutsche Oper am Rhein
Heinrich-Heine Allee 16A
4000 Düsseldorf, Germany
tel. 49-211/890-8211
fax 49-211/329051

Aalto Theater und Philharmonie
Rolandstrasse 10
4300 Essen 1, Germany
tel. 49-201/812-2200
fax 49-201/812-2172

Städtische Bühnen
Theaterplatz
Untermainanlage 11
6000 Frankfurt 1, Germany
tel. 49-69/236061 or 256-2434
Do not confuse this new building with the Alte Oper, on the Opernplatz, which reopened as a concert hall in 1981 after being damaged during the Second World War.

Freiburger Theater
Bertoldstrasse 46
7800 Freiburg, Germany
tel. 49-761/490-9412

Hamburgische Staatsoper
Dammtorstrasse 28
2000 Hamburg 36, Germany
tel. 49-40/351-721

Hamburg was the first German city to have a public opera house, and it has enthusiastically supported opera in various theaters ever since. The Hamburgische Staatsoper enjoys a solid artistic reputation and attracts world-class stars on a regular basis.

Niedersächsische Staatstheater
Opernplatz 1
3000 Hannover, Germany
tel. 49-511/368-1711
fax 49-511/368-1768

Musik und Theater in Herrenhausen (late June–early September)
Ernst-August Platz 9
3000 Hannover, Germany
tel. 49-511/168-6146 or 168-3903
Performances held in stately gardens.

Heidelberg Schloss Spiele Konzertkasse (late July–late August)
Theaterstrasse 8
6900 Heidelberg, Germany
tel. 49-6221/583521

Schleswig-Holstein Music Festival (July–August)
Postfach 3840
2300 Kiel 1, Germany
tel. 49-431/567080
fax 49-431/569152

Badisches Staatstheater
Baumeisterstrasse 11
7500 Karlsruhe 1, Germany
tel. 49-721/60202
fax 49-721/373223

Oper der Stadt Köln
Offenbachplatz
Opernkasse, Postfach 180241
5100 Köln 1, Germany
tel. 49-221/221-8400 (box office) or 221-8210

Oper Leipzig
Postfach 35
7010 Leipzig, Germany
tel. 49-341/258
fax 49-341/293-633

Ludwigsburg Castle (May–September)
Postfach 1022
7140 Ludwigsburg, Germany
tel. 49-7141/25035 or 28000
fax 49-7141/901011

Staatstheater Mainz
Gutenbergplatz 7
6500 Mainz 1, Germany
tel. 49-6131/123365
fax 49-6131/122706

Nationaltheater
Am Goetheplatz
6800 Mannheim 1, Germany
tel. 49-621/24844
fax 49-621/168-0385

Bayerische Staatsoper (Bavarian State Opera)
Max Joseph Platz 2
8000 Munich 2, Germany
tel. 49-89/21851 or 218-5368
fax 49-89/218-5304

The Bavarian State Opera, housed in the National Theater, is one of the world's leading companies. The strengths here are the operas of Richard Strauss, a native son, and those of Wagner, but the general artistic level is quite high.

Munich Biennale (May)
Kulturreferat des LH München
Rindermarkt 3–4
8000 Munich 2, Germany
tel. 49-89/290-4183
fax 49-89/224659

Munich Opera Festival (July)
P.O. Box 100148
Maximillianerstrasse 11
8000 Munich 2, Germany
tel. 49-89/21851 or 22136
fax 49-89/218-5304

Great operas, conductors, and singers every night make for huge ticket demand at this popular festival.

Staatstheater am Gärtnerplatz
Gärtnerplatz 3
P.O. Box 140569
8000 Munich 5, Germany
tel. 49-89/263-041, 202411 or 201-6767
fax 49-89/202-41237

Municipal Theater
Richard Wagner Platz 2
8500 Nuremberg, Germany
tel. 49-911/163-808

Stadttheater
Bismarckplatz 7
8400 Regensburg, Germany
tel. 49-941/507-2427

Opernhaus Saarbruecken
Saarbruecken, Germany
tel. 49-681/30920

Schwetzingen Festival (April–June)
Schlossplatz
6830 Schwetzingen, Germany
tel. 496202/4933
Or contact:
Postfach 106040
7000 Stuttgart 10, Germany
tel. 49-711/288-3138
fax 49-711/288-2600

Württemburgisches Staatstheater
Oberer Schlossgarten 6
Postfach 104345
7000 Stuttgart 10, Germany
tel. 49-711/21951 or 221795

Ulmer Theater
Olgastrasse 73
7900 Ulm, Germany
tel. 49-731/161-4400
fax 49-731-137

Hessiches Staatstheater
Christian Zais Strasse 1–5
Postfach 32 47
6200 Wiesbaden, Germany
tel. 49-6121/1321
fax 49-6121/132337
Every May the Internationalen Maifestspiele, founded in 1896, is held.

Stadttheater Würzburg
Theaterstrasse 23
8700 Würzburg, Germany
tel. 49-931/58686

Mozartfest (June)
Haus zum Falken
8700 Würzburg, Germany
tel. 49-931/37336

Sommerfestspiele in Archaologischen Park (August)
Touristbüro
Karthaus 2
Postfach 1164
4232 Xanten 1, Germany
tel. 49-2801/37238
fax 49-2801/37209

GREECE

Every Greek opera lover will tell you that Maria Callas was the country's greatest opera singer. In fact, Callas was born and raised in New York City and did not move to Greece until she was thirteen years old. Many Italians also claim Callas as a native daughter because she had many of her great successes at La Scala.

Megaron Musikis (Athens Concert Hall)
Vas. Sofias Ave. & Kokkali Street
Athens, Greece
tel. 30-1/729-0391

Athens Festival (June–September)
Herod Atticus Odeon
4 Stadiou str.
10564 Athens, Greece
tel. 30-1/322-1459 or 322-0049
fax 30-1/322-4148
Features international opera performances.

Lyriki Skini (The Opera House)
59–61 Akademias St.
Athens, Greece
tel. 30-1/361-2461

HUNGARY

Erkel Szinhaz (Erkel Theater)
Koztarsasag Ter 30
Budapest VIII, Hungary
tel. 36-1/133-0540
tickets by phone: 36-1/133-0540 or 112-0000

Magyar Allami Operahaz (Hungarian State Opera House)
Nepkoztarsasag u. 22
Andrassy Utca 22
1061 Budapest VI, Hungary
tel. 36-1/312-550 or 153-0170
tickets by phone:
tel: 36-1/153-0170 or 112-0000

ICELAND

Icelandic Opera
Gamla Bio
Ingolfsstraeti
Reykjavik, Iceland
tel. 354-1/62-1077 (box office)
tel. 354-1/27033 (admin.)
Although Iceland has only 250,000 people, it maintains a full season at the Icelandic Opera.

IRELAND

Waterford International Festival of Light Opera (September)
600 Morrissons Avenue
Waterford, Eire
tel. 353-51/75437

Wexford Festival (October–November)
Theatre Royal
High Street
Wexford, Eire
tel. 353-53/22144
fax 353-53/24289
Wexford is gradually developing a reputation as one of the real up-and-coming festivals.

ISRAEL

New Israel Opera
1 Allenby Street
Tel Aviv, Israel
tel. 972-3/57227

ITALY

Festival Internazionale Opera Barga (July)
Municipio
55051 Barga (LU), Italia
tel. 39-583/723745
Barga, not far from Puccini's hometown of Lucca, is the site of a training program for young singers trying to improve their skills in Italian language and style. The Barga Festival includes performances by many of these young talents.

Teatro Petruzzelli
Corso Cavour
70100 Bari, Italia
tel. 39-80/521-1438
fax 39-80/521-0740
This beautiful theater, opened in 1913, was practically destroyed in a devastating fire in October 1991. As this book was being written, funds were not yet raised to rebuild, so the future of the Teatro Petruzzelli is uncertain.

Teatro Donizetti
Piazza Cavour, 14
24100 Bergamo, Italia
tel. 39-35/249631
fax 39-35/217560
Bergamo was the birthplace of commedia dell'arte, the theatrical form that influenced Italian opera buffa. The town is also the birthplace of Gaetano Donizetti. In addition to a year-round calendar of performances by all composers, a Donizetti festival takes place in September and early October.

Teatro Comunale di Bologna
Largo Respighi, 1
40126 Bologna, Italia
tel. 39-51/529-999
fax 39-51/529-934

One of the better Italian companies is in one of Italy's most beautiful cities. Many artists native to Bologna's region of Emilia-Romagna, including Luciano Pavarotti, Mirella Freni, Ruggero Raimondi, and Leo Nucci, appear frequently in Bologna. This theater stages a wider range of operas than do many Italian houses, often to satisfy the particular interests of certain singers. For example, Freni and Raimondi have added roles in Russian, and the Bolognese audiences have proved very receptive to their efforts. An added plus is the superb food of Bologna, which you can have before or after a night at the opera. Rossini attended the music conservatory of Bologna and, I suspect, spent as much time at the dining table as he did at the writing table.

Orchestra Sinfonica Haydn di Bolzano
Piazza Domenicani, 19
39100 Bolzano/Bozen, Italia
tel. 39-471/975-031
fax 39-471/975-132

Occasionally performs opera in concert.

Teatro Grande
Via Paganora, 19
25122 Brescia, Italia
tel. 39-30/42400

Teatro Lirico di Cagliari
Via Regina Margherita, 6
Cagliari (Sardinia), Italia
tel. 39-70/662850
fax 39-70/650326

Teatro Bellini
Via G. Perrotta, 12
95131 Catania (Sicily), Italia
tel. 39-95/312024

A beautiful theater in a sadly depressed city that claims Vincenzo Bellini as a native son. The façade of the Teatro Bellini contains busts of eleven great Italian composers, with pride of place being given to Bellini, Verdi, and Rossini. The company also stages summer performances at the Teatro Greco in Siracusa.

Associazione Autunno Musicale (Autumn)
Villa Olmo
Via Cantoni, 1
22100 Como, Italia
tel. 39-31/571150
fax 39-31/570540

Teatro Comunale Amilcare Ponchielli
Corso Vittorio Emanuele, 52

26100 Cremona, Italia
tel. 39-372/407273
Cremona is the birthplace of two great innovators in music, Claudio Monteverdi, the first great opera composer, and Antonio Stradivari (1644–1737), maker of the world's finest violins, but its opera house is named for another son, Amilcare Ponchielli (1834–86), composer of La Gioconda *(1876).*

Festival di Fermo (July–August)
Comune di Fermo, Assessorato alla Cultura
63023 Fermo, Italia

Teatro Comunale di Ferrara
Piazzetta Sant'Anna, 3
44100 Ferrara, Italia
tel. 39-532/202675 *(tickets)*
tel. 39-532/202312 *(information)*
fax 39-532/47353

Teatro Comunale di Firenze
Via Solferino, 15
50123 Firenze (Florence), Italia
tel. 39-55/277-9236
fax 39-55/239-6954
Each May and June there is a great concentration of opera in Florence, the birthplace of opera, during the Maggio Musicale festival.

Teatro della Pergola
Via della Pergola 12
50137 Firenze, Italia
tel. 39-55/247-6351
fax 39-55/610141
Built in 1600, this theater was a performance site for many early operas.

Teatro Comunale dell'Opera Carlo Felice
Passo al Teatro, 4
16121 Genova, Italia
tel. 39-10/5381-1225 or 839-3589
fax 39-10/538-1233
Box office:
Via Frugoni 15/6
16121 Genova, Italia
tel. 39-10/53811.

Teatro delle Vigne
Via Cavour, 66
20075 Lodi, Italia
tel. 39-371/425862

Teatro Rossini
Piazza Cavour
46022 Lugo (RA), Italia
tel. 39-545/33037

Macerata Festival (mid-July–mid-August)
Arena Sferisterio
Casella Postale 92
62100 Macerata, Italia
tel. 39-733/256286
fax 39-733/41603

In this strange, spherical (hence the name) arena, one can hear good casts in outdoor performances. Montserrat Caballé is a frequent visitor. The capacious arena has enough room for grand spectacles, but the almond shape of the structure means that ticketholders with relatively central locations will be very close to the stage. Macerata is yet another of the dozens of attractive small cities in Italy that are routinely over-looked by tourists. The local version of lasagne, called vincisgrassi, *is worth a trip by itself.*

Martina Franca Valle d'Itria Festival (July–August)
Palazzo Ducale
74015 Martina Franca, Italia
tel. 39-80/701030 or 705100
fax 39-80/707191 or 705120

Teatro alla Scala
Via dei Filodrammatici, 2
20121 Milano, Italia
tel. 39-2/887-9211
tel. 39-2/807041 (information)
fax 39-2/887-9297 (ticket office)

Opened in 1778, La Scala is synonymous with opera. Many of Verdi's and Puccini's greatest works were first staged at the Milanese theater. La Scala sits next to the Galleria Vittorio Emanuele, which connects it to the Piazza del Duomo. This ar-chitectural assemblage forms the heart of Milan, and in the mind of every Milanese, whether they are operagoers or not, their opera house is one of their treasures. Every December 7 the city celebrates Sant'Ambrogio, the feast of St. Ambrose, Milan's patron saint. The entire city shuts down, delicious meals are served and concluded with Asti Spumante and panettone, the Milanese sweet bread. That evening marks the opening night of the La Scala season, one of Europe's great social events. It is unlikely that you will get tickets for opening night, and tickets for other perfor-mances are also hard to come by. It is often best to apply by mail for tickets or, if you find yourself in Milan unexpectedly, to visit concierges of major hotels, who will, for a handsome tip, probably be able to procure a pair. Dealing with scalpers in Milan, as in all cities, is a dicey endeavor and one I fully discourage. Whether or not you attend a performance, make sure to spend a couple of hours in La Scala's wonderful museum, which is open to the public most days in the mornings and after 2 P.M. If a rehearsal is not in progress, you will be able to have a look at the auditorium. Il Museo Teatrale has wonderful paintings and busts of great composers and singers and oddities such as a lock of Mozart's hair, Verdi's piano, and plaster models of Toscanini's hands. No opera lover should fail to visit this museum, which has a good gift shop as well.

Musica nei Cortili (late June–late July)
Comune di Milano

Settore Cultura e Spettacolo
Via T. Marino 7
20122 Milano, Italia
tel. 39-2/862418

Though it may not appear to be a leafy city, Milan has more trees and green than any other Italian city. But much of this vegetation is to be found in courtyards, such as the ones that are opened for musical performances in the early summer.

Teatro Comunale
Corso Canal Grande, 85
41100 Modena, Italia
tel. 39-59/214775

Modena is the hometown of Mirella Freni and Luciano Pavarotti.

Cantiere Internazionale d'Arte
Teatro Poliziano
Via del Teatro 4
53045 Montepulciano (SI), Italia
tel. 39-578/757089

This beautiful little town, which produces some of Italy's best wine and cheese, also has a lovely opera house that seems perfect for the size of this ancient and gracious part of Tuscany.

Teatro San Carlo
Via San Carlo, 98f
80132 Napoli, Italia
tel. 39-81/797-2111 or 416305
fax 39-81/797-2306

Teatro Civico Faraggiana
4 Corso Vittoria
Novara, Italia
tel. 39-321/27676

Teatro Comunale Verdi
32 Via Livello
Padova, Italia
tel. 39-49/876-0371

Teatro Massimo
Piazza Verdi
90138 Palermo, Sicilia
tel. 39-91/583600
tel. 39-91/581512 (ticket office)
fax 39-91/585974

Teatro Regio
Via Garibaldi, 16/A
43100 Parma, Italia
tel. 39-521/795685 or 218678
fax 39-521/795216

The citizens of Parma pride themselves on being the most exacting operagoers in Italy. They point out with pride that Arturo Toscanini and Giuseppe Verdi were both born and raised in the province of Parma, which the Parmigiani feel entitles them to be considered real opera cognoscenti. What is startling for the newcomer to the opera in Parma is not only how well people there know opera but how demonstrative they are when they approve or disapprove of singers. In Italy, an encore is known as a bis, *a word Italians cry when they admire the way a singer has rendered an aria. A theaterful of "bis" may sound like booing to an American, but in fact this is a sign of approval. At one time, it was common in Italy for a famous singer to repeat an aria if the audience demanded it. In recent times, the prevailing wisdom (with which I concur fully) is that opera is a theater piece rather than a showcase for one singer in which everyone and everything else is a backdrop. At one performance I attended in Parma in the 1970s, a particular tenor sang an especially pleasing rendition of "Una furtiva lagrima" in* L'Elisir d'Amore. *So great was the clamor for an encore that the tenor gestured that he would humbly oblige. Whether he was overcome with emotion or just didn't have it the second time around, the encore was a disaster, and the adoring crowd turned into an angry mob that jeered mercilessly. This should be a lesson to any singer: leave them with a good memory if they liked you the first time.*

Pesaro Rossini Festival (August–September)
Via Rossini, 30
61100 Pesaro, Italia
tel. 39-721/30161, 697212 or 33184
fax 39-721/30979

In only a few years, the Rossini Festival has deservedly become one of the leading music festivals in Europe. The Rossini Foundation devotes year-round effort to producing critical editions of Rossini scores. Pesaro is a popular seaside resort, so you may spend the day at the shore, go to hear a great cast sing a seldom-heard opera by the "Swan of Pesaro," and then dine on the superb cooking of the Marche that Rossini so enjoyed.

Teatro Municipale
Via Verdi, 41
29100 Piacenza, Italia
tel. 39-523/492251

Ravenna Festival (late June–early July)
Via Gordini 27
48100 Ravenna, Italia
tel. 39-544/32577 or 482494
fax 39-544/36303

Teatro Romolo Valli
Piazza Martiri 7 Luglio
42100 Reggio Emilia, Italia
tel. 39-522/434244
fax 39-522/46605

Musica Riva (July)
Via Pilati, 5
38066 Riva del Garda (TN), Italia
tel. 39-464/554073 or 516161
fax 39-464/505643

Accademia Nazionale di Santa Cecilia
Via Vittoria, 6
00187 Roma, Italia
tel. 39-6/678-0742
fax 39-6/678-2796

St. Cecilia is the patron saint of music. While most performances here are symphonic, there are also operas in concert.

Teatro dell'Opera
Via Firenze, 72
00184 Roma, Italia
tel. 39-6/481-601, 463641 or 461755
fax 39-6/461-253

Teatro Chiabrera
Piazza Dia, 2
Savona, Italia
tel. 39-19/820409

This seaport on the Riviera, west of Genoa, is the hometown of soprano Renata Scotto.

Accademia Musicale Chigiana (July–August)
Via di Città, 89
53100 Siena, Italia
tel. 39-577/214992

Festival dei Due Mondi (mid-June–mid-July)
Via Duomo, 7
06049 Spoleto (PG), Italia
tel. 39-743/40396 or 44097
fax 39-743/43284
for information:
Associazione Festival dei Due Mondi
Via Cesare Beccaria, 18
00196 Roma, Italia
tel. 39-6/321-0288
fax 39-6/320-0747

This festival is the child of Gian Carlo Menotti, the Italian composer who has spent great amounts of time in the United States. Many of his operas are produced here, along with others by four centuries of composers. There are also plays, films, dance, and other art forms. There is now a Spoleto USA in Charleston, South Carolina.

Teatro Greco (outdoor festival in July)
Siracusa, Sicilia
For information, contact Teatro Bellini in Catania, listed above.

Stresa Musical Weeks (August–September)
Via R. Bonghi 4
28049 Stresa (NO), Italia
tel. 39-323/31095
fax 39-323/32561

Taormina Arte (July–September)
Via Pirandello 31
98039 Taormina (ME), Sicilia, Italia
tel. 39-942/21142 or 23220
fax 39-942/23348

Performances take place in an ancient Greek amphitheater, so you might want to bring along a cushion to soften the hard stone on which you sit. But don't be deterred: performances here are magical. To see Strauss's Elektra *in this timeless place provides an unforgettable night at the opera.*

Todifestival (late August–early September)
Palazzo Ciuffelli
06059 Todi (PG), Italia
tel. 39-75/894-3611
fax 39-75/894-3429

Teatro Regio
Piazza Castello, 215
10124 Torino, Italia
tel. 39-11/88151
fax 39-11/881-5214

Auditorium RAI
Via Verdi, 16
10124 Torino, Italia
tel. 39-11/8807-4653

The national radio orchestra has recorded many memorable live performances in this hall.

Festival Pucciniano (July–August)
Belvedere Puccini, 4
55048 Torre del Lago Puccini, Italia
tel. 39-584/343-322 or 359322

Torre del Lago was Puccini's residence for much of his life, although he remained in touch with nearby Lucca, the town of his birth, and spent much time in Milan to be at La Scala and near his publisher, Giulio Ricordi.

Teatro Comunale
31 Corso del Popolo
Treviso, Italia
tel. 39-422/410130

Teatro Comunale Giuseppe Verdi
Piazza Giuseppe Verdi, 1
34121 Trieste, Italia
tel. 39-40/367816
tel. 39-40/366300

Given Trieste's former status as the port of the Austro-Hungarian empire, the German repertory is better represented here than in most Italian theaters.

Teatro La Fenice
Campo San Fantin 1977

30124 Venezia, Italia
tel. 39-41/786562, 786511 or 786500
fax 39-41/522-1768

This is the chief opera house of Venice, the city that turned opera from a royal enter-
tainment to a popular art form. Many operagoers say that La Fenice is the most
beautiful opera house in the world.

Arena di Verona
Ente Lirico Arena di Verona
Piazza Bra, 28
37121 Verona, Italia
tel. 39-45/590109 or 590726
fax 39-45/590201 or 801-1566

Gigantic productions are staged every July and August in the Arena di Verona, the
second-largest Roman arena in the world, after the Colosseum in Rome. Ticket
prices range from the very cheap to the very expensive, depending on where you sit.
The acoustics are pretty good, and even in the best seat it's hard to see the singers. So
I tend to opt for the cheaper seats and rent a cushion to place on the stone surface. By
the way, bring along a candle or a cigarette lighter. A beautiful Verona tradition is
that, once the sun has gone down, audience members light a candle to illuminate the
night. Hotel reservations are hard to come by, so you may wind up staying in nearby
Lake Garda or Vicenza, neither one a hardship.

Teatro Filarmonico
4/1 Via Mutilati
37121 Verona, Italia
tel. 39-45/800-2880

This theater, a few steps from the Piazza Bra in the direction of the train station, is
where opera is staged in Verona in the colder months when the arena is closed.

Vicenza Festival (July–October)
Assessorato alla Cultura
Palazzo del Territorio
Via Levà degli Angeli
36100 Vicenza, Italia
tel. 39-444/547022

Teatro Olimpico
Piazza Matteotti
36100 Vicenza, Italia
tel. 39-444/323781

Many performances, opera and otherwise, are held in one of the world's great the-
aters, the splendid Teatro Olimpico, designed by the Renaissance architect Andrea
Palladio.

JAPAN

While Japan does not have any permanent companies that produce Western-style
opera, the Japanese are among the world's most devoted opera fans, who travel the
world to go to opera in other cities and also import the world's finest opera compa-

nies. Among the companies that frequently appear in Japan are La Scala, Vienna, Berlin, and the Metropolitan Opera. Tickets in Japan tend to be prohibitively expensive, but if you can afford to travel in Japan, money might not be a problem for you. Listed below are three theaters that frequently present Western opera. For program information you can visit a tourist information booth in Japan or contact the Japan Tourist Office in New York (tel. 212/757-5640).

Tokyo Metropolitan Festival Hall
Taitou-ku, Ueno-Kouen, 5-45
Tokyo 110 Japan
tel. 81-3/338282111

Tokyu Bunka-Mura
Orchard Hall
Shibuya-ku
Dogen-Zaka, 2-24-1
Tokyo 150 Japan
tel. 81-3/34773244

Kamagawa Kenmin Hall
Yokohama-Shi, Naka-ku, Yamashita-Cho, 3-1
Kamagawa 231 Japan
tel. 81-45/6625901

LUXEMBOURG

Théâtre Municipal
Rond-Point Robert Schumann
Luxembourg City, Luxembourg
tel. 352/470895 (box office)
tel. 352/47962710 (information)

MEXICO

National Auditorium
Chapulteple
Av. Reforma
Mexico, D.F., Mexico
tel. 52-5/520-3737

Opera de Bellas Artes
Palacio de Bellas Artes
Av. Hidalgo 1, 3er piso
06050 Mexico D.F., Mexico
tel. 52-5/521-3668 or 521-6776
fax 52-5/521-6944

This beautiful theater, opened in 1910, is made of Carrara marble from Italy and is a source of great pride to Mexicans. Tenors Francisco Araiza and Plácido Domingo appear there frequently (although born in Spain, Domingo grew up in Mexico).

Teatro de la Ciudad
Donceles 36
Mexico, D.F., Mexico
tel. 52-5/510-2197

MONACO

Opéra de Monte-Carlo (January–March)
Salle Garnier
Atrium du Casino
98007 Monte Carlo Cedex, Monaco
tel. 33-93/306-931 or 506-931

Printemps des Arts Monte Carlo (Spring)
4, rue des Iris
98000 Monaco
tel. 33-93/255804 or 301921
fax 33-93/506694

NETHERLANDS

De Nederlandse Opera
Waterlooplein 22
Postbus 15465
1001 PG Amsterdam, The Netherlands
tel. 31-20/551-8922
fax 31-20/551-8311

Nederlandse Operastichting
Korte Leidsedwarsstraat 12
1017 RC Amsterdam, The Netherlands
tel. 31-20/255-454

Friesche Opera Vereniging
It Himpsel 30
9035 GE Dronrijp, The Netherlands
tel. 31-5172/1777

Opera Forum
Perikweg 97
Postbus 1321
7500 BH Enschede, The Netherlands
tel. 31-53/878787
fax 31-53/321882

Holland Festival (June)
Netherlands Reservation Centre
P.O. Box 04
2260 AK Leidschendam, The Netherlands
tel. 31-70/320-2500
fax 31-70/320-2611

Utrecht Early Music Festival (late August-early September)
Organisatie Oude Muziek
Postbus 734
3500 AS Utrecht, The Netherlands
tel. 31-30/340921

NEW ZEALAND

Aotea Centre
Performing Arts and Convention Centre
Wellesley Street (near Queen Street)
Auckland, New Zealand
tel. 64-9/309-26277
fax 64-9/309-2679

NORTHERN IRELAND

Belfast Festival of Arts at Queen's (November)
Queen's University
Festival House
25 College Gardens
Belfast BT9 6BS, Northern Ireland
tel. 44-232/667687
fax 44-232/247895

Grand Opera House
Great Victoria Street
Belfast BT2 7HR, Northern Ireland
tel. 44-232/241919

NORWAY

Bergen International Festival (May–June)
Box 183
5001 Bergen, Norway
tel. 47-55/216100 or 320400
fax 47-55/315531

This festival is devoted primarily to the music of Edvard Grieg, Bergen's native son. Although he did not write any operas, he wrote dozens of gorgeous songs. In addition, there are often visiting opera companies at the Bergen Festival.

Den Norske Opera
Storgaten 23
Oslo 1
tel. 47-1/337-985

The Norwegian Opera is now housed in a converted cinema, although plans are afoot to construct a new opera house for Oslo by the year 2000.

POLAND

Teatr Wielki
Place Teatralny 1
00-950 Warsaw, Poland
tel. 48-22/263-001 or 263-286
tickets (up to two weeks before the performance):
tel. 48-22/265-019
fax 48-22/260-423

PORTUGAL

The first three present operas periodically. Check local listings.

Coliseu dos Recreios
Rua das Portas de Santo Antão
1100 Lisbon, Portugal
tel. 351-1/346-1997

Fundação Calouste Gulbenkian
Av. de Berna, 45
1000 Lisbon, Portugal
tel. 351-1/301-3534

Teatro Municipal de São Luis
Rua Antonio Maria Cardoso, 38
1200 Lisbon, Portugal
tel. 351-1/346-1260

Teatro San Carlos
Largo de San Carlos, Rua Serpa Pinta 9
Lisbon, Portugal
tel. 351-1/368-664 or 327172

This theater is famous as the locale of the "Lisbon Traviata," *a 1958 performance with Maria Callas and a young Alfredo Kraus that was captured on tape and is now legendary. Playwright Terrence McNally, a true opera lover, has written a play called* The Lisbon Traviata *which includes a hilarious character, Mendy, who is a priceless example of what is called an opera queen. This person is an operatic equivalent of a baseball fan who can tell you how many triples Lou Gehrig hit in 1936. The opera queen, who is often gay, follows the intimate details of performers' lives and always knows who sang what where, when and with whom. Mr. McNally's Mendy can tell the difference between the "Lisbon* Traviata" *and the "London* Traviata" *after hearing "Maria" sing just a few notes. The San Carlos still has great artists who appear in modest but straightforward productions that please audiences.*

ROMANIA

Opera Româna
Bd. Gheorghe Gheorghiu-Dej 70-72
Sector 5, COD 70609
Bucharest, Romania
tel. 40-0/157-939

RUSSIA

Russian opera performed in Russian by a native cast is a real treat. The great theaters of Moscow and St. Petersburg have long and glorious histories thanks to the superb artistic education Russian performers receive and also because the Bolshoi and the Kirov helped foster the creation of most of the great works in the Russian repertoire. While Moscow has always been steadfast in its devotion to Russian works, St. Petersburg was always more open to the West. Italians were brought to write opera for the court of Catherine the Great, and Verdi wrote La Forza del Destino on a commission from the Imperial Theater of St. Petersburg. The Bolshoi and the Kirov opera companies have sensational orchestras and choruses that bring extra quality to each performance.

Bolshoi Opera
Sverdlov Square
Moscow, Russia
tel. 7-095/228-4091

Kirov Opera
St. Petersburg, Russia
tel. 7-812/216-5924

SCOTLAND

Aberdeen International Youth Festival (August)
Town House
Aberdeen AB9 1AQ, Scotland
tel. 44-224/642121

Dumfries and Galloway Arts Festival
Gracefield Arts Centre
28 Edinburgh Road
Dumfries DG1 1JQ, Scotland
tel. 44-387/56479

Edinburgh International Festival (August)
21 Market St.
Edinburgh EH1 1BW, Scotland
tel. 44-31/226-4001 or 225-5756
fax 44-31/225-1173

Often called the world's largest arts festival. Usually includes performances by the Scottish Opera and sometimes has a visiting opera company.

Scottish Opera
The Theatre Royal
39 Elmbank Crescent
Glasgow G2 4PT, Scotland
tel. 44-41/248-4567 or 331-1234
fax 44-41/221-8812 or 332-3965

The Scottish Opera also tours regularly to Aberdeen, Edinburgh, Inverness, and Newcastle upon Tyne.

St. Magnus Festival (late June)
Strandal
Nicolson Street
Kirkwall, Orkney Islands KW 15 1BD, Scotland
tel. 44-856/2669

Perth Festival (May)
Perth Theater
185 High Street
Perth PH1 5UW, Scotland
tel. 44-738/21031

SLOVAKIA

Bratislava Music Festival (September-October)
Michalská 10
81536 Bratislava, Slovakia
tel. 42-7/334528
fax 42-7/332652

SLOVENIA

Ljubljana Festival (July–August)
Trg Francoski Revolucije 1–2
SLO-6100 Ljubljana, Slovenia
tel. 38-61/221948
fax 38-61/221288

Slovensko Narodno Gledalisce
Zupancicava 1
Ljubljana, Slovenia
tel. 38-21/401

SOUTH AFRICA

Opera House
Nico Performing Arts Center
Capetown, Republic of South Africa
tel. 27-21/21-7695

Natal Performing Arts Council (NAPAC)
Durban, Republic of South Africa
tel. 27-31/304-3631

Civic Theatre
Bounded by Loveday, Hoofd, Simmonds and Jorissen Streets
Johannesburg, Republic of South Africa
tel. 27-11/724-9591

In Johannesburg, the Performing Arts Council of the Transvaal presents opera at the Civic and other theaters. The best source for information is the Johannesburg Publicity Association, Ground Floor, Markwell House, Cnr. Market and Von Wielligh

Streets; mailing address: P.O. Box 4580, Johannesburg 2000, Republic of South Africa. There is a twenty-four-hour tele-tourist information phone: 27-11/337-2727.

State Theatre
Church Street
Pretoria, Republic of South Africa
tel. 27-12/21-9440

SPAIN

Gran Teatro del Liceu
Rambla de Capuchinos, 61
08001 Barcelona, España
tel. 34-93/412-3532 or 318-9122
fax 34-93/412-1198 or 302-2979
fax 34-93/412-1498 (to reserve seats)

Don't say this to people in Madrid, but the opera house in Barcelona is surely the leading lyric theater in Spain. Audiences here are extraordinarily enthusiastic, as well they should be. This theater has launched many great stars, including Montserrat Caballé and José Carreras. Sadly, the Teatro del Liceu was practically destroyed by fire in early 1994. As this book went to press, the future of opera in Barcelona was still uncertain.

Palau de Musica Catalana
Sant Francesc de Paula, 2
08003 Barcelona, España
tel. 34-93/301-1104

Teatro Coliseo Albia (opera throughout the year, with a festival in September)
Alameda de Urquijo, 13
Bilbao, España
tel. 34-94/415-3954

To reserve tickets contact:
Asociación Bilbiana de Amigos de la Opera
Rodriguez Arias, 3, 1a
48008 Bilbao, España
tel. 34-94/415-5490
fax 34-94/415-2200

Festival Internacional de Musica
Cotxe, 2
17488 Cadaques, España
tel. 34-972/258315

Amigos Canarios de la Opera (February–April)
Teatro Perez Galdos
Malteses, 22
35005 Las Palmas de Gran Canaria (Canary Islands), España
tel. 34-928/370125 or 369394

Birthplace of the elegant and wonderfully musical tenor Alfredo Kraus.

Teatro Colón
Riego de Agua, 27 bajo
La Coruña, España
tel. 34-81/211443

Festival Internacional de Musica y Danza (June)
Gracia, 21, 3o
18002 Granada, España
tel. 34-58/267442
fax 34-58/267447
or contact:
P.O. Box 64
18080 Granada, España
tel. 34-58/220022 or 229681
fax 34-58/222322

Teatro Lirico Nacional de la Zarzuela
Jovellanos, 4
28014 Madrid, España
tel. 34-91/429-8225
fax 34-91/429-7157

Teatro Principal
Ayuntamiento de Mahon
Mahon (Minorca)
tel. 34-971/369800

Teatro Campoamor
Melquiades Alvarez, 20
33003 Oviedo (Asturias)
tel. 34-98/521-1705
fax 34-98/521-2402

Festival Internacional de Musica y Danza de Palma de Mallorca (February)
Teatro Principal
07001 Palma de Mallorca, España
tel. 34-971/713346 or 725548

Festival Internacional de Musica de Castell de Peralada (mid-June–mid-July)
Peralada (Girona), España
tel. 34-972/538125
fax 34-972/538087

Quincenza Musical de San Sebastian (August)
c/Republica Argentina, s/n
20003 San Sebastian, España
tel. 34-943/481238
fax 34-943/430702

Santander Festival (July–August)
Av. Calvo Sotelo, 15, 5o
39002 Santander, España

tel. 34-942/210508
fax 34-942/314767

Auditorio de Galicia
Palacio de la Opera, Exposiciones y Congresos
Avda. del Burgo de la Naciones, s/n
15705 Santiago de Compostela, España
tel. 34-981/573855
fax 34-981/574250

Teatro de la Maestranza
Paseo de Colón, 4
41010 Sevilla, España
tel. 34-95/422-3344 or 456-0899
fax 34-95/446-2505 or 456-0698

This theater was built to coincide with the start of the Seville World's Fair in 1992. Few cities can claim to be the setting of more classic operas than Seville: Don Giovanni, Le Nozze de Figaro, Fidelio, Il Barbiere di Siviglia, *and* Carmen *are but a few of the many that draw on Seville's colorful atmosphere.*

Palacio de la Musica y Congresos de Valencia
Paseo de la Alameda, s/n
46023 Valencia, España
tel. 34-96/360-3212
fax 34-96/369-9985
Friends of the Opera:
tel. 34-96/321-7004

SWEDEN

Drottningholm Court Theater (May–September)
Drottningholm Slottsteater
P.O. Box 27050
10251 Stockholm
tel. 46-8/660-8225
fax 46-8/661-0194

A wonderful summer festival with especially strong performances of Mozart operas.

Folkoperan
Hornsgatten 72
Stockholm, Sweden
tel. 46-8/658-5300

Jarlateatern
Kongstensgaten 2
Stockholm, Sweden
tel. 46-8/201602
Operetta.

Royal Opera Stockholm
Gustav Adolfs torg

103 22 Stockholm, Sweden
tel. 46-8/248240
Sweden's most important opera house.

Sodra Teatern
Mosebacketorg
Stockholm, Sweden
tel. 46-8/644-9900

Vadstena Festival (July–August)
Vadstena Academy
Lastköpingsgatan
59200 Vadstena, Sweden
Box office:
Wetterheds Bokhandel
tel. 46-143/19400

Visby Festival (mid-July–mid-August)
Tranhusgatan 47
62155 Visby, Sweden
tel. (July–August) 46-498/12144
tel. (September–June) 46-498/11068

SWITZERLAND

Stadttheater
Theaterstrasse 7
4051 Basel, Switzerland
tel. 41-61/295-1133
No credit cards accepted.

Theater Basel
Billettkasse
Postfach
4010 Basel, Switzerland
tel. 41-61/221133

Stadttheater Berne
Kornhausplatz 18
3000 Berne 7, Switzerland
tel. 41-31/220777

Grand Théâtre de Génève
Place Neuve
1204 Geneva, Switzerland
tel. 41-22/311-2311 or 212318
fax 41-22/311-5515 (not for ticket orders)

Gstaad Summer Festival (August–September)
c/o Verkehrsbüro
3780 Gstaad, Switzerland
tel. 41-30/47173
fax 41-30/45620

May contain the occasional opera-in-concert with big stars. There is also the Alpengala in early September. Check with the Gstaad Tourist Office, 3780, Gstaad, Switzerland, tel. 41-30/41055.

Théâtre Municipal
Opéra de Lausanne
Case Postale 3972
1002 Lausanne, Switzerland
tel. 41-21/326437

Lucerne Festival (mid-August–mid-September)
Hirschmattstrasse 13
6002 Lucerne, Switzerland
tel. 41-41/235272 or 236618
fax 41-41/237784

Stadttheater St. Gallen
Billettkasse
9004 St. Gallen, Switzerland
tel. 41-71/252511

An open-air opera festival is also held in St. Gallen the last weekend of August. Contact the Swiss National Tourist Office, 608 Fifth Avenue, New York, NY 10020; tel. 212/757-5944; fax 212/262-6116.

Opernhaus Zürich
Falkenstrasse 1
8008 Zürich, Switzerland
tel. 41-1/262-0909
fax 41-1/251-5896 (no ticket orders)

TURKEY

Istanbul International Festival (June–July)
Yildiz Kültür ve Sanat Merkezi,
Yildiz-Besiktas
80700 Istanbul, Turkey
tel. 90-1/160-4553
fax 90-1/161-8823

UNITED STATES

ALABAMA

Mobile Opera
Civic Center Theater
Mobile, AL
tel. 205/460-2900

ALASKA

Anchorage Opera
Alaska Center for the Performing Arts

Anchorage, AK
tel. 907/263-2787

ARIZONA

Arizona Opera Company
2332 N. Stone Avenue
Tucson, AZ 85705
tel. 602/884-7980

ARKANSAS

Opera Theater at Wildwood
Wildwood Park
Little Rock, AR
tel. 501/821-7281

CALIFORNIA

Music from Bear Valley
Festival Tent
Bear Valley, CA
tel. 209/753-2574

Carmel Bach Festival
Sunset Theater
Carmel, CA
tel. 408/624-3996

Opera Pacific
Orange County Performing Arts Center
Costa Mesa, CA
tel. 714/979-7000

Long Beach Opera
Terrace Theater
Long Beach, CA
tel. 310/596-5556

Los Angeles Music Center Opera
Dorothy Chandler Pavilion
135 North Grand Avenue
Los Angeles, CA 90012
tel. 213/972-7211

Monterey Opera
Steinbeck Forum, Conference Center
Monterey, CA
tel. 408/649-6772

Oakland Opera
Zellerbach Hall
Oakland, CA
tel. 415/841-2800

West Bay Opera
Lucie Stern Theater
Palo Alto, CA
tel. 415/321-3471

Sacramento Opera
Community Center Theater
Sacramento, CA
tel. 916/449-5181

San Diego Opera
Civic Theater
Write:
P.O. Box 988
San Diego, CA 92112
tel. 619/236-6510

Pocket Opera
Beale Street Theater
San Francisco, CA
tel. 415/989-1855

San Francisco Opera
War Memorial Opera House
San Francisco, CA 94102
tel. 415/864-3330
fax 415/621-7508

One of the nation's oldest and best opera companies receives enthusiastic support from local audiences. San Francisco has long been an international city with a pronounced taste for opera. The Metropolitan Opera was on tour there when the devastating earthquake shook the city in April 1906, and some of our best accounts of the events there came from tenor Enrico Caruso. The San Francisco opera house, which was built some years after the earthquake, sits in a place of honor opposite City Hall. The opera season begins in the early autumn and runs until around the end of the year. San Francisco often has a spring season, usually in the form of a festival honoring a particular composer or style. The company also does a good Ring cycle, which it stages every few years during the spring season.

Opera San Jose
Montgomery Theater
San Jose, CA
tel. 408/288-7077

Marin Opera
Memorial Auditorium
San Rafael, CA
tel. 415/472-3500

COLORADO

Aspen Music Festival
Wheeler Opera House
Aspen, CO 81611
tel. 303/925-9042
fax 303/925-3802

Central City Opera
Central City Opera House
Central City, CO
tel. 303/292-6700

Enjoyable productions are staged in the summers at this Old West opera house. The Central City Opera House is one of the best surviving examples of the opera houses that appeared in frontier towns throughout the West in the late nineteenth century. Though most were not built as opera houses, some now fill this function.

Colorado Opera Festival
Pikes Peak Center
Colorado Springs, CO
tel. 719/520-7469

Opera Colorado
Boettcher Hall
Denver, CO
tel. 303/778-6464

Four Corners Opera
Fine Arts Auditorium
Durango, CO
tel. 303/259-0987

CONNECTICUT

Connecticut Grand Opera
Klein Auditorium
Bridgeport, CT
tel. 203/359-0009

Connecticut Opera
Bushnell Auditorium
Hartford, CT
tel. 203/527-0713

Shubert Opera
Shubert Theater
New Haven, CT
tel. 203/562-5666

DELAWARE

Opera Delaware
Grand Opera House

Wilmington, DE
tel. 302/652-5577

DISTRICT OF COLUMBIA

Catholic University Summer Opera Theater
Hatke Theater
tel. 202/526-1669
fax 202/319-6280

Washington Concert Opera
Lisner Auditorium
Washington, D.C.
tel. 202/797-4671

The Washington Opera
Eisenhower Theater
The John F. Kennedy Center for the Performing Arts
Washington, D.C. 20566-0012
tel. 202/223-4757
tickets:
tel. 800/87-OPERA

FLORIDA

Ruth Eckard Hall
Clearwater, FL
tel. 813/538-0775

Fort Lauderdale Opera
Broward Center for the Performing Arts
Fort Lauderdale, FL
tel. 305/728-9700

Treasure Coast Opera
Civic Center
Ft. Pierce, FL
tel. 407/468-1530

Capella Cracoviensis
Tennessee Williams Fine Arts Center
Key West, FL
tel. 305/296-9081

Greater Miami Opera
1200 Coral Way
Miami, FL 33145
tel. 305/854-1643
performs at:
Dade County Auditorium
tel. 305/854-7890
Miami Opera holds the distinction of having given the American debut of Luciano

Pavarotti. The company has an enthusiastic following and ambitious artistic direction.

Orlando Opera
Bob Carr Performing Arts Center
Orlando, FL
tel. 407/896-7664

Palm Beach Opera
Kravis Center for the Performing Arts
701 Okeechobee Boulevard
West Palm Beach, FL 33401
tel. 407/833-8300

Gold Coast Opera
Omni Auditorium
Pompano Beach, FL
tel. 305/973-2249

Sarasota Opera
Sarasota Opera House
Sarasota, FL 33578
tel. 813/953-7030

Tampa Bay Opera
Tampa Bay Performing Arts Center
Tampa, FL
tel. 813/538-0775

GEORGIA

Atlanta Opera
Symphony Hall
Woodruff Arts Center
tel. 404/892-2414

Augusta Opera
Imperial Theater
Augusta, GA
tel. 706/722-8341

South Georgia Opera
Thomas County Cultural Center
Thomasville, GA
tel. 904/386-3812

HAWAII

Hawaii Opera Theatre
Blaisdell Hall
Honolulu, HI 96813
tel. 808/537-6191

ILLINOIS

Chicago Opera Theater
Atheneum Theater
Chicago, IL
tel. 312/663-0048

Grant Park Music Festival
Grant Park
Chicago, IL
tel. 312/294-2420

Lyric Opera of Chicago
20 N. Wacker Dr.
Chicago, IL 60606
tel. 312/332-2244

An outstanding company, founded in the 1950s, that attracts great international stars and directors. Maria Callas had many of her greatest American triumphs here. The Lyric proudly advertises that it sells out every performance and that it is a leader in the commissioning and production of new operas, especially by American composers. Chicagoans show a civic pride in the Lyric Opera that equals their love of the basketball Bulls and the football Bears. In this they create a model for American arts support, which, unfortunately, is not necessarily emulated elsewhere. The season in Chicago usually runs from September through February.

Light Opera Works
Cahn Auditorium
Evanston, IL
tel. 708/869-6300

Peoria Civic Opera
Civic Center Theater
Peoria, IL
tel. 309/674-7811

Ravinia Festival
Ravinia Park, IL
tel. 312/728-4642
fax 708/433-4582

INDIANA

Indiana Opera Theater
Ayres Auditorium
Indianapolis, IN
tel. 317/257-7464

Indianapolis Opera
Clowes Hall
Indianapolis, IN
tel. 317/283-9696

Whitewater Opera
Centerville Arts Center
Richmond, IN
tel. 317/962-7106

IOWA

Des Moines Metro Opera
Blank Performing Arts Center
106 West Boston Avenue
Indianola, IA 50125
tel. 515/961-6221

KENTUCKY

Kentucky Opera
Macaulay Theater
Louisville, KY
tel. 502/584-7777

LOUISIANA

Baton Rouge Opera
LSU Union Theater
Baton Rouge, LA
tel. 504/388-5128

New Orleans Opera
333 St. Charles Ave.
New Orleans, LA 70130
tel. 504/529-2278

Shreveport Opera
Civic Theater
Shreveport, LA
tel. 318/227-9503

MARYLAND

Baltimore Opera
40 W. Chase Street
Baltimore, MD 21201
tel. 301/727-0592

Prince George's Opera
Queen Anne Fine Arts Theater
Largo, MD
tel. 301/864-7326

MASSACHUSETTS

Berkshire Opera
Cramwell Opera House
Lenox, MA
tel. 413/243-1343

Boston Lyric Opera
Emerson Majestic Theater
219 Tremont Street
Boston, MA
tel. 617/248-8660

Opera Company of Boston
539 Washington St.
Boston, MA 02111
tel. 617/426-5300

Salisbury Lyric Opera Company
Mechanics Hall
Worcester, MA
tel. 508/752-0888

Tanglewood Festival
Koussevitzky Music Shed
Tanglewood
Lenox, MA
tel. 617/266-1492

Tanglewood is one of America's great summer music festivals, with the Boston Symphony as the resident orchestra. Although most of the music is symphonic, there is usually an opera-in-concert or two with a top-notch cast.

MICHIGAN

Michigan Opera Theater
Masonic Temple
Detroit, MI
tel. 313/874-7464

Opera Grand Rapids
DeVos Hall
Grand Rapids, MI
tel. 616/456-3333

West Michigan Opera
21 Ottawa N.W.
Grand Rapids, MI 49503
tel. 616/451-2741

MINNESOTA

Minneapolis Viennese Sommerfest
Orchestra Hall
Minneapolis, MN
tel. 612/371-5600
fax 612/371-0838

Minnesota Opera
850 Grand Avenue
St. Paul, MN 55105
tel. 612/221-0122

or:

Ordway Music Theater
Minneapolis, MN
tel. 612/333-6669

MISSISSIPPI

Mississippi Opera
Jackson Municipal Auditorium
Jackson, MS
tel. 601/960-1528

Opera/South
Mississippi Arts Center
201 E. Pascagoula St.
Jackson, MS 39201
tel. 601/968-2051

MISSOURI

Lyric Opera of Kansas City
Lyric Theater
1029 Central
Kansas City, MO 64105
tel. 816/471-7344

Opera Theater of St. Louis (June)
Loretto Hilton Theater
P.O. Box 13148
St. Louis, MO 63119
tel. 314/961-0644

Springfield Regional Opera
Landers Theater
Springfield, MO
tel. 417/869-1960

NEBRASKA

Opera/Omaha
1200 City National Bank Bldg.
Omaha, NE 68102
tel. 402/346-0357

Nebraska might be one of the last places you would think to find an ambitious opera company with creative productions and an emphasis on unusual old operas and the occasional new one. But Opera/Omaha has carved itself a niche as the presenter of deserving works that other companies are reluctant to stage for fear of alienating traditional audiences.

NEVADA

Nevada Opera
Pioneer Center
Reno, NV
tel. 702/786-4046

NEW HAMPSHIRE

Monadnock Music Festival
Pine Hill School
Peterborough, NH
tel. 603/924-7610

Opera North
Lebanon Opera House
Lebanon, NH
tel. 802/649-3750

NEW JERSEY

Metro Lyric Opera
Paramount Theater
Asbury Park, NJ
tel. 908/531-2378

Opera Classics of New Jersey
DeNooyer Auditorium
Hackensack, NJ
tel. 201/592-5821

Opera Festival of New Jersey
Kirkby Arts Center
Lawrenceville, NJ
tel. 609/292-6130

New Jersey State Opera
1020 Broad Street
Newark, NJ 07102
tel. 201/675-6665

New Jersey Association of Verismo Opera
Park Theater
Union City, NJ
tel. 201/224-6911

NEW MEXICO

Santa Fe Opera
P.O. Box 2408
Santa Fe, NM 87504-2408
tel. 505/982-3855

An unbeatable natural setting makes summertime attendance at the Santa Fe Opera one of the great operagoing experiences anywhere. The 1,889-seat opera house is a semicovered outdoor theater, so that occasional cloudbursts will drench audience members who are not under the overhang (the stage is covered and largely immune to rain). But the beauties of the desert air, the mesas, the Sangre de Cristo mountains, and the huge sky add a dimension to the enjoyment of the operas you hear. Santa Fe produces five operas each summer, one of which will always be by Richard Strauss, a great favorite of General Director John Crosby. The Santa Fe Opera was founded in 1957.

NEW YORK

Tri-Cities Opera
Forum Theater
Binghamton, NY
tel. 607/797-6344

Bronx Opera
Lehman College Theater
Bronx, NY
tel. 212/365-4209
Information: 718/625-2332

Brooklyn Academy of Music
BAM Opera House
Brooklyn, NY
tel. 718/636-4100

"BAM" is probably the nation's leading center for avant-garde opera. Contemporary composers such as Philip Glass and John Adams and directors such as Peter Sellars find BAM a congenial environment with a devoted audience that comes by bus, subway, taxi, and limousine from Manhattan. BAM opened at the turn of the century and was a site for the Metropolitan Opera when it went on tour. Don't forget that moving scenery, orchestra, and chorus was a much bigger enterprise in the days before large trucks and modern transport. Enrico Caruso sang his last performance at the Brooklyn Academy of Music in 1920.

Brooklyn College Opera Theater
Walt Whitman Hall
Brooklyn College
tel. 718/434-2222

Il Piccolo Teatro dell'Opera
Brooklyn Academy of Music
Brooklyn, NY
tel. 718/643-7775

Regina Opera Company
Regina Hall
Brooklyn, NY
tel. 718/232-3555

Greater Buffalo Opera Company
Shea's Auditorium
Buffalo, NY
tel. 716/852-5000

Chautauqua Opera
Chautauqua, NY 14722
tel. 716/357-4493

Glimmerglass Opera
Alice Busch Opera Theater
Cooperstown, NY
tel. 607/547-2255
fax 607/547-6030

Two operas are staged each summer in this charming little town on the shores of Lake Otsego. You can visit the Baseball Hall of Fame during the day (many opera fans are also avid baseball fans), go boating or for a drive in the idyllic countryside, stay at a bed-and-breakfast, and then enjoy one of Glimmerglass's fine productions. Many creative directors and talented singers make Glimmerglass part of their schedules, so this company offers more than most troupes that stage summer opera in pretty locales.

Lake George Opera Festival
P.O. Box 425
Glens Falls, NY 12801
tel. 518/793-3858

Queens Opera
Little Theater
St. John's University
Jamaica, Queens, NY
tel. 718/837-8726

Caramoor Festival
Box "R"
Katonah, NY 10536
tel. 914/232-4206

After Dinner Opera Company
New York, NY
tel. 212/477-6212

Founded by Richard Flusser in 1949, with encouragement from Leonard Bernstein and Aaron Copland, for the production of American operas. Free performances are given year-round at sites all over New York City. Call for performance details.

Amato Opera
Amato Opera Theater
319 Bowery (at Second Street)
New York, NY
tel. 212/228-8200

Full productions are staged in this 107-seat theater. How often can you sit so close to a singer? A good local company.

John Brownlee Opera Theater
Borden Auditorium
Manhattan School of Music
New York, NY
tel. 212/749-2802

Center for Contemporary Opera
John Jay College
New York, NY
tel. 212/308-6728

For information:
4 West 76 Street
New York, NY
tel. 212/874-0245

Gilbert & Sullivan Society
New York, NY
tel. 718/259-6431

Presents all of the famous works by G & S at theaters around town. Call for details.

Hell's Kitchen Opera Co.
Sacred Heart Church
457 West 51 Street
New York, NY 10019
tel. 212/489-7938

An ambitious troupe that specializes in early operas such as L'Incoronazione di Poppea.

Henry Street Settlement Music School Opera Production Group
Harry de Jur Playhouse
466 Grand Street
New York, NY
tel. 212/598-0400

La Gran Scena Opera Company
New York, NY
tel. 212/929-3597

A wonderful company that is a delight to opera fans. Continuing the great travesti tradition, the men of La Gran Scena appear as some of those great divas whose artistry must be seen to be believed. Among the legendary singers who might appear are the last of the Golden Age divas, 105-year-old Gabriella Tonnoziti-Casseruola,

Mme Vera Galupe-Borszkh, a "traumatic soprano" from somewhere east of the Danube and west of the Dnieper, and America's most beloved retired diva, Sylvia Bills (not to be confused with Beverly Sills, unless you want to). There is no funnier night at the opera, but what also astonishes is what excellent singers these divos-turned-divas are! Many famous opera singers attend Gran Scena performances. The company has a large following in Europe and is frequently on tour, but usually does a spring season in New York. Call for details.

Juilliard Opera Center
Juilliard School of Music
Lincoln Center
New York, NY 10023
tel. 212/874-7515 or 769-7406
The stars of tomorrow.

Liederkranz Opera Theater
Liederkranz Foundation
6 East 87 Street
New York, NY
tel. 212/534-0880
Specializes in well-known and seldom-seen German works, such as Wagner's Das Liebesverbot.

Majestic Opera Company
P.O. Box 3307 Church Street Station
New York, NY 10008-3307
Another of New York's many small companies. This one, founded in 1992, presented an unusual debut season that included L'Ebreo *(1855) by Giuseppe Apolloni,* Iolanthe *(1892) by Tchaikovsky,* L'Oracolo *(1905) by Franco Leoni, and* Manon Lescaut *(1856) by Daniel François Esprit Auber, one of the originators of grand opera in France. Write for details on future repertory.*

Manhattan School of Music
Borden Theater
Broadway at 122nd Street
New York, NY 10027
tel. 212/749-2802, ext. 497

Mannes Opera Ensemble
Mannes College of Music
150 West 85 Street
New York, NY 10024
tel. 212/580-0210

Metropolitan Opera
Metropolitan Opera House
Lincoln Center
New York, NY 10023
tel. 212/362-6000
Founded in 1883, this mecca of the lyric art is in a class by itself. With a budget larger than that of many corporations and an awesome fundraising capacity, the Met can set its heights higher than anyone else and, for the most part, makes good on its promise. With 3,786 seats, the opera house can hold more people than other theaters,

with the result that prices here are lower than at the Vienna State Opera, La Scala, Covent Garden, and most of the other international houses. The Met's extraordinary stage machinery permits scenic effects that other theaters can only dream of. The Met has a magnificent orchestra and an excellent chorus, so that even when solo singers are not always up to snuff, there is usually much to appreciate from these other musical forces. The company presents seven operas a week from late September through mid-April, and for any opera lover visiting New York during its season, a night at the Met is a must. While performances often sell out, if you attempt to purchase tickets by phone or mail at least six weeks in advance, you stand a decent chance of getting a location.

Mostly Mozart Festival (July–August)
Avery Fisher Hall
Lincoln Center
New York, NY 10023
tel. 212/875-5030
Performances include operas in concert, mostly by you-know-who.

New York City Opera
New York State Theater
Lincoln Center
New York, NY 10023
tel. 212/877-4727
Just across Lincoln Center Plaza from the Metropolitan Opera is another of the nation's greatest opera companies. If the City Opera were located anywhere else, it would be much more famous than it is. With low prices and a great emphasis on presenting unusual repertory and talented young singers, the City Opera brings variety to New York's operatic life. While the standard repertory is generally better served at the Met, City Opera's audacious productions of contemporary works and older neglected masterpieces attract devoted audiences. The company has been the launching pad for many of the greatest singers, most of them Americans. To cite but a few: Beverly Sills, Plácido Domingo, Carol Vaness, Samuel Ramey, and June Anderson.

New York Grand Opera
Central Park
New York, NY
tel. 212/245-8837
Free performances in the summer, with an emphasis on Verdi.

New York University/Kurt P. Reimann Opera Studio
University Theater
35 West 4th Street
New York, NY
tel. 212/998-5278

Opera at the Academy
New York Academy of Art
419 Lafayette Street
New York, NY
tel. 212/966-0300

Opera Ebony
Aaron Davis Hall
New York, NY
tel. 212/874-7245
A fine company composed of African-American singers.

L'Opéra Français de New York
Florence Gould Hall
French Institute/Alliance Française
55 East 59th Street
New York, NY
tel. 212/355-6160
Presents excellent, carefully crafted performances of French operatic rarities.

Opera Orchestra of New York
Carnegie Hall
57th Street and 7th Avenue
New York, NY
information: tel. 212/799-1982
Three or four times a year New Yorkers pack Carnegie Hall to hear great stars in often little-known works performed in concert by the Opera Orchestra of New York, led by Eve Queler. One of Maestra Queler's strong suits is discovering talented singers abroad and introducing them to New York audiences. Typically, Carnegie Hall will be full of arts executives and famous singers who turn out to hear the next Pavarotti or Callas and then can say, "I was there." Queler has carved a special and important place in New York's musical life.

Repertorio Español
Gramercy Arts Theater
138 East 27th Street
New York, NY
tel. 212/889-2850
This company performs opera of all nations translated into Spanish. You can also see performances of zarzuela, occasionally with artists from Spain.

Hudson Opera Theater
SUNY Purchase
Purchase, NY
tel. 914/633-2929

Opera Theater of Rochester
P.O. Box 8359
Rochester, NY 14618
tel. 716/461-5839

Thalia Spanish Theater
41-17 Greenpoint Avenue
Sunnyside, Queens, NY
tel. 718/729-3880
Specializes in zarzuelas.

Opera Theater of Syracuse
Civic Center
411 Montgomery Street
Syracuse, NY 13202
tel. 315/435-2121 (box office)
315/435-2151 (information)

NORTH CAROLINA

Brevard Music Festival
Whittington-Pfohl Auditorium
Brevard, NC
tel. 704/884-2019

Charlotte Opera
110 E. 7th Street
Charlotte, NC 28202
tel. 704/332-7177

Opera Carolina
Ovens Auditorium
Charlotte, NC
tel. 704/372-7464

Triangle Opera
Durham, NC
tel. 919/560-2737

Greensboro Opera Company
War Memorial Auditorium
Coliseum Complex
Greensboro, NC
tel. 919/273-9472

Piedmont Opera Theater
Stevens Center
Winston-Salem, NC
tel. 919/725-2022

NORTH DAKOTA

Fargo-Moorhead Civic Opera
Fargo Theater
Fargo, ND
tel. 701/239-4558

OHIO

Cincinnati College Conservatory
Patricia Corbett Theater
Cincinnati, OH
tel. 513/556-4183

Cincinnati Opera
Music Hall
Cincinnati, OH
tel. 513/721-8222

Cleveland Opera
State Theater
Cleveland, OH
tel. 216/241-6000

Lyric Opera Cleveland
Kulas Hall
Cleveland Institute of Music
tel. 216/231-2910

Opera Columbus
Palace Theater
Columbus, OH
tel. 614/461-0022

Dayton Opera
210 N. Main Street
Dayton, OH 45402
tel. 513/228-0662

Sorg Opera Company
Sorg Opera House
Middletown, OH
tel. 513/425-0180

Southern Ohio Light Opera
Massie Theater
Shawnee State University
Portsmouth, OH
tel. 614/355-2212
Kathleen Battle's hometown.

Toledo Opera
Masonic Auditorium
Write:
3540 Secor Road, #212
Toledo, OH 43606
tel. 419/531-5511

Ohio Light Opera
Freedlander Theater
Wooster, OH
tel. 216/263-2345
Time *magazine called this company the "Bayreuth of Operetta."*

OKLAHOMA

OK Mozart International Festival
Bartlesville Community Center Auditorium
Bartlesville, OK
tel. 918/336-9800

Tulsa Opera
1610 S. Boulder Avenue
Tulsa, OK 74119
tel. 918/582-4035

OREGON

Eugene Opera
Hult Center for the Performing Arts
Eugene, OR
tel. 503/687-5000

Portland Opera
P.O. Box 8598
Portland, OR 97207
tel. 503/248-4741
(Civic Auditorium tel. 503/241-1802)

PENNSYLVANIA

American Music Theater Festival
Plays and Players Theater
Philadelphia, PA
tel. 215/567-0670
fax 215/988-0798

Opera Company of Philadelphia
Academy of Music
1518 Walnut Street
Philadelphia, PA 19102
tel. 215/981-1454

Pennsylvania Opera Theater
Shubert Theater
Philadelphia, PA
tel. 215/440-9797

Pittsburgh Opera
Benedum Center
Pittsburgh, PA 15222
tel. 412/456-6666

PUERTO RICO

Casals Festival (June)
Festival Hall Antonio Paoli
Santurce, PR
tel. 809/725-7334
fax 809/723-5843

RHODE ISLAND

Newport Music Festival (July)
The Breakers
Newport, RI
tel. 401/846-1133
fax 401/849-1857

SOUTH CAROLINA

Spoleto Festival USA
P.O. Box 157
Charleston, SC 29402
tel. 803/722-2764

The American branch of the famous Italian festival is held in gracious Charleston each year in late May and early June.

TENNESSEE

Chattanooga Opera
Tivoli Theater
Chattanooga, TN
tel. 615/267-8583

Knoxville Opera
Civic Auditorium
Knoxville, TN
tel. 615/523-8712

Opera Memphis
Memphis State University
Memphis, TN 38152
tel. 901/454-2706

Nashville Opera
Polk Theater
tel. 615/741-2787

TEXAS

Austin Lyric Opera
Austin, TX
tel. 512/472-5992

Dallas Civic Opera
3102 Oak Lawn Avenue, Suite 450

Dallas, TX 75219
tel. 214/528-9850
ticket orders:
214/443-1000
fax 214/443-1060

The site of some of Maria Callas's greatest American performances, this company has long attracted many of opera's greatest stars, although the productions tend to be standard issue.

Fort Worth Opera
3505 West Lancaster
Fort Worth, TX 76107
tel. 817/731-0833

Houston Grand Opera
Brown Theater
Write:
510 Preston Avenue, Suite 500
Houston, TX 77002
tel. 713/227-2787 or 546-0246
tel. 800/346-4462

Frequently ranked among the top five American companies, along with the Metropolitan, the New York City Opera, the Chicago Lyric, and the San Francisco Opera, Houston often attracts big stars who want to try out new roles before bringing them to the larger American houses and to Europe. The company has also produced memorable versions of Gershwin's Porgy and Bess *and Joplin's* Treemonisha.

San Antonio Festival (June)
Municipal Auditorium
San Antonio, TX
tel. 512/226-1573

San Antonio Grand Opera
Write:
109 Lexington Ave., #207
San Antonio, TX 78205
tel. 512/225-6161

UTAH

Utah Festival Opera Company
Ellen Eccles Theater
Logan, UT
tel. 801/752-0026

Utah Opera
Capitol Theater
Salt Lake City, UT
tel. 801/355-2787

VIRGINIA

Opera Theater of Northern Virginia
Arlington, VA
tel. 703/549-5039

Ash Lawn-Highland Summer Festival
Boxwood Gardens
Charlottesville, VA
tel. 804/293-8000

Virginia Opera
261 W. Bute Street
Norfolk, VA 23510
tel. 804/623-1223

Opera Roanoke
Mill Mountain Theater
Roanoke, VA
tel. 703/982-2742

Wolf Trap Opera
1624 Trap Road
Vienna, VA 22180
tel. 703/938-3810
fax 703/255-1986

Just outside Washington, D.C., this festival often presents great international opera companies such as the Bolshoi.

WASHINGTON

Seattle Opera
P.O. Box 9248
Seattle, WA 98109
tel. 206/447-4700

Seattle is famous above all for its Ring *cycle, which is presented most summers. Imaginative leadership and a devoted audience make Seattle a notable regional opera company.*

WISCONSIN

Pamiro Opera
Ralph Holter Auditorium
Green Bay, WI
tel. 414/437-8331

Madison Opera
Oscar Mayer Theater
Madison, WI
tel. 608/238-8085

or:

Wisconsin Union Theater
Madison, WI 53706
tel. 608/266-9055

Florentine Opera
Uihlein Hall

Write:

750 N. Lincoln Memorial Drive
Milwaukee, WI 53202
tel. 414/273-1474

Skylight Opera Theater
Skylight Theater
Milwaukee, WI
tel. 414/271-8815

VENEZUELA

Opera Metropolitana
Teatro Municipal, Ap. 4403
Caracas 101, Venezuela
tel. 58-2/418-522

WALES

Swansea Festival of Music and the Arts
City Centre Booking Office
Singleton Street
Swansea SA1 3QG, Wales
tel. 44-792/470002

Vale of Glamorgan Festival
St. Donats Arts Centre
St. Donats Castle
Llantwit Major
South Glamorgan CF6 9WF, Wales
tel. 44-446/794848
fax 44-446/7941-6883

Welsh National Opera
John Street
Cardiff CF1 4SP, Wales
tel. 44-222/464666
fax 44-222/483050

The Welsh National Opera is an ambitious company that boasts many of the fine voices that seem to be the birthright of the people of Wales. The company has no permanent home, but performs regularly in Birmingham, Bristol, Cardiff, Liverpool, Manchester, Oxford, Plymouth, Southampton (home port of H.M.S. Queen Elizabeth II, if you are traveling to Britain by ship), and Swansea. By contacting the address, phone, or fax listed above you can find out where and when the Welsh National Opera is appearing.

TRAVEL AGENCIES OFFERING OPERA TOURS

Several travel agencies cater to clients who journey to see the best in the performing arts around the world. In general, these tours do not come cheap, but they offer the considerable advantage of procuring tickets to hard-to-get performances which would be much more difficult to see on your own. In addition, they provide the companionship of fellow opera lovers from whom you can learn more about the art form. While most tours visit the hot spots of Europe, such as Vienna, Salzburg, Munich, Bayreuth, Milan, and Verona, others may be more esoteric, with visits to Eastern Europe or off-the-beaten-track festivals in Italy, France, or Britain. In the United States, many tours will typically be a long weekend featuring three performances at the Metropolitan, the Chicago Lyric, or the San Francisco Opera. Trips to special American festivals, such as Seattle, Santa Fe, St. Louis, or Spoleto USA, can also be arranged. Inclusion of the names below does not imply an endorsement, and, as with any travel purchase, you must carefully check what is included in your package, what is optional, and what is a required additional expense.

Adventure in the Arts
357 Tehama Street
San Francisco, CA 94103
tel. 415/433-1306

Allegro Enterprises, Inc.
900 West End Avenue
New York, NY 10025
tel. 212/666-6700 or 800/666-3553

The Colorado Connection
tel. 800/776-3065 or 303/321-1125
Tours include lectures.

Congress Travel
350 Sparks Street, Room 207
Ottawa, Ontario K1R 7S8
tel. 613/234-3360 or 800/267-8526

Dailey-Thorp Travel
330 West 58th Street
New York, NY 10019
tel. 212/307-1555

Great Performance Tours
1 Lincoln Plaza
Suite 32V
New York, NY 10023
tel. 212/580-1400

International Curtain Call Tours
3313 Patricia Avenue
Los Angeles, CA 90064
tel. 310/204-4934 *or* 800/669-9070
fax 310/204-4935

Metropolitan Opera Guild
Members Travel Program
70 Lincoln Center Plaza

New York, NY 10023-6593
tel. 212/760-7062

Morgan Tours
P.O. Box 6037
Station J
Ottawa, Ontario, Canada K2A 1T1
tel. 613/820-0221 *or* 800/667-4628

Mozart's Europe
Now Voyager Tours
Deer Lane
Pawlet, VT 05761
tel. 802/325-3656

Opera Education International
400 Yale Avenue
Berkeley, CA 94708-1109
tel. 800/675-6837

Opera Europe
P.O. Box 1427
Pomona, CA 91769-1427
tel. 909/629-2188

Ovations International
One Executive Concourse
Suite 104
Duluth (Atlanta), Georgia 30136
tel. 800/635-5576 *or* 404/476-4007

Rudolf Travel Service
77 Bloor Street West
Suite 1105
Toronto, Ontario M5S 1M2 Canada
tel. 416/964-3553
fax 416/964-3601

Viva Tours USA
12 Station Road
Bellport, NY 11713
tel. 800/645-1084
tel. 516/286-7051
fax 516/286-2626

Has tickets to the Bayreuth Festival in even-numbered years. Also, will custom-design tours to appeal to particular interests or groups. Guenter Jansen is the opera specialist.

INDEX